THE SHADOW ON THE HILLS.

Looming down the Khyber Pass – 'The Shadow on the Hills'. *(ILN)*

SPYING FOR EMPIRE

THE GREAT GAME IN CENTRAL AND SOUTH ASIA, 1757–1947

Robert Johnson

Greenhill Books, London
MBI Publishing, St Paul

Spying for Empire
The Great Game in Central and South Asia, 1757–1947

First published in 2006 by Greenhill Books, Lionel Leventhal Limited,
Park House, 1 Russell Gardens, London NW11 9NN
www.greenhillbooks.com
and
MBI Publishing Co., Galtier Plaza, Suite 200, 380 Jackson Street, St Paul,
MN 55101-3885, USA

British Library Cataloguing-in Publication Data
Johnson, Robert, 1967–
Spying for empire : the Great Game in Central and South Asia, 1757–1947
Spies – Asia, Central – Biography   Spies – Great Britain – Biography
Great Britain – Relations – Asia, Central   Asia, Central – Relations – Great Britain
Russia – Relations – Asia, Central   Asia, Central – Relations – Russia
Asia, Central – Politics and government
I. Title

ISBN-13: 978-1-85367-670-3
ISBN-10: 1-85367-670-5

Library of Congress Cataloging-in Publication Data available

For more information on our books, please visit
www.greenhillbooks.com, email sales@greenhillbooks.com,
or telephone us within the UK on 020 8458 6314.
You can also write to us at the above London address.

Edited and typeset by Donald Sommerville

Printed and bound in Great Britain by
Creative Print and Design (Wales), Ebbw Vale

Contents

Illustrations

Acknowledgements

The following abbreviations are used in the illustration captions

AC	Author's Collection
NAM	Reproduced by kind permission of the National Army Museum
MG	Reproduced by kind permission of the Mathaf Gallery, London
ILN	Illustrated London News
SRO	Reproduced by kind permission of the Somerset Record Office
ERM	Reproduced by kind permission of the Essex Regiment Museum

Maps

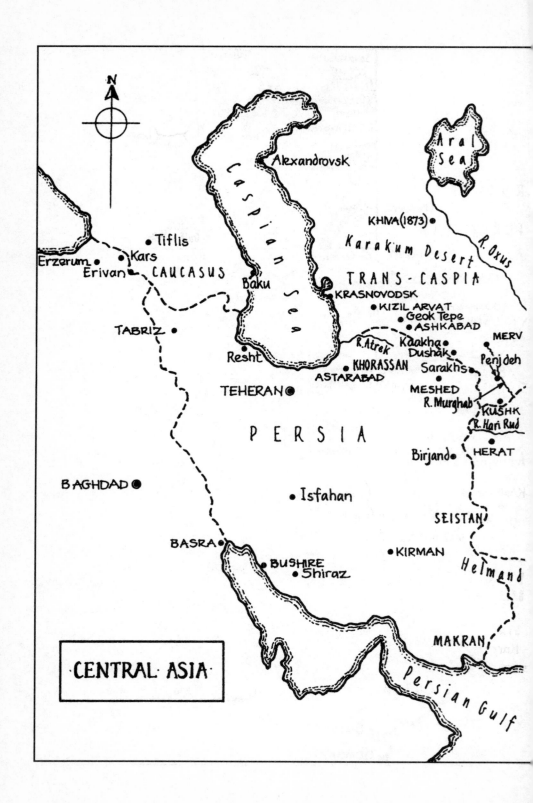

Alexandrovsk

Aral Sea

Caspian Sea

Tiflis

KHIVA (1873)

Karakum Desert

R. Oxus

Kars

Erzerum

Erivan

CAUCASUS

Baku

TRANS - CASPIA

KRASNOVODSK

KIZIL ARVAT

Geok Tepe

ASHKABAD

MERV

TABRIZ

Resht

R. Atrek

Kaakha

Dushak

Penjdeh

KHORASSAN

Sarakhs

TEHERAN

ASTARABAD

MESHED

R. Murghab

KUSHK

R. Hari Rud

PERSIA

Birjand

HERAT

BAGHDAD

Isfahan

SEISTAN

BASRA

KIRMAN

Helmand

BUSHIRE

Shiraz

MAKRAN

Persian Gulf

CENTRAL ASIA

Sevastopol • Orenburg
CRIMEA
Black Sea
CAUCASUS
CASPIAN SEA
TRANS-CASPIA
RUSSIAN TURKESTAN
CHINA
Constantinople
STRAITS
THE OTTOMAN EMPIRE
AFGHANISTAN
North-West Frontier
TIBET
Lhasa
CYPRUS
Mediterranean Sea
PERSIA
NEPAL
EGYPT
BRITISH INDIA
BURMA
Calcutta
Persian Gulf

RUSSIAN

TURKESTAN
Chimkent
•

TASHKENT • Khokand
Osh
R. Syr Daria → Khojend
The Tien Shan
• BOKHARA • SAMARKAND
• KASHGAR
Taklamakan
Kizilkum Desert
The Pamirs
Desert
• Kerki
• YARKAND
CHINA
/ Balkh • Kunduz
The Karakoram
The Hindu Kush
Chitral
Shahidulla
KABUL ◉
Gilgit
• Leh
KASHMIR
Srinagar •
AFGHANISTAN
• PESHAWAR
KANDAHAR
•
LAHORE
TIBET
• QUETTA
PUNJAB
• SIMLA
The Himalayas
LUDHIANA
Desert
BRITISH INDIA
• DELHI
BALUCHISTAN
SIND
Lucknow •
KATHMANDU
Karachi
R. Indus
Faizabad
CUTCH
0   200   400
·miles·
Surat
BOMBAY

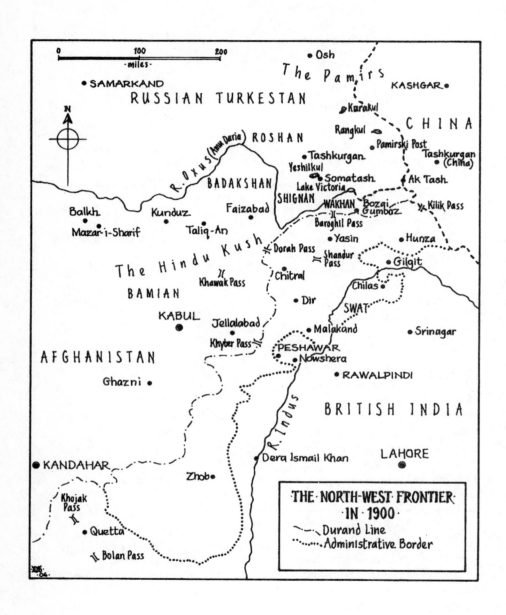

THE·NORTH-WEST·FRONTIER·
IN·1900·
—·—·—· Durand Line
·········· Administrative Border

Foreword

When everyone is dead the Great Game is finished. Not before.

Rudyard Kipling, *Kim*, 1901

It has always been the policy of the British-Indian government to prevent any other European Power from obtaining a foothold within the Asiatic States situated on the border of our actual possessions. Just as a fortress or a line of entrenchments requires an open space around or in front of it, so it is manifestly advantageous for the security of a kingdom to be surrounded by a ring of territories with which powerful neighbours must not meddle. Upon this principle we place the adjoining states under our protectorate, whether they desire it or not.

Sir Alfred Lyall

The Great Game is a subject which has been extensively written about, but mostly by those with political axes to grind – polemicists, armchair strategists, ambitious generals and statesmen – and by a number of players of the stature of Sir Francis Younghusband and Lord Curzon, knights and bishops rather than the pawns of the game. Rather more recently a number of writers who combined travel with research tackled the subject with considerable acclaim, most notably Peter Hopkirk and John Keay. More recently still the American academic Karl Meyer has greatly extended the scope of our knowledge, and I have made a couple of peripheral contributions myself. Yet the fact remains that the history of the Great Game is far from complete. This is where Robert Johnson's *Spying for Empire* comes in; why this is an important book that comes closer to revealing the full story than anything that has gone before.

The Great Game was played on many levels: diplomatic, military, overt and covert. One of my paternal great-grandfathers served in the Survey of India Department, which had responsibility for mapping the land both within and without India's borders. As a young officer he spent several years in the remotest corners of Afghanistan, ostensibly as part of a commission drawing up Afghanistan's western and northern boundaries but also helping to extend Britain's political authority in those regions; later, as a more senior officer, he 'ran' a number of locally recruited explorer-spies with coded identities who traversed unexplored regions of central Asia and Tibet, mapping with concealed instruments as they went. This was the Great Game at its least complicated – but also its most public, discussed in lectures at the Royal Geographical Society, and later given a romantic gloss in Rudyard Kipling's *Kim*, the book which more than anything else helped to raise the Great Game to the status of an imperial romance. 'Well is the Game called great,' muses the young Kim, after he finds himself deeply enmeshed as one of its players. 'Now I shall go far and far into the north playing the Great Game. Truly, it runs like a shuttle through all Hind.'

Kipling exaggerated, as journalists and novelists invariably do, but it was during his six-year apprenticeship in India that the Viceroy Lord Dufferin first established an Intelligence Department for the whole of India. And Kipling was well placed to know the truth, for his proprietor – who just happened to be my other paternal great-grandfather – was at this time paying out large sums of money to senior government officials to ensure that his newspaper, *The Pioneer*, was kept fully informed of what the Government of India was up to.

Armies in the field, of course, have always depended on good intelligence. The East India Company's Bengal, Madras and Bombay armies were no exception, the best of their commanders seeking out young officers with dash and enterprise, perhaps with a talent for languages or map-making, or who had the ability to win the respect of locally-recruited irregulars of foot or cavalry. As fresh territories were won it was from this same cadre of enterprising young men that successive Governors-General recruited their Agents – with a capital A – to be placed in sensitive forward postings, either on the borders of British territory or at the courts of local rulers and friendly powers with whom the East India Company had formed an alliance in the name of the British monarch. These 'politicals' reported not to the Government of India but to the governor-general through their own Political and Secret Department. They were to some degree self-selecting: ambitious young military officers, for the most part, risk-takers for whom (in the words of William Moorcroft) 'the game [was] well worth the candle'. Intentionally or not, they tended to force the political pace – sometimes with disastrous consequences both for themselves and their government. But the success or failure of a political officer in whatever capacity depended to a large extent on the quality of his intelligence, which in turn rested on the quality of his intelligence network, made up of local intelligence-gatherers, agents, informants and – to call them what they undoubtedly were – spies.

I had the good fortune to get to know a real player of the Great Game: Professor and Lieutenant-Colonel Kenneth Mason, RGS Gold Medallist, explorer, surveyor, academic and some-time spy. Mason's uncle had served on India's North-West Frontier as an intelligence officer and Afghanistan expert and was said to be Kipling's model for Kim's spy-master 'Creighton Sahib'. The younger Mason had followed his uncle out to India in 1909 as a member of the Survey of India, and over the course of twenty-five years' service had made a number of daring forays into the Himalayas and the Pamir. On one of these expeditions Mason had encountered one of his opposite numbers, a Russian colonel, and the two of them had spent the night swapping toasts in whiskey and vodka. Early next morning, with the other man stone drunk in his tent, Mason had packed up and left, taking the Russian's yak transport with him.

This was the Great Game as it has entered the public imagination. Essentially a game played by amateurs: gentlemen travellers, explorers and surveyors whose main purpose lay elsewhere other than raw intelligence gathering in the sense of obtaining secret information by secret means. But also being played out side by side with the amateur game was another altogether darker, infinitely more serious and more illicit one. It is this professional Great Game that Robert Johnson seeks to uncover in *Spying for Empire*. This is a task that has largely eluded earlier historians – myself included – simply because of the slippery nature of the subject, the paucity of the records that survive and the sheer size of the canvas across which the game was played. Yet, as Robert Johnson now demonstrates, there is enough evidence to show that the factual Great Game was not only as dramatic as Kipling's fictional one – but even more spectacular.

CHARLES ALLEN

Preface

In the pursuit of the Great Game, I have had the pleasure of trekking in the footsteps of historical characters through some of the most stunning scenery in the world. Fine travel writers have tried to capture the sensation of hiking in the Hindu Kush and Himalayas, and yet nothing can quite capture the exhilaration of the air, the great voids around the peaks, the crystal white glow of the glaciers, or the hard and unforgiving rocky slopes. The sticky scent of the deodar trees on the Lowari Pass remains locked in my consciousness. South Asia is a magnetic place, and, once experienced, can never be forgotten. The great lengths of service of British soldiers and administrators to India gave them strong feelings of attachment too. These feelings were perhaps not dissimilar to those of settlers in other Commonwealth countries, and give us a glimpse of the strong bond that developed between Britons and their adopted lands. Of course, it was not just the landscapes that did this: it was the people too.

The British Empire is frequently held up for criticism. Powerful attacks have been made on it, and many of them, in my view, are justified. However, there is a troubling tendency to give a two-dimensional and caricatured image of British colonial rule. In some work by post-colonial scholars, the Empire's officials and soldiers, the colonisers, are portrayed as distant, racist, greedy and immoral: the colonised are represented simply as victims. However, it is now widely acknowledged that the Empire could not have functioned without its 'sub-imperialists', and the willing co-operation of millions of imperial subjects. Rudyard Kipling, regarded as the 'poet laureate of Empire', took a great deal of trouble to create verse and story about all those who served the Empire, regardless of colour or background, from the world of the civil servants in *Departmental Ditties* to the heroism of *Gunga Din*. The British Empire was not just an exercise in power by a British oligarchy; it was also a great mixing of cultures, peoples and ideas.

The contact between the British and African or Asian peoples caused a sharp redefinition of their sense of place and identity. The British took on settler identities, or reinforced a sense of Britishness, often in an idealised form. For Africans and Asians the traditional layering of loyalties, from family, religion, clan, region, and nation was sometimes also extended to Empire. Indeed, many developed a pride in their own understanding of being 'British'. The Empire represented opportunity as much as it stifled and suppressed, and employment in the service of the Empire was sometimes attractive. This reorientation of identity has been the subject of intense debate in recent years. What emerges is a complex picture that encompasses many experiences, from the white convict to the Gurkha soldier; some were brutalised and crushed, others elevated and lionised. And hidden within this pantheon stand the shadowy figures of the intelligence world.

British intelligence was clearly less developed in the nineteenth century than it is today. However, it is misleading to credit the creation of a modern intelligence community solely to the advent of the two world wars, for the imperial network developed before the centralised Intelligence Division in London. Indeed, all over the British Empire, the casual employment of spies, the reconnaissance of territory, and the extension of colonial rule built up a comprehensive intelligence picture.

Traditionally too much emphasis has perhaps been placed on covert intelligence, or secret agents, which leads to the conclusion that British intelligence in the nineteenth century was amateur and almost negligible in extent. In fact, a broader and more accurate definition of intelligence, encompassing the gathering of information by a variety of means, shows how sophisticated the Victorians were. Until recently, it has suited British authorities to conceal the nature of British intelligence. There was a desire to protect the anonymity of the participants and even the memoirs make few references to Asian personnel who served their organisations. Indian historians since 1947 have also focussed on the personalities in the nationalist struggle: 'collaborators' have been a less attractive area for research. Yet a study of the imperial dimension of British intelligence offers a chance to re-examine the function, scale and achievements of the secret services. In the last two decades, post-colonial scholars have sought to show how important 'knowledge' was in extending British rule. Whilst some of this work gives an exaggerated picture of cynical centralised planning, almost to a level of totalitarianism, there is merit in the idea that knowledge made the business of governing easier. Given the speed at which the Empire grew in the last quarter of the nineteenth century, the volume of global intelligence that was gathered and processed is little short of miraculous. Moreover, British intelligence in the early twentieth century was able to thwart a series of conspiracies without erecting a 'police state'. The achievement was partly due to the development of more sophisticated systems, but the dangerous work of gathering intelligence was carried out by a relatively small group of British and Asian agents. It is their achievement, especially the latter, that forms the focus of this book.

In researching and writing this book I owe a debt of gratitude to many people. Special thanks must go to Professor Jeremy Black, Dr Iain R. Smith, Professor George Boyce, and Dr Bruce Coleman for their support and encouragement, and I am deeply grateful for the assistance of staff at the Public Record Office, the National Army Museum, the National Archives of India, the Oriental and India Office Collection at the British Library, and the Royal Society for Asian Affairs. Special thanks must go to David Watkins of Greenhill for his combined skills of encouragement, guidance and diplomacy: this book would not have been possible without him. There are many more, in South and Central Asia, that I should also like to thank for introducing me to their countries, culture and ideas – all have been an inspiration. Most of all I wish to thank my family who endure my absences and obsessions with selfless tolerance, and I dedicate this book to them.

R. A. JOHNSON

Note on Names and Dates

Throughout this book, the old names of places have been retained as they appear in contemporary records, hence Cawnpore not Kanpur, and Bombay not Mumbai. The only exception is in eighteenth-century spellings where a more modern form has been preferred, hence Baluchistan not Baloochistan, and Kabul not Cabool. Where names changed during the period covered by this book those changes are used, hence St Petersburg becomes Petrograd. In order to differentiate between the entire region and colonised Russian territory, again as they appear in nineteenth century references, the lower-case central Asia refers to the former and the upper-case Central Asia refers to the latter. The term Anglo-Indian refers here to the British personnel of India rather than men and women of mixed-race descent. Transliteration techniques for Asian languages seem to change too, but for simplicity it seems sensible to retain the usage as it appears in the original documents of the period. This leaves us with, for example, Abdur Rahman rather than Abd-al-Rehmen. However, with Russian names, generally the anglicised transliteration is used, hence Damagatsky, not Damagatskii. Throughout the text, there are a large number of references to locations that may not be familiar to the Anglophone world. It is therefore recommended that the maps provided be consulted for clarity. Finally, a note on dates. The Western European calendar is used throughout rather than the Russian. As a general rule, the Russian dates were eleven days ahead of those used in the west during the period covered in this book.

SPYING FOR EMPIRE

'I sent word that the roads for which I was paying money to the diggers were being made for the feet of strangers and enemies.'

'For?'

'For the Russians… Over the Passes this year after snow melting come two strangers under cover of shooting wild goats. They bear guns, but they bear also chains and levels and compasses … They are well received by Hilas and Bunar … They make great promises; they speak as the mouthpiece of a *Kaisar* [tsar] with gifts'.

Rudyard Kipling, *Kim*

* * *

'The importance of this portion of the frontier [Kashmir and Gilgit] lies mainly in the proximity of the Russian outposts … The Great Empire – the coming shadow of which Napoleon saw with a prophetic eye – is expanding in many directions. Central Asia is now hers. That her soldiers, and the ablest of them, consequently believe in the possibility of conquering India, no one who has had the chance of studying the question can now doubt.'

Colonel Algernon Durand, *The Making of a Frontier*

Chapter 1

The Great Game

Myth and Reality

In a secret journal hidden in the Public Record Office in London, enigmatically entitled *The Great Game*, lie the forgotten names of agents who risked their lives in the service of the British Empire. On these vellum pages, pungent with age, is a remarkable archive of men who worked for British intelligence. They were usually only referred to by their code-names: a letter to denote their area of operations, and a letter or a number for the individual. Their mission was to keep watch on the movements and strengths of the Russian Army, which lay apparently poised to strike at British India through Persia, Afghanistan, or the mountains of the Hindu Kush.

However, the tone of the records, detectable through the handwriting of the agents' 'Control' or handler, Colonel Charles Maclean, is one of anxiety. An entry of September 1887 concerned with recruitment notes that: 'No eligible men have come forward due to the dangerous nature of the duty.'[1] The previous month, two messengers had been arrested in Merv, a small oasis settlement in Russian Central Asia. Agents 'I' and 'J' had been compromised and had to be discharged. An agent in ring 'C' went missing in November 1888 after being despatched to get 'photos of Russian guns, troops and barracks'. Later it was discovered that his brother, living inside Russian territory, was being threatened in some way by the Russian governor of the area.[2] The situation deteriorated. Systematic searches were preventing agents from crossing the Russian border, and, despite precautions such as invisible ink messages, more agents were going missing.[3]

Who were the men in these stories? What motivated them to engage in such dangerous work for a foreigner's empire? And why, in the history of British intelligence, has their contribution been overlooked?

The Great Game

The Great Game was the nickname given to the struggle to secure and maintain geo-strategic supremacy in Asia in order to protect India, Britain's largest imperial possession. More specifically it involved the gathering of intelligence on potential threats and the winning over of Asian rulers who lay beyond the mountain ramparts of the subcontinent. For most of the nineteenth century Britain's chief rival in Asia was the Russian Empire, a power which appeared threatening not least because of its potentially vast armies and its seemingly inexorable advance across central Asia towards India. British personnel were thus employed in a number of related tasks in this period: gathering information about routes of likely invasion forces and their strengths; diplomatic offensives to ally or befriend khans, emirs and other potentates and thus deny their lands to foreign occupation (without the expense of governing them within the British Empire); and counter-intelligence work. In the twentieth century this pattern was unchanged, but new threats emerged from other powers – Germany, Italy, Japan – and there were fresh ideological challenges for the British Empire from nationalists and Communists. Yet the British had always to contend with a potential 'fifth column' too, namely Indian activists and all those others affected by periodic unrest in the subcontinent. The British learned to deal with each of these threats and in the process a sophisticated and modern intelligence system gradually evolved.

The aim of this book is to re-examine the Great Game and its pivotal role in the evolution of British intelligence. Many existing studies do not give sufficient weight to the 'imperial' dimension in the development of the secret services, and, as a result, too little attention has been paid to the British, but also particularly the Asian personnel who served them. Moreover, this book also tries to show the connections between the decisions being made by civilian ministers, the army and the British authorities in India. Usually, the internal security of India and the evolution of Britain's foreign intelligence are treated separately, but it is clear from the material in the archives that they were, in fact, inextricably linked. This book therefore takes a broad view, examining the development of British intelligence in the Great Game within wider contexts, but without losing sight of the very individual nature of espionage in this period.

The Challenging Topography of Central Asia

Dividing south and central Asia is the world's largest mountain complex. It is so vast that several of the greatest ranges lie within it, as well as many of the highest peaks, including Everest and K2. Radiating from this great spine are vast rivers, such as the Indus, the Oxus, and the Ganges. Between the richly watered valleys span huge deserts, which force their sparse inhabitants into a marginal existence. Climatically, this is a region of extremes. The deluge of the monsoon in the south gives the subcontinent tropical humidity interspersed with periods of furnace heat. Beyond the mountains, arid conditions prevail and all human activity is dependent on the oases that are studded across the region or the great rivers of the Oxus and Syr Daria. Yet, before European colonisation, the peoples of these lands had adapted themselves to their environment. Whilst the mountain dwellers, nomads and pastoralists remained poor, the city dwellers of the central Asian khanates and Indian states had grown rich. The wealth and the resources of south and central Asia acted like a magnet for the colonising powers of Europe.

Politically, the region was fragmented. By the late eighteenth century the sub-continent was divided into a number of states, the flotsam and jetsam of the old Mughal Empire. Religious and ethnic differences were overlaid with a variety of political systems, but the existence of lucrative industries (especially textiles and metals) and a vast peasantry that could be taxed for handsome revenues made the occupation of India irresistible to the British servants of the East India Company.

Across the mountain systems in the north were pockets of hill peoples living in tough, marginal conditions. A long tradition of rivalry for scarce resources and difficult access had meant the evolution of more bellicose cultures. In the north-west, for example, a particularly militant brand of Sunni Islam sustained the people whom the British were to call Pathans. To the west of the Indian subcontinent, across the Indus, lay the regions known as Sind and Baluchistan. Again a harsh desert climate and remote location had given rise to a deep distrust of all outsiders. Further west still lay the fading glories of Persia. Governed by an increasingly decrepit monarchy and corrupt state, the country had fallen significantly behind the West.

To the north of Persia was central Asia itself. A vast expanse of deserts and semi-arid steppe, broken by the mountains of the Caucasus, Pamirs and Tien Shan or by the great waters of the Black, Caspian and the Aral Seas. Once again, a number of independent states existed in the region, clustered around oases cities. Nomadic mountain Khirgiz in the Pamirs, and desert Turcomans in the Karakum owed little loyalty to these states beyond a nominal suzerainty. Indeed, a similar arrangement affected the area that came to be known as Afghanistan. The rulers of Kabul exercised limited authority beyond the city, and for long periods the other cities, such as Kandahar, Herat and Mazar, were entirely independent, as were all the rural areas. Although Europeans have tried to categorise the 'Afghans', in reality a complex mesh of families, clans, sections and ethnic loyalties have prevailed. Trying to create a nation state among the Afghans has long proved elusive.

During the nineteenth century, the inexorable advance of the Russian Empire southwards across Asia, and the threatening boasts of the tsar's officers, seemed to menace the pre-eminent British position in India, the so-called 'Jewel in the Crown' of Britain's colonies. The two empires had emerged triumphant from the Napoleonic Wars in Europe and were eager to capitalise on their success – but the advance of one was perceived as a threat to the other. Every assurance from the tsar's ministers that there was no warlike intention seemed to the British to be a deliberate smokescreen. The British felt compelled to despatch diplomats to negotiate in St Petersburg and to launch military expeditions to secure their Indian borders in the period 1839–98. Yet, the seizure of territory by Russian troops continued, decade after decade, including those regions which were supposed to act as buffer zones between the British and Russian Empires in central Asia. The British authorities in India were thus forced to send out agents to win over local chieftains and rulers beyond the borders but also to survey, map and monitor the approaches to the Indian subcontinent: an intelligence effort called the 'Great Game'.

The most likely route that an invasion force might take had historic precedent. Alexander the Great, Timur the Lame, the Mughal Babur, and Nadir Shah of Persia had all crossed into India in the proximity of the Khyber Pass in the heart of the mountains that came to be called, somewhat enigmatically, the North-West Frontier. Yet to the south, the mountains gave way to the deserts of Baluchistan and this appeared to be an 'open flank' for India. The river Indus was unsuitable as a defensive feature too. Indian forces had frequently suffered defeat there, so British imperial planners looked to stop their enemies where they would be weakest, namely in the barren mountains of the Hindu Kush. The high passes would be ideal to hold an opponent. But it was also vital to be forewarned of the advance of hostile forces and this meant being thoroughly acquainted with the most likely approaches. These appeared to be the rivers of central Asia, since they were the only sources of water in a parched land devoid of good roads and with scattered settlements.

Anxieties about Russian ambitions in central Asia were magnified in the 1870s by the Russian annexation of the ancient and fabled khanates of the old Silk Route, such as Khiva, Bokhara and Samarkand. As the Russian Empire's frontiers drew ever closer to British India, a debate developed amongst British officers and their politicians: what were Russia's real intentions in the region, and what should the response be? Whilst some deplored the alarmist reactions to Russian expansion, others pointed to the evidence of more sinister designs: the discovery of secret Russian military plans, border skirmishes between the tsar's forces and Britain's Afghan allies, or the arrival of so-called 'shooting parties', 'scientific explorers' and less covert armed Cossack patrols in the mountain passes on India's northern border. These Russian parties seemed to suggest there was an intention to stir up the peoples of Afghanistan and South Asia against British rule. Although the British had managed to crush the Indian Mutiny in 1857, there was widespread concern that it might be necessary to fight a border war against tribesmen and Russian forces, whilst trying to suppress an internal revolt at the same time. This internal dimension, in the context of the Great Game, is often overlooked, but the mood of the Indian population was an important element in the calculations of the British authorities – and their Russian adversaries.

The potential for conflict between Britain and Russia stemmed not just from their rivalry for imperial supremacy in Asia, but also from the vagueness of their frontiers, and there were several attempts to define the limits of their influence in the late nineteenth century. Nevertheless, even the settlement of the borders of Afghanistan, Persia, Russian Turkestan and India between 1885 and 1907 did little to abate covert intelligence activity. It was not until German intrigues began to threaten both British and Russian interests in the years before the First World War that the Great Game cooled in intensity. Nonetheless, after the Russian Revolution in 1917, a new episode of Anglo-Russian rivalry opened up so that British concern about subversion did not subside. Subsequently, new threats presented themselves: the Afghans disputed the settled borders and sought to stir up the independent hill men, the Pathans, who lived astride the North-West Frontier of India. Nationalist unrest developed throughout the 1920s and 1930s, and the Japanese assault on the eastern borders, which coincided with serious unrest in Bengal in 1944, was a great trial for the Raj. Eventually the British relinquished their exclusive hold on power, even though they had successfully held India against the Japanese and Indian Nationalist unrest. The Great Game in South Asia was brought to its conclusion with the end of British colonial rule in 1947. Just over forty years later, the Russian grip on central Asia was also broken.

Kipling's *Kim*: License of Literature or Reflections of Reality?

> Yes, and thou must learn how to make pictures of roads and mountains and
> rivers – to carry these pictures in thy eye till a suitable time comes to set them
> upon paper. Perhaps some day when thou art a chain man, I may say to thee
> when we are working together: 'Go across those hills and see what lies
> beyond ... I will give thee a hundred rupees for a picture of a river and a
> little news of what the people say in the villages there'.[4]

In Rudyard Kipling's enigmatic story *Kim*, the central figure of his story – an
orphaned boy of an Irish soldier and an Indian mother – is challenged in this
extract by Colonel Creighton, the head of the Intelligence Department, to join his
team of native agents. Trained by the British, men like Mahbub Ali or Hurree
Chunder Mookerjee are despatched on missions that range from listening in on the
conversations of Asian rulers to the interception of seditious intelligence.

The struggle between Russia and Britain for imperial influence over southern
and central Asia was immortalised in Kipling's fictional underworld of espionage.
Kim is portrayed as no stranger to intrigue. He acts as a courier even though he
does not understand the contents of the messages he carries – 'what he loved was
the game for its own sake'.[5] However, over time, he is drawn deeper into a secret
world of spying. He carries a vital document on the activities of 'The Northern
Power, a Hindu banker in Peshawar, a firm of gun makers in Belgium and an
important semi-independent Mohammedan ruler to the south' to the head of
British intelligence in India.[6] For his first mission, Kim is trained by a mysterious
figure, Lurgan Sahib, before setting off into the mountains to play the 'Great
Game'. It is there that he clashes with a Russian and a Frenchman, spies acting for
the 'Power in the North'. Kim bravely steals their survey plans of sensitive passes
through the mountains and passes them, at the cost of his cover – and almost his
life – to Colonel Creighton back in Simla.

Kipling himself was never an agent of British intelligence, unlike some
twentieth century authors of espionage fiction, so in trying to investigate the reality
of the Great Game, how much attention should be paid to his picturesque novel?
Some have written it off as a fanciful exaggeration. But Kipling was certainly better
informed about the Great Game than is generally supposed. When he was a young
journalist at Simla, the Commander-in-Chief of the Indian Army, Lord Roberts,
briefed him directly on the threat to India, and he read Major-General MacGregor's
Defence of India (1884), which was regarded as the handbook of the hawkish
'forward school'. Kipling was also well informed about the frequent border wars
on the North-West Frontier, although his only foray to Peshawar on the frontier, in
native dress, ended swiftly when he was stoned by children.[7] Of course, Kim is also
an autobiographical figure in the novel, and many of the questions he poses, and
the affection he feels for old India, are, in fact, Kipling's own sentiments.

The trademark of Kipling's work was always to represent the unsung heroes of
the British Empire, from lowly water carriers of the Indian Army, like Gunga Din,
to the overworked members of the Indian Civil Service who appear in *Plain Tales*

from the Hills. In *Kim,* Kipling engages his reader with unforgettable pictures of Indian people on the Grand Trunk Road and on the rail network, but he is also concerned to show that the Indian Raj is safeguarded by the unceasing and sacrificial efforts of the intelligence community. His conversation with Lord Roberts was critical in shaping the novel; deeply troubled by the potential of another popular uprising, Roberts believed that the Russian threat to India was the most important issue of his career. He produced no fewer than twenty reports on the Defence of India between 1877 and 1893, and he championed the creation and development of an Indian Intelligence Branch. As a novelist, Kipling seized these ideas from his own experience and adapted them in his story. Even the characters had personal connections. One of Kipling's former lovers, Gussie Tweedell, married Colonel Crichton of the Survey Department, providing Kipling with the name of his own fictional intelligence chief, Colonel Creighton. On his first visit to Simla, Kipling also drew inspiration from his brief hike in the Himalayan foothills and it is in a remote mountain setting that the climax of Kim's mission is acted out.

Indeed, in his story, Kipling fused together the real work of the Survey Department of India, which employed Asian agents with cryptonyms like 'The Mirza', with fictional British intelligence operations, to create a hybrid organisation deeply engaged in counter-intelligence activities on the frontiers, and within the Indian subcontinent.

Until recently, historians have rather neglected literature as a source, but the development of post-colonial studies, with a strong emphasis on the deconstruction of texts, suggests that an analysis of Kipling's novel may reveal more than previously thought. Whilst it is clear that Kipling exaggerated and invented a great deal, *Kim* is certainly *based* on reality.

In many studies of the historical, as opposed to fictional Great Game, there has been surprisingly little reference to the Asian and British agents who were the backbone of the intelligence effort. Derek Waller and Peter Hopkirk tried to redress the balance, but even though they dealt with individuals their efforts were not linked directly to the intelligence departments of London and Simla, or to the commanders of the British Army, the nucleus of the modern intelligence community.[8] This is curious since there is a remarkable and perhaps obvious clue left in Kipling's *Kim*. Kipling's heroes are, in fact, all Asian agents and they are portrayed as directly linked to British intelligence in India. Even Kim, the ideal agent who is able to move seamlessly between the world of the 'sahibs and the natives', is himself half Asian. The chief players, other than Colonel Creighton, the 'control', are the Afghan horse trader, Mahbub Ali; the Indian master of disguises, Hurree Babu (also known as R17); and the mysterious agent E23. Successful intelligence organisations are always eager to recruit men and women from a target region, expert linguists from home, or, and perhaps most valuable of all, those who already work in the enemy's senior ranks. Kipling's story reflects a fact now often overlooked or downplayed. It is clear that the British Raj was dependent on the willing co-operation and participation of millions of its subjects.

Is there any truth behind Kipling's world of agents *within* India? Richard Popplewell's excellent study of British intelligence in India deals with this issue.

He diminishes the importance and organisation of the nineteenth-century efforts in internal surveillance and intelligence, noting: 'A strong aversion to the use of spies was one of the alien traditions of government which the British brought to India.'[9] Tracing numerous episodes in which the British authorities were badly informed, he shows that they sought to avoid harassment of the people, concluding: 'What they could not afford was to alienate the Indian public on a substantial scale. The maintenance of British rule in India depended upon the acquiescence and participation of the ruled.'[10] Nevertheless, it would be wrong to see the work of Victorian intelligence only in comparison with the more modern techniques of the twentieth century. There are several references to work by spies and spy networks inside India, and the police were tasked to detect subversion, albeit with varying degrees of success. Indeed, Lawrence James noted that: 'In the broadest sense, every Briton abroad in India was a spy, expected to use his ears and eyes and record what he had seen and heard.'[11]

The Collaborative Empire

In the eighteenth century, military intelligence was a makeshift affair. In essence, commanders had to rely on the reports of their own light cavalry and forward units, or on the arrival of periodic pieces of information from civilians, prisoners or part-time agents. It is not surprising that, both at a tactical as well as a strategic level, there were spectacular failures. Governments were dependent on the reports of their ambassadors or consuls, while military attachés might, by accompanying another nation's army on campaign, learn something useful. On the whole military intelligence lacked coherence and consistency. However, it would be wrong to judge these intelligence efforts of the day by twenty-first-century standards. Such a judgement would create a totally misleading idea that all intelligence before the modern period was, at the least, worthless, and, at best, rather amateurish.

In fact, the British intelligence effort tended to ebb and flow, depending on the nature and severity of the threat. At the end of the sixteenth century, Walsingham had constructed a network of informers to protect the Elizabethan monarchy from Catholic conspiracies. In the seventeenth century, internal security continued to provide the focus of operations and Oliver Cromwell kept himself well informed about the loyalties and movements of royalist plotters, both in Great Britain and in Europe, through his spymaster John Thurloe. The Jacobite threat continued the trend of internal surveillance into the early 1700s.[12] From 1666 there had been a secret service fund, but it was not until 1797 that it came under parliamentary control with an annual vote. According to the eminent intelligence historian Christopher Andrew, much of this money was spent on: 'British propaganda on the continent, an assortment of part time informants, a variety of secret operations by freelance agents, and an elaborate system of political and diplomatic bribery.'[13] Some of the money was spent on the Decyphering Branch, an agency established in 1703 by the Reverend Edward Wills. However, when postal services replaced couriers (making intercepts harder), this organisation, re-titled The Post Office Secret Office, was run down and then abolished in 1844.[14]

The French Revolutionary Wars (1792–1802) caused considerable anxiety in the

British government and a remarkable increase in intelligence activity. Police surveillance was established in the United Kingdom to prevent the infiltration of agitators, and laws were passed against immigration and sedition. Secret Service operatives were sent to France and assisted in the escape of counter-revolutionaries. With the rise of Napoleon, British intelligence turned to recruitment of members of the European intelligentsia. At a tactical level, too, field intelligence also improved. In the Peninsular campaign in Spain and Portugal, agents in disguise operating behind enemy lines were a common feature of the fighting. A number of spies went into French camps dressed as pedlars and minstrels, and the cobbler at the bridge at Irun had sent accurate information of French units crossing the river over several years.[15] Furthermore, Lieutenant-Colonel Colquhoun Grant ably served the Duke of Wellington as one of the most successful 'exploring officers' over a long period. Whilst Assistant Quartermaster-General George Scovell broke French codes,[16] Grant used his Spanish contacts to intercept French despatches, and, although captured on the river Coa in 1812, he sent a stream of intelligence to Wellington from his captivity in Paris. He then escaped, disguised as a sailor. In 1815, he was again in front of Wellington's army in the Netherlands and was the first to report the movement of Napoleon from Condé, prior to the Battle of Waterloo.[17]

After the Napoleonic Wars, the threat to Britain receded. Funding was cut back and the efficiency of the army dwindled during the 'long peace'. Military intelligence, known from 1803 as the Depot of Military Knowledge and then from 1815 as the Topographical Department, was almost exclusively engaged on collating information from the foreign press and map making. This was used to build up a library of information on other powers, but until the 1850s it was hardly active at all. In the Crimean War (1854–6), the British Army was painfully short of maps. Field intelligence was also very poor. Small improvements were made, but the general view is that Victorian intelligence was small in scale, badly co-ordinated and inadequate. In his excellent work on the history of British intelligence, Christopher Andrew did not condemn the nineteenth century Intelligence Division (ID) of the War Office entirely, but wrote: 'By comparison with its efficient, up to date library, the ID's covert intelligence system remained amateurish.'[18] Andrew notes that the Secret Service was seriously under-funded: in the 1880s the annual vote was little more than £600.[19] This compares badly with the £26,000 that was spent on 'pensions' (payments to spies) in 1815.[20]

However, the danger in drawing conclusions based only on the intelligence effort in the United Kingdom is that it leaves out a good deal of the evidence. Although direct threats to the British Isles declined in the early nineteenth century, the growth of the Empire in the same period shifted the interest of British intelligence overseas. Across the globe, Britain's expanding imperial dominion compelled its servants, both military and civilian, to make contact with indigenous peoples. Partly as a result of the emphasis on trade, the British were obliged to involve the local peoples in the imperial enterprise. In China, British merchants were dependent on the Chinese *compradors*, or middlemen, who arranged transactions, translated, and acted as commercial agents for their employers. In the dark years of slavery on the West African coast, British merchants had been similarly dependent on the supply of human captives provided by the powerful tribesmen of the interior. In India, the states that had succeeded the old Mughal Empire remained far more powerful than the British trading settlements for decades and the British were, once again, dependent on local co-operation for trade, translation, and commercial concessions. In 1756, the Newab of Bengal, Siraj ud Dowlah, proved that Britain's presence in India was precarious when he stormed and sacked Calcutta, throwing his unfortunate prisoners into the infamous 'Black Hole'.[21]

On the other hand, when Robert Clive won his celebrated victory at Plassey the following year, a battle that began a process of expanding British territorial rule in the subcontinent, he did so with the assistance of Indian troops and the connivance of Indian allies. A key player in the acquisition of these allies was a Punjabi called Omichund. A merchant with both the British and the Newabs of Bengal, Omichund had lived on the fringe of Calcutta in great wealth, but he aroused suspicion when he suffered no loss during the sack of the city in 1756. Nevertheless, he was entrusted with the secret communications between the British and Mir Jaffar, one of Clive's potential allies.[22] Thus, from the outset, British imperial rule was characterised by the successful co-operation and collaboration of people who were not British-born.

The Indian states that allied with the British did so because they perceived the British to be useful partners against other Indian states. Indian troops who enlisted saw financial advantage in serving the British, although this mercenary motive was tempered by the cultural demands of their caste: military clans had to serve as soldiers to preserve their prestige. Collaboration with the British often meant mutual benefit. Traders enjoyed protection, peasants were relieved from oppressive landowners by formalised land settlements and many thousands enjoyed some form of employment. It would be wrong to suggest, of course, that every Indian lived a better life under the East India Company and the Raj. There were abuses by the British-Indian police, catastrophic famines, and millions were administered by a foreign regime which denied them either representation or a role in the government. But the relationship was a complex one, and Indians were not always the subordinate partners.

Whilst much has been written about the failures of British rule and the fundamental inequalities of imperialism, far fewer have adequately explained how this system, if it was as bad as it is now suggested, lasted so long. After much debate, some consensus is beginning to emerge that the British Empire neither rested solely on British bayonets, nor was it run in the 'black and white' way suggested by nationalists. The Indians were not simply 'the Oriental' or the 'Other'. To the British, they were, in fact, a combination of groups of varying levels of usefulness to the imperial enterprise. Amongst the most favoured in the military sphere were the Gurkhas and the Sikhs, whilst in agriculture it was the 'sturdy peasants' of the lower castes. In intelligence work, too, there were resourceful individuals who were well suited to positions of special trust. The secret of the success of the Raj, like the rest of the Empire, lay not so much in brute military force, but in its ability to connect existing social and political structures, ensure mutual economic gain and to incorporate or employ many thousands of the local populations. In this sense, the intelligence system represents just one small facet of how the British Empire actually 'worked'.

Myth and Reality

There are many strengths in current studies of the Great Game. The shifting relationship between London and St Petersburg and the global context of Anglo-Russian relations is now more thoroughly understood. Histories of European exploration have also highlighted the role of the British and Asian surveyors, and the missions of some of the more colourful characters who travelled across central Asia have been examined in depth.[23] However, there is still a strong tendency to see the agents and explorers concerned only with mapping and topography, and then fail to understand how the purpose of this work fitted into the wider needs of intelligence gathering.

Gerald Morgan believed that *Kim* 'owed practically everything to Kipling's imagination', and the only thing that was not an invention was his use of the name 'The Great Game'.[24] Morgan argued there was no secret world of spies and counter-espionage endemic throughout northern India and central Asia. He tried to show how little British institutions in reality matched the mythical inventions of *Kim* and he argued that even the Indian Survey Department, employing a number of Asian agents with code-names, was not engaged on intelligence work, for their tasks were strictly limited to gathering information on topography. Morgan played down the importance of the intelligence departments, both in India and Britain, maintaining that their tasks were only really those of 'collating information'. The Political Service, formed in 1820, was little more than a diplomatic corps designed to send agents to neighbouring states. The politicals' use of disguise, Morgan believed, fooled no one; it was for personal safety rather than clandestine operations. These agents rarely collected information on the Russians and had no powers to make treaties. Their 'special duty' was carried out quite openly, with letters of introduction for the rulers they visited, and British officers never entered Russian territory without permission. Morgan even questioned the success of the actual intelligence officers, doubting if there was anything, beyond some geographical knowledge, that they really achieved.[25]

Others are not convinced that Kipling's work is entirely an invention.[26] If the fictional struggle was between the Russians, who sought to encourage Afghans and frontier tribesmen to fall upon the British, and the loyal Indians and British agents who aimed to thwart them by observation and survey work, then the essence of Kipling's story is not an exaggeration, for the evidence is there. Morgan was prepared to acknowledge the existence of 'newswriters', the name given to local spies hired by British political officers when they were *en poste* in Teheran, Kabul, and Kandahar. He noted that they were often Indian merchants living in these cities and argued that they 'rarely contributed much of importance'.[27] Morgan admitted that on at least one occasion, Asian agents were despatched to spy on the Russian Army, but he promptly dismissed this as an *ad hoc* and isolated example.

Morgan's intention was to demolish the fanciful claims of the Soviet historian N. A. Khalfin who believed that the British intelligence network was highly organised and aimed ultimately at ejecting Russia from Central Asia.[28] Khalfin believed, like many Russian historians, that British agents had swarmed across Russian Central Asia 'for the purposes of reconnaissance and propaganda'. The Russian scholar had apparently misunderstood the role of the 'pundits', Asian surveyors who moved across central Asia and Tibet in disguise – he believed they had been specifically trained in intelligence work at the 'Captain Dalgetty School'. Morgan in turn pointed out that the reference to a special school for spies came from a memoir by Captain Rollo Burslem.[29] This officer had met a traveller who imparted information about Khokand, but he described him as a member of the 'Captain Dalgetty School'. This was not, Morgan explained, a centre for training spies at all, but a way of describing a mercenary – Dalgetty was a fictional soldier of fortune of the English Civil War created by Sir Walter Scott.

Khalfin's research revealed that the Russians had long feared the British annexation of central Asia. Count Ignatiev led a large trade mission to Khiva in 1858 to forestall British designs there. Unable to make any headway, he had moved on to Bokhara, only to learn that five British agents had recently visited the city. He also seems to have accepted the rumour that British officers were training the army of Khokand. The Russian anxiety about the British training central Asian troops, a recurrent theme in the nineteenth century, was, Morgan argued, a 'baseless rumour'.[30] According to Morgan, gun-running was ruled out by the British authorities too.

However, in trying to belittle the efforts of the 'intelligencers', and in refuting Khalfin, Morgan perhaps rather overstated the case.[31] British officers did train the Persian army for a time, and there was a British gun-running effort to support Imam Shamyl in his resistance to the Russian annexation of the Caucasus in 1836.[32] Even Sir Garnet Wolseley, an experienced general of colonial warfare who became Commander-in-Chief at the end of the nineteenth century, favoured the idea of recruiting central Asians to fight the Russians. After all, all over the Empire, Britain had successfully created colonial military forces.

Thus, whilst Morgan conceded that the hiring of local Asian agents was common practice, he remained unconvinced by the quality of the information they gathered, the extent of their secrecy, and their level of organisation, which the Soviet historian, Khalfin, was certain existed. Morgan perhaps failed to acknowledge properly the role played by British intelligence in India. Intelligencers were not solely concerned with 'producing maps' and 'collating information'. There were a number of locations across the region, which were covert or known 'listening posts', either permanently or partially occupied, including Peshawar, Gilgit, Chitral, Kandahar, Kabul, and Meshed. *Ad hoc* arrangements were made, for example, by boundary commissions and by agents. The role of these agencies, even 'innocent' ones like the Survey of India, was to gather 'intelligence'. Morgan argued that none of the institutions of the Raj, except perhaps the Indian Political Service, had any connections with intelligence. But there are grounds for challenging such a generalisation because of the measures the British employed to deal with the lack of information on the region. There was no one central organisation, except perhaps the Government of India itself, but India was the only possession in the British Empire in the nineteenth century to have its *own* intelligence branch.

It has to be said that there was firm opposition from the British Army Commander-in-Chief, the Duke of Cambridge, to the innovation of military intelligence which, as a traditionalist, he regarded as the manifestation of 'pwogress' [*sic*].[33] There was no counter-espionage service, or indeed, espionage, in the way it is understood in modern terms. Intelligence operations overseas (that is, beyond the Empire) were limited, and British officers usually sought command appointments, rather than less prestigious staff work. There were hysterical 'war scares' in the newspapers in the Victorian era, matched only by the equally exaggerated 'spy scares' of the Edwardian period. Yet a false impression has perhaps been created. Unlike previous eras, where intelligence was only considered when an actual war was in progress or a threat was evident, the nineteenth-century intelligence agencies gradually coalesced. Moreover, the Foreign and Colonial Offices made use of the War Office Intelligence Division to a far greater extent in the late nineteenth century. Major-General Sir John Ardagh, Director of Military Intelligence 1896–1901, became a respected figure with these two government ministries.[34] Intelligence operations invariably became more efficient when faced with the imperative of a specific threat. In the South African War (1899–1902), field intelligence developed significantly, and by 1909, with a greater German naval threat looming, Britain had a permanent Secret Service Bureau with agents in continental Europe. The same year, the rise of Indian terrorism led to the creation of a Department of Central Intelligence in India with officers deployed to the United States, China and south-east Asia.

In the face of the Russian threat, intelligence from central Asia was given a greater priority in India than perhaps it was in London, and a constant stream of information was provided. The difficulty, as in all intelligence operations, was to sift fact from rumour, and make sense of the information provided. Errors often occur with the gathering of intelligence, but perhaps more often it is the *way* that intelligence is used, which can be misleading or detrimental. In the nineteenth century, the consuls and political officers who were spread across central Asia from Constantinople to Peshawar, could detect Russian troop movements long before an invasion of Afghanistan, but contemporaries still recognised the limitations of their efforts. C. E. Callwell, the author of a handbook on colonial warfare, wrote:

> In every class of warfare uncertainty must exist as to the movements, intentions, and whereabouts of the enemy ... To correctly interpret the auguries derived from reconnaissances, from information brought in by spies, and from the various forms of circumstantial evidence provided by the theatre of war, is often one of the most difficult of military problems.[35]

It is not surprising that Callwell should have suggested the employment of locals as spies wherever possible. It was a familiar system which formed a crucial part of the Great Game. He acknowledged how quickly local people seemed to learn of new developments:

News spreads in a most mysterious fashion. The people are far more observant than the dwellers in civilised lands. By a kind of instinct they interpret military portents even when totally deficient of courage or fighting capacity. [Intelligence] flies from mouth to mouth ... The enemy has no organised intelligence department, no regular corps of spies, no telegraphs – and yet he knows perfectly well what is going on.[36]

The Great Game Re-examined

There is a need to re-orient the definition of the Great Game to examine, from the fragmentary sources, the role of the Asian agents and to link these together with the intelligence-gathering network in Afghanistan, Central Asia and Persia, and to show their connections with the work of the Intelligence Branch (in India), and the development of the Intelligence Department (in London). This book therefore takes a thematic approach, looking at both the internal and external intelligence efforts of British India, and sets these within a wider context of British intelligence and its development in the period.

There are perhaps many reasons for the gaps in our current knowledge. Asians were, to some extent, hidden within the British literature during the days of Empire. Memoirs of British agents, and biographies, tended to dwell on the activities of the Europeans. But it was also vital to conceal the secret role of the Asian and British agents. Whilst geographical knowledge was broadcast, and was perhaps used as a means to promote the achievement of individuals, some of their publications did not contain the full details of their reports and journals, especially where sensitive mountain passes and potential military information was concerned. Although the survey work and techniques of Indian surveyors were printed in the mid-nineteenth century and made their way to St Petersburg, later reports and missions were not disclosed.

The acquisition of information is obviously central to the idea of intelligence, but the collation and analysis of that information, and conclusions drawn from it, constitute the correct definition of the term.[37] 'Espionage' really describes only the covert aspects of intelligence-gathering, and even today, covert intelligence supposedly represents only ten per cent of all intelligence activity.[38] With these definitions in mind, the Great Game can be recast in a more accurate context. The shift of emphasis to threats beyond the United Kingdom after 1815 (with the exception of the Fenian outrages and the periodic fear of French naval attack which prompted renewed intelligence activity at home) meant that the focus of the British intelligence effort was to the colonies. The greatest threat lay in the size and proximity of the continental Russian Army, which lay beyond the range of the Royal Navy and appeared to menace India from the landward side. With the government ever desirous of cutting expenditure, it was perhaps not surprising that cheaper Asian agents should be used to gather the necessary intelligence. Moreover, from a pragmatic point of view, it was far easier to disguise the covert activities of Asians than it was British officers and to 'disown' them if they were compromised.

However, as C. A. Bayly points out, British rule in India was dependent on the acquisition of knowledge far beyond topographical information for the creation of military maps or the assessments of which passes could be traversed by artillery. Information on languages, customs, loyalties, beliefs, and ethnicity had a part to play in helping the British to rule India. Classifying the various peoples of India gave the British: 'a reassuring certainty that they were all identifiably distinct elements which could be arranged legibly and clearly in the "living museum of mankind".'[39] The obsession with recording and collating can be traced back to the scientific traditions of the eighteenth century, but the Victorians faced the practical problem of how to govern a vast Empire of great diversity. As an example of how information made government possible, Bayly observes systemisation in the ordering of knowledge in anthropology, although it has to be said that the process emerged over time and in a piecemeal fashion.[40] There was no one central agency directing the acquisition of intelligence for the purposes of British rule. However, it is perhaps significant that 468 photographs recording the various ethnic groups of the subcontinent in *The People of India*, begun after the Mutiny in 1858, were kept in the Political and Secret Department of the Government of India. Moreover, there were attempts to discern whether caste had been a determinant of 'loyalty' during the uprising. The concept was developed into identification of 'martial races' and 'inherent lawlessness' in the late nineteenth century and became an important tool in the administration of India.[41] It is noticeable that commerce was also closely interlinked with intelligence assessments, both from its logistical potential and as a means to sustain the area administratively.

The history of Great Game intelligence is thus far from simple and in its course the British had to overcome some major problems. There were considerable difficulties with the interception of agents by Asian states, hostile tribesmen and Russian military personnel. As the archival sources indicate, there was a division of opinion in British military and political circles about the real or imagined nature of the Russian threat to India. There were the problems of communication and maintaining observation in an area larger than the continent of Europe. There were major problems in preserving alliances with unstable regimes, from Persia to Kashgaria. There was also the thorny question raised by the unresolved status of Afghanistan – was it an ally or an enemy? The Great Game was still further complicated by the instability of the Indian border area, a region through which British and Indian troops would need to operate in wartime, but which was inhabited by recalcitrant tribesmen unwilling to accept British rule without a fight.

The Russian side was just as complex. Despite inconsistency and changes of policy in St Petersburg, the tsars and the senior military commanders were unwilling to risk conflict with Britain in the late nineteenth century. However, there were more junior officers for whom a posting to the wastes of Central Asia was a prison sentence that could only be redeemed by military adventure. Willing defiance of official instructions clashed or coincided with occasional directives from the capital. The potential central Asian theatre was a convenient pressure point to divide the British effort and help counter-balance British naval supremacy in the eastern Mediterranean and North Sea. Plans for the invasion of Afghanistan were drawn up, but much of the belligerence at the turn of the century was generated at a popular level, and British statesmen were left in the dark about Russia's true intentions.

Collaboration was perhaps the secret of the Empire's success for it ensured that long periods of peace prevailed. Whilst the current trend is to highlight the Empire's negative features – not least its racial stereotyping, its rule without consent, and its military power – there is a danger of caricature superseding history. The Empire was not run solely by the British for the British: it was a vast, indeed global, collaborative effort. British officials went to great lengths to avoid intervention in the lives or customs of their subjects. Special distinctions and traditions were preserved in the Indian Army and European officers were required to use the languages of their men. Moreover, whilst political power lay in the hands of the viceroy, his council and the white-dominated Indian Civil Service, this elite numbered only a few thousand in a country of 300 million. Moreover, Indian princes continued to rule their own subjects, each under the supervision of a single British officer.

In the intelligence world collaboration was again a crucial factor. The chapters that follow seek to separate myth from reality and to explain how the imperial intelligence network evolved, and, through the individuals who participated, how it worked. The objective of this work is also to show how far the Asian contribution to the Empire's defence has been overshadowed, and how the threat of conflict with Russia, and later Germany and Japan, affected Britain's dealings with the people of south and central Asia.

Chapter 2

Agents of Empire

The Evolution of Political Intelligence, 1757–1830

In the British conquest of India in the eighteenth century, the primary function of secret intelligence was to provide tactical information. Locals were employed as guides and information was gathered by military commanders on a short-term basis. Off the battlefield, there was, as yet, no permanent cadre of secret agents. However, the British did make use of some other remnants of the Mughal system. The couriers and the *dak* postal system were retained, and one or two former *kufia naviss* ('secret writers') were hired to provide political intelligence, whilst the overt gathering of information via Asian envoys and representatives was an integral part of the British administration. In gathering knowledge of India, especially its languages, customs, and diplomacy, the British were dependent on the men they employed, and, until such alliances became unfashionable, on their Indian wives and mistresses. Bankers and money-lenders (whose interests were served by stability) sometimes reported on political and military changes beyond the borders of British India. For a few rupees, the co-operation of a number of midwives (who were at the heart of rural life), older women and labourers could be readily purchased. As Chris Bayly points out, these people were not traitors in the modern sense. Those of high birth in India felt that service to the state was more important than base or low caste 'rebellion'.[1] At the lower end of the social ladder, cash was always more attractive than lofty sentiments.

Nevertheless, British officers were the mainstay of intelligence-gathering. Their military skills and their interpretations were regarded as more reliable than the reports of their Asian personnel. The chief problem was their vulnerability: if deployed alone to remote locations, there was always a risk they could be tortured or killed. Moreover, although they could give a European's view of a situation, they were still dependent on the active collaboration of Indians for their information. These factors reveal the dual nature of the early British intelligence system in India. Covert intelligence-gathering was limited to the casual employment of locals for military campaigns and for limited political purposes. And whilst Europeans might still provide intelligence interpretations, Asians were used in overt information-gathering and communication, as envoys, heralds, couriers, negotiators, interpreters and linguists.

The Emissary: Mehdi Ali Khan

In gathering information, the Honourable East India Company made use of Asians from all walks of life as agents to support its European personnel. After all, they had the ability to pass unnoticed through sensitive border regions. There were countless numbers who provided relatively small amounts of information for a small financial reward, but their oral reports were not published. Without the records to go on, their names and their contributions are lost to us. However, within the reports, journals and memoirs of British officials, occasionally a name appears and a tantalising detail is revealed. For example, George Cherry, British Resident at Lucknow 1761–98, made contact with a number of pilgrims, merchants and exiles to gather information. In 1799 this enterprising officer served on the staff of Arthur Wellesley (later the Duke of Wellington) and ran a comprehensive network of agents, until he was tragically murdered.

Some of the agents that the Company employed turned out to be little more than swindlers. One of these was the mysterious Talamash, a half-Indian half-French clerk of the East India Company from Calcutta.[2] Talamash had a gift for languages and travelled to Afghanistan in the last years of the eighteenth century disguised as a 'dervish'. He attached himself to the court of Zemaun (1793–1801), the king of Kabul, as a servant and learned 'all the secrets of Afghan policy'. When Afghan intelligence was no longer in demand (or perhaps when he was compromised), he moved successively to Bushire, Bahrein and Surat before ending up, it is alleged, as a pirate in the Indian Ocean. Whether he provided much information to the East India Company or not is unclear, for he appears, in fact, to have been little more than an opportunist boasting to impress a potential foreign employer.

When Mountstuart Elphinstone, a British envoy of the East India Company, made a diplomatic visit to Afghanistan in 1808, he came across another adventurous character called Durie. The boy, the son of a European father and an Indian mother, was a dispenser's assistant at Poona and, although he spoke very little English, it was clear he had been educated in the classics. When Elphinstone came across him he was disguised as an Afghan and had made his way across the Middle East from Baghdad. Yet, he refused Elphinstone's offer of a newswriter's post and disappeared, apparently heading back to Baghdad as a pilgrim.[3] Clearly not all could be recruited in a mercenary fashion.

The Great Game did not begin in earnest until the emergence of a specific external threat. At first this came from France, the maritime power that had rivalled Britain in India for much of the eighteenth century. The French had allied themselves to Indian rulers, just as the British had done, and engaged in several local wars. Although the British successfully neutralised the French coastal stations and their political influence in the subcontinent after a succession of conflicts in 1744–61, Napoleon Bonaparte's military victories in Europe, and his occupation of Egypt in 1798, caused a reassessment of the threat to India and the East. It was already known that Tipu Sultan of Mysore, a long-standing enemy of the British in India, was seeking French support. Between 1796 and 1807, French envoys were active in Persia and Mesopotamia, prompting the Governor-

General, Marquess Wellesley, the elder brother of the Duke of Wellington, to take action.

With Napoleon's troops at Cairo, apparently set on marching across the Middle East preceded by his emissaries, Wellesley enlisted Mehdi Ali Khan, a Persian who was serving as the acting Resident at Bushire, to generate conflict between the shah, Fath Ali, and his allegedly pro-French court at Teheran.[4] Clearly no British envoy could have achieved this feat, and, with French agents already in the country, it was an excellent way to 'trump' his rivals. Mehdi Ali Khan was entrusted with a mission of considerable importance and he was a lone player, but, as if these obstacles were not enough, he had to fulfil a second, even more difficult objective. With news of Afghan preparations for an invasion of India, and suspicious contact between Tipu and Zemaun, the king of Kabul, Mehdi Ali Khan was tasked by Jonathan Duncan, the Governor of Bombay, to provoke a civil war in Afghanistan and encourage a Persian attack from the west. The experiment apparently succeeded, forcing the Afghans to retreat from Lahore on 4 February 1799.[5] Wellesley followed up this coup by sending Captain John Malcolm to Persia to conclude a commercial treaty in return for the exclusion of all French envoys and a generous subsidy.[6] However, the treaty was never ratified as Napoleon had been checked and forced to withdraw from Egypt. Moreover, Zemaun had been deposed and blinded by his brother Mahmoud. The threat had passed.

However, hostility between Persia and Russia over the Caucasus turned into a full-scale war in 1804. The shah's plea for British assistance was turned down, largely because Britain was focussed on Napoleon's preparations for an invasion of the United Kingdom itself. Unsurprisingly, when French envoys reappeared in 1807 (having sealed a pact with Russia at Tilsit that year), the shah concluded an alliance against Britain.[7] Malcolm returned to Teheran in 1808 but made little headway until the Foreign Office persuade the shah to accept British support against Russia in a treaty of 1809.[8] The shah was to receive £120,000 per annum and British officers to train his army. Nevertheless, in order to get a clear picture of this invasion route to India, the British intended to map Persia with or without the shah's permission too. Missions were also sent to Lahore and Kabul to impress the local rulers, and to convince them of the merits of siding with Britain.

Russia's alliance with Napoleon in 1807, and the discussions about joint operations, were a turning point. Increasingly the British came to see any Russian advance in central Asia as a move directed ultimately against India. The British saw Persia, even at this early stage, as the first outwork in the defence of India. It was regarded as a useful buffer state, a view reinforced by its war against Russia in the Caucasus (1804–12) and the shah's re-annexation of the province of Khorassan. British diplomacy had been instrumental in securing Persian support, but the success of the first phase of the British covert intelligence operation had been largely down to Mehdi Ali Khan. The next phase was to obtain information about Persia's topography, especially those routes that an invading army might take on its way to the subcontinent.

British Political Officers

Not surprisingly, British Army officers were in the forefront of intelligence work. More prepared to accept hardships and risks in the pursuit of their duty, they were well suited to the hazards of central and south Asia. They often spoke one or more of the Asian languages and they had a good eye for the military potential of topography, although they were not cartographers and they could only observe a narrow compass along the line of their journeys. They were not given any powers to make treaties, or even to negotiate with local leaders. However, they could be used to verify the political situation of a country and assess the resources of possible opponents. They could also be tasked to examine specific intelligence targets – routes, passes and defensive features. However, the lawlessness of the areas through which they travelled, especially the incidence of robbery and murder, made the missions exceptionally hazardous. Foreigners were unlikely to get a warm reception as the fear of strangers, and infidels at that, was strong. As far as incentives were concerned, the missions were challenging and adventurous with great responsibility and need for initiative – a strong appeal for young men of a certain stamp.[9] Moreover, a successful mission could significantly advance an officer's career. Three officers encapsulate the daring and the valuable work required of intelligence officers in this period: Grant, Christie and Pottinger.

Captain N. P. Grant was one of the first British officers to be sent to make a military intelligence assessment of Persia. He journeyed to the Makran area of Persia in 1809, with the specific aim of discovering whether a French or Russian army could march along the Persian Gulf coast to reach Karachi, and he decided that it was possible.[10] However, in 1810, as if to underline the dangerous nature of his work, he was murdered on a similar mission between Isfahan and Baghdad.

Lieutenant Henry Pottinger and Captain Charles Christie of the 5th Bombay Native Infantry were soon tasked with further reconnaissance of the region. Travelling into Baluchistan disguised as Muslim horse traders working for a Hindu merchant, their aim was to continue Grant's work and determine the strengths of the tribes, the nature of the terrain, potential invasion routes and the names of local leaders. Even before they had left Baluchistan, they were warned by their contact, the Khan of Khelat, that armed riders of the Emirs of Sind were on their way to arrest them. Pottinger and Christie split up on 22 March 1810, in accordance with their original plans, and disappeared into the desert. Both were able to verify that the border of Baluchistan and Afghanistan was separated by the great Helmand Desert, a formidable obstacle to any invading army. Pottinger continued along the southern fringe of the desert to enter the Makran, then turned north to end his mission at Kirman in southern Persia, avoiding detection by a variety of disguises, including that of a Baluchi peasant and a devout *hajji* (pilgrim to Mecca). It seems only one of his five-man party knew his real identity as a British officer. On several occasions, Pottinger was only saved from exposure by the people's ignorance of Europeans, but he was eventually compromised by a ten-year-old in Makran who had met Grant the previous year. Fortunately, by then, he was beyond the reach of the Baluchis who would have cut his throat for such a deception. In fact, for all the objective dangers of the desert, the greatest threat to his life was the use of an *agent provocateur* by his eventual host, the Khan of Kirman. Hoping to trick Pottinger, the agent claimed to want to become a Christian and to help lead a revolution against the khan. The attempt failed and Pottinger was able to continue his journey.[11]

Christie, meanwhile, had marched north to Herat and, to improve his personal security, he pretended to be a Muslim pilgrim returning from Mecca, a guise he apparently owed to a mysterious Indian merchant for whom he bore a secret letter. He spent four weeks in Herat, hosted by another Indian merchant (again he carried letters of introduction), drawing up a report on the defences of the city and the logistical potential of the valley. He rejoined Pottinger at Isfahan in July, disguised as an Afghan, and the two made their reports to General Malcolm, the military attaché at Teheran.[12] However, whilst Pottinger returned to India, Christie remained in Persia to help in the training of the Persian army. He was subsequently killed in a frontier battle with the Russians in 1812.[13]

These British officers had been deployed, despite the risks involved, because of the need for specifically military information. Yet, it is clear that, for all their undoubted courage and enterprise, they were dependent on the assistance of their guides and contacts. But who were they? The details will perhaps never be known for, apart from the letters carried by Christie, the identities of the contacts were passed by word of mouth. Whoever their assistants were, there can be no doubt that the missions of Grant, Pottinger and Christie were successful: they established that, whilst an invading army could use the coast of the Persian Gulf, it would be unable to traverse the great Helmand Desert. The Royal Navy could ensure that the coastal lines of communication would be severed, and, just as Napoleon had found in Egypt, without naval supremacy an operation to the Persian Gulf was out of the question.

The Russo-Persian war of 1812 on the Caucasus frontier crystallised the situation. In that year, after a military successful campaign in the mountains against the shah's forces, Russia concluded the Treaty of Gulistan, by which Persia lost its claims to Baku, the Caspian and its Caucasus provinces. Although British officers had taken part in the defence of the frontier alongside the Persian troops they had trained, the embarrassment of British officers fighting against an ally in the war against Napoleon caused the British military mission to be withdrawn. Yet, the following year, Captain John Macdonald-Kinneir collated all the data collected by the British officers on special duty in an intelligence report entitled *A Geographical Memoir of the Persian Empire*.[14] He concluded that, given the Russian presence at Orenburg, a landward invasion of India would have to be made via central Asia and Afghanistan. However, the Tartar tribes he considered too strong and the distances too great for such a venture to succeed. It was Constantinople the Russians would target. Nevertheless, there was already a growing chorus that condemned Russia's territorial ambitions. Sir Robert Wilson, the British military attaché to the tsar's army in 1812, was shocked by the atrocities committed by Cossacks against the French and warned that, after the war, Alexander I seemed 'inebriated with power'.[15] Peter Hopkirk concludes that Wilson may be considered the nineteenth century's 'father of Russophobia', a stance that was to have long-term consequences.[16]

Mir Izzet Ullah and William Moorcroft

Using Asians for local intelligence work was common practice for the British, but one man was charged with an altogether more ambitious mission. In 1812, Mir Izzet Ullah, a Persian *munshi* (translator), was selected to travel along the suspected central Asian caravan routes from Kashmir to Yarkand in Chinese Turkestan, then from Yarkand to Bokhara across the Pamirs, and finally from Bokhara to Kabul, across the Hindu Kush mountains. Ullah was the grandson of one of the last Mughal governors of Lahore and this pedigree was greatly respected by Ranjit Singh, the Sikh Rajah of the Punjab. Trained in the Islamic sciences, Ullah produced accurate reports and he caught the attention of the British whilst serving as the munshi of the Delhi Residency where he formed part of the city's prestigious intelligentsia. Mountstuart Elphinstone, the British envoy to Kabul, described him as: 'intelligent, well-informed and unusually methodical'.[17]

Mir Izzet Ullah's remarkable journey, completed in relatively short time, appeared in published form in the *Calcutta Oriental Quarterly Review* in 1825. His topographical survey was surprisingly accurate.[18] Once again the emphasis was on commercial possibilities and trade routes (and sites of religious significance), for Ullah was acting as agent for William Moorcroft who was a veterinary officer and the Superintendent of the Stud of the East India Company with his own ambitious designs on the future of central Asia. Moorcroft lobbied Calcutta to allow him to make his own expedition into central Asia, ostensibly to uncover more about caravans and the lucrative horse trade that Ullah had reported on. However, Moorcroft was also eager to discover potential invasion routes and he warned that a French or Russian embassy at Bokhara would presage hostile activity north of the Hindu Kush and would eventually constitute a serious threat to India. He urged the governor-general to allow Mir Izzet Ullah and Hyder Young Hearsey, a colleague, to make a second expedition with a purely military intelligence objective.

Hearsey was an Anglo-Indian adventurer, the illegitimate son of a British officer and a Jat woman. He was educated at Woolwich, but initially joined the army of the Newab of Benares and became second-in-command of the fort at Agra, before going on to form his own cavalry regiment which fought alongside the British in Mahratha Wars. At the age of thirty-nine, he married a princess of Cambay and acquired lands near Bareilly, but he provoked trouble with the Gurkhas in 1808 and did little to improve relations between the East India Company and the Kingdom of Nepal. Hearsey was, in a sense, a kindred spirit for Moorcroft. Both were looking for adventure and were, in H. W. C. Davis's words, 'individualists operating on the fringe of the empire'.[19]

Denied the chance to travel north-west in 1812, they decided to attempt to enter Tibet to secure some of the coveted shawl-wool goats (known to the West as 'cashmere' or pashmina). Since Tibet had closed its borders to foreigners, they readily accepted the advice of Pundit Harbalam, another co-opted member of their party, to disguise themselves as *gosains*, or Hindu pilgrims. Their outfits, white robes, red turbans and cummerbunds, were supplemented by staining their skin with lamp black, walnut juice and the ash of burnt cow dung. Moorcroft thus adopted the approach that was to become so common to later players of the Great Game: in disguise, he maintained a clandestine log, and relied on his Asian allies to acquire intelligence. Other than the disguises and learning the manners of the gosains, he needed the regular pacing of Harbalam's young nephew, Harkh Dev, to maintain an accurate record of the march. Hearsey carefully recorded each day's distance and produced a map of their entire journey.

However, this covert approach had its limits. The fifty-four strong caravan was halted near the Niti Pass by Bhotian Rawats, a Hindu clan who could pass freely into Tibet and who shared much in common with their Buddhist neighbours. Without the official status of government envoys, crossing borders was problematic. However, here Moorcroft used his medical knowledge to good effect and he soon won over two influential tribesmen, one of whom permitted his son, Amer Singh, to accompany the caravan as a guide. It was entirely due to Amer Singh that the expedition was able to pass through the Tibetan border posts and thus trade its cargo of Indian wares for the goats and their precious wool. Nevertheless, on the return journey (accelerated by the warning that the death penalty would be imposed on any trade in the goats to outsiders), Moorcroft's party was ambushed and detained by the Gurkhas.[20] Once again, Moorcroft was able to win over the locals. Despite his status as a private individual on a trading mission, he was tempted to inflate his position to acquire the respect needed in negotiations with his captors. Although he was eventually released, he had aroused the suspicions of the Nepalese and perhaps contributed to the deterioration of relations that would end in war in 1814. Significantly, though, his report included details on the military potential of the Gurkhas, noting prophetically: 'under our government they would make excellent soldiers'.[21]

The irrepressible Moorcroft was still refused permission to go to central Asia in a new venture he had concocted to find horses for the East India Company, because he had angered the government with his first expedition. The Nepalese had condemned the activities of this English 'spy', and the Company had no wish to suffer further diplomatic embarrassments with its neighbours, even though there had been some interest in his comments about the extent of Russian trade with the Tibetans.[22] In fact, Moorcroft had to wait seven years before the Political and Secret Department approved a second expedition, but only for the purposes of acquiring horses.[23]

It should be noted that the acquisition of Tibetan shawl wool and good horse stock were not simply covers for more clandestine objectives. Trade was an integral feature of the East India Company; indeed, for the directors the establishment of lucrative commerce was always preferred to formal rule. Wherever possible, the British aimed to work within existing structures and alongside native elites, tolerating all manner of rulers to preserve trade and stability – only their reliability and compliance were required and this would be enforced if necessary. Even when India was eventually relinquished, one quarter of the Indian population lived entirely under Indian princes (although they were, of course, suzerains to the British). Tibetan wool was a popular commodity that promised great wealth and

Moorcroft was prepared to go to considerable lengths to acquire a share of it. In his capacity as Superintendent of the Stud for the East India Company, his desire to obtain good horse breeds was also perfectly understandable. Yet Moorcroft was convinced that Russia intended to annex central Asia. He tended to see evidence of covert Russian activity everywhere, but it would be years before fears of tsarist intrigue and an advance towards India became widespread amongst the Anglo-Indian community.

Moorcroft's Afghan and central Asian expedition has been covered before, most ably in recent years by Gerald Alder.[24] Alder's research included a most hazardous retracing of the expedition's steps and it is an excellent biography. However, it is disappointing to note that, until now, attention has focussed on the decisions and fate of Moorcroft to the exclusion of the Asian agents who were so instrumental in its success. Admittedly, Moorcroft's journey, apart from its ill-fated end, is better documented than that of the reconnaissance of Mir Izzet Ullah. Yet, without Ullah's reconnoitring, and his accurate report, Moorcroft would not have been able to mount his expedition at all. When Moorcroft planned to reach central Asia via Chinese Turkestan, it was Ullah, for example, who suggested that Leh in Ladakh, which, until then, had not been visited by Europeans, would be a safe and convenient base from which contact could be made with the Chinese authorities to the north. Without that permission, the expedition could not even have begun.

For years, Moorcroft promoted plans to penetrate central Asia that went well beyond horse trading. To Hearsey, he suggested a trek across the Niti Pass into Tibet, pushing on to Lhasa, then west to Ladakh, up to Yarkand and across into Turkestan. Hearsey realised just how ambitious this expedition would be, and suspected that Moorcroft was pursuing too many objectives, including, perhaps, his own self-aggrandisement. If the real aim was to discover the extent of Russian and French influence, to prevent its spread and to promote British influence through commerce, then his own proposal was far more likely to succeed than Moorcroft's. Hearsey suggested that he, Moorcroft, and Moorcroft's companion, George Trebeck, should sail to Bushire through the Persian Gulf, and, with Persian permission, travel through the shah's dominions. They would then each establish British agencies: Trebeck was to be the commercial agent at Teheran, Hearsey would travel further into central Asia and remain at Bokhara (where he would assist the emir to resist the forces of the tsar), and Moorcroft would go on to Yarkand to establish a trade treaty with India. This plan would effectively give the British 'listening posts' across the central Asian caravan routes, for, although the Napoleonic Wars had ended, there was little doubt that Russia and France were the only two powers that could challenge Britain's military and commercial supremacy, and, since India was Britain's prize possession, it was here that pressure could be applied from the landward side.

It was not until after the Gurkha War was over in 1816, that Moorcroft's commercial plans were given any consideration by the Company and he was not permitted to set off until the end of 1819. Even then, he had no official position. Unable to cross the Niti Pass into Tibet as he had hoped, Moorcroft turned to march north towards Ladakh. However, in March 1820 his vast caravan, and its escort of hired Gurkhas, was mistaken for an invading army by the Sikh overlords of Sukhet in the Kulu Valley. Hoping to persuade Ranjit Singh that he had no evil intent, Moorcroft tried to reach Lahore, the Sikh capital, but he was arrested at Hoshiapur and it was only through Mir Izzet Ullah's negotiations that Moorcroft was released. Even so, it still took a month. It was not until June that Moorcroft, again relying heavily on Ullah, got permission to proceed. To avoid further protracted negotiations at Lahore, Moorcroft eventually made his way to the court of Sanser Chand, the Rajah of Kangra. There, cultivating a friendship with the rajah, he spent another six weeks. Unkindly perhaps, some have commented that Moorcroft indulged himself in the pleasures of the *nautch* girls, but, ever anxious to obtain information, his real purpose was to foster good relations with 'the best informed and most communicative natives of any the traveller might meet'.[25]

Moorcroft was delayed for a total of three years in Ladakh and Kashmir, the potential wealth of central Asian trade lying apparently just beyond his grasp. In the meantime, Mir Izzet Ullah was sent ahead to Yarkand to open the way into Chinese Turkestan. In fact, due to Chinese objections, Moorcroft was simply unable to progress any further and had to content himself with a brief survey of Kashmir. Having already upset the authorities in Calcutta by concluding his own commercial treaty with Ladakh, he rashly proposed that the East India Company should absorb the hill state, a suggestion that was flatly refused. The governor-general valued the alliance of 1809 with the Sikhs more highly than the remote and weak hill state of Ladakh. Moorcroft had exceeded his instructions by warning Ranjit Singh not to interfere in Ladakhi affairs in future. This earned him a severe reprimand from Calcutta, he was recalled, and an apology was offered for Moorcroft's unofficial meddling in Sikh affairs. Undeterred, and in defiance of his masters, Moorcroft began recruiting and training a private army in Kashmir, no doubt in an attempt to show the military potential of the mountain regions that bordered India, but this activity merely fuelled the growing suspicions in Lahore.

Despite further travels through the northern Punjab and subsequently in Afghanistan (ignoring an order to return to India), Moorcroft's expedition seemed doomed to failure. He lacked the official backing of the Company; he had barely a handful of bodyguards; and there was no chance of any relief force being sent to assist him if he got into difficulties. Moorcroft continued to take enormous risks. He had considered the idea of assuming control of the city of Peshawar, then under Pathan warlords, as a secure base beyond Sikh control, knowing full well this would not be accepted in Calcutta. He marched confidently at the head of an armed bodyguard and some Peshwari allies, using a Waziri guide he had cured and recruited to make the passage through Waziristan and the Khyber Pass, watched carefully by the Afridi Pathans. At Kabul, in July 1824, Moorcroft met Dost Mohammed, the Afghan leader who had just secured power. Moorcroft kept meticulous records, including notes on the trade and defences of the city, but civil unrest continued after Dost Mohammed's accession, prompting the expedition's rapid departure. Moorcroft recommended that Dost Mohammed's rival, Shah Shuja, would be more compliant to British interests and that a 'regime change' would require only a single British regiment. For all the official disapproval at the time, Moorcroft's comments were to find sympathy with his successors, with far-reaching consequences.

As the expedition travelled north, it entered the lawless fringes of Afghanistan. There, the chief of Kunduz, Murad Beg, trapped the party and imprisoned them all for six months in the hope of acquiring all their merchandise. Mir Wazir Ahmad, a member of the expedition who had joined the caravan at Kabul, suggested a solution – a desperate ride by Moorcroft, disguised as an Uzbek, to a rival chieftain, the respected Pirzada of Taliq-An, Syed Mohammed Khan (some accounts refer to a certain Kasim Jan Khoja), which enabled him to open negotiations for the release of the whole expedition. Fortunately, it worked, but the experience indicates just how vulnerable Moorcroft's party was.

They marched on to Bokhara where they obtained an audience with the emir, Khan Hyder, but even in the court they enjoyed little security. Moorcroft suspected that the protracted pauses between the emir's questions and his own answers indicated that their words were being recorded – effectively they were under interrogation. Moreover, to Moorcroft's dismay, *uruz* (Russian merchants, or their intermediaries) were already well-known in the bazaar. Indian merchants there were disdainful of Moorcroft's expensive British and Indian manufactures, preferring to trade in Persian and Russian goods. The nature of trade in Bokhara should not have been a surprise. The British Resident at Gwalior, Richard Strachey, believed there was 'nothing particularly formidable' about getting to Bokhara. Even if one accepts a degree of typical understatement or *sangfroid* here, it is likely that Strachey based his knowledge on what his Indian hosts told him. The presence of Indians at Bokhara, the flow of trade across central Asia, and the termini in Russia, China and Persia were all perfectly understandable, but Moorcroft was convinced that these facts were evidence of sinister designs.

Moorcroft kept copious records and his journals are filled with material on subjects ranging from flora to architecture. The small extracts of his papers printed by the Royal Geographical Society's first journals naturally concentrated on his geographical achievements. Yet the full, published version of his expedition, printed after his death in 1841, omits any detail on his stay in Kabul or Bokhara. The most convincing reason for this seems to be his covert activities. There is no doubt that, in Bokhara at least, Moorcroft recruited a network of 'newswriters', who corresponded with coded symbols if they came across evidence of the Russians.[26] The agents of the Khattri commercial houses were involved (an organisation with offices in Delhi, Lahore, Peshawar and Kabul), as were wealthy Kashmiri merchants.[27] What is more, Moorcroft's reports were sent directly to the Political and Secret Department during his expedition, for the eyes of Charles Metcalfe, its director. The absence of any official status was, as Metcalfe pointed out, to avoid the British government being committed 'unpleasantly and contrary to its design'; disowning the failure of its agents, or condemning them as independents, was to become a common practice in espionage.

Although they had reached Bokhara and acquired some of the horses they sought, the party never returned to India. Mir Izzet Ullah, sick and dying from something the party called 'Kunduz fever', was permitted to go to Peshawar in

September 1824 to recuperate but he never made it: he died in Kabul. As Moorcroft's party struggled to get out of central Asia, it was Mir Izzet Ullah's colleague Askar Ali Khan, sometimes known as 'Luskeree Khan', who provided a route south towards Peshawar via Badakhshan and Chitral, avoiding potential trouble in Kabul. However, Moorcroft, Trebeck, and the expedition's doctor, Guthrie, were soon dead in northern Afghanistan, apparently *en route* to Herat. The circumstances in which Moorcroft died are unknown but treachery by Murad Beg, the ruler of Kunduz who sought the expedition's merchandise, has been considered. Trebeck and Guthrie almost certainly succumbed to the fever that had claimed Mir Izzet Ullah, although Askar Ali Khan was convinced they had all been poisoned.[28] Ghulam Hyder, the loyal and industrious Afghan of the expedition, gave his own account in the *Asiatic Journal*, but, given that the expedition was travelling in separate parties, little light was shed on how Moorcroft and the others had died.[29]

Moorcroft was convinced that Russian influence was growing in central Asia and he was ahead of his time in predicting the region's annexation. He reported that a Persian Jew, known as Aga Mehdi (but in fact called Mekhti Refailov), acting for Count Nesselrode, the Russian Foreign Minister, had preceded him in Ladakh and was bound for Lahore. Although the agent had died on the Hindu Kush, Hayman Wilson, who edited Moorcroft's journals, believed he had already reported on the political situation in Afghanistan. A Russian envoy had also reached the Emir of Bokhara and there was plenty of bazaar gossip that the Russians meant to overthrow the Khan of Khiva before advancing on India. All this was, no doubt, rumour emanating from the conflict between Russia and Persia in the years 1826–8.

The two year Russo-Persian War for the Caucasus ostensibly broke out over a border dispute, but it was almost certainly planned by the Persians as a means to recover the territory they had lost in 1812. With Russia distracted by its involvement in the Greek War of Independence and by the death of Alexander I in December 1825, 30,000 Persian troops crossed the border and captured Tiflis (Tbilisi). The victory was short-lived. General Paskievich soon drove the Persians back out of the Caucasus. The shah appealed to Britain, but, unable to bring the Royal Navy to bear, and with priority given to delicate negotiations over Greece and the future of the Mediterranean, London refused to support him. Facing defeat, Persia concluded the Treaty of Turkmenchay in 1828. The terms dictated that Russia should acquire Erivan and Nakitchevan, but Britain's insistence that the shah should no longer appeal for a subsidy seemed evidence of British weakness: 'All through the East, we were thought to be afraid of Russia.'[30]

The year after Turkmenchay, Russia also defeated the Turks and concluded the Treaty of Adrianople (1829). This gave the Russians control of the Black Sea ports (although diplomatic pressure forced them to relinquish Erzerum and Kars) and Russia seemed to have embarked on a process of limitless expansion. In 1831, Russia sent a fleet to Constantinople for its 'protection' against the advance of the army of Mehemet Ali, and in 1833 it secured effective control of the Bosporus Straits by the Treaty of Unkiar Skelessi. In Britain, there was now a growing circle of Russophobes, and the notion that tsarist warships would enter the Mediterranean to sever one of the arteries of British trade to the East gained a wider currency.

John Gleason examined the extent to which Russophobia was a popular sentiment that interacted with, and eventually influenced, government policy. Curiously, British and Russian attitudes to the Near East were very similar, which explains their co-operation over Greece in the 1820s and a tradition of surprisingly good relations for much of the nineteenth century. Gleason argued, moreover, that colonial rivalry in Asia did not cause Russophobia, rather it was a product of British domestic affairs. A combination of factors, some deliberate and some accidental, gave rise to a fear of Russia. British trade with Russia declined significantly in the first half of the nineteenth century relative to other parts of the world at a time when British commerce was undergoing massive expansion.[31] A growing lobby of free traders despised the Russians' attempts to protect their own industries with tariffs and Russian customs were regarded as corrupt and inefficient.[32] In British domestic politics, too, the Great Reform Act of 1832 had been hailed as a victory against reactionaries everywhere and improving communications meant that the educated classes of Britain were learning more about the autocratic system of the tsar. Publications, like David Urquhart's *Russia and England* (1835) fuelled Russophobia and Russia became a caricature of oppression in the growing popular press.[33] Even in the House of Commons, partisan views could be reinforced or discredited by invoking the likeness of Russia. The British media also invented the romantic idea of 'rescuing' the Turks from the Russians. It took a series of diplomatic incidents to convert this hostile sentiment into government policy.

What Moorcroft interpreted as tsarist intrigue directed ultimately against India was little more than the process of Russian imperialism. Aggressive attempts to secure trade, a strong desire to wipe out slavery, missions to obtain a closer relationship with indigenous rulers, and attempts to gain knowledge of the strengths and weaknesses of secretive regimes were a mirror of the means by which the British, too, were developing their interests in Asia. Yet there was something unique about Russian expansion. It was not, according to Dietrich Geyer, some 'natural law of Russian history' as was so often the verdict in the West.[34] It was the result of a fundamental economic weakness compared with the Western powers that could only be offset by the acquisition of new territory and new victories. Geyer rejected the idea posited by Marxist historians, that capitalism was in decay in Russia, to show that it was a relative decline compared with the take-off of the West, which drove Russians to seek psychological compensation and greater security.[35] Moreover, Russian imperial policy was frequently a reaction to events in Europe. Geyer concluded that, faced with British power in Asia and limited power in the West, the Russian elites were eager for military success and prestige, dressed in the language of the 'civilising mission'.[36] As far as central Asia was concerned:

> The ambitions of military men hungry for medals and promotions played a large role in the conquests. They undertook operations without official

authority and continually confronted St Petersburg with new *fait[s] accompli[s]*. Military logic was such that new actions were deemed necessary.[37]

Whilst distant governments, or directors of the East India Company, tried to limit the activities of their local forces, both military and commercial, they discovered that the 'turbulent frontier' drew them further into Asian affairs.[38] It was to be a pattern repeated across the globe.[39] The focus of British interests in the 1820s, as far as any Russian threat was concerned, remained in Persia. The northern frontier of Persia and the vast expanse of central Asia were still unknown. Moreover Persia had been defeated – and ejected from the Caucasus. However, it was also clear that the states that lay on India's immediate border posed a problem of their own. The Sikhs were a powerful nation astride the Sutlej and Indus, with outlying tributary states in the northern mountains; the Afghans were still an unknown quantity; the Maratha Confederacy was powerful; and the smaller provinces of Gwalior, Sind and the hill states below the mountains of the Hindu Kush and Karakoram were lawless, unstable and apparently ripe for seizure by some hostile power. It was clear that further missions were needed to ascertain the strengths and weaknesses of these potential enemies.

The Intelligence Community of the 1820s

In his Raleigh Lecture of 1924, Professor H. W. C. Davis stated that there was no single centre for intelligence-gathering in India in the early nineteenth century, nor was their a single coherent strategy. This was largely because intelligence had emerged as a piecemeal effort, with informers hired locally from amongst the camp followers and paid for anything that seemed useful.[40] However, Davis also mentioned four places where intelligence officers could 'learn their business': Bombay, Cutch, Ludhiana and Teheran. It should be noted that, before departure to India, many officers of the East India Company's armies learnt Indian languages, but these locations appeared to offer more than language training. Officers could be trained for service in Teheran because the Government of Bombay was concerned with the future of Persia and the Indus Valley. It seems that the British residency at Cutch was also responsible for some form of 'training'. However, Gerald Morgan doubted whether these locations could have been used for intelligence instruction and believed they may have referred more to the 'schools of thought' about British policy in central Asia. Davis indeed hinted that there were differences of opinion between officers based at Teheran and Ludhiana, and Morgan wrote:

> On the face of it the four places are very unlikely; Teheran after all is Persian, whilst Cutch and Ludhiana were then no more than advanced army bases. We already know that there was no army intelligence in those days and Political officers would surely have never gone there to be trained.[41]

In fact, Ludhiana *was* an active British listening post, gathering intelligence from as far afield as Nepal. William Kirkpatrick, one of the first officers of the East India

Company to travel in Nepal, had recommended as early as 1793 that regular intelligence reports should be compiled on the Gurkhas' territories.[42] However, setbacks during border skirmishes made it difficult to penetrate the interior. As a result, the British employed Kumaon traders of Indian cloth as informants since these were people who had been displaced by the Gurkhas. *Harcarras* (couriers) were also recruited from certain tribes known to have a grievance against the Nepalese. This *ad hoc* arrangement prevailed until the war of 1814 when Thomas Rutherford, the civil surgeon of Moradabad, offered his knowledge of the transport, tribal loyalties and resources of the Gurkhas.[43] Despite initially being discouraged, other border officials copied Rutherford's employment of local men who knew the languages. Rutherford employed runners and a covert surveyor to find out more about the land beyond the border and in 1815 Lieutenant Roper of the Intelligence Department run by Colonel Nicholls incorporated Rutherford's system.[44] New tactics were then employed: letters were intercepted and more harcarras were recruited from a variety of tribal groups, including Kashmiri Muslims.[45] Nevertheless, it proved difficult to penetrate the Nepalese hierarchy. Whereas on the plains of India the British had been able to negotiate with individuals and to play on ancient rivalries, the Gurkhas proved more homogeneous. In fact they proved adept at negotiating with their neighbours and they maintained a strict counter-espionage network to capture British-Indian harcarras. Tragically, some of them were tortured for being spies.[46] But cash was a more reliable way of winning allies. Hyder Hearsey, Moorcroft's companion, was the intelligence officer for the west of Nepal responsible for the payment of couriers and informants until William Fraser took over from him.

All the border officials fed their information to the Company, but significantly, this was not the only source of intelligence. The Sikh hill state of Patiala had its own newswriters in Nepal and their information was passed to Ludhiana. General Ochterlony was able to make use of this intelligence during his campaign. This perhaps demonstrates that Ludhiana, like Teheran, had an intelligence function after all, albeit one dependent on Asian sources.[47]

Morgan also argued that there was nothing covert about the role of the Political Department. Created by the East India Company in 1820, the Political Department was apparently little more than a diplomatic corps whose missions were well publicised. It was merely unfortunate that the department should refer to its officers as 'agents', a point that led to confusion amongst Soviet historians.[48] However, the legation at Teheran was on the front line of intelligence work and Morgan admits that local intelligence networks, recruited by the British, existed there as 'normal practice'. The officers here had the responsibility of watching the Caucasus frontier and of training the Persian army in 1810 and in 1834. But it was also here that the differences in British policy towards central Asia emerged.

John McNeill (later Sir John) arrived at the legation in 1824 having served as a surgeon in the Bengal Army, but he rose to become the minister there. In 1836, he published a pamphlet warning of Russian ambitions in the region.[49] His views seemed justified when, just one year later, a joint Russo-Persian army attacked Herat and the Persian authorities made little secret of their anti-British attitude.

Despite McNeill's concerns that Persia should be the focus of British efforts to block Russian expansion, and thus protect India, Colonel Claude Martine Wade, the officer in command of the residency at Ludhiana, took a different view. Wade believed that the threat to India came less from Russia and more from the capabilities of the Sikhs and Afghans. He believed that Britain's best policy lay in fostering a close relationship with Lahore, and he was keen to maintain Ludhiana as a listening post in the region. Wade favoured the continual disruption of Afghanistan to preserve its weakness and he also promoted the idea that Shah Shuja, a claimant to the Afghan throne, should be installed because he was compliant and could easily be controlled from India. In 1833, the Government of India supported an attempt by Shah Shuja to invade Afghanistan, but it failed and Ranjit Singh used the opportunity to secure Peshawar from the Pathans (who owed a loose loyalty to Kabul). Dost Mohammed, the Amir of Afghanistan, made no attempt to recover the lost province, largely because of all the threats from within his own state and because any large Afghan army might be tempted to secure power for itself in Kabul.

The British alliance with the Sikhs and the continued weakness of Afghanistan were entirely satisfactory to the Company's security in India, but the whole policy was thrown into jeopardy by the ill health of Ranjit Singh. Intelligence reports suggested that the demise of the old Rajah of Lahore would be followed by a power struggle and civil war. This prediction coincided with reports that Dost Mohammed was strengthening his hold over Afghanistan and news that Persia was falling under Russian influence. The key problem remained the same: how to acquire sound intelligence on these issues in Afghanistan, the Punjab and Persia. There was precious little known about the Muslim gentry of the Punjab and where their loyalties lay. Beyond the Indus, the Pathans were also something of a mystery except that they seemed to be dominated by charismatic *mullahs* (teachers of law or religion). In Kabul, the British envoy, Mountstuart Elphinstone, had managed to interview notables and religious leaders, whilst runners and itinerant merchants furnished him with some information about the country, but the picture was far from complete.[50] Furthermore, despite a resident being established at the Sikh court from 1815, it was difficult to obtain reliable information about any of the territories extending to the north beyond the Indus. The solution appeared to be a new round of missions, most of them political and overt, but whose officers were always alert to opportunities for secret intelligence.

Chapter 3

Misreading Intelligence

The Consequences of Exaggerating the Threat, 1830–1842

Arthur Connolly and Syed Karamut Ali

In the dry and dusty streets of Kandahar one afternoon in 1830, multitudes passed to and fro on every imaginable trade and business. Veiled women hurried out of the sun, cacophonous stall holders announced their wares whilst serious imams moved through the throng with a distant air. Beneath the long mournful cry of the muezzin, one man stole away from the crowds to attend a colleague in hiding just outside the city who was suffering from a fever. Secrecy was paramount, not because of his sickness, but because the patient was an infidel close to a city of the devout. The man who attended him was Syed Karamut Ali, a Muslim from India who acted as guide and was later to become a 'newswriter' for the Governor-General of India. The infidel was Arthur Connolly, on a reconnaissance mission for the British envoy to Persia, Sir John Macdonald. Thanks to Syed Connolly survived his sickness, and it was Syed's efforts that produced the bulk of the intelligence on the city that the British required. Yet it was one thing to gather information, but quite another to interpret it correctly. Within eight years, convinced that the Russians intended eventually to advance on India via Herat, Kabul and Kandahar, the British were at war with Afghanistan.

Captain Arthur Connolly was the first to use the expression 'The Great Game'. In two letters to Henry Rawlinson, then a fellow policital officer of the East India Company, whilst at Kandahar prior to a clandestine mission to Bokhara in 1837, Connolly had written enigmatically: 'you've a great game, a noble one, before you', and later, 'if only the government would play the grand game'.[1] Connolly believed that the Russian Empire, Britain's only serious rival in Asia, would use the existence of banditry and slavery in the central Asian khanates as a pretext for annexation. Once installed in Khiva and Herat, he was sure that the Russians would exploit any unrest in India.[2] India was not yet the consolidated Raj so often depicted in the popular histories of the twentieth century. It was still a patchwork of territories more or less under British influence, but not yet under British control. Intrigue was rife, and Connolly was aware of how susceptible the Indian states might be to the temptations offered by Russia. He was advocating that Rawlinson should participate in the battle for influence, if only to bring the benefits of Western civilisation to the peoples of Asia.

Despite an undercover mission across Persia, the territories of the Turcomans and Afghanistan, Connolly saw his role, not as a spy, but as an honourable officer and envoy who would explain the Russian tactics to local rulers, befriend them, and persuade them to release slaves, not only to neutralise the Russian interference, but also for humanitarian reasons.[3] Connolly was a man of deep religious convictions, part of the breed of officers who went out to the Empire convinced 'there was nothing but God above and duty below'.[4] He had joined the 6th Bengal Light Cavalry aged sixteen in 1823, having been orphaned just four years before. Given the high death rate in India – three of his five brothers would die in India in the service of the Company – it is perhaps not surprising that he was so careless about his own fate.

In the autumn of 1829, Connolly made his way back to India at the end of furlough, not on board ship, but overland via Moscow. For the first stage of his journey he had the permission of the Russian government, and he was entertained warmly by Russian officers when he reached Tiflis. Nevertheless, Connolly took note of all the military details he could gather and concluded that, despite guerrilla action by the 'ferocious mountaineers' of the Caucasus, Russian pacification of the area was inevitable. He was also impressed by the endurance of the Russian troops on the Persian frontier who slept without blankets in the snow and demonstrated great stoicism in all conditions. These observations were to influence his subsequent conclusions about Russian capabilities in central Asia.[5]

It is not clear at what stage Connolly had been given his mission objectives for the next phase of his journey, but we do know that Sir John Macdonald had designed them.[6] He was to set off for Khiva, across northern Persia and through one of the most dangerous regions of central Asia, the Karakum Desert. Once at the ancient city, he was to ascertain the degree of Russian influence and any signs of a Russian threat. Macdonald was convinced that any advance against India would first necessitate the capture of Khiva from a base of operations at Orenburg. The vast distance and the semi-arid nature of the terrain made supporting an army, encumbered by wagons, guns and livestock, extremely difficult. In the modern age of mass communications, armoured warfare and air power, it is difficult to appreciate the fundamental lack of knowledge about this region, but Connolly's mission was to simply go and find out. Today, his mission would be regarded as low-tech 'humint' (human intelligence, that is, people deployed 'on the ground'), but at the time it was really the only way of securing reliable information.

What made the Karakum Desert so hazardous was the banditry of the Turcomans who lived there. So effective was their plundering, usually carried out as cavalry raids, that large armed caravans were essential for any trading activity at all. Many of the settlements of northern Persia and Afghanistan had simply been abandoned and the whole region was depopulated.[7] Those that resisted were killed; the rest were taken into captivity to be sold as slaves in the bazaars of the central Asian cities, including Khiva. Around those villages that were still inhabited, small towers were dotted amongst the fields. At the first sign of a raid, these were places of refuge, the ladders being drawn up inside to prevent capture. Connolly wanted to ride across the desert and link up with a well-protected caravan, but it was a mission of enormous risk. He considered two types of disguise: as a humble *hakim* (doctor) or as a Persian merchant.

Syed Karamut Ali was ostensibly Connolly's guide and interpreter whom he met at Teheran, and when he is mentioned at all in the more recent histories of the Great Game, it is only in this capacity. Yet there is a strong possibility that Syed was more than what he appeared to be. Given that it was the envoy at Teheran, Macdonald, who had tasked Connolly with the mission, and that Teheran was an acknowledged 'listening post' for activities on the Russo-Persian frontier, it seems highly likely that Syed was an experienced agent. Connolly noted that 'Syud Karamaut Allee was indefatigable' in seeking information on trade, people, passes and routes – and on the defences of Kandahar.[8] Professor Davis praised Syed's 'courage and presence of mind' and noted that he 'supplemented Connolly's own work in collecting information'.[9] Perhaps it was not surprising that, after the mission, the directors of the East India Company appointed him newswriter at Kandahar in a permanent and salaried post.

Syed Karamut Ali's value to the mission was demonstrated from the very beginning. It was clear to him that, without the apparatus of a hakim, it would be pointless for Connolly to pose as a doctor. Instead, he could disguise himself as a merchant and thus still slip unnoticed into the caravan from Herat to Khiva. Several days into the march from Persia, four armed Turcoman horsemen arrived and addressed Syed, claiming to be a protection squad, but it soon became apparent that Connolly and Syed were effectively captives. Clearly Connolly's disguise had failed: the Turcomans meant to rob them, and perhaps kill them too. However, Syed's negotiations, and the robbers' fear of retribution, caused a stay of execution and eventually Connolly was released for a ransom, arranged via the envoy in Persia.

Despite being prevented from reaching Khiva, and this near miss, Connolly and Syed were able to learn that rumours of a Russian presence in the city were groundless. Valuable information was also obtained on an area hitherto completely unknown to the British but potentially important. Once again, they were able to verify that there was, as yet, no Russian force on the eastern Caspian shore.

Connolly now embarked on the second phase of the operation which was just as dangerous. He aimed to reach Herat, a city not visited by a British officer for twenty years and now governed by the fanatical Kamran Khan, a brutal ruler with a reputation for great cruelty. Connolly seemed to know in advance that the greatest threat to his life was Kamran Khan's use of informers. Yet, marching via Meshed, Connolly managed to enter the city and for three weeks made records about its defences and about its potential to provision a large army. How he did this, and managed to evade the informers, is not disclosed in his published report, except a reference to a new disguise as a hakim, but it seems likely that it was Syed Karamut Ali who made his way about the city and who reported back to Connolly.

The final stage of the journey was a 300-mile march across central Afghanistan to Kandahar. Once again, the greatest threat came from bandits and slavers; the Afghans of the region were even known to cut off the ears of their human traffic to make escape attempts less likely. If these hazards were not formidable enough, the sheer difficulties of the march were surely a deterrent. There are long stretches of barren and waterless terrain, and the route took them across the grain of the mountains. Connolly nevertheless made light of the challenging environment and enjoyed the intellectual stimulation provided by a party of Muslim scholars who accompanied him. However, at Kandahar, he was struck by a sickness, possibly amoebic dysentery, from which he almost died. The care of Syed Karamut Ali enabled him to recover, and his warning that Connolly's cover was compromised allowed the British officer to escape the city and make for the border town of Quetta with a group of horse traders.

Arthur Connolly had achieved a remarkable feat. He had completed a journey of 4,000 miles, and, by taking the route it seemed most likely that a Russian army would follow, he answered many of the questions posed by the Russophobes. His very survival was an achievement, given the lawless nature of the region. Had he been captured at Kandahar, his death was certain, for the city was then at war with Kamran Khan and there was a rumour that an English officer was abroad, spying for the Herati chief. By any standards, Connolly's journey was an epic of courage and endurance, worthy of the great names of European exploration. Yet, too often, the narrative ends there, without acknowledging the achievement of his colleague, Syed Karamut Ali, and the worth of the intelligence he gathered. Of the information on Kandahar, there is no doubt that what appeared in Connolly's book was collected by Syed, and this helps to explain his later appointment as news-writer there.[10] Syed left no memoir, and any announcement of his part in the mission, either by Connolly or the East India Company, would have compromised his appointment in Kandahar.

Connolly's conclusions did little to dispel anxieties about the threat to India; indeed, they added to them. Despite the hardships of his odyssey, Connolly concluded that the Russian Army had two options if it wished to strike against India. Until then, it was thought that an invasion force would have first to defeat or befriend Persia and then march on to Sind and Baluchistan before crossing the Indus into India. Now, for the first option, Connolly believed that the Russians would choose to advance through central Asia. Using their base at Orenburg, they would first seize Khiva, and, after a period of consolidation, they would use the river Amu Daria as an axis to Balkh in northern Afghanistan. From Balkh, they would then cross the Hindu Kush by the Khawak Pass, following in the footsteps of Alexander the Great, and then secure Kabul. Access to India would be via the Khyber Pass.[11]

The second option was for the Russians to advance via northern Persia, or from the shores of the Caspian, to Herat. Once again, a river, this time the Hari Rud, would provide the axis and water the troops and horses on the long march. Once Herat was taken, the fertile valley there would support the army before it made its next move towards Kandahar, the Bolan Pass and into India. It was possible, thought Connolly, that both of the options could work in concert, but the chief difficulty was in the vulnerability of the lines of communication. The Turcomans and the Afghans were likely to offer stiff resistance to any invaders, and students of the Peninsular War would realise how easy it was for guerrillas to harass, and perhaps even defeat, a regular army. However, Connolly's concern was that the divided nature of Afghan politics would render them weak in the face of a Russian invasion. In a rejection of the old theories about maintaining Afghan weakness and supporting Persia, Connolly suggested a radical new plan. He advocated the creation of a strong, united Afghanistan, capable of withstanding invasion. Moreover, its ruler, Connolly stated, would require British support in the face of Russian 'inducements'. His conclusion was that Kamran Khan, with Herat under his command, would provide the ideal leader for the country.

It is interesting how closely Connolly's thoughts coincide with an actual Russian invasion plan drawn up in 1886 by General Kuropatkin, and which fell into British hands shortly afterwards.[12] Kuropatkin wrote of the need to advance by stages toward India, each phase being followed by a period of consolidation. Kuropatkin also mentioned how two routes presented themselves as the most practicable. Meshed and Herat would be important centres on the southern advance, whilst Balkh and Kabul would be crucial in the north. Like Connolly, the Russian officer concluded that the presence of a Russian army in Afghanistan would be enough to excite the population of India, and fatally weaken the British there, but Kuropatkin discounted the Afghan resistance, suggesting they would join Russia willingly.

Connolly's suggestions coincided with interest in a report by Colonel George de Lacy Evans that to counter a Russian threat to India, a screen of 'agents' should be established in Peshawar and Afghanistan. De Lacy Evans suggested that Bokhara should be an intelligence outpost.[13] He also believed Britain should be prepared to use force to compel the Afghan and other regional rulers to conform to the British defence system. Of course, as Gerald Morgan points out, the British 'agents' need not have been necessarily covert and would act as consuls for the purpose of promoting trade and carrying on negotiations with local rulers, but there can no doubt that the primary function of the agents would be to provide early warning of Russian troop movements. It was an idea later promoted by Lord Salisbury in the 1870s, although he envisioned a long curtain of agents from Asia Minor to northern India.

Lord Ellenborough, the President of the Board of Control for India, was impressed by the new thinking about the defence of India.[14] In 1829 he ordered that information should be collected on the regions beyond India's borders. Convinced that the Russians would advance stealthily towards Khiva and the oases of central Asia, Ellenborough believed that Britain should also move forward to occupy Lahore and Kabul. It was Ellenborough, the architect of this 'forward policy', who had prompted Sir John Malcolm in Teheran to send Connolly, even sending him a copy of de Lacy Evans's work.[15] However, in the first instance, it was Lord Heytesbury, the ambassador to St Petersburg, and a spy he had recruited within the Russian court, who obtained the information about Russia that mattered. What emerged was the picture of a country not poised to strike at India, but impoverished and militarily weak. Although grand on paper, the scale of Russia's armed forces was misleading. Thousands of troops were deployed on internal security duties and could not be released for operations outside Russia. Logistically, the army was in an abysmal state. Connolly's observations about stoic Russian troops in the snows of the Caucasus may have seemed impressive, but they revealed a fundamental logistical weakness in the Russian Army that was to dog the tsar's forces for decades. These shortcomings were to be dramatically revealed by the Crimean War, although they have been overshadowed by an obsession in Western historiography with only British and French logistical mismanagement.

Nevertheless, as Edward Ingram has argued, Ellenborough's advocacy of a pro-active policy in Persia and Afghanistan showed 'the truer perception of the needs of a continental state', which Britain now was through its possession of India.[16] The British government still believed that naval power was sufficient to protect its Empire since, apart from India and Canada, it was no more than an assemblage of littorals, but there was growing concern about Russia's grasping policy in Greece and Turkey, and therefore Russia's broader ambitions with regard to Asia.[17]

Ellenborough dismissed Heytesbury's findings on the Russian Army, believing the ambassador to be a Russophile. Instead, he turned to the Duke of Wellington for an expert's opinion on how to defend India. Whilst Wellington agreed with Ellenborough that it would be preferable to halt an invading army before it reached the Indus, he still felt that it was perfectly possible for the British Army to hold the river.[18] However, Wellington was concerned that, if a foreign power was able to establish itself at Kabul permanently, there would be a more serious threat to India. He was also anxious about the effects on the minds of Muslims in India if Britain opposed Muslim Turkey in Europe. Ellenborough was more concerned by the instability of the buffer states and felt that, although Russia was still too distant to be an immediate threat, it was vital to seize advantages whilst there was still time. This was all the more pressing when news arrived that Persia had now aligned itself with Russia. Moreover, rumours that an envoy of Ranjit Singh had reached St Petersburg meant that closer relations with the Sikhs were also vital. But what Ellenborough wanted above all else was a clearer picture of the situation beyond India's borders. His solution was to despatch a cordial diplomatic mission up the Indus to the Sikh capital of Lahore, making covert observations *en route*, before establishing a more permanent network in Afghanistan and beyond.

The Missions to Afghanistan

The diplomatic mission to Lahore fell to Lieutenant Alexander Burnes, formerly an officer of the 1st Bombay Light Infantry and now a political officer. He was a natural choice, for he had already explored the lower Indus in 1828, and was described as genial and sympathetic towards Muslims of all classes. He was also an excellent linguist. After learning 'Hindustani' in just two months before leaving Britain in 1821, he quickly became his regiment's interpreter. He took part in his first active service operations in Cutch when just eighteen years old, but it was evident that his greatest passion was for languages. He was soon fluent in Persian, learning the necessary Muslim etiquette at the same time. One of his biographers described him as: 'undeniably an able man, self-confident, brave and intelligent. He was tough, determined and ambitious – probably over-ambitious.'[19]

The 700-mile journey to Lahore in 1831 was not without incident. Much of the surveying had to be done at night, local emirs had to be bribed and there were occasional snipers to contend with. The mission was a success but Sir Charles Metcalfe, the former secretary of the Political and Secret Department felt the subterfuge was 'unworthy of our government' and likely to generate suspicion.[20] Indeed, the risk was that it would prove counter-productive to the diplomatic side of the mission.[21] Yet for all the misgivings, Ranjit Singh was delighted with the British gift of six dray horses and a state coach and he entertained the British party lavishly for two long months. In that time, Burnes made some acute observations about the Khalsa (the Sikh army) and its formidable artillery arm.[22]

Burnes returned to India and reported directly to the governor-general, Lord William Bentinck, at Simla. Apart from the military information, there was much enthusiasm for the potential for trade up the Indus and on into Afghanistan that would enable British and Indian wares to compete with Russian goods in central Asia. Efforts were made to secure the compliance of the Sind emirs for the passage of caravans, and Burnes was granted permission for a second mission to Kabul, to assess the defences of the city and the Afghan forces there, before pushing on across the Hindu Kush to Bokhara. Having gathered as much intelligence as possible on the city state, he intended to return via Persia.

For the mission to Kabul in 1832, Burnes was accompanied Mohan Lal, a Kashmiri munshi, and Mohammed Ali, an accomplished surveyor who had joined Burnes on the mission to Lahore. Mohan Lal was merely described as the 'Hindu lad' who helped with correspondence in Burnes's published *Travels to Bokhara*, but he was fluent in several languages and became the 'eyes and ears' of the mission. His father had taken part in Mountstuart Elphinstone's diplomatic visit to Afghanistan in 1808, and Mohan Lal had been talent-spotted by Charles Trevelyan, the founder of the Delhi English College and a friend of Sir Charles Metcalfe.

Once again, the mission was to serve the double purpose of gathering intelligence as well as opening diplomatic relations. After crossing the Indus on 17 March 1832, they travelled in disguise, in the vain hope it might prevent robbery, although Burnes himself doubted the effectiveness of such a ruse. Like Connolly before him, he considered it was simply too difficult to conceal their identity since the local people walked, ate and even dismounted in such a different fashion to Europeans. Burnes always told the people he met that he was an 'Englishman' (as Scots referred to themselves overseas), but pretended to avoid pork so as to protect Muslim sensibilities.

Crossing the mountains to avoid the Khyber Pass, Burnes's party arrived in Kabul on 1 May. Whilst Burnes presented himself to Dost Mohammed and waxed lyrical about the city, the climate, the wildlife and the amir's achievements, Mohan Lal took a more sanguine view. Dost Mohammed was undoubtedly an able administrator. He had acquired power in 1826 by defeating his brothers through alliance and intrigue. He had restored order in the capital and his influence extended across much of what is today central Afghanistan. The conclusion of years of civil war also brought prosperity and he welcomed the commercial overtures that Burnes seemed to represent. Mohan Lal acknowledged that he was 'prudent and wise in cabinet and an able commander in the field', but warned that he was also renowned for 'treachery, cruelty, murder and falsehood'.[23]

Dost Mohammed lost no time in interrogating Burnes about Europe and European practices over a range of subjects, but he also understood that Burnes was a vain man. It was perhaps just flattery that he offered the British officer command of a cavalry force numbering 12,000 men. But he probed Burnes on the question of the Punjab too, suggesting that Britain and Afghanistan should reduce the power of the Sikh state. Burnes declined, mindful that it was Calcutta's policy to maintain both Afghanistan and the Punjab as stable and friendly nations, but he could see that keeping Dost Mohammed on the throne at Kabul was the surest means of achieving stability and he wrote as much to his superiors.

Taking leave of the amir, Burnes's party continued on their journey to Bokhara. Again, the published version of the expedition contains references only to the hunt for coins of antiquity near Bamian and a visit to the grave of Moorcroft at Balkh, but the secret report of the mission gives details of the navigability of the Oxus (for the purpose of transporting Russian troops), the availability of fodder and supplies, and passes that could be traversed with artillery.[24] These details were clearly of interest to the army and were also stored in the military records of the India Office Library.[25]

Burnes's party crossed the Kizilkum Desert under the protection of a well-armed caravan in just ten days, but he noted that the terrain here, and between Herat and Merv, was waterless, barren and uninhabited. He concluded that artillery and heavy transport wagons could only be dragged across the desert with the utmost difficulty, the first sign that he had begun to doubt the possibility of the Russian Army advancing by this route.[26] Once in Bokhara on 27 June 1832, Burnes was invited for an audience with Kush Begee, the grand vizier of the city. He announced quite openly that he was a British officer but the vizier granted Burnes the freedom of the city in exchange for some customary gifts. In the month that followed, the party acquired a mass of information, including details of the slave trade, in which a significant number of victims were Russian citizens. Burnes concluded that the central Asian khanates were not about to fall under Russian control, and Bokhara at least would resist vigorously.[27] He could not foresee that, some thirty years later, Bokhara would fall after a token Russian artillery demonstration.

Burnes also concluded that only two invasion routes were practical for the Russian Army. The first, between Herat and Kandahar, was surveyed by Captain Gerard to make sure. Gerard completed this journey in 1832 even though it 'almost killed him'. Although he reached Simla safely, and he completed a map on a scale of five miles to the inch on a sheet ten feet by three feet, he died just two years later from the effects of his illnesses and exhaustion.[28] The second invasion option that Burnes considered was the route which followed the river Oxus as far as the Pamirs. From there, an army could cross the Hindu Kush into Chitral or Kashmir, thus ensuring itself supplies and some grazing along the whole route. Yet, like Connolly, he suggested that the two routes would be used at the same time.[29]

Travels into Bokhara was a best-selling book when it was released in 1834, earning Burnes praise in London, Paris and Berlin. He was made a gold medallist of the Royal Geographical Society, a member of the Royal Asiatic Society and was granted an audience with the king. All the reviews were favourable, and the appeal of the book lay not just in the verve of a piece of travel literature, or in the exotic-sounding names that conjured up Byron or Shelley, but in the idea of a Russian threat to India. Up until then, reports about Russian designs had been confined to military men and the administrators of India: now they were public property and fed the growing popular prejudice against Russia and tsarism. But little credit was given for the sources of information contained in the book. It was not until 1846 that Mohan Lal published his own account of the mission and Burnes did not acknowledge how he relied on his colleague's work throughout the journey.[30] As John Keay notes, he failed to mention the group of merchants from Badakshan who gave him a wealth of information on the tea trade between Yarkand and Bokhara, as well as details of the routes across the Pamirs and the situation in Kashgaria (now Xinjiang Province in China).[31] He also learnt about the Karakoram Pass and the formidable mountain barrier between Leh and Yarkand, but this did not stop him believing that Britain should develop stronger commercial ties with central Asia to replace the Russian goods he had seen with his own eyes in the bazaar of Bokhara.

Burnes turned down promotion to a post as secretary of the legation at Teheran, arguing instead to be allowed to lead another mission to Kabul.[32] Although it was designed to promote trade, Sir Charles Metcalfe, the acting Governor-General (1835–6), was in no doubt that, with Burnes at its head, it would develop political overtones.[33] The anxiety of the newly arrived Governor-General, Lord Auckland, meant that Burnes was granted permission to return to Kabul. For Auckland, the real reason for the mission was to establish the sort of political resident who became a feature of many Indian states in the nineteenth century, a British supervisor who came as a reminder that, whilst independent in theory, the ruler would have to acknowledge the supremacy of the British as the 'Paramount Power'.

There can be little doubt that the efforts to maintain a watch over Afghanistan and Persia were unceasing. In the summer of 1833, a mysterious European had settled in the Armenian quarter of Kabul having spent years travelling about the region, often penniless, in search of antiquarian curiosities, particularly those relating to Alexander the Great. He claimed he was Charles Masson, an American from Kentucky, but this did not fool Colonel Wade at Ludhiana: his real name was James Lewis and he was British and a deserter from the army of the East India Company. Nevertheless, Wade realised that, for a pardon and a small salary, this European might be able to provide a permanent listening post in Afghanistan to augment the Hindu merchants who were currently paid for their snippets of bazaar gossip. Masson agreed but it soon became clear that he had little respect for Burnes, later writing a highly critical account of the mission of 1836–8.[34]

As soon as Burnes reached Kabul and began his negotiations with Dost Mohammed, the covert aspect of the mission began. Percival Lord, a political officer and doctor, Lieutenant Leech of the Bombay Engineers, and Lieutenant John Wood of the Royal Navy were all surveyors who explored the passes of the Hindu Kush for more information of which routes were practicable for Russian troops. However, very quickly, the officers were re-tasked. Leech was sent south to keep watch on Kandahar. From Kunduz Lord established, between treatments of the ageing Murad Beg's brother, a network of informers across northern Afghanistan. Lieutenant Wood was sent to see whether the Oxus was navigable downstream from Kunduz, and to examine any passes of the Hindu Kush further to the east as it was still a blank on British maps. However, the first attempt by Lord and Wood to cross the Hindu Kush, in December, was thwarted by the weather, and the conditions convinced Wood that no Russian troops could force the passes at that time of year.[35]

Wood continued to make an epic reconnaissance of the southern Pamirs in the depths of winter, and several of his seven-man party suffered frostbite; one man even lost an arm. He penetrated as far as Wakhan, the valley that would eventually become the no-man's-land between British India and tsarist Russia. Crossing ridges at 14,000 feet in deep snow and freezing temperatures, Wood located Lake Sar-i-Kul, temporarily named Lake Victoria, as the origin of the Oxus, in the manner of those European explorers who sought to establish the sources of the world's greatest rivers.[36] Despite the success of their respective reconnaissances, by the time Wood rejoined Lord and they re-crossed the Hindu Kush, events in Kabul and Herat had overtaken them.

Henry Rawlinson and Eldred Pottinger

The British ambassador to St Petersburg, Lord Durham, was unconvinced by the alarmist reports of Russian designs in central Asia. In March 1836, in a memorandum to Lord Palmerston, the Foreign Secretary, Durham pointed out that Russia was too weak to pose any threat to India. Its only power, he argued, was in defence, as the fate of Napoleon's *Grande Armée* of 1812 had shown. However, to Sir John McNeill, the minister at Teheran, the threat in central Asia was real enough. Publishing an account of Russia's territorial acquisitions since the 1720s, McNeill calculated that the central Asian khanates would be the next to fall.[37] He had already observed, whilst serving under Sir John Macdonald, growing Russian influence in Persia.

Lieutenant Henry Rawlinson, the political officer of McNeill's staff to whom Connolly had written, was patrolling the northern Persian border in the autumn of 1837 and came across a party of Cossacks led by Lieutenant Yan Vitkevich. The Russian commander was evasive, pretending that he did not speak any of the languages in which Rawlinson addressed him, but his story, that he was carrying gifts from the tsar to the shah of Persia, did not seem convincing. In fact, the shah was at that moment visiting the encampment of his army, preparing itself for an attack on Herat. The shah had been encouraged to take back Herat, once a Persian possession, in the hope that Kamran Khan would himself make a bid, with Persian approval, for the throne at Kabul. Kamran's refusal had precipitated military action, but there was no doubt that the Russian envoy to Teheran, Count Simonovich, had encouraged the shah's belligerence, for Russian troops accompanied his army. Rawlinson managed to reach the shah first and tested Vitkevich's story. The shah had no knowledge of Vitkevich's party and Rawlinson realised that the Russian was heading for Kabul to open negotiations there. He immediately set out to ride the 700 miles back to Teheran to warn McNeill. What the British did not know was that Dost Mohammed had opened correspondence with St Petersburg as early as October 1835, even though he still hoped that a close association with the British would enable him to wrest Peshawar from the Sikhs and open a window on the subcontinent.

When the Persian army laid siege to Herat its leaders did not know that a British officer, Lieutenant Eldred Pottinger, was within its walls. Pottinger had made his way across Afghanistan, apparently in a 'private' capacity, using the regulation disguises as horse trader or holy man. Pottinger described his status as follows:

> It might be alleged from my having a commission in the Indian Army, that I was a secret agent for Government, whereas I was a free agent, Government having most liberally given me *carte blanche* as to leave and action, in return for which I offered to lay before it my acquisitions in geography and statistics; and I was very apprehensive that my actions might be disapproved of.[38]

Taken at his word, it would appear that Pottinger had simply obtained approval for a journey across Afghanistan where he would acquire information almost casually. There is, however, another explanation. None of the British officers involved in the Great Game wanted the stigma of 'spy' and tended to describe their activities as adventurous expeditions which would add to the stock of geographical knowledge of the world. Many writers seem to have accepted these officers' explanations at face value, but, despite the 'Boys' Own' appeal, there is no doubt these officers were engaged in gathering intelligence-worthy material.

Whether it was the fact that the Hazaras had detained him *en route* to Herat because they were suspicious of the 'holy man of the land of mountains', or because he was unsure how long it would take to be identified in the back streets of that city, Pottinger decided to approach the *wazir* (chief minister), Yar Mohammed, and announce his nationality. Believing that the Englishman might be a useful tool to procure British support against Persia, Yar Mohammed gave Pottinger freedom to move about the city as an observer. However, when the walls were breached and supplies ran low, Pottinger eventually participated more actively in the defence, no doubt conscious that the fall of the city would be greeted with alarm in India. However, he played down his own role in the fighting, particularly his efforts to stem the critical Persian attack of 13 June 1837. His biographers have attributed this, perhaps correctly, to Pottinger's modesty, but his eagerness to avoid actions that 'might be disapproved of' by the government was also uppermost in his mind.[39] His brief was to gather intelligence, not co-ordinate the defence of Herat.

Pottinger remained in contact with Burnes at Kabul, updating him on the progress of the siege. Pottinger also came to act as the negotiator with the Persian army. On 8 February 1837, he tried to obtain terms favourable to both sides, conversed with the Russian advisor, General Samson, and a British observer, Captain Arthur Connolly. Connolly had been sent to accompany the shah by McNeill to convey British disapproval, but eventually McNeill had to make the journey from Teheran himself in April when it appeared that Herat would fall. He brought a warning from the British government that the shah's attack should be halted, but Count Simonovich then hurried from Teheran, offering the shah enough gold to pay the army and assistance with the siege operations, thereby trumping McNeill's negotiations. In fact, Cossacks acted as the shock troops in the final attempt to storm the city in June. McNeill broke off negotiations and Auckland authorised the government of Bombay to send two steamers with troops up the Persian Gulf. When they landed at Karrack Island, the Persians believed a full-scale invasion was in progress. Consequently, when Connolly delivered an ultimatum, the siege was abandoned.[40]

Gerald Alder believed that the British obsession with Herat as the 'key to India' was wholly misguided.[41] McNeill and Connolly had argued that if the city fell to a hostile Persia, Russia, its ally, would have secured for itself a base within Afghanistan from which to harass the Indian border. Dost Mohammed himself remarked: 'If the Persians once take Herat, all is open to them as far as Balkh, and neither Kandahar nor Kabul is secure.'[42] The city was variously styled the 'Gate of India' and the 'Garden and Granary of Central Asia', and even those who did not think it was likely to open up Afghanistan to occupation believed it would provide a means for Russia to dominate Persia. The debate about the city's value continued throughout the nineteenth century, but Canning, echoing the view that any Russian attack would have to cross 500 miles of barren terrain inhabited by hostile Afghans, summed up the solution to the problem:

> If Herat be the key to India, that is, if a power once in possession of it can command an entrance into India, our tenure of this great empire is indeed a feeble one . . . The country of Afghanistan rather than the fort of Herat is our first defence.[43]

The problem was that Afghanistan was far from a united country at all – it was perhaps, to borrow Metternich's phrase, a 'geographical expression'. In April 1836, the tribal chiefs of Kandahar had sought an alliance with the shah in order to reduce the power of Herat, and few of the outlying clans owed any loyalty to Kabul. Auckland therefore considered three options. The first was to leave Afghanistan to its fate through non-intervention. This he rejected as it would give a free hand to Persia and Russia, and constitute an 'absolute defeat'. The second option was to follow Burnes's advice and support Dost Mohammed more pro-actively, but Auckland was concerned that the Afghans' bitter enmity towards the Sikhs over the city of Peshawar threatened to destabilise his ally and thus the security of the frontier. The third option was to encourage Ranjit Singh to advance on Kabul and install the puppet ruler, Shah Shujah.[44]

When Vitkevich arrived in Kabul, Dost Mohammed hoped it would concentrate British minds on the importance of an alliance, but it merely confirmed Auckland's suspicions that the Afghans could not be trusted. Burnes's suggestions that Dost Mohammed was sincere and should still be supported were no longer reaching the government because his despatches were being doctored to suit a policy shift. This was because Burnes's correspondence was being transmitted via Colonel Wade at Ludhiana and Wade made little secret of his desire to see Dost Mohammed ousted. In addition, Wade was more inclined to believe Masson's intelligence which was becoming ever more critical of Burnes. Clearly Masson and Burnes were still co-operating, but Masson believed Burnes was too ready to accept Dost Mohammed's word. Nevertheless, Masson too was inclined to agree that Dost Mohammed, for all his faults, was the best bet for a secure Afghanistan. Wade did not listen; he was more interested in the idea that Burnes had no further use in Kabul. His greatest failure was to dismiss the possibility that Vitkevich was probably not acting for the tsar at all after Masson revealed that the tsar's seals on Vitkevich's despatches were forgeries. Moreover, St Petersburg denied any knowledge of the 'envoy', which, although a frequent refrain in the years to come, may have been correct. Vitkevich was, in fact, a former Polish revolutionary, conscripted and exiled to Siberia. He had risen through the ranks and was eventually appointed to the mission to Kabul under the direction of the official envoy in Teheran, Count Simonovich. Whatever the nature of Vitkevich's origins, the purpose of a diplomatic mission to Kabul was clear: it was designed to gain influence with the Afghans against Britain.

Unaware that the 'intelligence' he received from Wade had been doctored, Auckland reacted decisively. In the 'Simla manifesto' of 1 October 1838, he issued an ultimatum calling for the immediate deportation of the Russian envoy and a renunciation of all Afghan claims to Peshawar. Burnes had been recalled in April 1838, by then realising that the governor-general clearly had a preference for Shah Shujah on the throne of Kabul, which Auckland thought would result in a weak and compliant Afghanistan. The political officer who would ensure the success of the operation was the chief secretary of the government in Calcutta, William Hay Macnaghten. Macnaghten had been a diligent bureaucrat and was an accomplished linguist, but he, and Henry Torrens, his assistant secretary, and John Colvin, the governor-general's private secretary, all encouraged Auckland on the grandiose plan to turn Afghanistan into a protectorate.[45] Attempts to get Sikh co-operation were a failure and Ranjit Singh insisted that the Army of the Indus, as the invasion force was styled, would have to enter Afghanistan via the Bolan Pass. Some 9,500 troops from the Bengal Army formed the core but an additional 6,000 men were called Shah Shujah's force, even though not one of them was an Afghan. But for some sniping and cattle rustling, the Army of the Indus, swollen to 38,000 by camp followers, sweated its way up the Bolan Pass, with Burnes still in the vanguard, threatening or issuing subsidies to the local Baluchis to ensure safe passage.

The First Afghan War, 1838–42

The military aspect of the operation was a complete success. Kandahar was taken without a shot being fired, Dost Mohammed fled to Bamian (and then Bokhara), and, after the fall of the fortress of Ghazni, his army melted away. However, problems were evident from the outset. When Shah Shujah entered Kabul on 25 April 1839, it was a sullen crowd that greeted him, suggesting that, as soon as the British force withdrew, he would be overthrown. There had also been some fundamental errors in logistics which stemmed from poor field intelligence. It could easily have been established that crop failures in the summer of 1838 in Afghanistan meant that living off the land was impossible; the villagers had been reduced to collecting roots even before the troops arrived. It was simply not foreseen that Burnes would be forced to purchase 10,000 sheep from the Baluchis to feed the army. The climate had also been misjudged. The men were stifled in their uniforms; heat stroke killed off some of the soldiers as they marched and dehydration caused immense suffering to the rest. Two officers died in their tent, killed by a temperature of 106 degrees.[46] Nevertheless, there were some intelligence successes, too. Mohan Lal, Burnes's secretary, managed to bribe one of the Afghans, Abdul Rashid Khan, who had deserted from inside the fortress at Ghazni. His vital information revealed that all but one of the gates had been walled up from the inside. This made it possible for all effort to be directed against the Kabul gate, and the position was carried by storm.

Once installed in Kabul, Macnaghten tried to win over the Wazir of Herat, but Major D'Arcy Todd, his political agent, was simply seen by Yar Mohammed as a means to acquire British rupees. Eventually, Todd withdrew, fully expecting that Herat would soon be annexed. In fact, Macnaghten disapproved of Todd's action. He had anticipated that Herat would become a new buffer, friendly to the regime in Kabul, even though this assumption was contrary to all the intelligence that both Todd and Pottinger had supplied him with. The fact was that Macnaghten had become blindly optimistic. He grew accustomed to dismissing reports that did not accord with his own personal view, and, observing the tranquil cricket matches, the gaiety of ice skating, and the arrival of the families of the soldiers, he believed that Afghanistan had indeed become just another possession of the East India Company.

The departure of the bulk of the fighting troops was almost immediate, but criticisms about the costs were expressed in India and in London. The levying of taxation in a more efficient manner than Afghans had ever witnessed before was one of the first things to ignite a fiery discontent.[47] The punishments meted out by Mullah Shikore, Shah Shujah's minister, added more fuel to the fire. The liaisons that had sprung up between some British officers and Afghan women turned resentment into a blaze. An old Pushtun proverb noted that three things will always generate conflict: *zar, zan* and *zamin* (gold, women and land). But to this list should be added the presence and power of infidels and foreigners. Many Afghans were insular, suspicious of outsiders and felt humiliated by the British garrison. Intelligence reports confirmed this. Henry Rawlinson, now a major serving as political officer at Kandahar, noted in August 1841:

> The feeling against us is daily on the increase and I apprehend a succession
> of disturbances in this part of the country till the winter. The moolahs are
> preaching against us from one end of the country to the other, and we may
> now be said to hold our position by our military strength.[48]

Rawlinson suggested either withdrawal, or a policy that would 'carry fire and sword through some of the insurgent districts' as the only solutions. Macnaghten responded by telling the government in India that 'the country is perfectly quiet from Dan to Beersheba.'[49]

Even Burnes, who felt redundant as the political officer attached to Shah Shujah, was complacent, despite Mohan Lal's warnings. Mohan Lal had remained active in the bazaars of Kabul, learning that Akbar Khan, Dost Mohammed's son, was mustering a confederacy of Afghan chiefs. Moreover, Mohan Lal also discovered that Abdullah Khan, an influential figure in Kabul, was planning to murder Burnes as the signal for a general rising. Burnes appears to have ignored this warning. Two days later, on 2 November, Burnes was attacked by a mob in the city and killed. Mohan Lal witnessed the event, and it was said that an Asian collaborator had originally offered to disguise Burnes and spirit him away when the crowds first gathered, but, on getting him outside had shouted: 'This is Sekunder Burnes!' In the confusion of rioting that followed, Mohan Lal managed to recover the journal that Burnes had been compiling since his arrival. The mystery of who betrayed Burnes has never been solved.

General Elphinstone, the ageing officer sent to command the garrison, failed to act swiftly against the rioters, encouraging further Afghan resistance. Macnaghten also refused to let the British garrison shelter inside the walls of the Bala Hissar, the immense fortress that dominated the city, believing that it would be an affront to Shah Shujah who occupied it. Instead the garrison and the families remained in their peace-time cantonment, where their supplies were cut off. Macnaghten clung to the mistaken belief that he could play the tribal leaders off against each other, but the policy backfired when he agreed to meet Akbar Khan; he was seized and killed – his dismembered parts being paraded through Kabul.

Elphinstone then tried to make terms, agreeing to surrender 130 hostages and evacuate the cantonment in order to return safely to India.[50] The 4,500 troops and their family members were accompanied by a stampede of 10,000 camp followers when they set out on 5 January 1842. Three days into the march, conducted in freezing weather conditions, the Ghilzai tribesmen began attacking the column. Brigadier Sale had already taken a portion of the garrison as far as Jellalabad to clear the road, but he had pitifully few men to hold open the entire route. Gradually, as the column wended its way through the passes, it was reduced by sniping, cold and starvation. A handful of officers and men, a mixture of units, made a final stand at Gandamack, and although some fugitives subsequently made their way back to India or Kabul, only one man, Dr Brydon, completed the whole journey to Jellalabad.[51]

To avenge the defeat, Auckland despatched the 'Army of Retribution' into Afghanistan under the command of Major-General Sir George Pollock. As Pollock pushed through the Khyber Pass, crowning the heights with protective picquets as he advanced, Major-General Nott advanced from Kandahar. Akbar Khan withdrew, and Kabul was abandoned to the British who sacked the city in revenge. Nevertheless, no army of occupation was to remain behind. The universal opinion was that Afghanistan had proved too expensive and troublesome to hold. It lay on an over-extended and vulnerable line of communication, with intervening mountains that were all but blocked in winter. Within weeks, the British withdrew, and, predictably perhaps, Shah Shujah was assassinated soon after. Finally, Dost Mohammed was permitted to return to his kingdom; he ruled there for a further twenty years.

A Failure of Diplomacy or Intelligence?

It was a misreading of intelligence that led to war with Afghanistan. Auckland and his advisors had misunderstood the local politics, underestimated the gravity of the situation in 1841 (and the feelings of the Afghans), and over-estimated the Russian capability. However, it has to be said that the Russians did attempt what the agents and newswriters were predicting – the seizure of Khiva as a first step in a broad policy of annexation. In 1839, General Perovsky, the commander-in-chief at the garrison of Orenburg, set out with 5,000 men to capture the ancient khanate. The expedition soon foundered in deep snows and Perovsky's transport animals died in scores. It was an unprecedented winter. After three months of painful progress, the march had to be abandoned. When the force finally returned to Orenburg in May, a fifth of the troops and ninety per cent of the camels had died. Burnes had been right to highlight the problems of the region for an advancing army, but soon all attention in Britain and India was on the failure of their own Afghanistan adventure.

Gerald Morgan was disparaging in his summary of the types of officers who had gathered information, 'all religious and bachelors', and their missions, which added little to the real defence of India. Their ideas, formed without corroborative evidence, tended to influence those in high places, and at least one, Henry Rawlinson, had the ear of the prime minister. As they travelled openly as Europeans, and carried letters of introduction, Morgan believed that: 'as part of any real espionage system they simply do not qualify'.[52]

But what was the role of these political agents – was it primarily diplomatic and commercial? Did it have any intelligence dimension at all? For the Europeans, disguises were deemed necessary for their protection, even though in most cases they failed to conceal their identities from the Afghan people. There is also no doubt that each mission had a diplomatic function. For the Asian personnel, their employment was often casual – most were not entrusted with missions of importance – but, because of their ability to slip unnoticed through the bazaars and to question local people without arousing suspicion, they were the most important in information gathering. The European missions were always accompanied by one or two, and, although styled as munshis or guides, clearly some were qualified beyond mere translation. In Burnes's party Mohammed Ali was a surveyor of some note. Mohan Lal was well educated (producing his own memoirs and a biography of Dost Mohammed) and he established a network of informers in Kabul. Moreover, he survived the destruction of the Kabul garrison and later travelled to England to be presented to Queen Victoria. Syed Karamut Ali was also important enough to be entrusted with the post of newswriter in Kandahar.

Previous histories have tended to concentrate on the just the geographical achievements of the European officers and on the details of their consular missions. They were simply servants of the East India Company, or travelling gentlemen, and their memoirs confirm that impression. But they did glean sensitive information about the areas they travelled through and this was kept in the political and secret files of the government of India. Much of this material, including the voluminous reports of the newswriters, was transferred to the India Office where it was used by military planners. Burnes's Military Memoir and other reports can still be seen in the military files of the India Office Library to this day.

In fact, taking the missions of Connolly, Pottinger, Rawlinson and Burnes together, it is clear that there was more being attempted than a diplomatic push to secure Afghanistan's alignment with Britain. It was a major intelligence effort across the whole region. Their reports and maps were designed to provide the British in India with comprehensive details of potential invasion routes and resources. It was also important to record the names of local rulers and to sound out their ambitions. The Europeans may have been little more than roving consuls, but as army officers they would have been on the lookout for information that would be useful for military purposes.

Spying can be a cause of instability between states – there was certainly concern about Burnes's mission being interpreted that way – but the causes of the Afghan War were essentially the misreading of intelligence, and the ambitions of Auckland and his advisors to seize vital ground before it was lost to the Russians. In the political climate of the day, and given the success of the Russians in the first half of the 1830s, this attitude is understandable, but its translation into a 'forward policy', based on several assumptions about the intelligence gathered, was a folly. What turned folly into disaster was the incompetence of those in command of the mission. Yet, within British India itself there was a similar story of intelligence success and failure.

Chapter 4

Internal Insecurity

The Development of Intelligence Within India, 1776–1859

Indian spies were recruited by the British on a routine basis to secure military, political and social information. The origins of the intelligence practices used beyond the frontiers were to be found within the subcontinent, and, by the early years of the nineteenth century, the British had build up a system (if it was so complete it merited the term 'system') based largely on the older Mughal intelligence and communication networks. In the struggle for supremacy in India between 1765 and 1804, the British scored some remarkable intelligence successes, but in every case they were dependent on Asian personnel. By the 1830s, the same methods were being used against the remaining princely states and against organised gangs of criminals. Despite this progress towards order and stability, the British gradually abandoned the co-operation of their Asian personnel in the administration of the subcontinent. Cut off from the roots of information, the East India Company faced unrest, mutiny and rebellion. And yet, at the lower levels, collaboration within the British-Indian Empire survived and continued.

The Mughals had not presided over a police state, with comprehensive eaves-dropping on their subjects. They were primarily concerned with the attitude of their powerful subordinate rulers who were the most likely to threaten their rule. The Mughal emperors had their own royal agents, most of whom functioned as envoys or heralds, but some were deployed in the disguise of holy men and located at sites of pilgrimage to pick up on the feelings of certain religious sects. This was especially important where religious groups jealously guarded their own sources of information. Below the royal agents was a range of other informants with specialist tasks. The imperial newswriter collated the reports of subordinate newswriters at the courts of the most prominent subjects. The newswriters had a role akin to that of a diplomatic service in that they were expected to relay conversations of the subject to the emperor and from time to time they employed their own secret agents to dig deeper. The newswriters were something of a *corps d'élite*, and served as chief negotiators in the final decades of the Mughal Empire. But secret agents were also employed directly by the monarch to listen at bazaars and to check the reports of officials.

Couriers and security forces supplied a stream of intelligence to the imperial capital. Communication within the old Mughal Empire had been maintained on a system of *dak chaukis* (postal networks), served by *harcarras*. These runners, or couriers, were far more than just fleet-footed postmen; they were trained in several languages and expected to be able to report on military strengths, deployments and weaponry. The security men, such as police chiefs (*kotwals*), and village watchmen (*chaukidars*), also sent reports up the chain of command, and these were in turn supplemented and collated by royal scribes, record keepers and the highly respected and well educated munshis.

Yet, in the Mughal era, intelligence was not centralised or exclusively hierarchical. Information flowed between members of religious groups, through bazaars (where it was picked up by *bazarians* – gossip mongers – and passed on), and from thousands of itinerants, such as the doctors, barbers, traders, astrologers, and many others who performed some small, specialised service. When the Mughal Empire began to fragment, the system of intelligence-gathering was disrupted, although it was never entirely destroyed. Newswriters remained an important conduit for negotiations and could bring conflicts between rival states to a speedy conclusion. They also enabled rulers to see which allies of the enemy might be turned to their own side. Daks and agents might be knocked out more readily, however, and so the whole system was duplicated and increased. The rising costs of wars also put more pressure on the collection of accurate and timely military information. Thousands were employed as casual spies, couriers and informants, and private daks and newswriters emerged across the subcontinent.

'John Company' and Intelligence

The East India Company had its own intelligence needs from the beginning. In the early years, information on south Asian textiles was particularly valuable. In 1639, Henry Bornford had written a report on the location, production and types of cloth in India.[1] The main sources of information were Indian merchants and Indian employees of the East India Company, known as *banians* or *dubashes*. On commerce, not surprisingly, the Company was well informed, although initially it lacked detailed knowledge of manufacturing processes. Nevertheless, it was political information that impinged on trade which came increasingly to dominate the intelligence effort. This, in turn, drew the Company into the complex web of alliances and allegiances of the subcontinent. Nevertheless, the British found it hard to unravel the relations of castes and rulers and this forced them to depend on their Asian employees and intermediaries.

The networks of the Mughal system lent themselves easily to British penetration. When Bengal was transferred to British rule, for example, the former Newab of Bengal's administration was not entirely destroyed. Mohammed Reza Khan was the deputy appointed by Robert Clive to administer Bengal, and it was through him that the British gained knowledge of commerce, revenue systems and the arts of Indian diplomacy.[2] The British also made extensive use of 'Persian letters', that is, reports from the networks of spies, newswriters and couriers that extended throughout Bengal and westwards as far as Delhi.[3] However, Warren Hastings sought to streamline the system. He abolished the post of *akbar navis* (subprincipal newswriter) and relied heavily on his own, newly appointed agents, such as Krishna Kanta Nandy, a landed magnate, or entrepreneurs like Ramchandra Pandit, and Muslim former courtiers such as Taffazul Hussain Khan and Ali Ibrahim Khan.[4] But faced with the threat of other hostile states, the British still needed to supplement their intelligence system with relatives of employees, merchants, and, as they acquired new territory, the personnel of older networks who found themselves suddenly without any other employment.[5] The outbreak of hostilities in 1776 also prompted Hastings to try and extend the intelligence-gathering capacity of the residency system. In 1782, James Grant, the British resident at Hyderabad, tried to glean information of military value on the Deccan.[6] In the fashion that was to become the classic style of the Great Game, Grant relied on Indian merchants, the route maps of British officers travelling through the region and on their Indian informants.

Yet there were always weaknesses in the system. The *peshwa* (chief ministers) and Mysore authorities deliberately tried to starve British agents of information, or fed them deliberately misleading 'intelligence'. The problem was always getting reliable information, and, in a climate of competition, even British officials could not be trusted entirely. The resident of Lucknow between 1782 and 1784 was John Bristow, a personal rival of Hastings, who intercepted the letters of British officers and tried to undermine Hastings's authority in Oudh by sowing misinformation to his Indian hosts.[7] Hastings himself complained about the interventions of European 'adventurers' who polluted the sources (probably to serve their own interests). The problem of interpretation by subordinate British officials in the chain of intelligence was another perennial difficulty, and some Company officers used the parallel Indian networks to cross-check their own sources.

Hastings was aware that the fundamental weakness in British authority was its lack of knowledge about India and its people. The subsequent search for politically useful information inspired a wave of benign Orientalism, a thirst for knowledge of Indian literature, law and religion, made famous by the works of William Jones, H. T. Colebroke and Charles Wilkins. Post-colonial scholars have made much of the British desire to 'know' the Indians so that they could more easily govern them. Whilst this effort has been portrayed as sinister, centralised, and cynical, in fact it reflected the trend of British intellectual thought in this period. The nineteenth-century British historical obsession was with constitutions and government systems, partly to legitimise their own colonial rule but also to make sense of the bewildering array of native systems they encountered across the world. The reign of the Mughal Emperor Aurangzeb (1658–1707), for example, was likened to that of James II in Britain, and both tyrannies had been overthrown by forces of English liberty. This *raison d'être* of British rule continued to be reinforced throughout the nineteenth century. Major Owen Tudor Burne, secretary of the Political and Secret Department in the 1870s, summed up the mission statement of colonial rule: 'Everyone knows what our Indian government is trying to do, namely to govern India justly, to make the native Princes strong, and the people happy, as far as we can, and thereby add to the material progress of the country, and strengthen our position internally.'[8] The result was the development of systems for the collection of revenue, and the systemisation of information-gathering on politics and society in south Asia. In short, the British search for information was designed to make India 'progress and pay'.[9]

By the first decade of the nineteenth century, British intelligence networks in India were more firmly established. There were British residents at all of the princely courts accompanied by newswriters (and their own covert agents), the Company's armies made use of intelligence through their scattered posts and garrisons, and British surveyors had crossed the subcontinent, producing the first scientific maps of the interior in 1788.[10] The small legions of amateur ethnographers, writers and artists were also adding to the growing stock of knowledge of India, and books and journals had appeared specialising in agriculture, commerce and society.

From the period when Lord Cornwallis was governor-general (1786–93), independent channels of information such as daks were closed down in an attempt to make Indians dependent on British systems of communication. It was, perhaps, a first attempt at counter-intelligence in India. In its place, a system of patronage was established. When Indian princes protested, arguing that depriving them of their own dak and harcarra systems diluted their authority, they were overruled and gently reminded of their client status. Native agents representing independent states were threatened and replaced with more compliant figures.[11] Misinformation was fed to them too, and they were then discredited by sending British officials directly to the rulers, persuading the princes they could no longer trust their own men in British territory. Where agents could not be detected, the minister who was acting as their controller was located and then threatened. Existing Indian networks continued to be absorbed. In Mysore, the Bedar tribesmen, who had provided the sultans with daks, harcarras, spies and guides, were recruited by the British. This was a particular success since the British had lacked reliable intelligence on Mysore for years, and Tipu Sultan had once maintained an extensive system. It was clear that money was the crucial factor. British agents in the first Mysore War (1767–73) had been so badly paid they had invented information to collect a reward. Many had avoided dangerous missions. Colonel William Fullarton, an agent handler, had condemned those that 'skulk for a day among the bushes conversing only with camp followers' and he had advocated a more comprehensive system.[12]

In the Second Mysore War (1778–84), Fullarton acquired five trustworthy agents (recommended by the resident of Tanjore and the Newab of Arcot) who employed their own harcarras, but Fullarton also ensured they were in competition with each other and threatened that treachery would result in execution. They were posted on bridges and certain routes, and each was interrogated on his return. Fullarton would test them by asking them to name the places they stopped at on each day, and threw in fictitious locations to check their honesty.[13] When reports failed to come in, it was clear that Mysore cavalry had severed the links and this gave him an indication of the location of fast-moving enemy forces. A regular Corps of Guides was formed during the war and their reports, along with those of the harcarras, contributed to the creation of large-scale maps of the province.[14] When

Arthur Wellesley led a Company army in the Assaye campaign, he benefited from Fullarton's system of espionage, but he was still compelled to have his chief harcarra hanged for treachery.[15]

The main problem in the fighting with the Maratha Confederacy was the loyalty of the people on whom the British were dependent for their agents. The solution was to recruit selectively from certain tribes. In southern India, Kallars, Coorgs and Bellars were favoured; in the west, the Mewias and Mehars, and throughout India, high caste Brahmins, merchants and gosains. Off the battlefield, a variety of sources was still used: heralds, midwives, old women, and low-caste men who supplied information for a few rupees; this information was passed on to independent agents or secret writers who, in turn, were employed by known newswriters.

The comprehensive development of intelligence under British rule was exemplified by the governor-general's personal secretary and chief intelligence officer, George Cherry, former resident of Lucknow (1761–98). He was typical in his tactics of intelligence-gathering, making contacts with pilgrims, merchants and native exiles who had some grievance with the Oudh authorities. In addition, Cherry made use of women of the court to acquire useful information, and of the ubiquitous eunuchs who had long served south Asian courts as couriers (eunuchs enjoyed a status of special trust as they were not regarded as a dynastic threat). By this means, which Cherry extended to southern India, letters were acquired that were to have far-reaching consequences. Wellesley used the interception of diplomatic correspondence between Mysore and the 'neutral' state of Arcot as an excuse to overthrow the latter's independence. Interpreting the warmth of the language used in Indian diplomacy between the Newab of Arcot and Tipu Sultan of Mysore as evidence of treason contrary to the 'established maxims of the public law of nations', Arcot was brought under Company rule. Although Cherry was murdered in 1799, Mysore was eventually captured and Lord Edward Clive, the governor of Madras, set up a comprehensive system of espionage to monitor Tipu Sultan's heirs who had been exiled to Vellore.[16] Penetration of the princely courts was relatively easy, given their tradition of 'openness'. By the summer of 1805, Company agents had access to the correspondence and conversations, states of finances and military strengths of many courts, including those of the Maratha leaders Jaswant Rao Holkar and the Rajas of Bharatpur and Jaipur.[17]

The close connection between revenue and the British military conquest of large parts of the subcontinent is well documented, but the intelligence effort by independent states and their British adversaries was no less reliant on money; it might even be said that cash was the lubricant of loyalty. In the fighting of 1790–2, Tipu's own commissary officers had taken the grain and rice they had requisitioned to the Company's army, knowing they would be paid in cash, rather than the promises of a near-bankrupt state.[18] The Company was able to attract the services of military victuallers, the *brinjaris*, and pay for enormous numbers of transport animals through its formidable financial system. Moreover, surveys of newly acquired territories were more than assessments for future revenue possibilities to facilitate British rule. They were essential for the accurate acquisition of resources for future wars. Surveys had other military purposes.

Roads were assessed for their suitability for military transport and artillery, whilst fortifications and river crossings were the focus of particular intelligence interest.

Even so, up to date field intelligence on campaign was still essential in the early years. Light cavalry probed and reconnoitred ahead of every army, and commanders had to interpret their findings rapidly. Few ever enjoyed comprehensive intelligence on either the topography or the enemy. Wellesley had made use of harcarras in the Deccan campaign in 1803–4, with Mountstuart Elphinstone as translator. At Assaye, Wellesley deduced that the presence of villages on either side of a river suggested that some ancient communication, such as a ford, existed between them, even though his guides assured him there was none. Despatching a sepoy volunteer, Ramdin Missir, to test the depth of the water, Wellesley was able to complete his brilliant flank march prior to the hard fighting of the battle itself.[19] Despite the occasional failure of his guides, Wellesley's harcarras were able to bring him detailed information about the strengths of the Marathas, particularly their artillery.[20] As a result, Marathas who caught British harcarras at Deeg had them tortured and mutilated.[21] The use of field intelligence in this campaign suggests the British had already established a precedent some time before the emergence of a foreign threat to the north-west.

Once British rule was firmly established in India, the intelligence network continued to function wherever there was a threat. Mountstuart Elphinstone, the former envoy to Kabul who became resident of Poona, employed a broker who collected intelligence from a variety of sources. Disguised agents were sent to hunt down Trimbakji Danglia, an anti-British agitator from Poona who had fled to Maratha territory. Not only was he successfully located, but he was also kept under surveillance.[22] A servant of the Gaikwar of Baroda betrayed information about his employer's anti-British sentiments to the assistant resident in 1812, and agents serving the British revealed similar correspondence by the Raja of Nagpur in 1817.[23] Nevertheless, without a specific threat, intelligence tended to atrophy. Indeed, a general trend of complacency accompanied the change of emphasis on the plains from war to administration. This gave rise to occasional scares about plots and conspiracies, especially when unrest turned into rebellion or disorder. Yet, the most celebrated of the internal intelligence efforts to combat the hidden menace of crime and conspiracy was the struggle against Thuggee – the stranglers of the highways.

William Henry Sleeman, Indian Informers and Thuggee

The first European report on *Thugs*, or highway stranglers, was produced in the seventeenth century by a French traveller named Thevenot.[24] The term Thug was translated as 'deceiver', and Thevenot's account described how roadside robbers would pretend to befriend travellers until, on an appointed signal, they would throttle their victims and steal their possessions. Thomas Perry, the magistrate of Etawah, noted in 1808 that a defendant called Ghulam described himself as a Thug, but it seems Hussein understood the term to mean cheat, rather than *phansighar* (strangler). Nevertheless, in return for a pardon, he agreed to elaborate on thug gangs and their murders. Christopher Bayly believes that it was Hussein's exaggerations which prompted the British to establish a separate Thuggee department, and that they confused ordinary banditry on the highways with a widespread network of organised crime.[25] Moreover, Bayly suggests that the specialised language of the Thugs, penetrated by the British after months of research, was little more than working-class Hindi slang. Nevertheless, it is interesting that the rituals of Thug murder were similar across large areas. The peculiarity of the language, slang or not, was striking. The use of scarves was ubiquitous, as were certain tools for burial, talismans and omens. Not all worshipped Kali as the British initially believed, since some were Muslims with a strong dedication to certain tombs or shrines, but there were many Thugs who believed in the divine protection of this particular goddess.

At first, the intelligence on the Thugs was patchy, but interrogations by William Henry Sleeman, the magistrate of Nursingpur, produced a collection of confessions in 1822–4. These early reports suggested that roadside murders accounted for 40,000–50,000 deaths every year.[26] From the robberies, certain landed magnates received cash bribes and in return they agreed to harbour the criminals.[27] Thugs operated in family groups, and Thuggee was common in certain tribes, as well as attracting criminal opportunists. Demobilised Pindari soldiers were also amongst their ranks. They flourished in areas where agriculture was unstable, major shrines and route ways existed, or where traditional systems of village watchmen had broken down. Some seemed to relish the ritualised nature of the killings, with graves sometimes prepared in advance, and, in rare instances, stabbing replacing the scarf-strangling.[28]

Sleeman's success was due to the wealth of information he was able to glean from voluntary or pressed informants. Thugs who were captured were offered the chance either to turn evidence and join the band of 'approvers' who gave information on other Thugs, or be hanged (although some were in fact transported to the Andaman Islands). After compiling the informers' confessions, troops or police were then deployed to net the next gang. Sleeman spent months drawing up detailed family trees of Thug gangs, and kept records of all their vocabulary (the *Ramasi*), practices and ruses. Excavations of burial grounds helped in the process of identification of the criminals by the idiosyncrasies of their methods.

His first informant was Kalyan Singh, a man recently released from prison, who identified the members of a Thug gang.[29] Bringing the gang in without disclosing that he knew their real purpose, Sleeman recognised the slang vocabulary of *dacoits* (robber bandits). Having incarcerated them, Sleeman used Kalyan Singh and his brother, a member of the gang, to locate the graves of recent victims, buried in a sacred site called a *bele*. Three corpses were found at first, then many more. These discoveries enabled Sleeman to convict ninety-eight Thugs.[30] It is striking that even amongst this first haul of gangsters, Sleeman found a courier and a policeman. This made him all the more determined to ensure that the conspiracy of silence was broken. He ensured he had clear and substantiated evidence of each murder, and he obtained the legal authority to have any association with Thugs recognised as a criminal offence which carried a sentence of life imprisonment.

From his own province, Sleeman extended his networks. He made sure that police and military patrols were furnished with lists of information about gang movements, names and identifying data.[31] But it was the approvers who offered the most reliable means to intercept Thugs. In 1829, a British force managed to corner a hundred-strong gang led by a man called Umrao. They all protested their innocence until an approver called Khaimraj, a blacksmith who had once been part of the same group, revealed the location of graves. Sleeman identified a certain 'Feringhea' as a co-ordinator of Thugs in 1830 and set himself to discover the real identity and location of this guiding hand. The break-through came when several of Feringhea's relatives were imprisoned and Dhan Singh, an approver, gave Sleeman vital information on his most recent movements. Feringhea was captured and confronted with the same bleak choice as other Thugs – death or information. He chose to explain to Sleeman the whole process and justification of Thug murders, as well as the identities of many other Thug gang members. By 1837, 'Thuggee' Sleeman had acquired the services of 483 informers and they were later rewarded with jobs in the Jabalpur Gaol weaving carpets and making tents. In all 3,266 Thugs were arrested between 1829 and 1837, of whom 412 were hanged.

Whether Sleeman had mistaken common banditry for Thuggee seems immaterial when he and his followers helped to reduce the numbers of deaths on India's highways. Nevertheless, criminal gangs were not limited to the roads. Dacoits were the scourge of rural India.[32] Like the Thugs they often operated in large gangs and occasionally enjoyed the connivance of village watchmen whom they bribed. The travelled widely and attacked both rich and poor alike, sometimes disguising themselves as pilgrims and holy men to operate amongst the pious and vulnerable. Torture was frequently used as a way of discovering the location of hidden valuables. For the British, combating this menace followed the Thuggee model. The Thagi and Dakoiti Department was established under Lord Bentinck in 1829 on the initiative of Sleeman, and its methods were those that Sleeman had established. For example, acting on intelligence from a variety of informants, James Paton, the assistant resident of Lucknow, took part in one of the many operations against dacoits in 1834 at the Bheera forest. Using Indian cavalry, he ambushed a party of 500. Sixty were slain and 200 taken into captivity for the loss of one dead and sixteen wounded.

Sleeman also tackled dacoit gangs himself after 1838, employing the same tactics as he had against Thugs, but this time calling his informers 'spies' or 'intelligencers'.[33] One of the most prominent of these men was Chandal who helped Sleeman's officers locate Mangal Singh, a notorious gang leader. Chandal disguised himself as a pedlar selling sugar and mixed freely with Mangal's men. His report explained that the gang moved in three groups and he gave details of their strengths and weaponry. Although Mangal Singh escaped briefly to the Terai borders of Nepal, malaria forced him out, and his group was neutralised.[34]

It may have been, as Bayly suggests, that the British effort to break Thuggee was the result of a desire to penetrate native networks of crime and information, so as to prevent Asians combining against them.[35] Whilst accepting that a Thug language and religious motivation were probably exaggerations, Bayly rightly points out that there was no centralised direction, as Sleeman had feared initially.[36]

However, the British were not entirely wrong in their 'orientalist' judgements. The categories of Thugs clans and families would not have been unfamiliar within the Mughal lexicon, whilst the extent and ritualised nature of the violence made British concerns entirely understandable. The means by which Sleeman defeated the Thugs is of even greater interest. Once again it indicated that, in the face of a perceived threat, the British could enlist Asian personnel and break down the networks of information that confronted them within India. Nevertheless, without centralised direction, the system was always in danger of failing at precisely the moment it was needed. If Sleeman's methods had been a success, it was because he had led by personal example and he had inspired others with a similar zeal. Without an established and permanent organisation, this dependence on charismatic personnel was doomed to periodic failure.

Intelligence in the Great Mutiny, 1857–9

When Sleeman returned to his old province of Bundelkund after unrest there in 1842, he noted:

> I was concerned to find that there was no longer that sympathy between the people and the agents now employed in these regions by our government. The European officers no longer showed the courtesy towards the middle and higher classes and that kindness towards the humbler which characterised the officers of our day, while the native officers rather imitated or took advantage of this.[37]

Sleeman's warning about the growing gulf between British and Indian was also remarked upon by other 'old hands' of the Company, but few appeared willing or able to change the trend.[38] There was disdain for the 'gossip' of the locals, and European officers spent less time learning their military craft from the older Indian NCOs.[39] Officers no longer hosted nautch dancing for their men, or took them hunting. Better communications with England meant that there was a longing for home news and more attention paid to English society and events. The old habits of cohabiting with Indian mistresses, or of marrying them, were dying out too in a climate of prejudice and contempt. In short, there was a withering of the connections between the Company Raj and the Indian people as British administration became ever more distant, hierarchical, and less dependent on its roots of personalised leadership.

In contrast to the complacency of Anglo-Indian society, the Indian population was increasingly alarmed by the signals of impending unrest. Using their traditional networks of bazaar gossip and news from itinerants, the people seemed conscious that trouble was brewing. There were plenty of signs: the demand for cash and the price of gold rose steeply in Oudh, merchants appeared to be anxious about the future, and sepoys asked repeatedly for news. In intercepted letters, Sir Robert Montgomery, a tough Ulsterman and the chief commissioner of the Punjab, noted that coded phrases were being used to describe the apparent weaknesses of British military power, such as: 'hats were hardly to be seen and turbans very plentiful'.[40] Less coded expressions of discontent were evident in the Indian press.

The *Sadik-ul-Akhbar* and *Dihli Urdu Akhbar* printed anti-British sentiments both before and during the Mutiny.[41] Despite the growing signs of unrest, many British leaders assumed that the Indian troops would simply carry out their orders and contain any disturbances. Major-General Hearsey, commander of the Presidency Division in Calcutta, refused to spy on his sepoys to obtain 'secret information' because he said 'it would not be proper for me to do it'.[42] Captain Richard Lawrence of the Thagi and Dakoiti Department nevertheless sent a Brahmin agent into the sepoy lines and received a typical report: they were 'full of *fissad* [sedition]'.[43]

Most enigmatic of all was the mysterious passage of chapattis from village to village in January 1857. Few actually understood what they were supposed to herald, and the British regarded them as evidence of some widespread conspiracy, but it seems likely that they belonged to a far older superstition of rural India whereby bad luck, disease or misfortune could be removed from a village by sending out food.[44] However, what made this occurrence so unusual was that they spread so far and wide. From an epicentre in Indore, they were transmitted through Gwalior, across the British North-West Provinces to Oudh and Rohil-khund, carried up to an astonishing 200 miles every night. Although cholera was prevalent at the time, they had not appeared in such abundance during previous outbreaks. British suspicions were fuelled when it was noted that the mutiny at Vellore in 1806 had been preceded by chapatti distribution.[45] British officials who interviewed Indians about the affair disagreed on its meaning, and it seems that the chapattis had a different significance in each district.[46]

But was the Mutiny planned by a centralised group of conspirators that British intelligence failed to detect? James Cracroft Williams, a special commissioner appointed after the Mutiny to punish the guilty and reward the loyalists, concluded that the sepoys had not known of any plans except that they should act as other regiments did in the event of trouble. Major G. W. Williams, another special commissioner, believed that the rapid spread of the Mutiny suggested that some co-ordination had taken place, but the large numbers involved only indicate that many were drawn in by the lure of loot or fear that their religion was about to be overthrown. The religious dimension was certainly mentioned time and again by participants, as were omens and 'signs'. There is little doubt that each group in Indian society had some particular reason for joining or resisting the rebellion. All the sources agree that the trigger factor for the sepoys was the greased cartridges affair, but landowners and officials who had been displaced by British annexations, peasants unhappy about taxation, and the difficulty of getting grievances redressed through British administration also played a part.

If British intelligence systems had failed to read the mood of the Indian troops and the people of the North-West Provinces, then intelligence certainly helped in the military effort to crush the Mutiny. After the initial outbreak of fighting at Meerut, the mutineers instantly set out for Delhi, the first mounted contingent arriving there at dawn on 11 May. The sacking of European quarters in Delhi quickly followed, with the desecration of Christian churches, and the execution of women and children in the courtyard of the Red Fort. The rebels used the old harcarras to communicate their triumph across the north-west. Agents, who had clearly been waiting for some news of mutiny, were captured at Allahabad on 24 May whilst trying to incite sepoys there.[47] The British information network was assisted not only by loyal troops who refused to join the mutineers and brought in reports from the affected stations, but also by the newly erected electric telegraph. This was a vital asset which the mutineers failed to attack, although the Meerut mutineers did sever the line to Delhi.[48] Nevertheless, news of the risings was transmitted within hours to the Punjab where the bulk of the army was still stationed after the recent war against the Sikhs. The first message from Delhi read: 'We must leave office. All the bungalows are on fire, burning down by the sepoys of Meerut. They came in this morning.'[49] Informers also passed messages to the Lahore police enabling Sir Henry Lawrence, the governor in the Punjab, to disarm battalions whose loyalties were in doubt.[50] Reliable harcarras transmitted messages between British stations whilst the dak between Indian merchants was carefully scrutinised.[51] However, it has to be said that British officers, both civil and military, could see with their own eyes what was happening and the news of atrocities, murders and mutiny was soon conveyed to every British post in India.

The immediate action against the rebels included closing down, as far as possible, their communications. Having disarmed battalions in the Punjab, Robert Montgomery, the acting lieutenant-governor of the province, ordered the occupation of all the river crossings. At these choke points he insisted that all suspicious travellers were to be checked.[52] Elsewhere, transport was seized and the native press was censored. Muslim clerics suspected of spreading anti-British propaganda were placed under surveillance.[53]

It was evident from the outset that, alongside resolute action by the British themselves, Indian allies would help to turn the tide. The Maharaja of Jodhpur immediately offered his troops to the British to crush the mutineers, and Maharaja Jaijii Rao Scindia of Gwalior did the same, although not all of the soldiers followed their instructions. Sikhs and Gurkhas, loyal remnants of the mutineer battalions and many of the Europeans' own servants nevertheless fought on the British side. The merchant classes of Dehli, both Hindu and Muslim, regarded the insurrection as a threat to the prosperity they had enjoyed under British rule. Many of them passed information to agents like Mohan Lal.[54] One British magistrate was approached by the Seth family, who were influential bankers at Mathura, and offered their entire intelligence network and two cannons.[55]

Reinforcements were brought to India from Malta, South Africa and Burma and troops *en route* to China were diverted. All had been alerted by telegraph and the passage of steam shipping. Yet until they arrived, there were precious few men to hold the isolated positions at Cawnpore, Lucknow and on the ridge outside Delhi. At this point, it was imperative to prevent the further spread of mutiny so as to concentrate the available manpower at the most threatened points. The difficulty to begin with was knowing who could be trusted. To the south-west, the officers in the Bombay Army were taking precautions against insurrection, and, in so doing, secret correspondence between Bombay sepoys and the mutineers was discovered on 14 June.[56] Rumours were rife and it was almost impossible to be sure of information. When a sepoy of the 13th Native Infantry warned his officers that the Lucknow garrison meant to join the mutiny, his information was ignored because it could not be verified.[57]

The news of terror tactics by British troops who advanced to the relief of the besieged garrisons, itself a response to the widespread murders and mutilations of Europeans, confirmed the resolve of many mutineers that there could be no going back and no negotiation.[58] After much bitter fighting, the British secured victory after victory, but not one was a foregone conclusion; it was, to use the Duke of Wellington's expression, more of a 'near run thing'. Flying columns eventually reached Lucknow and relieved the garrison there, and reinforced the meagre numbers on the Delhi Ridge. In time, stronger columns converged on Oudh, and the fall of Delhi, a six-day battle of intense street fighting, broke the back of the rebellion. In all these engagements, the British needed reliable information on the strengths of the rebels that opposed them. In this endeavour much use was made of Asian agents since it was impossible for Europeans either to pass themselves off as Indians or cover the ground adequately with cavalry reconnaissance.

The methods for gathering intelligence employed by William Muir, the magistrate of Agra, were perhaps typical.[59] His agents were well paid and numerous, deployed to observe the rebel lines and to maintain communications between the separated British columns. He used these reports to create a digest of facts so as to dispel the rumours that sapped morale. He also scoured the rebel newspaper of Lucknow for information on enemy movements.[60] His most reliable source was the newswriter for Gwalior who was stationed in Delhi. Through the British resident at Gwalior, the newswriter's reports were passed directly to Agra.[61] Mukdum Bash was another commercial spy active in Delhi for Muir, and he was later moved on to Bareilly until captured and executed by his quarry Nana Sahib.[62] The nephew of the Raja of Jorhat, Khan Jehan Khan, worked for the British in Delhi, too, and for this he was later rewarded with a horse and robes worth 1,500 rupees. Muir's best agent though was Chaube Ghyanshyam Das, a landed and pious Hindu who joined the British fearing the mutineers' real intention was to restore Muslim hegemony.[63] Once again, little more is known of these agents. The archives reveal a name, a reward, or a glimpse of some information they brought in; then they are gone, like a wisp of gun-smoke.

Intelligence networks were also established by Lieutenant Herbert Bruce, the Inspector of Police of the North-West Provinces, in May 1857. His primary objective was to keep open communication with Havelock's force during the relief of Lucknow, but he also fed the column intelligence on rebel strengths and movements. He was assisted by Man Raj, a clerk of the Etawah district office, who maintained a network of secret agents to observe rebels in the countryside.[64] Abbas Ali, the sub-divisional officer of the same district, assisted Man Raj by intercepting Nana Sahib's correspondence with the local landowners. But Bruce used his initiative to introduce 'black propaganda'. He had placards announcing British victories secretly posted up around Lucknow by his agents to break the morale of the rebels. Mirza Abbas Beg, an agent inside the city, also passed on crucial intelligence about the positions of the mutineers' guns which contributed to British success.[65]

The third highly prominent officer in the gathering of information during the Mutiny was Major William Hodson, the Assistant Quartermaster-General and therefore the official chief of intelligence. He was a colourful character. Nicknamed the 'Company's Blade' for his skill in swordsmanship, he had a mercurial temper, his charm turning to blind rage in a flash. But he was a 'man of action' and wasted no time in making decisions, vital attributes in the crisis of 1857. He first established a dak between the theatre of operations and the Punjab and then helped to co-ordinate the intelligence gathered from around Delhi. Moreover, Hodson was able to glean reliable information from the newswriter of Jhind Raj, a small Sikh state, inside the capital, which was copied by G. Barnes, the Commissioner of the cis-Sutlej (southern Punjab) states, before being passed on. Penetrating Delhi was made easier by the lacklustre field security offered by the mutineers. Mabub Khan, a trooper of the Guides cavalry disguised as a rebel, simply walked into the city through the Lahore gate without being challenged. He freely asked questions of the mutineers he met and walked out of the city to report his findings to the Delhi ridge force. On the British side, Sir Colin Campbell was alive to the threat to security posed by the mass of camp followers with the column he commanded. He told William Howard Russell, the journalist for *The Times*, to be cautious of what information was discussed publicly.[66] Colonel Thomas Pierce operating in Rajasthan made it a standing operational procedure not to act on any information unless it could be verified by at least two sources.[67]

Despite the problems of misinformation and rumour which inevitably were swept up into the intelligence reports, Hodson's main difficulty was the interception of his own agents. The mutineers were on the lookout for *cossids* (messengers) of the British. Those that were caught were either beheaded, as befell one pair captured between Delhi and Agra, or blown from cannon, a punishment inflicted on two Sikhs in British service. To protect the couriers, letters were sometimes written in French or Greek. Maulvi Rajab Ali, one of Hodson's agents (and formerly the munshi of the governor-general), received information from the newswriter of Jhind on small pieces of paper rolled up and hidden inside sticks.[68] The cossids protected themselves by demanding higher wages: ten times the normal rate was charged in May 1857.[69] After the fall of Delhi, some of the agents were retasked, but increasingly the reports that came in spoke of the rebels losing heart. The mutineers in Delhi lost their chance for offensive action because they were dependent on astrology and paralysed by a fear of the reprisals the British would take. The only pro-active elements seemed to be the Pathans who had come in from the frontier region. As the rebellion petered out, more and more Indians came forward to offer information to the British.

The hunt for former rebels and mutineers went on into the early 1860s. In contrast to the pre-Mutiny years, it was a period where information was valued more highly and security measures were draconian. Suspects were publicly flogged; there were demands for arms to be surrendered; extra police were deployed to monitor certain villages. Robert Montgomery, the chief commissioner in Lahore, was one who offered financial rewards for information on any fugitives.[70] Allies of the British gave valuable intelligence; the Maharaja of Banares, for example, forced his servants to provide information on named rebels. Many others were tracked down by police informants.[71] There were also attempts to improve the quality of the Indian police, especially in rural areas, and to have early warning of any unrest.

However, like their Mughal forebears, the British were anxious to avoid India becoming a 'police state', and hoped to create the sort of consensus policing that they had achieved at home.[72] As part of the process, village watchmen were to be centrally co-ordinated, although, in practice, it proved hard to break the influence of the landowners over them. Increasing the numbers of rural police also failed to improve the quality of policing. In years of hardship, robbery and banditry increased and some policemen threw in their lot with the malcontents. However, the British never attempted to set up a centralised and systematic police apparatus over rural India, and their efforts were directed against crime, not political opposition. In the end, improvements in communications and military technology made the likelihood of another rebellion very remote, and the spread of mass media made it easier for the British to eavesdrop on Indian opinion without the need for a secret police force. The British made use of the local elites, used the power of the law, and worked hard to maintain the prestige and inviolability of the government to maintain their rule. In this effort, the continued involvement of Indians was crucial.

Security, Knowledge and Intelligence

Backed by a ready supply of cash, the British were able to purchase the employment of many Asians in low-level espionage. But collaboration went beyond the 'money motive'. For the wealthier classes, the British secret service offered the chance to maintain their status when the old indigenous system was falling away; the alternative was ruin or anarchy. Moreover, the existence of a far older network of Mughal espionage, which the British could exploit, gave the Europeans critical intelligence on court politics, princely rivalry, military strengths and topography. Above all, it was the willingness of Indians to co-operate with the Europeans, because of their own interests and a certain consciousness of where political power lay, which enabled British intelligence to flourish. As Lawrence James so ably put it: 'They [the British] could always rely on the active collaboration of thousands of Indians who, for a variety of reasons, were willing to co-operate with those who seemed destined to become their new masters.'[73]

The success of the British in extending political control of the subcontinent during the late eighteenth and early nineteenth centuries depended, in part, upon developing intelligence systems to 'know' the country and its peoples (although the accusation that knowledge and power rested entirely in the hands of the colonisers, as many post-colonial scholars assert, seems grossly exaggerated).[74] As a result, understanding and using indigenous forms and practices of knowledge were vital, even though these, at first, carried the latent threat of dependence, and therefore of subversion. As the Company's jurisdiction expanded, and the territories of the plains were secured, the emphasis of British rule changed from an attempt to work closely with Asians, to a more distant attitude. The British concern was to gather information and statistics themselves, and thus reduce the reliance on the native informant. But the post office, telegraph, press and railway were communication systems without the intelligence dimension, and, whilst Asians were forewarned about the unrest of 1857, the majority of British personnel were taken by surprise. Despite their efforts to penetrate and control the channels of communication, the British networks proved frail, and failed altogether in the initial stages of the Great Mutiny of 1857.

The British learned several lessons about intelligence in the Mutiny, not least their dependence on Asian personnel to gather information. Internally the British preferred to leave security in the hands of their Indian police, and, despite the risks, they were still reluctant to carry out any systematic monitoring of the population for fear of antagonising the people. They fell back on their idea of a mission to help India progress, for the best form of security was not the Russian model of secret police, they argued, but good government, justice and the upholding of British prestige. This desire helps to explain the emphasis on cultivating the support of the Indian princes, and a strong focus on economic prosperity, rather than developing a widespread intelligence and security network.

However, in the aftermath of the Mutiny, letters and reports suggest there were, although unspoken, anxieties about subversion, and the fundamental gulf between Briton and Asian. Many Anglo-Indians sought to heal the divisions of the two by emphasising the success of imperial collaboration. Indeed, unity was the recurrent theme of imperial literature. Yet, depressingly, there were many others who saw the differences between European and Asian as an unbridgeable abyss founded on racial characteristics. The Great Mutiny's greatest tragedy was that it had provided this latter group with ample evidence of treachery, so that the loyalty and co-operation of so many Indians in that traumatic period were often forgotten or downplayed.

Chapter 5

Penetrating Central Asia

The Great Game and the
Russian War, 1842–1864

To many British observers in the mid-nineteenth century, Russia appeared to be a threat to India because of its inexorable advance across central Asia. In 1839 Russia was 1,500 miles (2,400 km) from the Indian border; by 1873 the tsar's armies had annexed all the ancient khanates of Tashkent, Samarkand, Khokand, Bokhara and Khiva, bringing them within 300 miles of India. One British officer pointed out that a Russian regiment on the shores of the Caspian was nearer Lahore or Delhi than its own capital.[1] Mountains, deserts and fierce tribal resistance had not deterred them, and they had annexed 70,000 square miles in thirty years. It is easy to condemn the alarmist reaction of the British with the benefit of hindsight, particularly as there was no war between Britain and Russia on the frontiers of Afghanistan. Eventually, in the 1890s, the borders were settled peacefully between the two powers. Indeed, the East India Company's folly of trying to control Afghanistan in the war of 1839–42 and the long standing military weaknesses of Russia – so graphically exposed by the wars fought between 1854 and 1917 – suggest that all the anxiety of the 'Great Game' was 'not worth the candle'.

Yet placed in its wider context across the continent, the threat that Britain and Russia posed to each other was a deadly reality. Russian aspirations to take control of the Straits near Constantinople, for both strategic and commercial reasons, clashed with British attempts to retain the Mediterranean as an 'English lake' for similar motives. Ottoman Turkey was to be the British bulwark against Russian expansion in the Near East. However, by the 1850s the so-called 'Sick Man of Europe' seemed to be on the verge of disintegration.[2] The Eastern Question, which dominated European diplomacy for decades in the mid-nineteenth century, was in essence: who would replace the Ottomans as the pre-eminent power in the region? This issue was also inextricably linked to the question of who would eventually dominate the entire continent.[3]

The rivalry between Britain and Russia in this period led ultimately to a costly war. British envoys tried to release slaves in central Asia to remove a pretext for Russian intervention there; there was the attempt to conquer Afghanistan in 1838–42; and there were new efforts to gain information on topography, invasion routes and the political situation in the 'buffer states' that surrounded India by means of agents and spies. But these could not prevent a war between Britain and Russia in 1854–6.

Although history has recorded the name of this conflict as the Crimean War, the initial name for it in Britain was 'the Russian War' as the Crimean Campaign was in fact only one aspect of the fighting (the Royal Navy also conducted operations in the Baltic with landings on the Åland Islands). Moreover, whilst the diplomatic exchanges in Europe and the details of the Crimean campaign have been well documented, too often the Asian dimension of this war has been neglected.[4] The causes of the conflict are usually ascribed to a nebulous dispute over the control of the Holy Places in Palestine which developed into a question of the right of the Russian Empire to intervene in Turkish affairs. The British reaction ran far deeper than the newspaper hysteria which apparently prompted Lord Aberdeen's coalition government into action. It was concern for India and the growth of Russian power (and Nicholas I's growing confidence to assert himself) in the decades before that really compelled the government to act. As Lord Russell remarked: 'If we don't hold them on the Danube, we shall have to stop them on the Indus'.[5]

After the war, Russia underwent substantial internal reform, but central Asian conquests offered a chance to restore the country's prestige, arrest its economic decline and challenge Britain's position of supremacy in the continent.[6] It was difficult to see, from the British perspective, that Russian policy was directed from a position of weakness, not strength, and anxiety, not confidence. Nevertheless, Russian officers were far more ambitious than the civilians of the tsar's court and belligerent personnel in the Military and Asiatic Departments actively supported them. The result was a dramatic expansion of Russian power in central Asia and a new, intense phase in the Great Game.

Diplomacy or Intelligence? Abbott, Shakespear and Stoddart

The war in Afghanistan between 1839 and 1842 has overshadowed the other efforts, both diplomatic and covert, to forestall the Russian annexation of central Asia in the same period. It was nevertheless significant that British officers were sent, or volunteered, to travel into Turkestan in the early 1840s in an attempt to persuade the city states to free their slaves as part of a strategy to deprive the Russians of any pretext for annexation. Among them were Captain James Abbott, Lieutenant Richmond Shakespear, and Lieutenant-Colonel Charles Stoddart.

Colonel Stoddart had set out for Bokhara whilst the British garrison was in the process of establishing itself more permanently in Afghanistan. His aim was to persuade Emir Nasrullah to align himself with Britain, and to release the Russians he had enslaved, a mission entrusted to him by Sir John McNeill at Teheran. Nasrullah would certainly have looked favourably on British offers of support, but news of the disaster that had befallen Perovsky's column convinced him that he did not need to fear the tsar. Indeed, when Stoddart arrived, Nasrullah was more interested in the threat posed by the Kokendis. It did not help therefore that Stoddart was unfamiliar with the etiquette of the Bokharans. He did not dismount on entering the holy city, and he failed to use the essential prefixes of flattery and exchanging gifts. His military background, particularly the reserve and formality of the British officer corps, meant that his stilted diplomatic overtures were unlikely to succeed. Inevitably perhaps, Stoddart was seized and imprisoned in August 1839. He was to be incarcerated for two years, with a temporary reprieve (with continuing house arrest) when he was forced to convert to Islam on pain of death.[7]

Captain Abbott was already on his way to Khiva on a similar mission to Stoddart's when he learned that Perovsky's column was approaching the city. However, news of the Russian advance did not improve the mood of the Khivans towards any Europeans. On his arrival, Abbott was instantly suspected of being a Russian spy disguised as an Englishman. This was an alarming accusation because two men accused of spying had recently been tortured and executed, their corpses and entrails being thrown over the city walls. Fortunately for Abbott, the khan was in a state of panic about the impending Russian attack. He was prepared to accept Abbott's explanation that a release of slaves might persuade the Russians to call off their attack. However, he was more interested in British military assistance and hoped that the British garrison in Afghanistan would now march to confront the Russians. But Abbott had no freedom to offer either troops or formal diplomatic agreements. He had only a letter of introduction from Major Todd, the officer commanding at Herat, and he admitted that he had been sent in haste and was therefore unable to conclude any treaties.[8]

If Abbott had such a limited diplomatic role, it begs the question: what, in fact, was the real purpose of his visit? The Khivans did their best to deprive Abbott of any military intelligence on Khiva, but it is clear that he kept his eyes open, commenting on the construction of the city's fortifications and artillery. But the intrigue was not one-sided. The khan tried to probe Abbott on Britain's military strength and intercepted his messages to Todd in Herat. When news of Perovsky's disaster reached the khan, he requested that Abbott should travel to St Petersburg via Alexandrovsk on the Caspian to obtain the release of Khivan hostages. Initially the khan agreed to release some Russian slaves too, but he rescinded the offer, fearing treachery, so Abbott left the city on 7 March 1840 empty handed.

Deprived of Abbott's despatches, Todd sent Lieutenant Richmond Shakespear to find out what had happened in Khiva and to complete Abbott's humanitarian–intelligence mission if necessary. Shakespear left Herat on 15 May with an escort of eighteen mounted men, and was appalled to find fresh slaves being led to Khiva on the caravan routes. Despite the long stretches of waterless desolation, and his dependence on his guide, Shakespear made the 700-mile crossing of the Karakum Desert to the Oxus in just one month. The Khivans were in a celebratory mood after the Russians' setback, but Shakespear's warnings that the Russians would return in strength, and his persistent negotiations, eventually paid off. On 3 August, he recorded that the Khan had agreed to release all the Russian slaves. Nevertheless, the Khivan people were reluctant to comply and it took further patient discussions to secure the rest. By mid August, Shakespear was able to leave Khiva with 416 released slaves and he delivered them all to the astonished Russian garrison of Alexandrovsk. While his Herati escort retraced their steps, Shakespear pressed on to Orenburg where Perovsky set free 600 Khivans in gratitude. He made notes on this military frontier town but he found no evidence of a second attempt to take

Khiva, although the Russians were eager to see the observant British officer depart for St Petersburg. There, he received the public thanks of the tsar before returning to London where he was knighted.[9]

A different fate awaited Colonel Stoddart. Whilst he was still imprisoned in Bokhara, hoping for a relief column from Afghanistan, Captain Arthur Connolly was petitioning for his rescue. It is extraordinary that some of Stoddart's letters were spirited out of Bokhara, eventually reaching his family in Britain, but it was proof for Connolly that Stoddart was still alive. The emir varied in his temper towards his British captive. He even corresponded with Macnaghten in Kabul for a short period, giving rise to hopes that Stoddart might be released. Macnaghten suggested an expeditionary force should advance on Bokhara, although Auckland prevented this dangerous over-extension of British forces, especially as the Afghans were growing restive under Shah Shujah and his foreign backers. The British government of Sir Robert Peel was anxious to avoid any new commitments as it was already engaged in a protracted war with China, and there was antagonism with the United States and France. Nevertheless, Auckland was prepared to let Captain Connolly go and negotiate Stoddart's release as long as no promises of British security for Bokhara were offered.

Connolly had a specific vision for the future of central Asia. Like Abbott, Todd, McNeill and Shakespear, Connolly believed that the Russians were using the existence of banditry and slavery in the central Asian khanates as a pretext for their annexations. In letters to Rawlinson which contained the enigmatic phrase 'the Great Game', Connolly argued that Britain should influence the khanates in order to bring the benefits of Western civilisation to the peoples of Asia, and in this civilising mission he did not exclude the Russians. In short, Connolly's Great Game was not a political struggle between Russia and Britain, but a spiritual and moral crusade to reform the people of central Asia. He wrote: 'we should help Russia cordially to all that she has a right to expect', and advocated that Afghanistan should be unified, and Persia befriended. He did not rule out Russia as a rival completely, but he believed Britain's mission in the whole region was to 'civilise and Christianise'.[10] With that certainty of convictions so redolent of the early Victorians, Connolly was prepared to wage war on slavery, open up the Oxus to steam navigation and develop the commerce of the region with a flood of British goods. But the first step was to unify the khanates into one state.

Alexander Burnes opposed Connolly's idea simply on the grounds that it would not work; the khanates were too divided, too confident of their strength and were too committed to Islam. Burnes also doubted Britain's ability to defend these 'barbarous hordes' against Russia when it was far more effective to put pressure on St Petersburg from London. Nevertheless, Connolly set out on 3 September 1840 on a mission that, at least in his own mind, went beyond the rescue of a British officer in Bokhara. He reached Khiva first, but his proposal for a central Asian union was turned down. He continued to Khokand, but, with the Kokendis on the verge of war with Bokhara, his plans were again rejected. Connolly's personal mission had thus failed but he still hoped to obtain Stoddart's release. Stoddart was able to correspond with Connolly while the latter was in Khokand, and Stoddart believed that Nasrullah appeared to be more favourable towards a British alliance. In fact, Nasrullah thought that the British envoy was encouraging the Khivans and Kokendis to fall on Bokhara, and that Connolly would only want to visit the holy city to discover details of its defences. Nasrullah had had Connolly followed throughout central Asia by his own corps of spies and he was convinced of treachery.

When Connolly finally reached Bokhara, Nasrullah felt he had two other vital pieces of information that proved both officers were merely spies. First, a letter he had despatched to Queen Victoria was acknowledged by Lord Palmerston rather than the queen herself, and Nasrullah had not heard of the British prime minister. Second, Lord Auckland had sent a despatch that described the two officers as 'private travellers' and he demanded their release, which Nasrullah immediately interpreted as a deception: clearly neither were diplomats.

A young Persian man who was employed by Connolly brought the news of the two officers' execution to Teheran.[11] Connolly and Stoddart had been forced to dig their own graves in the main square.[12] Stoddart had denounced the emir before he was beheaded. Connolly was offered the chance to convert to Islam, but, a devout Christian to the end, he chose to die by the axe. His death was a further shock to a country that was coming to terms with the debacle of the retreat from Kabul.[13]

Not all the intelligence officers perished. Captain Shakespear joined the Army of Retribution that made its way into Afghanistan in 1842, and he was charged with negotiating the release of all the British hostages taken before and during the fateful retreat. In fact, he discovered that Eldred Pottinger had not only overthrown his captors but he had turned his prison-fortress at Bamian into a defensive position. The main negotiator in buying the support of the local Afghan commander at Bamian was none other than Mohan Lal, and within days the former captives had recruited an armed group of Afghans, run up a Union Flag, and imposed a system of taxation on the local community. When news of the fall of Kabul reached the little garrison, they marched out to meet Shakespear on his way to relieve them.

The movements of British officers across central Asia, even as envoys, were clearly hazardous. Yet the nature of their missions was also unique. They were not given the authority to make any treaties or offer British military assistance. In this sense, there was no attempt to turn the central Asian khanates into satellite states, but the attempts to release slaves and thus deter Russian annexation hint at some effort to form buffer states, particularly as the British frontier had shifted to northern Afghanistan. The British officers were despatched from Teheran and from occupied Herat, and, as usual, they were accompanied by their munshis, servants and guides. As army officers, they kept their eyes open for military information, and they were able to establish how volatile the political situation in central Asia was, particularly with regard to the intense rivalry between the khanates.

The Soviet historian N. A. Khalfin argued that British agents in central Asia were directed from a 'Control' in Herat. This city was, Khalfin wrote, the centre of communications for British spies and the headquarters of a network that radiated across the region. Abbott and Shakespear, Khalfin maintained, used the excuse of accompanying released slaves to enter Russian-held territory for the purpose of gathering military intelligence. He argued that, far from the British being the cause of their release, the slaves would have been granted their freedom anyway as a result of Russian military pressure. Khalfin went on to argue that Shakespear was carrying documents, intercepted by the Turcomans and handed over to the Russians in 1873, that proved he was trying to establish communication with the British and Foreign Bible Society, a front for a British-inspired espionage ring inside Orenburg itself. Khalfin suggested that Shakespear did not seem to realise the Bible Society had been closed down by the Russian authorities, although he believed that Shakespear was probably trying to make contact with the remnants of the ring.

Neither Abbott nor Shakespear made any mention of the Bible Society in their memoirs, and it seems unlikely, as Peter Hopkirk points out, that any agent would have been carrying sensitive documents other than letters of introduction. According to Khalfin, the bundle of letters is deposited in the Soviet Military Archives in file 6996, but they are dated 1831–38, almost two years before Abbott's and Shakespear's missions took place. Their headers of 'Secret and Confidential', and the absence of any names make them intriguing documents, but it seems unlikely they were really connected with these two men.

All the British agents, Abbott, Shakespear, Connolly and Stoddart, were on official missions, but they were hardly 'secret'. Although Shakespear adopted Afghan clothes, they all made clear their identities as British officers. To categorise them as diplomatic missions would be to offer them a status they did not have, but they were, in a sense, conveying the wishes of the authorities in India (or British-held Afghanistan). They therefore had more in common with McNeill and the French envoys at Teheran during the Napoleonic Wars than with the clandestine missions of Grant, Pottinger and Christie. Khalfin misjudged the role of these British officers and indeed the focus of Britain's military effort. It was not central Asia that interested the British, but the threats that lay within the subcontinent.

Consolidating the Frontiers

Lord Metcalfe, the provisional governor-general in 1835–6, once remarked that to pursue a policy beyond the Indus 'would lead to wars and embarrassment, expensive and unprofitable at the least'.[14] The war in Afghanistan had been designed to create a balance of power in central Asia favourable to Britain, but it had proved too difficult to sustain a garrison across the mountainous eastern fringe of Afghanistan, and the potentially hostile powers of Sind, Gwalior and the Punjab. The policy was thus changed to incorporate or neutralise these three regions and to establish a frontier on the Indus.

Before the second campaign against the Punjab in 1848, British personnel had been appointed to administer the new frontier areas, so that there was some continuity before and after 1849. Henry Lawrence had been appointed as resident at Lahore and his elder brother, George, was made the political agent at Peshawar. They were assisted by James Abbott, who settled the borders of Hazara and became its political, John Nicholson – 'The Lion of the Punjab' – who acted as observer in Kashmir, Frederick Mackeson who became the first commissioner of

Peshawar, and Harry Lumsden who raised a specialist Corps of Guides that was to become the nucleus of the Punjab Frontier Force (or 'Piffers') in 1865. Lieutenant Herbert Edwardes characterised the outlook of this group of British officers in his march through Bannu on the frontier. He restrained his Sikh troops who had traditionally plundered the area, rewarded those who brought in tribute, and, as a result was able to recruit local men to fight on the British side in the Second Sikh War.[15] This sort of personalised and charismatic leadership, delivered from the saddle, was envied by later generations of imperial officials who resented the dull procedures of government 'red tape'. To the Victorians they were 'a special breed of British hero: saints militant fired with Christian grace; *beaux sabreurs, sans peur et sans reproche'*.[16] They were certainly young and self-confident, and driven by deep religious convictions to take huge risks.

Lumsden was appointed head of the India Commander-in-Chief's intelligence department, charged with keeping the army informed of the movements of Sikh forces. As expected, the Guides performed the tasks of both cavalry screen and intelligence gatherers, although it was James Abbott in Hazara who first learnt of alarming secret negotiations between Chattar Singh, a Sikh resistance leader, and Dost Mohammed of Kabul. The Afghans had agreed to join their former enemies, the Sikhs, to throw the British back across the Sutlej. In return, the Afghans would receive the city of Peshawar and all the territory west of the river Jhelum. Other intercepted reports included the rumour that Queen Victoria had died without issue and that, as a result, 'the *Angrez* (English) were in confusion'. Jellalabad fell to the amir in December 1848, but the defeat of the Sikh army and the Afghan cavalry at Gujrat convinced the Afghan ruler to withdraw back up the Khyber Pass. Hazara, Peshawar and Kohat then came under the jurisdiction of the commissioner of Peshawar, whilst Bannu, Dera Ismail Khan and Dera Ghazi Khan went to the commissioner of Derajat. The North-West Frontier was the responsibility of the Government of the Punjab, and all border intelligence was filtered through this body before being forwarded to the governor-general in Calcutta. On the ground, political officers were sent to liaise with the tribesmen of this new mountainous frontier.

In the hills, there was little chance that the sort of intelligence networks that existed down on the plains could work. In a sparsely populated region of close-knit clans, the presence of any outsiders was immediately obvious. The British were therefore dependent on the political officers forging a close connection with the tribes of the North-West Frontier. Theodore Pennell, a missionary, believed this personalised contact was respected by the tribesmen:

> It has always been the man, and not the system that governs the country; and there are names of officers now dead and gone which are still a living power along that frontier, because they were the men who thoroughly knew the people with whom they had to deal, and [they] exerted such a mesmeric influence over those wild Afghans that they were ready to follow their *'feringi'* masters ... with the most unswerving loyalty.[17]

Nevertheless, the political's life was not without its hazards and some of the unlucky, or perhaps unsuccessful ones were shot by the tribesmen.[18] They refused to accept British authority being extended over them, and they found it difficult to abandon the habits of raiding (usually for cattle or women) and clan feuding which were endemic in their culture. Recalcitrant tribes were chastised by punitive operations by the special border units of Scouts and Militias raised for the purpose.[19] Henry Lawrence told the government at home: 'The people like us, but they do *not* fear us. I should try to reverse the case – to conciliate when quiet, and hit them hard when troublesome.'[20] The need for quiet borders was soon pressing as Russia and Britain went to war in 1854.

The Russian War, 1854–6

In April 1849, when the Austrians failed to defeat the Magyar Revolution, Tsar Nicholas I freely offered Russian troops in order to maintain the hegemony of conservative powers in Europe.[21] In order to preserve Russia's security, Nicholas also ordered the occupation of the principalities at the mouth of the Danube, Moldavia and Wallachia, where Russian troops remained until 1851. He put further pressure on the Turks in October 1849 by demanding the extradition of Polish officers who had fled to Ottoman territory from the Russian invasion of Hungary. The demands prompted Palmerston to despatch a fleet to the Dardanelles, but the Russians withdrew their requests before the Royal Navy arrived. Nevertheless, Nicholas believed he had emerged from the Year of Revolution immeasurably stronger than the other European powers. Already emboldened by what he thought was a clear understanding with Britain, namely that the Ottoman Empire should be replaced by Russian, French and British control, Nicholas assumed he could play the leading role in European affairs. When Louis Napoleon came to power in France and apparently threatened Belgium, St Petersburg offered to send 60,000 troops to oppose the French. Anti-French sentiment in Russia grew when the Ottomans effectively handed control of the Near East to Catholic authorities, in the teeth of the Greek Orthodox Church of which Nicholas was the head. The tsar was convinced that the European powers would rally against another Bonaparte. As a first step he despatched Prince Menschikov to Constantinople to resurrect the terms of the Treaty of Kutchuk Kainardji of 1774, a treaty which had given Russia the right to represent the interests of the Christian churches in the Ottoman Empire. When the Turks were reluctant to overturn their concessions to France, the Russians mobilised.

The over-confidence of the tsar was to lead him into direct confrontation with the French and the British. Stratford Canning, the British ambassador at Constantinople, described Nicholas as 'drunk with power', referring to the fact that the tsar was truly convinced of Russia's overwhelming military strength.[22] Menschikov added to British suspicions by proposing a Russian protectorate over the Balkans. Despite a British fleet being at the Dardanelles, Russian troops crossed the river Pruth on 2 July 1853. At this stage, both sides held back from war, hoping to resolve the dispute by diplomacy. However, vague Turkish concessions merely fuelled the tsar's impatience, whilst the movement a joint Anglo-French fleet, which made its way through the Bosporus, added to the sense of crisis. The Turks took the initiative and declared war on 4 October, and the Russian naval victory at Sinope on 30 November committed both France and Britain to military action.

Whilst the campaign in the Crimea unfolded, there was every expectation that Russia would be able to raise some 800,000 men, many of whom would be deployed against the small expeditionary forces of France and Britain. What the Allies did not realise was that Russia struggled to find 350,000 combat troops and that supplying these, let alone transporting them to the periphery of the Russian Empire, was too great a logistical challenge. Nevertheless, some advance towards India seemed a distinct possibility, particularly as a means for diverting British troops from European Russia. General Duhammel, the Russian minister to Teheran, proposed an invasion of India, advising the tsar that Russian forces should announce themselves as the 'liberators of India'. He envisaged Sikhs and Afghans joining a relatively small Russian column from Persia or the Caspian, then moving across Afghanistan and down the Khyber Pass to Delhi.[23] More credence was given to the schemes of Generals Chikhachev and Khruliev who suggested sending a force of 30,000 men via Askhabad and Herat to Kandahar.[24] The British did not learn about these plans until 1873.[25]

When Tsar Nicholas I died on 2 March 1855, the belligerence of Russian foreign policy in Europe died with him. Negotiations stumbled on. Sevastopol fell on 8 September, and the Austrians mobilised on the Galician border, giving rise to a pressing desire in St Petersburg to concentrate on Russian affairs. As a consequence of this new domestic focus, Gorkachov was appointed as the Foreign Minister to replace the hawkish 'German' Meyendorff. Far reaching internal changes were proposed, including the emancipation of the serf peasantry, the modernisation of industry, and reforms of the army and the civil service.

In February 1856, whilst Britain planned new amphibious operations in the Black Sea and the Baltic (having concluded an alliance with Sweden), negotiations began to end the war in the Crimea. However, whilst it has often been thought that the war 'shattered both the myth and reality of Russian power', it certainly did not terminate Russia's aggressive foreign policy in Asia.[26] Indeed, the internal reforms under consideration were designed to prevent another invasion of Russian soil, and, since Russia had been defeated on the periphery of its own empire, the government in St Petersburg was determined to make the frontiers more secure. It is therefore not surprising that, under the new Tsar Alexander II, Russia acquired more territory and fought more conflicts than it had under Nicholas.

When the war in the Crimea ended, the struggle between Britain and Russia was transferred to central Asia. Britain had insisted that Persia remain neutral during the war in 1854, so reports that the shah was entertaining a treaty with the Russians in order to regain lost possessions in the Caucasus led to the despatch of a warship to the Persian Gulf as a warning. Dost Mohammed then informed the Government of India that Persia, encouraged by Russia, was planning to seize Herat. The alert came too late: Herat fell to the Persians on 25 October 1856. With no communications or intelligence network across Afghanistan or eastern Persia, the news took a month to reach London, and there was considerable anxiety that the Russians would open a consulate in Herat, prior to the development of espionage aimed at the subversion of Afghanistan.[27]

Although Dost Mohammed appealed for weapons, there was a great deal of reluctance by Lord Canning, the Governor-General of India, to send either arms or men into the country when memories of the Afghan War were still so fresh. Instead, it was decided to launch an amphibious operation from the Persian Gulf. Bushire was bombarded and captured on 10 December 1856, and, after a short campaign inland, the shah quickly agreed to a complete withdrawal from Herat.[28]

Russian efforts to improve the security of their own frontiers in the 1850s concerned three regions: the Caucasus, central Asia and east Asia. In the Caucasus, the tsar's forces were engaged in a bitter guerrilla war against a collection of tribesmen inspired by the Muslim generalissimo Shamil. Fired by a religious fanaticism, the guerrillas were welded together by a combination of Shamil's uncompromising tyranny, the sanctuary offered by the mountains and a terror campaign by the Russians. In 1854, the British had attempted to supply these fighters, through the Turks, with rifles, but Shamil's campaign was beginning to disintegrate before the weapons reached him. Having suffered a series of setbacks, including the destruction of General Mikhail Vorontsev's column in 1845, the Russians changed tactics. Instead of burning crops and destroying villages (to deprive the guerrillas of their supplies) and thereby antagonising the people, the Russians promoted the authority of the local chiefs, encouraged dissent with Shamil's dictatorship, and reduced the impact of Russian law, customs and immigration. Whilst this did not subdue levels of resistance in Shamil's heartland, today's Chechnya, it secured the areas Russia already occupied. It also provided an important template for future colonial conquests: the crushing of guerrilla or conventional forces, followed by patient and thorough consolidation. In 1859, Shamil's strongholds were conquered.

In central Asia in the spring of 1858, Nikolai Khanikov was despatched to Afghanistan to establish diplomatic relations between St Petersburg and Kabul. The timing was significant for the British were at that moment fighting to regain control of India during the Great Mutiny. Khanikov was able to cross the Caspian and rode on to Herat, which at that time was still in the hands of Dost Mohammed's rebellious subjects (it was not retaken until 1863). But if the Russians intended to seize an opportunity to extend their influence, they received an early setback. Dost Mohammed refused to grant the Russian envoy an audience, even in secret. This was for two reasons: one, the Vitkevich mission of 1839 had prompted a British invasion, and, two, he had just concluded an alliance with Herbert Edwardes, the commissioner of Peshawar.[29]

Nonetheless, other Russian initiatives were more successful. In the summer of 1858, a Russian diplomatic mission under the command of Nikolai Ignatiev reached Khiva, mapping the Oxus and approaches to the khanate *en route*. It proceeded to Bokhara, and concluded a treaty that released Russian slaves, encouraged trade and even schemed the partition of Khiva. However the important clause was the exclusion of all British agents.[30] Ignatiev then returned to Russian territory furnished with plenty of intelligence on the armies and defences of the central Asian khanates. In addition, further to the east, the Russians' annexation of the region that would one day come to be known as Kyrgyzstan brought them up to the ancient border of China.

The Russian anxiety that their frontier regions might be annexed, or that their peripheral possessions might be subverted by British gold and guns, prompted the next forward move in east Asia. In 1859, whilst China was absorbed by the Tai'Ping Rebellion, Russian forces annexed the Amur province in order to forestall any British attempts to acquire Chinese territory. Acting as mediator for the Chinese at the conclusion of the Second Opium War in 1860, Ignatiev convinced the emperor that the British and the French intended to carve up China. He deftly 'reduced' the demands of the British and French and had the Chinese recognise the Russian annexation of Amur province in return. In addition, he insisted on the opening of Russian consulates in Kashgar (Chinese Turkestan) and Ugra (Mongolia).

Taken together, the conquest of the eastern Caucasus and the defeat of Shamil, the annexations in east Asia, and the reconnaissance of central Asia represented a more vigorous Asian policy by St Petersburg. There was a determination amongst the upper echelons of the Russian government to thwart the British in Asia. Ignatiev, now urging the annexation of all the khanates, especially the fertile Ferghana valley of Khokand, was appointed the head of the Asiatic Department of the Foreign Ministry.[31] The Governor-General of Eastern Siberia, Count Nikolai Muraviev, was just as eager to prevent further British encroachments in China. The Governor-General of the Caucasus, Prince Alexander Baryatinski, was convinced his region was the springboard for operations against the Turks, Persians and the British. Against these belligerent voices, the calmer counsels for the tsar included Count Dimitri Miliutin, the cautious reformer of the War Ministry, Prince Alexander Gorchakov, the Foreign Minister, and the domestic reformers such as Count Mikhail Reutern, the Minister of Finance. By the mid-1860s, rival factions in St Petersburg were battling it out over Russian foreign policy. In one way they were united by a common anxiety about Russia's military and financial weaknesses, especially in the face of British power in Asia, but the policy that emerged was contradictory and piecemeal. In central Asia, it was the army that drove forward the expansion of Russia's frontiers, with or without official sanction.

The Intelligence Department in London

The mid-nineteenth century was an age of increasing volume and variety in communications, and, by the 1850s, the British Foreign Office was handling eight times the number of despatches as it had at the turn of the century. The reason for this was only partly new technology. This was the era of a gradual extension of Britain's imperial dominions. The need for secret intelligence had always been driven by the nature of the threat to British interests, and the diminishing of the threat in Europe after the Napoleonic Wars meant that the focus of intelligence shifted out into the Empire. This would explain why the intelligence efforts in central Asia and India were being extended, but why, at the same time, there seemed to be so little determination to improve secret intelligence at home. In 1844, the Decyphering Branch of the Foreign Office was closed down, but the Foreign

Office extended its handling of information and processed its 'intelligence product' for Cabinet instead of simply recording it.[32] It also maintained (until 1864), a listening post on the Ionian Islands where all foreign mail that passed through under 'quarantine regulations' was routinely opened and processed.[33] However, as Keith Hamilton and Richard Langhorne point out, the funding of secret intelligence had fallen to £40,000 in the decades after the Napoleonic Wars, and a public scandal over the interception of the mail of Mazzini, the Italian nationalist, indicated the diplomatic risks that secret intelligence created.[34]

The Topographical Department, the intelligence and map-making wing of the Army Quartermaster-General's department, had a low profile in a period when colonial authorities in the Empire carried out their own field intelligence, map making and secret intelligence work on a demand-led basis. However, when troops were sent from home during the Russian War in 1854, they landed on the coast of the Crimea without any intelligence support at all. Raglan complained that he had no more idea of the topography of the Crimea than 'Jason and his Argonauts'.[35] In response, a retired Royal Engineer officer, formerly of the Bombay Army, Major Thomas Jervis, had maps copied at his own expense, and subsequently acquired 1,476 maps from the French Dépôt de la Guerre.[36] Jervis, a cartographer once tipped to succeed George Everest as the Surveyor-General of India, was then appointed head of the reconstituted Topographical and Statistical Department in 1855 under the control of the War Office.[37] His energy led to a proliferation of reports and proposals, including the suggestion that brigades of topographers should be formed to serve as a 'secret intelligence corps' in wartime.[38] The staff of the Topographical and Statistical Department grew to fifty-five, but overwork had killed the selfless Jervis by 1857.[39]

This concern to acquire maps was not exclusive to the British. In 1857, Nikolai Ignatiev, then serving as the military attaché to London, was discovered buying maps of British ports and railways.[40] Although the need for a better counter-intelligence service had been highlighted strongly by this incident, the conclusion of the Crimean War meant that the threat had once again diminished in Europe. A special government committee recommended that, on grounds of cost, the T and S Department should be scaled down and merged with the Topographical Depot and Ordnance Survey.[41] For a time, foreign intelligence work was in the hands of the military attachés who were posted after the Crimean War to Berlin, Paris, Turin, Vienna and St Petersburg, but the store of knowledge on foreign armies was still thought inadequate ten years later and the collection of foreign maps on European theatres was incomplete. The Topographical and Statistical Department was tasked with mapping British forts and coastal defences, copying historical documents and compiling dress regulations.[42] Until the appointment of Captain Charles Wilson as head of the T and S Department in 1870, British intelligence lacked a centralised structure. It was Wilson's view that the department should change its emphasis from compiling data on British defences and concentrate on collating and processing intelligence of military value from across the world.[43] Events then unfolding in central Asia were to make that a far more pressing issue.

The Russian Annexation of Turkestan, 1864–73

In 1864, Prince Gorchakov issued his famous court circular to Russian representatives abroad in an effort to explain Russia's creeping annexations in central Asia. He stated:

> It always happens . . . that the interests of frontier security and of commercial relations demand the more civilised state to exert a certain ascendancy over neighbours whose nomadic, turbulent habits make them very disagreeable . . . All have inevitably been constrained to follow this pro- gressive path. Ambition plays a lesser role than imperious necessity and the greatest difficulty lies in knowing where to stop.[44]

The document was little comfort to the British in India, and there were many who predicted that Russia would make other forward moves. Lord Augustus Loftus, the British ambassador to St Petersburg, felt that the Russian Army was the principal problem:

> Where an enormous standing army is maintained, it is necessary to find employment for it. Every officer is anxious to gain the St George or some other decoration, while both officers and men seek to enrich themselves. When a system of conquests sets in, as in central Asia, one acquisition of territory leads to another and the difficulty is where to stop. Fresh conquests of territory are laid at the tsar's feet, gained by the prowess and blood of his troops. He cannot refuse them without offending his army; and troops so far distant are difficult to restrain.[45]

There seems to be little agreement amongst historians about why the Russian Empire expanded into central Asia, but from the evidence it seems likely that a search for imperial prestige coincided with an opportunist forward policy within the army.[46] Nevertheless, David Saunders believes St Petersburg was perfectly capable of restraining its officers when it needed to and suggests that Gorchakov and Miliutin only had to 'tread softly when explaining Russia's central Asian policy to foreigners'.[47]

The army certainly had a key part to play in the process of annexation. Russian outposts on the Syr Daria had been attacked in 1852 by Yakub Beg, the commander of Kokendi forces. The counter-attack launched by General Perovsky the following year indicated that local tribal forces could not stand against the Russians. However, it was not evident until 1864, when Chimkent fell to the tsar's troops, that the balance of power had changed in Russia's favour. Khokand's rival, the khanate of Bokhara, led by the Emir Mirzaffar al-Din, saw the opportunity to open a second front by taking Tashkent. But, far from co-operating with the Bokharans, Gorchakov urged his regional commander, General Cherniaev, to avoid any operations that might bring Russia into collision with the British. Cherniaev either took this to mean he had a free hand, or, as others have suggested, that he should act before any British intervention was possible. Thus, regardless of orders and with just 1,900 men and 12 guns, he attacked and captured Tashkent on 15 June

1865. The local elders, anxious to avoid the sacking of their city, agreed to Chernaiev's generous terms of surrender. Chernaiev's initiative and daring earned him a reward that would inspire others to follow his example: he was decorated with the Cross of St Anne.

After just three years, Russia's relations with Bokhara had broken down to the extent that the *ulema* (council of religious leaders) of the Holy City declared a *jihad* (holy war). General K. P. Kaufman quickly laid siege to Bokhara and cut off its external water supply, but it was internal dissent that caused resistance to collapse; the imams were disappointed that the response to the cry of holy war had not been heeded, and, blaming their own head of state, they led an attempt to overthrow the emir. Kaufman then marched into the city to 'restore order'. Thus only Khiva remained independent, until, in 1873, after failed attempts to persuade the khanate to join the Russian Empire voluntarily, this city was annexed by a bold offensive on three fronts.

If the British Foreign Office had convinced itself that central Asia was a buffer region for the defence of India, then it was sadly deluded. The Royal United Services Institute recorded:

> It is seen that Russia by thus steadily pursuing her career of conquest, may gradually be able to creep up to a position so near to our frontier as to exercise at pleasure a disturbing force, and to render us uneasy for the tranquillity of our dominions. This ... is a danger which we are bound, if possible, to prevent.[48]

The Foreign Office quickly concluded a new agreement with St Petersburg, settling a line on the northern frontiers of Afghanistan which ran on the same latitude as the east–west flow of the river Oxus. The problem was that the region was virtually *terra incognita*. Worse still, the Amir of Afghanistan, Sher Ali, was rebuffed by the Liberal government when he offered to conclude a defensive treaty against Russia in 1873, because Prime Minister W. E. Gladstone was convinced that direct negotiations with St Petersburg were the only means by which agreements could be reached. However, later events would show this confidence was misplaced.

The Genesis of the Russian Threat

The missions to central Asia by British officers in the 1840s had produced some useful information on the rulers, the nature of government, the trade and the military resources of the khanates, but there was no extension of British influence and the First Afghan War had shown how dangerously over-extended the Company Raj had already become. Consolidating the control of the subcontinent by the conquest of Sind, Gwalior and the Punjab, the British obtained a defendable frontier that was to last until their departure in 1947.

Whilst European disputes led to the Crimean War in 1854–6, the genesis of Russophobia that contributed to that conflict can be traced to both the Near East and the central Asian theatre. The war with Russia, and the victory at Sevastopol did little to quell anxieties about the continental approaches to India. Indeed, the

Great Mutiny of 1857 seemed to indicate that the British were vulnerable to subversion or the rallying cry of a foreign 'liberator'. Russian attitudes to the British were also unchanged by the Crimean War. If anything, the Russian Army became even more determined to restore its military prestige. But there was also a deep conviction in Russia that they were acting defensively, and they were securing their frontiers against British imperial expansion. Reflecting on the annexations in the 1870s, one Russian official wrote:

> Our movements in central Asia have been dictated in the first place by our own interests, and also by the need to ensure a defensive position against the hostility towards us of which the English government has given proof since the Crimean War.[49]

Furthermore, British commercial dominance threatened to eclipse Russian power in Asia unless a robust policy was adopted.

The wave of Russian annexations that followed in the decade and a half after the Crimean War convinced many Anglo-Indians that a conflict with Russia in central Asia was, sooner or later, inevitable. In contrast to the state of British intelligence at home, the Indian Army therefore began to increase its efforts to accumulate information of military value on topography, native communities, governments and resources.

Chapter 6

The Pundits, Topography and Intelligence

Surveyors and Intelligence Gathering, 1800–1883

Asian surveyors, or 'pundits', gathered important topographical data both within and beyond the borders of India, and, armed with secret equipment, they operated in a highly clandestine fashion. They made extensive journeys, often travelled in disguise and used cryptonyms, such as 'the Mirza' or 'the Havildar' instead of their names. Yet, according to Gerald Morgan, Indian surveyors were never part of the secret service. He believed the Survey Department must be 'entirely ruled out as a cover for espionage' as it was responsible only for the survey of India and 'there was nothing secret about that'.[1] Certainly the results of the surveys, including those carried out in secret, were published in the renowned journals of the Royal Geographical Society (RGS). Controversially, even the details of the surveyors' disguises and methods were made known publicly. Moreover, there were sometimes clashes of interest between the Survey's thirst for geographical knowledge, supported by ambitious explorers and the RGS, and the Government of India which had its own more secret political and strategic agenda. However, despite the efforts of some writers to show the Survey of India as totally devoid of any connections with espionage, the pundits were not as innocent as has been claimed. They were not purely geographers, but part of a broad intelligence-gathering fabric, interwoven with other departments and objectives, not least the acquisition of information useful to the Indian Army. They were funded by the Government of India, worked alongside 'political' agents, and were subject to the directives of Calcutta. They also functioned in a world limited by the geopolitical considerations of the day, including the attitude of the Russian and Chinese Empires.

The Topographical Department in India had already accumulated route surveys of the subcontinent, but concerns for accuracy, the deaths of several Europeans beyond the frontiers, and the closing of Tibet's borders by the Tibetans and the Chinese, prompted the employment of Asians in survey work from the 1860s. Before 1800, route surveys had been made by British personnel using a 'perambulator' (cyclometer), a compass and astronomical readings from the stars, and the first map of all 'Hindoostan' was printed in 1782. The inaccuracies of astronomical readings were soon apparent and so William Lambton suggested that the Madras Government support a triangulation survey of southern India. The work, which began in 1800, was extended and later, in 1818, became the Great Trigonometrical Survey of India (GTS). This Herculean task was not completed until 1883. Lambton wrote that the survey would offer a 'true delineation of the river valleys, ranges of mountains, with some noted points near the ghauts [gorges] and passes, will also be a foundation for more minute topographical surveys such as are immediately wanted for military purposes'.[2] This close connection between the needs of the army and the work of surveyors cannot be downplayed, since British survey work had hitherto always been in the service of the armed forces.

The work was, in itself, an arduous and sometimes dangerous undertaking, but the important intelligence value of the survey was evident from the outset. The Government of India funded and controlled the work of the GTS through the Military Department, appointing Lambton as its first Superintendent with George Everest as his assistant. When Everest succeeded Lambton in 1823, he combined the established post of Surveyor-General with that of Superintendent of the GTS. By 1837, the survey had mapped the plains of India and reached the foothills of the Himalayas whereupon Everest designed new lightweight equipment for his teams. Nevertheless, the death toll was high, particularly in the malaria-infested swamps of the Nepal Terai, and, as the surveyors climbed into the hills of the north, mountaineering skills were frequently needed to haul their plane tables and sextants to the best points of observation. Yet the survey was not just about taking and recording heights, bearings and distances. The GTS teams were expected to collect information on the peoples of the area, the nature of their livelihood, crop types, transport and livestock. Crucially, alongside this information of a logistical nature, military and commercial data were also required. Surveyors often worked for years at a time in one region and they effectively became intelligence agents of the Government of India, but the Military Department was also eager to obtain valuable intelligence for its own purposes from those enterprising men.

A British Army officer, Lieutenant-Colonel Andrew Waugh, took over from Everest in 1843 and he was eager to extend the survey of India into the mountains that fringed the subcontinent. The Nepalese had closed their borders to the British but the conclusion of the First Sikh War in 1846 opened up the possibility of surveying Kashmir. This task was delegated to Captain Thomas G. Montgomerie, who, like Waugh, was an officer of the Royal Engineers.[3] Montgomerie was an intelligent twenty-five-year-old, the son of a colonel of the Ayrshire Yeomanry. He was joined by William Johnson, an experienced high-altitude surveyor, and a team of assistants in the spring of 1855. From the beginning, the conditions were hard: they were beset by snow blindness, they had to scale 15,000-foot peaks, and they had to plough through great drifts that hampered all movement even in the summer months. The surveying party counted itself 'lucky' when it had only eleven feet of snow to excavate to reach the rock of a summit. By 1858, the survey had migrated as far north as Ladakh, the peaks rising ever higher, until, in 1864, Montgomerie declared the Kashmir survey complete. He had covered an area of 7,700 square miles and he earned the universal praise of his colleagues for his tact, skill and leadership.[4]

The Government of India was always eager to avoid deaths of Europeans at the hands of natives when they could not be investigated, punished or avenged. There was a concern, commonly held amongst Anglo-Indians, that the prestige on which the British Empire rested would be jeopardised by such incidents. Accordingly, Montgomerie's instructions were that, whilst he was to 'obtain the means of rectifying our imperfect geographical knowledge of the regions beyond British influence', he was not to 'risk the safety of the party nor to entangle the Government in political complications'.[5] Major James Walker of the Survey of India, reflecting on the deaths of Moorcroft and of a German explorer, Adolf Schlagintweit, noted that the Afridi lands astride the Khyber Pass, like much of the frontier region, were lawless: 'to go into their country excepting by force is never possible for a European, and is at all times dangerous for a native'.[6]

Abdul Mejid, Abdul Hamid and Nain Singh

Given the record of using Asian agents for intelligence work within the subcontinent, it was not surprising that Montgomerie began to consider the use of Indians to gather information beyond the borders. In 1860, Abdul Mejid had been recruited for secret intelligence work in central Asia. Brought up in Kabul, Mejid was a mullah and also a merchant who had travelled widely in Afghanistan and the central Asian khanates. Although it is unclear how Mejid was recruited, he was despatched from Peshawar on the authority of the governor-general, Lord Canning, to carry a letter and presents (including music boxes, watches and rifles) to the ruler of Khokand. In fact, this was really a front for a covert mission to ascertain the extent of Russian influence in the area, for Khokand was by then adjacent to Russian possessions beyond the Syr Daria. Travelling via Kabul and the Pamirs, Mejid completed his mission successfully and returned to Peshawar the following year. His report included details of the military and political situation in Khokand and the strength of the Russians.[7] The intelligence was so valuable that it was recommended Mejid should receive 'suitable substantial acknowledgment'.[8] Significantly, back in London, the Royal Geographical Society made no reference to Mejid's intelligence mission, and praised only his geographical achievements, especially that of crossing the Pamirs from north to south. He was described merely as a 'meritorious native traveller'.[9]

Observing the Asian travellers, namely merchants and pilgrims, who crossed the border of Kashmir heading north, Montgomerie submitted his first proposal for Indian surveyors to Major Walker on 20 August 1861.[10] The following April, he reiterated the plan to the Asiatic Society of Bengal, focussing on a grand scheme to map Chinese territory including Tibet.[11] Walker was particularly enthusiastic about the idea because he was in favour of driving British influence across the borders of India. In contrast to the closed border of Nepal and Tibet, the military operations on the North-West Frontier of India offered a chance for surveyors to accompany British troops and map the area. Similar sentiments were shared by Sir Robert Montgomery, the Lieutenant-Governor of the Punjab.[12] Something of the way the Great Game was really behind the scheme to train Asians as clandestine surveyors can be glimpsed from the first letters that outline the type of personnel who would be required. Montgomerie initially proposed that the Asian surveyors should be 'Mohammedans' from the North-West Frontier deployed in central Asia.[13] It is interesting that he said nothing of China, Tibet or the peoples that fringed those countries, so if, as so many scholars assert, Montgomerie's aim was purely geographical, it is curious that he started with the idea of sending men into an area that was regarded as the next target for Russian imperial expansion. Subsequent efforts would concentrate on Western China and Tibet, but this too, of course, was a potential Russian sphere of influence once the tsar's forces had secured central Asia.

The surveyors were to be disguised as pilgrims and traders, and they would conceal their specialist surveying instruments. They were equipped with a sextant, a dark-glass or mercury 'artificial horizon' (for fixing a baseline), a boiling point thermometer for fixing altitude, a compass and a clinometer (for reading slope gradient). In addition, to measure longitude, a chronometer was used, but these proved vulnerable to moisture and rough treatment on the march. Each surveyor was trained to make a measured pace and to count them over long distances. Buddhist rosaries were altered from 108 beads to 100 to make the recording of paces easier, whilst a devotee's prayer wheel was used to conceal survey notes and a compass. Along with a detailed and accurate route survey, the agents were expected to record information on the people of the area through which they travelled, their customs, economic activity, political leaders and military potential. It has been argued that this information was gathered because 'they knew so little about these countries', but such an innocent motive seems highly unlikely given that the survey was being directed by British military personnel.[14]

Montgomerie's chief concern was getting 'natives with sufficient nerve' and ones that were capable of using survey instruments. As he was later to discover, the question of loyalty would also give him problems, but the majority of those selected were exemplary.[15] By 1863, the Government of India had approved training expenditure of Rs 1,000 and a monthly salary for recruits at sixteen to twenty rupees.[16] The approval was timely for an expedition through China, led by two British officers and which was supposed to return to India via Nepal, was thwarted.[17] Another British officer, a certain Major Smyth, was prevented from entering Tibet via Ladakh the same year.[18] News of unrest in Chinese Turkestan, and rumours of Russian advances on the Syr Daria must also have moved the 'forward school' to action. It all must have seemed particularly pressing when the Government of India at that time apparently favoured a policy of 'masterly inactivity' beyond the frontiers.

Sir John Lawrence, the 'plain-spoken' Governor-General of India and brother of the famous defender of Lucknow in the Mutiny, was determined to maintain a 'close border' along the North-West Frontier in the early 1860s. Essentially this meant avoiding any actions that might be interpreted as a prelude to annexation, entanglements with tribesmen on the border or any attempt to make treaties with the khanates of central Asia. Britain's experiences of waging war in Afghanistan and the North-West Frontier had so far been expensive in treasure and prestige. The disasters of the First Afghan War could not, at least in the minds of the British in India, be separated from the outbreak of the Indian Mutiny. The pundits offered a chance to carry out militarily useful surveys without the risk of losing British officers or of entangling the Government of India in expensive expeditions. As Gerald Morgan points out, they had 'no military or political training', and assessments of the Russians were 'quite outside the scope' of their reports, but they did add to the store of knowledge about central Asia, and, like all secret agents, they were expendable if they were compromised.

The first destination for a pundit mission was Yarkand, where, rumour had it, there was a state of ferment against Chinese rule. The population who lived in the city, like much of Chinese Turkestan, were Muslim and ethnically Uighur, more akin to the peoples of central Asia across the Pamir and Tien Shan ranges to the west, than to the Chinese. The agent selected was Abdul Hamid (or Mahomed-i-Hameed), a Muslim from the northern territories of India who was described as a munshi. He had been recruited by Sir Robert Montgomery of the Punjab and sent to the Survey of India in May 1863, and the Government of the Punjab paid all the expedition's costs.[19] In just one month, Hamid was trained in the use of his equipment and then set off, adding a spiked staff to his baggage that, whilst common to other travellers of the area, could also be used to steady a compass and conceal its readings. Hamid's companion was to be Mohammed Amin, a guide who had served the Schlagintweit expedition of the 1850s, but Amin was investigated by the GTS officers in Ladakh and found to be 'of doubtful character'. He was therefore dropped. Hamid was ordered to join a *kafila* (caravan) heading towards Yarkand through the harsh Karakoram and Kun Lun ranges, disguised as a trader and accompanied by two servants and pony.[20]

Leaving Leh on 24 August 1863, Hamid must have been conscious that he was taking a considerable risk. Other than the objective dangers posed by the mountains, the altitude and the climate (with which he was, in fact, familiar), there was also the threat of banditry. Most dangerous of all was the threat that discovery of his surveying activity could lead to imprisonment or execution. But Hamid managed to record details of his route, distances, rivers and lakes, observations of the people, and the locations of settlements. It was an arduous journey. In the Karakoram, headaches caused by altitude and dehydration plagued the caravan, and several of the ponies died of starvation. It took nineteen days to reach the first signs of habitation on the northern side of the range, and Hamid estimated the distance across this belt of infamous mountains was 400 miles. Taking bearings during the day, Hamid wrote up his findings at night and made other observations whilst cloaked by the darkness.

In Yarkand itself, Hamid chanced upon an old friend, Awaz Ali, who introduced him to the governor of the city. Without giving away his real intentions, Hamid was able to obtain information about the population of the region, its political factions and even construct a general map of the area. Moreover, Hamid was able to make an assessment about the extent of Russian influence, an important overlap with other 'political' agents of the period. Whilst the origins of Abdul Hamid are largely unknown (since the archives yield frustratingly little detail), it seems likely that his recommendation by the Lieutenant-Governor of the Punjab, and his experience of travelling in central Asia were no coincidence. The British had chosen someone who already knew the area.

Rival merchants from Kashmir believed that Hamid, still in his disguise as a commercial traveller, was a threat to their trade given his closeness to the governor. Fortunately he was able to obtain the patronage of the Kashmir *aksakal* (consul) to protect him from their intrigues. However, by March 1864, the Chinese authorities were becoming suspicious of Hamid's activities and he was advised by his ally the governor to return to Leh. Although he crossed the Karakoram safely, he died within British territory, just when he was within reach of a GTS camp manned by William Johnson. Johnson was told that Hamid had fallen ill after eating wild rhubarb, but he suspected that he had been poisoned – an ironic prediction, since Johnson was to die exactly the same way a few years later.

Fortunately, Johnson was able to recover all of Hamid's books and instruments and he sent them on to Montgomerie.[21] What the British had lost was the explanation of his findings, and the services of an excellent agent. Hamid's political observations were passed on to the Government of the Punjab and Montgomerie returned to England to write up his reports and recover from the strain imposed by a 'low jungle fever'.[22] Later he was to receive the plaudits of the Royal Geographical Society for his enterprise, a precedent that would be repeated even at the expense of his agents' secrecy. But for Abdul Hamid, there was no glory.

Whilst Hamid was still on his mission, Montgomerie had arranged for the selection and training of more recruits. He had approached Major Smyth, the officer who had been turned back from Tibet in 1863, to see if he had any suitable candidates from amongst his charges at the Education Department at Kumaon.[23] This district, which had been annexed by the British at the conclusion of the war with Nepal in 1816, lay just to the west of the Gurkha kingdom and was a source of potential agents who shared a close likeness to the Nepalese. In the same way, alongside British India's border with Tibet, lived the Bhotia people whom William Moorcroft had used to help him cross the Tibetan frontier fifty years before. Indeed, it was amongst the Bhotias, in the village of Milam, that Smyth eventually found two cousins, Nain Singh and Mani Singh, who were experienced in trading with the Tibetans in the summer months. Nain Singh was Smyth's choice because he was a man with intellect: he was a schoolmaster, or *pundit*, of a local school. Nain Singh was referred to by this code-name, 'The Pundit', or sometimes 'The Chief Pundit', for the rest of his life. Mani Singh was known as the 'Patwar' or 'GM' (reversing the first and last phonetic letters of his name). They were also recommended for other reasons: they were in fact the sons of two Singh brothers who had assisted Moorcroft and Hearsey in 1812. Moreover, Nain and Mani had worked with the Schlagintweit expedition and two British explorers, Richard and Henry Strachey in the 1850s.[24] The long family connection was maintained when Kishen Singh, another descendant, later became a pundit too.

Once recruited, the two men were despatched first to Dehra Dun, the headquarters of the Survey of India, and then the Engineering College at Roorkee in early 1863.[24] Both Walker and Montgomerie, on his return from England, supervised the training which lasted all year.[26] They were not taught how to make calculations of latitude in the hope that they would not be tempted to falsify the data, but they were tested in the handling of boiling-thermometers, compasses and sextant. Records were to be written up as if they were prayers, mercury was hidden in a coconut and some cowrie shells, whilst the special 'rosary' of 100 beads was concealed in the folds of their sleeves. Having practiced the pacing of precisely 31½ inches, chanting prayer-like to remember figures over large distances, they memorised the characteristics of different peoples in the region to make their disguises more effective. Finally, Nain Singh and his cousin set out to explore Tibet and to establish the precise location of Lhasa.

Although prevented from entering Tibet from Kumaon by suspicious border officials, they made a second attempt to enter Tibet via Nepal, claiming that some of their property had been seized during recent arrests by border guards.[27] In Nepal, their baggage was repeatedly searched, and, whilst detained in Kathmandu, Mani Singh decided he had had enough of the risks, returning to Kumaon and surveying *en route*. Nain Singh thought it better to press on, adopting the disguise of a Ladakhi on a mission to buy horses to get into Tibet. On the way to Lhasa he teamed up with Bashahri merchants and managed to cross the hazardous Tsangpo River, even though three men who preceded him were drowned when their flimsy coracle overturned. Nain Singh's intelligence on the river crossings was supplemented by the discovery of a maintained road between Gartok and Lhasa. This hitherto unknown route was broken up by staging posts which could accommodate up to 200 people, but most important of all was the pundit's uncovering of the Tibetan riders who maintained a vital communications link across the country. These haggard but hardy men paused only to eat and change horses, secret messages being sewn into their clothes to preserve security. The effect of the icy winds and hard riding left them in a terrible state: 'their faces cracked, their eyes blood-shot and sunken, and their bodies eaten by lice into large raws, the latter they attributed to not being allowed to take off their clothes'.[28] Here, the pundit had discovered the key to Tibet's legendary border security system, for the riders could cover the 800 miles to the capital in just twenty days. And so the subterfuge continued. Nain Singh found the route cairns along the road useful for compass bearings and often he would hang back from the caravan in 'religious devotions' to make his observations. On 10 January 1866, he finally reached Lhasa.

In the published version of the pundit's report in the *Journal of the Royal Geographical Society* some of the more sensitive military and political data are missing.[29] But Nain Singh gathered a wealth of material on the Chinese army's presence, the geography, economy and defences of the city. Bluffing his way through an audience with the Dalai Lama, Nain was eventually unmasked by two Muslims of Kashmiri descent. He bribed them to keep quiet since discovery at this point would probably have resulted in a public beheading, a common occurrence in the city. After three months, he left the capital with a Ladakhi merchant, returning to India in October 1866, some seventeen months after first setting out. Walker and Montgomerie (initially absent in England again through ill health) both interviewed Nain Singh, and compiled his data into a route survey and map.

Montgomerie described Nain Singh as a 'most excellent and trustworthy observer'.[30] The RGS was so impressed it presented him with a gold watch, a reward hitherto only given to Europeans like Johnson. However, for the Government of India, this was a breakthrough in intelligence work. Inspired by Nain Singh's success, the Home Department authorised the expenditure of no less than £5,000 for further pundit training and exploration. The Foreign Department recorded its broader motive for secret survey operations:

> The Governor-General in Council cordially approves of the proposal to employ Asiatics in the exploration of the Trans-Himalayan regions, and directs that it be intimated to each explorer who may be sent out by the Trigonometrical Survey that any important political intelligence he may bring back will receive a separate pecuniary acknowledgement, according to its value, from the Foreign Secretary.[31]

Pundit and Secret Agent: The Mirza

It was disturbing for British military officers to note that the North-West Frontier had been the route through which all the historic invaders of the subcontinent had come. Russian annexations in central Asia between 1864 and 1873 seemed to indicate that another threat of invasion now loomed on the horizon. Each annexation brought the tsar's armies closer to the Indian borders until even those who did not believe that Russia could actually invade thought the Russian Empire might just use its proximity to stir up trouble amongst the border tribes and subsequently the people of India. There can be little doubt that Russian officers were driving the process of expansion, even if they were not the only factor. The conquest of Turkestan meant that Russian prestige was satisfied on two counts: fearing that the British intended to control central Asia, the Russians believed that their annexations successfully forestalled British influence; in addition, the defeat of the khanates, and their raiders and slavers, opened up a new economic potential for Russia in the region. But British concerns about Russia's intentions were fuelled by the contradictory or misleading remarks of Russian diplomats. Cherniaev's capture of Tashkent in 1865, the effective annexation of Bokhara, and the fall of Khiva in 1873 had all been preceded by diplomatic smokescreens against the British, and few Russian officers made a secret of their view that the 1873 border settlement with Britain gave them a free hand in central Asia. The Foreign Office produced a list of broken assurances by St Petersburg to remonstrate with the Russian ambassador, but it was easy for the tsarist government to reiterate Gorkachov's famous remarks about the difficulty of halting the advance of a modern civilisation that bordered lawless neighbours. Moreover, many British politicians were prepared to accept St Petersburg's line that Russian officers sometimes acted beyond their instructions.

In 1869, Britain and Russia had begun negotiations over the border line between Afghanistan and the khanates of central Asia, and the preliminary agreement of 1873 defined the border as running along the Oxus as far as a post at Khwaja Sahar, which turned out to be a ferry crossing point seen by Alexander Burnes in 1838.[32]

From there, the border extended vaguely westwards towards Sarakhs on the Persian frontier, but neither the Russians nor the British could be sure of the line because no surveys had been carried out there. There was little clarity from Teheran either, since Persian claims extended as far north as Merv where they had conducted (unsuccessful) military operations against Turcoman tribesmen as recently as 1865. Nevertheless, even the use of the river Oxus as a frontier line turned out to be fraught with difficulties. The decision was based on an interpretation of Lieutenant Wood's mission to the source of the Oxus in 1838. What Wood could not have known was that the Afghans who lived further down the river to the west inhabited not just the provinces south of its course, but the whole region astride it. They owed a loose suzerainty to Kabul but few really acknowledged it. To all intents and purposes, the people there were independent. However, Sher Ali, the Amir of Kabul who had emerged triumphant from years of civil war, was eager to establish his authority across Afghanistan. Thus Britain, Russia and Afghanistan had a vested interest in this sensitive border region. With so much resting on the course of the Oxus, who lived there, and what their allegiances were, it is not surprising that the Survey of India turned its attention to this political matter.

It is perhaps curious that those who have researched the pundits dismiss this political objective.[33] Any purely geographical organisation could hardly have selected this region through pure coincidence. Moreover, it if had been a case of simply wishing to define the border in co-operation with the Afghans, then it would have been far simpler to work directly with Kabul and even despatch a joint mission, as happened in 1885. In fact, there were no fewer than three secret missions extending from Kandahar to Kashgar between 1868 and 1870, all of which were aimed at filling in the 'Great Blank' between Russian and British possessions.[34] The speed at which these expeditions were mounted suggests that the boundary issue was, indeed, the driving force. The final clue is perhaps the route taken by the first of the pundits through Afghanistan. The Afghan territories were in fact already well known to the Survey of India. Elphinstone, Burnes, Pottinger and Wood had all contributed to the geographical knowledge of the country, and there had been a permanent occupation during the First Afghan War. But the first pundit marched this way in 1868 and this strongly suggests that the pundits were tasked with more than simply acquiring topographical information; they were trying to determine the political climate of Afghanistan and the areas to its north.

The first agent was Mirza Shuja, code-named 'the Mirza', who set out in 1868, with orders to carry out a survey of the southern Pamirs. Abdul Mejid had already traversed the Pamirs and Oxus in 1860, and five years later four Indian agents had been sent to collect intelligence on the Russian advance after the fall of Tashkent (*see p. 119*). None of these men had been trained as surveyors and what was needed was a more detailed picture of the topography that the Russians were likely to cross. The Mirza was selected on the basis of his familiarity with Afghanistan. He was a Muslim, fluent in Pushtu, and had been raised in Meshed in northern Persia. His mother was native born, but his father was a Turkish trader who had settled in the holy city. He had come to the attention of Lieutenant Pottinger during the siege of Herat and Pottinger had employed him as a munshi in Kabul where he learned to speak English. Ten years later, the Mirza reappeared in the service of Lieutenant Walker whilst he was mapping the northern borders of the Punjab (before he became the Surveyor-General of the Survey of India). Short of surveyors, Walker had himself trained the Mirza to collate data. After a time spent in public works for Peshawar, the Mirza was transferred to the Survey again for further training in 1857. It seems he was employed in taking secret bearings in the Swat Valley with a prismatic compass, but Walker was disappointed by his mathematical abilities.[35] Later the same year he approached the tribesmen south-west of Peshawar to negotiate the passage of European surveyors across their lands.[36] In October 1857, he was rewarded with six months' furlough in Kabul, but at the end of that period he failed to return, writing to Walker to say that he was employed teaching the sons of the Amir Dost Mohammed.[37] Here he stayed for ten years, remaining as a court teacher when Sher Ali, the third son of Dost Mohammed, came to the throne. Throughout this whole period, the Mirza provided a stream of intelligence to Major Pollock, the Commissioner for Peshawar. When Montgomerie requested that Pollock provide 'men to explore beyond the North-West Frontier', it is understandable that such an experienced and well connected man as the Mirza should be recalled from Kabul.[38]

Thus, in 1867, the Mirza was retrained at Dehra Dun and then, like Nain Singh, at Roorkee, before being posted to Peshawar. He left the frontier city in the autumn of 1867, hoping to travel to Chitral, but the passes were blocked with early snow and he found the borderlands of Afghanistan too unsettled to get through safely. After three attempts, he decided to head south. His fourth attempt to cross the mountains began with a journey down the Indus to Dera Ghazi Khan where he took a steamer for Sukkur before striking west towards the Bolan Pass. Once again winter snows meant he could not get through and so he switched to the Mula Pass, a broken defile 100 miles in length. Finally, in May 1868, after an arduous eight-month odyssey, he reached Kandahar to find the country in the midst of a civil war.

Back in India, the rivalry of different departments almost caused the Mirza's mission to be called off before it had begun. Sir Robert Montgomery had been replaced as Lieutenant-Governor of the Punjab by Sir Donald McLeod in January 1865, and McLeod was surprised to learn of the Mirza's existence; out of the blue Montgomerie had asked him for a letter of introduction to 'our agent in Khokand'. McLeod took the view that sending any agents into central Asia would excite jealousy and hostility amongst the Russians and the Kokendi authorities.[39] There was certainly some truth in this. Russian historians believed that central Asia was teeming with British agents intent on undermining Russian influence. The Viceroy, Sir John Lawrence, was in sympathy with McLeod's view, and asked Walker to hold the Mirza until the Punjab governor had investigated.[40] Walker replied that he could not since the Mirza was already 'beyond recall'. When McLeod had been mollified, Walker suggested that letters of introduction from traders might improve the agents' cover story, and this gave Lawrence the opportunity to reiterate that no agents should be sent without 'special sanction', that is to say, without his personal approval.[41]

Meanwhile the Mirza was in further trouble. Having sent his baggage on ahead of him from Kandahar, it was captured, and he was denounced as a spy. After much anxiety and effort, he managed to talk his way out of imprisonment, and hurried on. Fortunately he was able to join the army of Sher Ali which was marching to Kabul, and he arrived there in June. Once at the amir's court, he was able to cultivate his old friendship with Sher Ali and his son, Yakub Khan.[42] Nevertheless, few in the city were prepared to travel to the north and the Mirza had difficulty recruiting a party to accompany him to the Pamirs. He also clashed with the former British-Indian agent, the newswriter called Munphool, accusing him of deliberate obstruction. Although Munphool was recalled to India to explain his lack of co-operation, there was no conclusive evidence against him. Given the nature of the civil war in Afghanistan, it is more likely the Mirza was frustrated at the lack of progress he was making in preparing for a major trek to the north. Part of the reason was the draining of resources to support the civil war. He reported that Kabul, in contrast to the years he had spent there as a British agent, was now 'filthy' and 'in anything but a flourishing state'.[43]

With winter threatening to close the passes of the Hindu Kush, the Mirza was at last able to push northwards with supplies and porters. He kept notes on all that he saw and he reported on the fortress town of Kulm-Tashkurgan, a settlement not previously reconnoitred. However, the Mirza faced many hazards in the northern provinces. Attacked by robbers, almost trapped by a Persian-speaking *agent provocateur* claiming to be a helpful European, and constantly hindered by deep snow, the Mirza showed remarkable courage in sticking to his mission. At Faizabad, the capital of the province of Badakshan, the Mirza made notes on the political allegiance of the country and the attitudes of the people towards the *mir* (ruler). The weather deteriorated still further. One of the Mirza's servants was so reluctant to leave the safety of Faizabad to face the howling gales and frozen wastes of the Pamirs, that he denounced the Mirza as 'an infidel, spying on the country for the English'. Luckily the Mirza was able to bribe the man and bluffed his way through the exposure.

The party travelled on into Wakhan, the Mirza keeping yet more secret records on the topography and political situation. He noted, for example, that the Oxus could easily be crossed in winter as it was completely frozen. He also wrote about the allegiances of the people of Sarikol, some of whom he met fleeing south, refugees from reprisals of the *atalik ghazi* (governor) of Kashgar, Yakub Beg. The Mirza demonstrated his utter loyalty to his handlers by regaling the Mir of Wakhan with the power of the British *feringhees*, and why, therefore, it was a good idea to side with them and not the Russians. Eventually he crossed over the Pamirs to Kashgar, subjected the whole way to biting winds and intense cold. Snow blindness and frostbite affected the porters, and they grew mutinous. Yet, despite all these hardships, the Mirza continued faithfully to record his topographical data.

On the Chinese side of the Pamirs, the Mirza noted the abundance of forts near Tashkurgan (not to be confused with Afghan Kulm-Tashkurgan) and the suspicious nature of the governor of the area, the atalik's brother. At one point, the governor demanded a full examination of the Mirza's baggage, an alarming moment which could have exposed all his surveying equipment, but the Mirza offered him some gifts, claiming they were specimens of all that he carried in his baggage. It worked. Under escort, he made his way to Kashgar, charting new ground for the Survey. Once again he was almost discovered, this time using his compass to take bearings. Switching his prismatic for a rough compass he had in his pocket, he told his inquisitor it was for finding the direction of Mecca. When he then gave it to the man, it seemed that he was a traveller of genuine and impressive devotion. He was safe again.

At Kashgar, the Mirza made many observations about the traders' nationalities, the volume of commerce and the degree of Russian influence. A Russian consulate had been agreed since a Sino-Russian treaty in 1860, but they had only established a presence in 1868, the year the Mirza arrived. In fact, it was a critical moment. There was every chance the Russians would take advantage of the decay in Chinese rule in Kashgar to establish their own hegemony. The Tai'ping Rebellion to the east (in the central provinces) had absorbed much of China's resources, and the Chinese personnel who ruled the native Muslim Uighurs regarded their posting as a punishment. In 1862, the condescending attitude of Chinese officials, and their blatant misrule eventually provoked a rebellion amongst the Tungani Muslims and it spread quickly to Kashgar. Two years later, Yakub Beg, an adventurer who had fought the Russians on the Syr Daria, took control of the city, whilst the Russians responded by seizing Chinese territory including the Ili Valley, a strategic gap in the Tien Shan range. The Mirza noted that Yakub Beg had fortified the city, adding watchtowers at regular intervals and some sort of conflict with the Russians seemed likely. The Mirza gathered as much intelligence as he could on the atalik's armed forces, concluding that he was evidently a 'good soldier'. He also noted that all the routes towards Russian territory were well fortified. Taking an excursion from Kashgar itself, the Mirza was then able to gather information about the nearest Russian fort, just nine days' march away.

Although the Mirza was able to meet the atalik on several occasions, and even get along with him, he was constantly alert to intrigue. An *agent provocateur* was sent with some surveying instruments and asked to be shown how to use them. Sensing a trap, the Mirza pretended not to know how they functioned. But he continued to slip out of the city to take observations at night in secret. However, ironically, it was the arrival of two British explorers that almost cost him his life.

Between 1868 and 1872, central Asia was attracting a great deal of popular interest in Britain. Newspapers like the *Illustrated London News*, and popular journals like *Macmillan's Magazine* carried articles about the fabled cities of the ancient Silk Route. Something about the antiquity of the civilisation there and its status as largely 'unknown' (to the Europeans, of course) appealed to the Victorian imagination. For a time, Ladakh, Kashgar and Yarkand even rivalled the intensity of interest of African exploration.[44] The glamour of discovery gave explorers a celebrity status, and a reputation for heroism. It was a chance for a generation, brought up on the stories of Alexander the Great and other classical giants, to walk in their footsteps. There was also something 'imperial' about the idea: exploration offered the chance to act in the national interest, to enhance the prestige of one's country and to make history.

Yet, for the Government of India, this popular appeal was something of a nuisance. Europeans who crossed the frontier could easily cause offence, and consequently commit the government to unwelcome entanglements with central Asian rulers. Calcutta did what it could to prevent explorers swarming over sensitive border regions, denying them access or support, but even Sir John Lawrence was unable to control the enthusiasm of the Royal Geographical Society. The RGS directly funded two men who deliberately crossed the borders of British India in defiance of the Indian Government and the instructions of Douglas Forsyth, the commissioner at Peshawar responsible for the management of the North-West Frontier. The first was the explorer Robert Shaw, who was interested in the 'commercial possibilities' of Kashgaria. The second explorer, or adventurer, was the enigmatic George Hayward.[45] Hayward travelled disguised as a Pathan, but Shaw made no attempt to conceal his identity. Both were eager to be the first to 'discover' the area, but, arousing suspicions, they were detained in Yarkand. Hayward gave his guards the slip and made an arduous crossing of the Pamirs in mid-winter to escape his captors.[46]

Eventually both explorers were allowed to enter Kashgar, but they were soon detained again. Their servants, Indian and Ladakhi, were nevertheless permitted to wander the bazaars and they brought back information about the atalik's uncompromising rule. Women, they noted, were strictly controlled. But for a generally benign, if strict code of conduct, Yakub Beg was occasionally given to fits of rage and had, in one shocking instance, strangled one of his subjects with his own hands.[47] Most impressive of all was his system of secret police. Informers were everywhere and dissent was punishable by death.

It was at this point that the Mirza tried to approach Shaw, sending a message that he needed a watch (to record longitude) and explaining that he too had been sent to explore the region. Shaw was afraid that this was a Kashgari attempt to trap him, and, eager to stress the commercial nature of his mission, he refused. When Hayward had arrived, the Mirza made no attempt to contact him, but by then, all three were in detention. Shaw heard that the Mirza was chained up to a log like a common criminal. The atalik clearly believed they were all spies and he only decided to free the Englishmen in the hope of some favourable British alliance against Russia. Yakub Beg certainly believed that he could counterbalance the threat posed by the Russians on his border by appealing to the *Malika* (Queen) of England and the Lord Sahib (Viceroy) in India.

In desperation, and fearing he might be imprisoned indefinitely, the Mirza appealed to Yakub Beg to be allowed to leave too, and, finally on 7 June 1869, he did so, burdened with the customary presents. He eventually reached Leh in August that year and reported to Dehra Dun. His achievement was outstanding. He had surveyed a route of no less than 2,179 miles which included large sections of unknown territory, over a period of two years. The scale of his survey undoubtedly attracted the attention of geographers, but what particularly interested Montgomerie was the evidence that the Hindu Kush and Pamirs were actually joined and were themselves part of the Himalayan chain. Such discoveries must have been of some comfort to military officers looking at the defences of India.

Something of the military value of the Mirza's report was also hinted at by Montgomerie. The Mirza's accounts of the Afghan army, and its battles outside Kabul, 'at the time were rather valuable, as it was difficult to get any other information'.[48] In fact, the Mirza passed on intelligence on northern Afghanistan and routes from Kashgar to Russian territory with accuracy. Given his intelligence background before being employed as a surveyor, this is perhaps not surprising, but his work should finally dispel the myth that the Survey of India was somehow unconnected with the gathering of military and secret political intelligence. Montgomerie concluded: 'The Mirza is a very intelligent man, and has, as a native, an Asiatic, got a very considerable insight into the state of affairs in eastern Turkestan.'[49] Despite all the praise, which came later in 1871 from the Royal Geographical Society and from the viceroy himself, the Mirza did not live to enjoy the plaudits. Despatched on another mission to Bokhara (again, hardly a journey for geographical purposes, although it was Montgomerie who promoted the mission), and accompanied by his son-in-law, the Mirza was murdered by his guides whilst asleep somewhere beyond Maimena on the Afghan border.[50]

Pundits: the Havildar and the Mullah

On 12 August 1870, a small party of travellers, apparently in search of falcons, made their way out of the city of Peshawar on the North-West Frontier. Amidst the caravans, mullahs, itinerants and families of Pathans, they were indistinguishable from any other of the frontier peoples, lost in the swirling dust on the road. But they were led by a soldier on special duty who went by the code-name of 'the Havildar'. His real name was Hyder Shah.

Hyder Shah was a *havildar* (sergeant) in the Bengal Sappers and Miners of the Indian Army who had been born at Kohat, south of Peshawar. He had been recommended by Major Pollock, the former Commissioner of Peshawar, to Montgomerie, but Pollock had himself been alerted to the special aptitude of this man by Lieutenant-Colonel Frederick Maunsell, the Commandant of the Sappers and Miners. In fact, this was not the first time that this link had been used. Maunsell had also recommended, through Pollock, another Indian soldier in 1862. He had been described as: 'a Pathan of the Native Sapper and Miners – a very intelligent man indeed, and one who promised exceedingly well'.[51] He had been trained for a year before being tasked with a mission from Peshawar to Chitral, but he had apparently been killed in Swat as a result of a long-standing family blood feud, a phenomenon typical amongst the rival clans of the North-West Frontier.

Finding a replacement had not been easy.[52] Some of the Pathans were attracted by the pay of the Indian Army, especially the Punjab Frontier Force, but their loyalties were often divided. It was not unknown for them to change sides, or to continue to pursue a feud against some of their comrades for generations. But they never lacked for courage or spirit, and this was attractive to the British, who saw something of their idealised selves in these mountain warriors. By the 1890s, the preferred recruits for the entire Indian Army were either from the highlands of Nepal or the North-West Frontier, the so-called 'martial races', and it is remarkable that these hardy and independent people stuck so closely to their British officers throughout campaigns in India and elsewhere. It suggests something of a bond of mutual respect, built on the shared experiences of hardship and the common cause of duty.

The Havildar's mission was very similar to that of his ill-fated predecessor. Montgomerie had no topographical data on the states that lay immediately to the north of British India. Travellers and merchants could supply information about the people, and secret agents had already visited Chitral, Swat and Yasin, but where were the passes through the Hindu Kush? Could they be traversed by artillery? What distances lay between the strategic points? With the Russians now in possession of Bokhara, it was even more pressing to obtain intelligence on the northern approaches to India. There was also an added attraction in the form of the mysterious land called Kafiristan. Kafiristan exercised the imagination in much the same way that Prester John and the lost Christian civilisation of Ethiopia did in Africa. During his mission to Kabul in 1808 Mountstuart Elphinstone had sent an Asian agent into the region known as the 'land of unbelievers' which confirmed other reports that the people who lived in its inaccessible valleys were of fair skin, with light hair, and they worshipped gods. Romantics liked to believe they were the lost descendants of the armies of Alexander the Great, but the modern Kalasha tribesmen are now thought to be indigenous people who resisted migrants and the tide of Islam. Montgomerie was anxious to settle the identity of these strange people, but contact was difficult because of the perpetual state of war that existed between them and their Muslim neighbours. If this task was not hazardous enough, the Havildar's mission would not end with the survey of the northern states. He was to proceed on, through Badakshan, across the Pamirs and end at Khokand, now on the front line against Russian expansion. Once again, any idea that this was simply a journey to advance the knowledge of geography has to be challenged. It seems too great a coincidence that an intelligent army sergeant should be tasked to reconnoitre this region at such a crucial point in the Russian offensive in central Asia, unless it was to gather intelligence on the avenues of advance or the military activity of the tsar's forces in the area.

Accompanied by another surveyor code-named 'the Mullah', the Havildar marched north from Peshawar, over the Malakand Pass and into the Swat Valley. The tribesmen who lived here were also styled Pathans but, unlike their democratic cousins further west, here it was clear that an unpopular khan ruled an impoverished valley. Far more respect was accorded the religious leaders who inspired, roused, admonished and guided the people. This information was valuable to the British, for they regarded it as a valley of great strategic significance, linking, as it did, the northern states with the borders of British India.

As he traversed the region, the Havildar faced several hazards. Dangerous river crossings, brigandage and an endless probing curiosity about the purpose of his journey were common. Amongst tribesmen deeply suspicious of outsiders, being compromised would have meant a grisly death. But soon he had ascended the steep pine-forested slopes that led to Dir, the capital of the province of the same name. For a moment he was safe. Once at Dir, the Havildar expected to pause whilst large groups of travellers assembled into great caravans that could resist the predatory raids of the Kafirs to the west. Unfortunately the latest caravan had just left so the Havildar paid the local chieftain for an escort of twenty-five armed men. For six days, the party passed the memorial cairns and flags that marked the victims of Kafir raids, but the Havildar's party was lucky and reached Chitral safely on 31 August 1870.

Chitral is a small town nestling in the valley of the river Kunar, and surrounded by immense scree-covered slopes and outcrops of shattered rock. In summer, temperatures rise to a furnace heat whilst in winter the thermometer plunges and the region is cloaked in snow. The people, rivals of the Pathans to the south and west, jealously guarded the vital river terraces that were their only supply of food, but the Havildar noted that the fractious nature of local and dynastic politics led to frequent unrest. Aman ul Mulk, the *mehtar* (ruler) of Chitral, heeding an old Afghan proverb that 'kings sleep on an ant heap', was alive to the intrigues against him. He had conquered Yasin and Mastuj, married his children well into the most prestigious families and established himself as master, or *lott* as the locals called him.[53] But he himself was an intriguer and the Havildar reported that he was now in league with Mir Wali, the petty chief of Yasin. It was Mir Wali who had murdered George Hayward, and the mehtar knew it. Despite officially disapproving of what had happened, it was rumoured that it was he, in fact, who had ordered the assassination, an idea which Hayward had himself predicted. The Havildar noted that the mehtar now possessed some items that had formerly belonged to Hayward, including one of his rifles. When the Havildar was summoned to meet the mehtar and Mir Wali, he kept his hand on a loaded revolver under his cloak and expected at any moment to have to sell his life dearly.[54]

Fortunately, the Havildar's cover was not exposed and he learned that the road to Bokhara through Badakshan was closed. Sher Ali, the Amir of Afghanistan, had taken the precaution of preventing anyone passing into the country through this remote province after he received intelligence that conspirators were using the route to reach Kabul. His nephew, a claimant of the throne in Bokhara, had sent three men along the Badakshan road to convey secret letters to plotters in the Afghan capital, but Sher Ali had intercepted them and had them 'blown away from guns' in the old Mughal tradition.

Undeterred by this alarming story, the Havildar set off for Badakshan on 5 September. Crossing the Nuksan Pass proved extremely difficult. His party had to cut trenches between six and twelve feet deep through the snowdrifts to cross the summit plateau.[55] It took twenty gruelling days to reach Faizabad, the capital of Badakshan, but the details of the pass, its approaches, gradient and condition were all faithfully recorded. Once at the town, the Havildar was able to confirm that the road to Kabul was indeed closed. However, he did not leave empty-handed. He spent a month gathering information about Russian troop movements and strengths to the north, as well as on the political situation in the region as a whole, before turning back towards India.

On the way back, the Havildar crossed the Dorah Pass, a lower and wider gap in the mountains which was nevertheless often avoided because of the raids of the Kafirs. In November, amidst appalling conditions, the Havildar recorded that his party were at 'the height of misery'. Chitral was no haven either. The mehtar was noticeably cooler, it having been rumoured that the Havildar was, in fact, a British spy. Hurrying out of the mountain state, he re-crossed the treacherous Lowari Pass north of Dir, arriving back at Peshawar on 13 December.

Montgomerie was delighted. From the Havildar's remarkable notes, it was possible to construct at least a route survey map of the northern provinces, with the exception of Kafiristan. Sir Henry Rawlinson, the President of the Royal Geographical Society, described the Havildar, with unintended condescension, as: 'a most remarkable man ... a bold, energetic and well-trained officer [with] a combination of boldness and discretion which is very rare in an Asiatic'.[56] He had been lucky to survive. If the Mehtar of Chitral had been able to confirm his actual purpose, there is no doubt he would have been murdered. Moreover, in the climate of suspicion that prevailed in northern Afghanistan, it was indeed fortunate he was not exposed. If one adds the risk of being enslaved, butchered by the Kafir raiders, or killed in the sub-zero temperatures of the Hindu Kush in winter, there is no doubt that the Havildar was a very brave man.

However, there were doubts about the veracity of his information on two subsequent missions. In 1870, shortly after the first journey to Chitral, he was again sent to gather intelligence in Bokhara (now under Russian control) via Kabul, Balkh and Karshi on the Oxus. The mission was apparently a success but a mystery hangs over the results. No report of the mission was ever published. Derek Waller discovered that Montgomerie had written to Colonel Walker complaining that he could not understand the observations that the Havildar had brought back.[57] Waller suggests that the Havildar may have been falsifying the data, but Captain Trotter, Montgomerie's successor, wrote: 'No account of this journey has been published, as the greater portion of the route traversed has previously been described by others.'[58] If so, what *was* the purpose of the Havildar's second mission? Surely, it suggests that he was sent to gather intelligence rather than topographical information. Montgomerie said, referring to the observations, that he 'could make nothing of [them]', but he sent him on a third mission all the same. Trotter concluded that the Havildar was 'trustworthy' although he concurred with Walker that the data were 'somewhat meagre'.[59]

Further clues are perhaps suggested by the Havildar's third expedition. Initially he travelled as far as Jellalabad again with 'the Mullah', but also with two assistants, a *naik* (corporal) of the Bengal Sappers and Miners, and his nephew (the last two having accompanied him before). Here they split up, the Mullah departing for another task set up by Montgomerie. The Havildar turned north from Kabul, crossing the Saralong Pass which had not been surveyed before.[60] At Faizabad, he halted for five months, claiming in his report that snows prevented any crossing of the Oxus, a point which Trotter doubted. Nevertheless, in late April, the Havildar was able to cross the river on a raft of inflated skins and marched south-west, along the line that was at that moment being settled in London and St Petersburg as the boundary between Russian and Afghan territory. In places, the 'road' was a narrow path and one section in a defile consisted of no more than metal pegs driven into solid rock above the raging waters. At Shignan, the Havildar's party was halted, but he returned to Faizabad and, making a big loop, he tried to follow the river from the opposite direction. Once again he was halted, but he now switched to surveying the lands across the Oxus to the north. This sensitive area, claimed by the Russians as the southernmost fringe of Bokhara (which was under their 'protection'), was obviously of great political and strategic importance. It was not surprising then that the Havildar, on his return across the Hindu Kush via Kabul and Peshawar, was lauded for his achievements.

The importance of the region was such that another mysterious surveyor, Abdul Sabhan, code-named 'the Munshi', had also been in the area two months before without the Havildar's knowledge.[61] Corroborating the surveys was vital to avoid inaccuracy, and, but for a gap of twenty-five miles, the entire length of the river Oxus was now known. The information reached the British in the nick of time as Russian surveyors were also active in the region. In 1873, when the Imperial Geographical Society of St Petersburg published its findings, the surveys of the two imperial powers overlapped for the first time.[62] The problem was that the Oxus was a very unsatisfactory line for a border. Rather than dividing two communities, it was in fact the artery of trade and the centre of a region which had strong cultural and ethnic connections. Indeed, few in the Oxus valley had much interest in the directives of either Kabul or Bokhara. The Kirghiz nomads who grazed their livestock on the summer pastures of the Pamirs migrated through the valleys that fed the Oxus with little concept of national frontiers. Moreover, beyond the source of the Oxus, still disputed in 1873, the tangled complex of mountains, watersheds and basins of the Pamirs offered little chance of a clear boundary. The issue was to plague Britain and Russia for another twenty years. The Havildar, sadly, did not live to see the resolution of the problem. He disappears from the records until 1879, when, at the height of the Second Afghan War, it was reported he had died of cholera in the Afghan town of Jellalabad.[63]

The 'Mullah', who had accompanied the Havildar on the first stage of his final mission, was, in fact, Ata Mohamed. It says much for the Havildar that Ata Mohamed was taught clandestine surveying skills on the march, but his recruitment reveals the tragedy of intelligence work: he was the brother of the first agent, the Pathan Sapper who had been killed in a blood feud in 1869. Ata had recovered his dead brother's papers and instruments, but little else is known about his background except that he was educated at the Newab of Rampur's college and was fluent in Arabic as well as his native tongue.

His cover was as a merchant, and he travelled from Jellalabad on 28 September 1873 with a pony, a servant and bales of silk and cloth. His mission was to map the entire length of the Kunar River, cross the Hindu Kush at the Baroghil Pass and then march into Wakhan.[64] From there he was to continue to Yarkand before returning through Ladakh. This survey would therefore link together many of the previous expeditions and was expected to coincide with another mission led by a British officer, T. Douglas Forsyth. After taking meticulous care over the bearings and other data, the Mullah was praised for his work.[65] The accuracy of his records was remarkable given that the task had to be conducted in secret over an arduous twelve months.

After a break of one year, the Mullah was again deployed into the mountains, this time to chart the route of the Indus from Gilgit to the plains near Kohistan. This route was thought to be another potential avenue for invasion and was marked by a hypothetical dotted line on the maps. The region was dangerous in several respects, but hostile tribes and the precipitous terrain ranked above all else as the most hazardous. For the second mission, the Mullah was assisted by Syed Amir, a man who knew the area already. The Mullah had befriended him at Peshawar in 1875 and they agreed to adopt the disguise of traders. Together they traversed the Indus before the Mullah struck off on his own towards Gilgit. Here, in order to preserve his cover, he spent two weeks trading cloth before continuing on treacherous paths to Yasin and then on to Mastuj, to the north-east of Chitral. He returned to British territory successfully on 21 October 1876, having contributed a great deal to British intelligence on the topography and societies of the northern states.[66] When the British conducted military operations there in the 1890s, much of the information needededwas derived from the Mullah's original survey.

The last region to the north of the British Indian border not yet surveyed sufficiently was the Swat Valley. The Mullah was selected for this final task in 1877, but, in order to dispel any idea that he was working for the British, he was ordered to return to his home for a year.[67] He then left Peshawar on 23 April 1878 in his usual disguise as a trader, this time seeking timber. But he was to get a shock when he entered the Swat Valley. The ferryman told him that on the bank where he had just been standing, another Peshawar man, just like himself, had been murdered many years before whilst washing. It was immediately apparent that the ferryman was describing the Mullah's very own brother.

Undaunted, the Mullah pressed on. He endured avalanches, bandits, dysentery and fever but he managed to link together his own surveys and cover all the valleys that extended throughout Swat. Walker, now a lieutenant-general, described him as: 'the most painstaking and reliable of any of the Musselman explorers that have been employed by this department'.[68] Nor did his dedication end there. Although difficult to trace with certainty, he may have been part of the Afghan Boundary Commission in 1884–5 and he was certainly paid for 'secret and confidential explorations across the frontier' as late as 1888.[69]

A Forgotten Contribution

The dedication of the pundits was remarkable, and tragically so many of them paid the ultimate price for their loyalty. Their achievements have hitherto been seen only in terms of geography, but there can be little doubt that the real purpose of their topographical work had less to do with extending knowledge for some academic purpose than acquiring intelligence that had a specific military or political objective. It was clear that the Indian Government had no wish to broadcast this aspect of their missions, for fear of antagonising the peoples of the region. Moreover, their inspirational service to the British Empire was unpalatable to later generations of Indian nationalist historians who tended to focus on the heroes of anti-British resistance. Consequently, until now, it seems the true purpose of the pundits has been overlooked. Furthermore, the real significance of the pundit missions was in the continuity of Asian personnel serving British intelligence. However, in the 1870s, with the Russians sweeping southwards through central Asia, intelligence work was about to acquire an even greater importance.

Chapter 7

The Missions to the Frontiers

Central Asia, Afghanistan and the Formation of the Intelligence Division, 1865–1880

The British had used Asian agents in the native states on the plains of India from the eighteenth century; they had extended the use of agents into the hills of the frontier, and then sent them as far as the khanates of Central Asia. British officers had themselves adopted disguises and tried to travel incognito to gather intelligence in Persia, Afghanistan, and Turkestan. The missions had different emphases: some were essentially diplomatic, others more concerned with routes and topography. Yet all of them can be grouped under one design: to extend British influence and enhance the defence of British India through the acquisition of vital military intelligence. It would be wrong to draw distinctions between 'political' missions and 'military' ones, because the information the agents gathered served both needs. If one considers for a moment Clausewitz's famous dictum that 'war is the extension of politics by an admixture of other means', then it follows that political information was just as important as the sources of food and water, the location of strategic passes, and the strength of native forces to the creation of a comprehensive military analysis of the region. The gathering of intelligence in central Asia was underscored by the concern to maintain states that could act as 'buffers' against Russia, thus preventing the tsar's armies from reaching the borders of India where they might stir up unrest. However, a new urgency can be detected when the Russians annexed the khanates of Tashkent, Bokhara, and Khiva. The buffer states policy had not only failed, this failure had occurred at a time when Afghanistan was still in an unsettled condition having emerged from years of civil war.

The chief problem the British faced was trying to find out what was going on several hundred miles beyond their border. The rumours that trickled back from central Asia to trading centres like Peshawar were just too unreliable. Furthermore, information from St Petersburg was 'filtered' by the tsar's Foreign Ministry, the anglophobic Asiatic Department, or the Russian Army. In the late 1860s, the British had relied on specific missions to obtain information in central Asia, but there were soon calls for a permanent intelligence screen of covert agents based around consulates. The growth of telegraphic communication would aid this development, but in the mountains of the frontier, traditional systems of dak runners and mounted couriers remained essential. There were other continuities. The difficulty of getting reliable agents, the problems of sifting fact from rumour in the information acquired, and the incomplete nature of the intelligence also remained. Moreover, even the processing of the intelligence 'product' (such as the publication of a secret report on what was happening) could not guarantee that the correct decisions would be made by the 'consumers' (those that received the intelligence product). Some British ministers contemptuously dismissed the intelligence they received, whilst others were perhaps too inclined to believe that disaster was imminent.

Faiz Baksh, Pundit Munphool and Missions to Central Asia

Lord Lawrence, Viceroy of India 1864–9, instructed the Government of the Punjab to send four secret agents into Central Asia in 1865. Although Lawrence is always associated with the 'close border' policy, it says much about the importance of intelligence to the British authorities at this time that he was eager to acquire information on the regions to the north of the Hindu Kush. Four men were selected and, typically, the viceroy himself approved the list of questions they were to answer. The mission was designed to ascertain the Russian Army's strengths, its deployment and the state of local politics in Badakshan, Balkh, Bokhara and Khojend. Among the personnel was Faiz Baksh, who went by the alias Ghulam Rabbani. Like the others, he adopted a disguise, and with one companion he made his way to Bokhara. He was able to bring back a great deal of information on the Russians, even obtaining an audience with General Chernaiev.[1] The other pair included Pundit Munphool, who made an equally thorough reconnaissance of Badakshan, returning in 1866.[2] Such was the value of the intelligence acquired that Munphool received a payment of Rs 5,000.[3] He also appears to have been transferred from his original post in the Government of the Punjab to become a newswriter in Kabul. When the Pundit Mirza arrived in the Afghan capital in the summer of 1868, Munphool certainly was in communication with him. Accusations by the Mirza that Munphool was obstructing his preparations to reach Badakshan led to the temporary recall of the newswriter, but no misconduct was proven. Instead, there was some thought given to his redeployment in Bokhara to act as an unofficial consul under the guise of a Hindu merchant, but in the end he was not despatched. Much of the activity of this man is shrouded in mystery, but another glimpse of the value of Munphool's work is possible when we find, in the private papers of Lord Lawrence, the recommendation that he should receive the coveted Star of India.[4] This was perhaps a just reward for years of secret intelligence work which began with the missions through Baltistan, Chitral, and Swat between 1860 and 1865.

The Punjab Government had sent many agents across the administrative border of British India to ascertain the attitudes of the neighbouring tribes. The lawless tribal belt between the borders of the Raj and Afghanistan was not under the direct control of either, and the limits of jurisdiction were not settled until 1893.[5] Lawrence wanted to avoid any question of entanglement with the tribes and therefore with Kabul, but the result was that cross-border raids, cattle rustling, murders and kidnapping could only be checked by sending military expeditions periodically into the mountains of the frontier. Unable to bring the guerrilla tribesmen to battle, commanders were forced to destroy the fabric of tribal settlements: blowing up houses with explosives, burning crops and carrying away livestock. These punitive campaigns were referred to rather disparagingly as 'butcher and bolt' and there was widespread concern that, although they successfully subdued the tribesmen, they built up a store of resentment.[6] In the event of a war with Afghanistan or Russia it was feared the tribesmen would attack lines of communication tying up thousands of men.

The solution was provided by the example of Sir Robert Sandeman, a British political officer who lived and worked amongst the Baluchis, championing their cause and allaying their fears with a personal charisma. He used British expertise to improve the infrastructure, organised a land revenue system to replace the tyranny of the old rulers and suggested alterations to the tribal *jirgas* (councils) to improve the judicial system.[7] As a result, British officers known as 'politicals' went into the hills of the North-West Frontier to follow the Sandeman model. They did so knowing that they were backed by the might of the Indian Army and supported by the intelligence of Asian agents. Some of these agents were surveyors, but there were also intelligence agents, such as 'Bozdar'. Little is known of his work, but it must have been substantial to have merited his reward: a grant of land by the Survey of India and the title of *khan bahadur* in 1883.[8] Another man active in the 1880s was 'The Hakim', who gathered topographical and political intelligence on the North-West Frontier.[9]

Whilst Lawrence was confident that the Afghans and tribesmen of the North-West Frontier would maul any Russian troops that attempted to force their way through to the Indus, there was less certainty in the late 1860s over Kashgaria, Yakub Beg's new dominion across the Karakoram and Kun Lun mountains to the north. Despite initial misgivings, T. Douglas Forsyth, then the British commissioner for Kanggra, Kulu and Lahaul, persuaded the reluctant viceroy to establish a British representative at Leh.[10] Forsyth then dramatically stated that there was now a 'Leh agency', which implied rather too much for Lawrence. Forsyth was hoping that new exploration would reveal easier passes to develop commerce with Kashgar, but the agency was really no more than a 'listening post' for news across the mountains into Kashgaria.

Shortly after the return of the Mirza, Shaw and Hayward from that region Mirza Shadee, an envoy from the Atalik of Kashgar, arrived. Shaw and Hayward had stressed that the fall of Kashgaria to the Russians seemed imminent, opening up the possibility of Russians harrying the northern approaches to India. The new viceroy, Lord Mayo (1869–72), accordingly seized this opportunity to send an official mission to Kashgar. Mayo tried to conceal the purpose of the team he despatched, led by Forsyth, insisting publicly that it had no official, political or commercial status. But the fact that it contained military and intelligence personnel and was acting directly on the orders of the Government of India makes it plain that Mayo was trying to open permanent diplomatic relations with Kashgaria and develop strong links through commerce.[11]

Forsyth's mission did not get off to a good start. The arrival of Nain Singh, the Pundit, now a known agent of the British, fuelled the suspicions of the Kashgar envoy that the British intended more than simply settling a commercial treaty.[12] Consequently, Nain Singh was ordered to return to Dehra Dun. However, Faiz Baksh was ordered to join the expedition as one of the intelligence agents and he set off from Peshawar, traversed Afghanistan, crossed the Pamirs and joined the main party at Yarkand.[13] A second agent, Ibrahim Khan, a former police inspector, completed a long intelligence-gathering mission from Kashmir to Yarkand, via Gilgit and Yasin.[14] Nevertheless, when Forsyth arrived at Kashgar, he found that Yakub Beg was almost a thousand miles away supervising his border with China. The party therefore returned to India empty handed.

The assassination of Mayo in 1872 led to the appointment of a new viceroy, Lord Northbrook. From the outset, he was determined to take a firmer line with the Russians in central Asian affairs. The Russians were alarmed at the news of the Forsyth mission, fearing that the British intended to foster an alliance with Yakub Beg against them. To contain the new threat, they defeated local forces in a decisive battle on 24 June 1871 in the Ili Valley and then occupied it. Northbrook understood this to be further evidence of Russian expansionist ambitions in the region. However, from an intelligence point of view, the Russian annexation revealed a blind spot for the British: it took three months for the news of the fall of Ili to reach India. Consequently, Forsyth was despatched a second time in 1873 at the head of a mission consisting of 350 men and a caravan of 550 pack animals. Its objective was not only to foster better diplomatic relations with Kashgar, but also to acquire intelligence of a scientific, geographical and strategic nature. Forsyth was to be assisted by Lieutenant-Colonel T. E. Gordon, Captain Biddulph (one of the viceroy's own aides-de-camp), a medical officer, quartermaster and Captain Henry Trotter of the Royal Engineers and GTS. The armed escort was provided by men of the Guides, the elite frontier unit of the Indian Army.

The Forsyth mission also included Asian agents, some of whom were surveyors and others of a purely 'political intelligence' nature. Nain Singh, the Pundit, Kishen Singh (known as 'AK' or 'Krishna'), and Kalian Singh ('GK') were the pundits with three assistants. Faiz Baksh, Abdul Sudhan (the 'Munshi') and Ibrahim Khan were styled 'secretaries' to conceal their real profession of spy. The first task for these agents was to investigate the strategic passes across the Trans-Alai and Tien Shan ranges, the mountains that connected Kashgaria and Russian territory. Splitting up to cover more ground, the agents surveyed a large swathe of the Karakoram between Leh and Shahidulla.[15] However, a lack of time, freezing temperatures (to -25 degrees Centigrade) and bad weather curtailed some of the work. Moreover, as they approached Kashgar, the need for security meant that surveying had to be carried out in secret. Forsyth's concern was that survey apparatus might be considered 'instruments of the Black Art'.[16] Nonetheless, once he had had an opportunity of explaining the purpose of the surveys to Yakub Beg in Kashgar, Captain Trotter and Colonel Gordon made their way to the Russian border in the Tien Shan to begin more overt surveying. There they planned to make observations on the routes that the Russians might take and their forts on the Terekty Pass.[17]

In the event, the cautious Yakub Beg controlled the British officers by limiting the number of their transport animals and Trotter had to accept he could only manage a reconnaissance of the Turgat Pass. However, as they crossed over into Russian territory, it meant that the surveys of the two Great Powers had finally over-lapped.[18]

By February 1874, Forsyth had obtained a commercial treaty and a good picture of the heart of Yakub Beg's dominion. As he withdrew the mission to India, another survey was made of the eastern Pamirs and Wakhan, with the Munshi assisting in gathering yet more vital information on the topography and confirming that, as yet, there was no Russian presence in northern Afghanistan. In winter, the conditions were exceptionally hard, but Gordon and Biddulph exhibited typical sangfroid by commenting only that they had had 'an uncommonly rough time' and 'happily we are none of us the worse for it, except that we have lost the skin off our noses'.[19] Meanwhile, Ibrahim Khan had been sent to Kabul to negotiate with Sher Ali for a passage for the mission through his northern territories. He did not get as far as the Afghan amir was in contretemps with the Government of India, so the British officers made their way back to Yarkand through the southern Pamirs. However, although they had been checked, they despatched the Munshi on a more covert mission that was no less important.

The Munshi left the British officers at Tashkurgan on 29 April 1874 with the intention of surveying the Pamir provinces north of the Oxus, but he was also tasked to gather intelligence on the rulers and the political situation in the region. Crucially he was able to establish that the peoples who lived on the northern bank of the Oxus owed allegiance to the Mir of Badakshan, who, in turn, was a tributary to the amir in Kabul.[20] Despite the conclusion of the Granville–Gorchakov Agreement in 1873, which put the border of Afghanistan on the Oxus, it now seemed that Afghan claims extended into the Pamirs. This was to have severe consequences in the early 1890s.[21]

The British officers continued to survey and map the area to the north of the Karakoram, including the strategic Baroghil Pass, but eventually, in June 1874, they returned to Leh. The pundits however, remained in Shahidulla throughout the winter, before making further attempts to locate all the passes through the Karakoram. Nain Singh made a valuable survey of the Yangi Pass which Forsyth and Trotter also went to examine themselves.[22] The conclusion drawn was that it would be extremely difficult for a Russian army to cross the mountains to the north of India. Although Biddulph feared the Baroghil could be used even by wheeled artillery, a point confirmed by the Mullah a week later, the general feeling was that, in fact, only small raiding parties would be able to cross the watershed.[23]

The solution to this threat, according to Forsyth, was to establish a British agent at Gilgit (in addition to the one already at Leh) and a screen of native agents. In contrast, the view in Calcutta was that the most reliable solution was the extension of Kashmiri rule into Yasin and Chitral. Supporting the Maharajah of Kashmir in the event of a Russian advance was thought easier, safer for British officers, and perhaps cheaper, than maintaining an intelligence web in the northern states. The only risk of the 'Kashmir policy' was that other native rulers might throw in their lot with the 'Power in the North'. The safeguard against this was, so the argument ran, to impress the Oriental mind with the power and prestige of the British Empire, to make natives rulers see that their power and material benefits rested entirely with remaining alongside the British.

Establishment of an Intelligence Division

The sudden fall of Khiva to General Kaufman in May 1873 was a turning point. Despite a steam of assurances from St Petersburg that each Russian occupation was 'temporary' or the 'limit', one by one the khanates of central Asia had been annexed.[24] The driving forces behind Russian expansion were the War Ministry and the Asiatic Department of the Foreign Ministry, but more particularly the close advisor to the tsar, General Dimitri Alekseevich Miliutin. In response to Gorchakov's call for caution to avoid antagonising the British over central Asia, Miliutin retorted: 'It is not necessary to apologise to the English Minister for our advance. They do not stand on ceremony for us, conquering whole kingdoms, occupying alien cities and islands; and we do not ask them why they do it.'[25] The settlement of a border for Afghanistan in 1873 was regarded by the Russian forward school as a signal that they had a 'free hand' in central Asia, and to them the capture of Khiva seemed entirely justified.

In contrast, the British Liberal government regarded the border agreement of 1873 as a triumph, because they thought it would preserve the *status quo* in central Asia and end years of anxious speculation about Russian designs on India. They took the view that only dialogue between London and St Petersburg could avoid misunderstandings in the future. Furthermore, they reasoned that Russia would wish to avoid an unnecessary war over deserts and mountains of doubtful strategic value. Indeed, there were many who felt that Russia's civilisation was infinitely preferable to the slavers, tyrants and bandits of Turkestan. John Lawrence had written:

> I am not myself at all certain that Russia might not prove a safer ally, a better neighbour, than the Mahomedan races of Central Asia and Kabul. She would introduce civilisation, [and] she would abate the fanaticism and ferocity of Mohamedanism, which exercises so powerful an influence in India.[26]

Whilst the Russian government had plotted in secret to take Khiva, the Russian Foreign Ministry had carefully prepared a smokescreen. The British ambassador, Sir Andrew Buchanan, reported that they 'denied positively the existence of any such intention' to seize Khiva. The Russian popular 'boulevard press' took a different view and through 'evidence from other sources', about which he did not elaborate, Buchanan had warned the British government that Khiva was indeed the next target.[27] Lord Granville, the Foreign Secretary, met Count Shuvalov in January 1873, but received the same reassurances that the tsar had given 'special orders' not to take Khiva.[28] In fact, the tsar had ordered General Kaufman to take the khanate only a few weeks before, and it was he who had despatched Shuvalov, his chief of secret police, to confound the British.[29] When the city fell to Kaufman's troops, Shuvalov repeated the mantra that the generals were beyond the control of the

Russian government, but, by the following August, the British consulate at Teheran had picked up intelligence that Russian troops were already preparing to advance into the Turcoman provinces along the border with Persia, some 400 miles south of Khiva.[30]

Lord Northbrook, Viceroy of India 1872–6, reflected Anglo-Indian opinion that Russian interference in Persia would be a prelude to further annexations and eventually a springboard against India: ' ... a Russian protectorate to the shores of the Persian Gulf would be so direct a menace to India that it would, in my opinion, justify a resort to arms for the purpose of securing our present supremacy in the Persian Gulf.'[31] He proposed a military attaché be sent to Teheran, and that communications be improved between the coast and the interior. General Napier, the Commander-in-Chief in India, wanted to go further, with British officers being placed in command of Persian units and an alliance with the shah.[32] The Liberals, and later the Conservatives, would not commit themselves to the defence of Persia for the risks it entailed. The likely battlefields were simply too far from the protection of the Royal Navy, and the supply lines too long for it to be realistic to defend the shah's borders.

There were other options. Northbrook had been under-secretary to Edward Cardwell, the minister charged with the reform of the British Army in the early 1870s, and he had been appointed to develop the Topographical and Statistical Department (known as the T and S) in light of intelligence deficiencies during the Franco-Prussian War.[33] Prompted by the memoranda of Captain Charles Wilson (Royal Engineers) and Captain Evelyn Baring (Royal Artillery), the two officers of the T and S Department, Northbrook was impressed by the potential of a military intelligence branch.[34] After years of opposition to its expansion and development by the conservative voices of Horse Guards, the headquarters of the British Army, Northbrook recommended more officers and more money be provided for a new T and S Department in London. Wilson divided the organisation into three sections, each responsible for a third of the world. His officers scanned the international press for details useful to the army, and added attachés' reports, the narratives of travellers and articles from military periodicals. Major-General Patrick MacDougall was then appointed as the head of the new, and retitled, Intelligence Department on 24 May 1873.

The first issue that the Intelligence Department turned its attention to was, not surprisingly, the situation in central Asia. Wilson rapidly revised A. C. Cooke's, *Russia's Advances in Asia*, which had been published in 1869 by an enterprising intelligence officer, and sent it to Lord Salisbury who had taken over at the India Office. Salisbury was impressed that it contained not only information on the methods the Russian Army had used to annex territories, but also the order of battle in the region, strengths and deployments, with a time and space analysis showing how Russian forces would be canalised into certain axes of advance southwards through the rest of central Asia. His conclusion was that Russia would eventually try to take Herat.[35] The chief recommendation was that there should be a more reliable system for gathering intelligence on the ground. Cooke had complained that information that reached India was:

... derived from the tales of native merchants and travellers, whose stories, magnified in the bazaars of the different cities through which they pass, reach India and Persia in a most distorted state, and give rise to rumours utterly devoid of foundation.[36]

He also admitted that regular information about Turkestan was dependent on Russian sources such as the Invalide Russe and Journal de St Petersburg.

However, Captain Baring was posted as private secretary to Lord Northbrook and he helped to pass on, through private correspondence, the translations of the Russian press by D Section (Russia and Asia) of the London Intelligence Department, a practice that survived into the late 1870s at least.[37] This information, and the knowledge that an intelligence department existed in London, prompted Indian Army officers to consider a similar arrangement for India. As early as 1868, General W. R. Mansfield, the Commander-in-Chief in India, had complained that vital information about the 'dynasty at Cabul' came via border officials who passed that intelligence on to the Government of the Punjab, or, if the information came via Baluchistan, to the Government of Bombay. This merely created 'delay, lukewarm interest [and] weakening of responsibility'.[38] Salisbury therefore recommended that an intelligence screen be established beyond India's borders to the west and north. Acting like antennae, permanent agents would be able to detect Russian probes the moment they began. When the Russians began to move towards Merv in 1874, Salisbury told Northbrook that the existing intelligence arrangements were 'inadequate'.[39] It seems that the 'native agent' in Kabul, who had been there for thirty years, 'writes exactly what the Ameer tells him'.[40] He urged Northbrook to find ways of being 'thoroughly informed on all matters strategical, geographical, [and] political' especially in the area around Herat.[41]

Whilst Northbrook was inclined to hope for agreement with Russia through the Foreign Office in London, the Indian Army needed no such prompting. Its two leading officers, General Robert Napier and Lieutenant-Colonel Frederick Roberts, his deputy quartermaster-general, set up their own Intelligence Branch at Simla in October 1874. Roberts quickly wrote to Sir Charles Metcalfe MacGregor, a brother officer, asking him to make an intelligence-gathering mission. He stated:

> What we want are routes. Any number of them will be most valuable; and you will assist the Department greatly if you will send me every route you can get hold of. I have got sanction for two additional officers, to be attached to our office for six months, to collate information; and I intend to set them to work at routes beyond our border, so as to have a Central Asia Route-book.[42]

Captain George Napier, son of the Commander-in-Chief, set out a little in advance of MacGregor to make a high-profile reconnaissance of northern Persia. Although Napier was interested in topographical information, his travels were widely interpreted to mean that the British intended to arm or support the Persians and perhaps even the Tekke-Turcoman nomads of the frontier region. Colonel Frederick Wellesley, the British military attaché at St Petersburg, learned that the

Russians were also reacting to Napier's presence. The Russian minister at Teheran, M. de Beger, had just informed his government that the British were intending to make a move 'forward' in northern Persia.[43] MacGregor's mission to Herat confirmed the Russians' suspicions, and they despatched their own men to 'shadow' the British officers.[44] The Foreign Office was anxious lest General Kaufman, the Governor-General of Turkestan, tried to arrest MacGregor and Napier, but Salisbury continued to urge the formation of an intelligence screen which might avoid these high-profile expeditions. He clearly had reliable Asian agents or British consuls in mind when he wrote:

> Sir Douglas Forsyth – the recent envoy to Kashgar – says that his agents report to him that Russia is engaged in purchasing the allegiance of the turbulent chiefs, whose obedience to the Ameer [of Afghanistan] is almost nominal. This may be mere alarmist gossip: but it is very uncomfortable to think that for all we know Russia may have covered the country with intrigue: and that to all suggestions of this kind – I receive them from many quarters – I have not a shred of trustworthy information to oppose. I told you of the anxiety I felt on this subject four months ago. I propose therefore to instruct Northbrook formally to take measures for placing a Resident either at Herat or Candahar. Cabul is too fanatical to be quite safe.[45]

To Northbrook, Salisbury wrote that the failure of Afghanistan to admit a British envoy was more than a rejection of diplomatic protocol: 'It has the effect of placing on our frontier a thick covert, behind which any amount of hostile intrigue and conspiracy may be masked.'[46] Northbrook was only prepared to countenance the idea of a British officer at Herat, fearing that the Afghans would be roused to anti-foreign sentiment, but Salisbury continued to urge that intelligence was required on tribal movements, foreign and domestic intrigues and military matters, and by late 1875 he was beginning to consider that a British resident in Kabul was a necessity.[47] Northbrook still found it difficult to permit the idea of secret agents, believing he could not spend secret service money 'on moral grounds'.[48] He did allow the appointment of a military attaché to Teheran and let Robert Sandeman assist the Khan of Khelat in his negotiations with Kabul, but, when Sir Henry Rawlinson, a member of the advisory group called the India Council, published a book using Intelligence Department data, he resigned on this issue of India's espionage.

However, W. T. Thomson, the Foreign Office minister at Teheran, was concerned that intelligence-gathering by untrained and inexperienced Indian Army officers would lead to inaccuracy or, much worse, encourage different factions in Persia to think they had British support.[49] Matters were not improved when Colonel Frederick Burnaby travelled through Russia to Khiva whilst on furlough. Evading the Russian fort on the border, he discovered the official assurances that the Russians had withdrawn from the ancient city were false. He also revealed that there was a ban on all Indian trade, and an attitude of great hostility towards the British over the central Asian question.[50] He cited the ominous remarks of Colonel M. A. Terentiaev, an anglophobe officer, to the effect that: 'Sick to death, the natives [of India] are now waiting for a physician from the north.'[51]

In India, Captain Collen, the assistant military secretary of the Viceroy's Council, had joined Roberts in promoting the idea of a larger Intelligence Branch.[52] Reconaissances were to be centrally co-ordinated and the Corps of Guides he hoped would become the nucleus of an Intelligence Corps. The Council's response was generally positive but they thought that intelligence work outside of India might require permission from the government in London. Roberts argued that, if the Intelligence Department was going to be really valuable, 'it is most desirable explorers should have access to the countries adjoining India' and he recommended the development of 'extended knowledge of adjacent countries'.[53] Collen added that special training and more awareness of the role of the new Intelligence Branch were needed amongst civil government officers. He suggested: 'The more agents the Intelligence Department have in all parts of India the better, provided these agents are shown how to observe or collect information, and how to record it'.[54] A year later, Collen returned to England and joined the Intelligence Division (as it was now styled) in London. On the basis of his report about the role and functioning of a military intelligence unit, which gained Salisbury's approval, a permanent Intelligence Branch was established in Simla in 1878.

Whilst the role of the Indian Intelligence Branch was being debated, the whole question of secrecy became more pressing. From the beginning, the reports of pundits under the Survey of India had been divided into political and geographical information. Political and military data were passed to the Government of India, whilst the Survey usually printed topographical and geographical information. As far as Tibet was concerned, it was felt that the country was sufficiently far away from Russian influence that there was no harm in publishing the results of the secret missions there in the *Journal of the Royal Geographical Society*. The sensitivity of the North-West Frontier and central Asia was, however, an entirely different matter. The findings of the first missions there were not published until a serious breach of security occurred in 1876. As Derek Waller points out, it was perhaps inevitable that the secrecy interests of the Government of India would clash with the lure of the prestige and accolades that accompanied a discovery, a lecture or a publication for the Royal Geographical Society.[55]

The system for handling secret material had been established after the Great Mutiny in 1858, when the Secret Committee of the East India Company was replaced by the Political and Secret Department. The new department was concerned with frontier matters and the countries that bordered India as much as it was with internal matters of security. But Colonel Walker, the Superintendent of the GTS, decided to publish the reports of the Mullah, Havildar and Pundit in February 1876 without the knowledge or permission of the viceroy. When Northbrook received news that reports had been published he issued a minute reminding all officials that the approval of the Foreign Department was essential for publication of all confidential material.[56] However, what Northbrook had not realised was that the contents of the reports were full and unedited. The Foreign Department noticed that there were disparaging remarks about Naib Mohamed Alum Khan, a prominent Afghan noble, which could be damaging politically if they were to reach Afghanistan.[57] Moreover, the methods used by the 'secret agents' to disguise their surveys were considered 'entirely unsuitable for publication' and there was a strong reiteration that only geographical information should be released. Walker tried to argue that to omit these details would mean that 'four fifths' of the report would be cut, representing the backbone of the whole article.[58] In response, Walker was informed by the viceroy's Foreign Department that, if it could not be edited, the report must be designated 'secret and confidential' which restricted its circulation. In summing up, one official of the Foreign Department recorded that: 'the objection of the Gov[ernmen]t [of India] was not so much to any particular passages as to the publication to the world of the personal adventures and experiences of our spies, for spies they are, though the Survey Dep[artmen]t euphemistically terms them "explorers".'[59] He recommended that, in the interests of the Empire, these 'explorations' must continue.

The Government of India was particularly concerned that, if the names of agents were known, they would become 'bywords in the mouths of persons interested in watching their movements'.[60] The feeling was that a 'veil should be drawn over the proceedings by means of which our intelligence in respect of Trans-Himalayan countries is acquired'. But to the alarm of the viceroy, the *Pall Mall Budget* and the *Daily News* of 7 April 1876 carried information on the Baroghil Pass and the work of the Mullah. A week later an article appeared in *The Times* referring to the Russian geographer Colonel Venouikov who claimed to have received information on the Pamirs and the missions of the Mirza, the Havildar and the Munshi. Despite the express instructions of the Government of India, there had been a security leak 'which may prove of the utmost political embarrassment'.[61] There were only two suspects: Captain Trotter of the Survey of India, who had written the reports of the missions of 1874–6, or Colonel Walker.

It was not difficult to trace the breach of security. Walker had not only visited St Petersburg in 1864, but he had exchanged maps with the Imperial Geographical Society and the Russian War Ministry. He had even sent a Russian geographer a prayer wheel used by one of the pundits to penetrate Tibet.[62] An enquiry revealed that Walker had indeed sent copies of the reports out *after* the instructions from the Government of India had expressly forbidden him to do so. The viceroy called him a 'very disobedient officer', and the Government of India conveyed its 'grave displeasure'. The Political and Secret Department referred to the affair as a 'grave scandal' and stressed that 'the curiosity of the public should certainly be regarded as a secondary consideration to the political considerations of the Empire, if not to the safety of the Agents employed on a difficult and hazardous service'.[63] Salisbury too commented that 'any repetition of a proceeding as insubordinate and detrimental to the interests of the public service shall entail upon the officer responsible for it the severe marks of the displeasure of the Government'.[64] Although Trotter had planned to read the report of Forsyth's mission to the RGS, the programme was changed, no doubt on Walker's advice, to a lecture on a mission to Tibet by another RGS member instead. The alteration was explained with the remark that Captain Trotter had been 'called away to the seat of war in Asia Minor'.[65]

Picturesque imitation: Captain Colin Mackenzie appears here in Afghan noblemen's dress but most Great Game players chose humbler disguises. (*NAM*)

Left: Kufia Naviss: the Mughal tradition of keeping watch in the bazaar. *(AC)*

Right: The unsung hero of the Great Game: the newswriter of central Asia. *(MG)*

Below: Afghan beggar spies in Peshawar; itinerants like these were a useful cover for espionage. *(AC)*

William McNair (*left*) and 'the Syed', Syed Shah, prior to their reconnoitre of Swat. *(AC)*

Agent 'AK': the pundit Kishen Singh. *(AC)*

Nain Singh, alias 'The Chief Pundit'. *(AC)*

Colonel Maksud Ali Alikhanov, Russian Governor of Trans-Caspia in the 1890s. *(ILN)*

Krasnovodsk harbour: part of 'Ring B' in British intelligence operations in 1887. *(ILN)*

The Bolan Pass to Afghanistan: taking guns across the Bolan River. The forward policy to forestall Russian control of Afghanistan led to the Second Afghan War in 1878 and a series of campaigns on the North-West Frontier of India. *(ILN)*

Russian troops at Baku: the build-up of troops at the harbour suggested an impending forward move in Central Asia. *(ILN)*

Left: Perfect cover for spies on the move: 'The Great Highway of Central Asia'. *(ILN)*

Right: Cossacks at the gates of India: a detachment on patrol in Central Asia. *(AC)*

Below right: A *sotnia* of Cossacks in training; but would they have proved as effective in action as the British planners feared? *(ILN)*

Below: One of the great perils of central Asia: Turcoman raiders. *(ILN)*

Above: 'The Physician from the North'. *(ILN)*

Above right: Abdur Rahman, the 'Iron Amir', who forged Afghanistan as a nation state. *(ILN)*

Right: Afridi tribesman keeps watch on the Khyber Pass. *(AC)*

World revolution: Bolshevik troops in Central Asia, 1918. *(AC)*

Quetta: advanced listening post on the Afghan border. *(ILN)*

The missions across the North-West Frontier remained secret until 1915, and, as a result of the 1876 scandal, security was tightened on all reports of trans-frontier expeditions. The circulation of reports, for example, was strictly limited. Nevertheless, Walker did not seem to learn his lesson and was challenged by Alan Hume of the Government of India in a private letter in 1878 about a release of information on the mission of the Mullah.[66] Hume advised Walker to reply to a forthcoming official despatch that it had been an 'oversight'. Without heeding this friendly advice, Walker pointed out that the Government of India's printers had already published details of the expedition with the Mullah's name in it, so he felt justified in releasing the whole report into the public domain. This editing error by the government printers meant Walker escaped censure, but he made few friends with his comments. He was ordered to follow the guidelines of the Government of India in future with 'undeviating strictness'.[67] However, this was not to be the last breach of security the government would face, and next time it would occur at the height of an international crisis that could have led to war.

While the Intelligence Department organised itself and the Government of India struggled to secure its secret reports on the frontier regions, the Russians acquired new territory in central Asia. A rebellion in Khokand against the unpopular Khan Khodayar provided General Kaufman with the excuse he was looking for to occupy the province. He defeated an army of 30,000 tribesmen at Mahram on 3 September 1876 and the War Ministry moved quickly to incorporate the territory with the support of the Asiatic Department.[68] Against a background of growing unrest in Russia, the belligerent right wing was looking for foreign-policy victories to distract the people, and ambitious officers saw their opportunity to advance themselves. Grand Duke Mikhail Nikolaievich, the commander of the Caucasus, suggested an immediate advance on the town of Askhabad as a prelude to the occupation of Trans-Caspia.[69] Concern about Britain's reaction caused the plan to be shelved, but the issue was soon revived when the Persians accepted a Tekke-Turcoman delegation at Teheran, implying that the tribesmen owed their loyalty to Persia. A Russian force seized the village of Kizil Arvat on the Persian border on 19 May 1877 to send a clear warning to both the Persians and the Turcomans. At this point, in mysterious circumstances, the British chargé d'affaires at Teheran obtained a report which detailed Russian plans.[70]

The document was drawn up by D. A. Miliutin, the Russian War Minister, and it began with a condemnation of Britain, the 'Despot of the Seas', and called for an 'advance towards the enemy' that would show 'the patience of Russia is exhausted', and 'that she is ready to retaliate and to stretch her hand towards India'.[71] The new aggressiveness in St Petersburg coincided with a fresh spasm of the 'forward policy' in India under the viceroyalty of Lord Lytton. Already, on appointment, Lytton had drawn up a new agreement with the Khan of Khelat and took Quetta as a forward base from which to strike towards Kandahar if need be. Lytton also considered Salisbury's idea for a British resident at Kabul as essential and he was determined to have one installed as soon as possible. He regarded the Russian move to Kizil Arvat to be clear evidence that the Russians were exhibiting a 'notoriously aggressive character'.[72] He called for the stationing of a British agent with a military escort at Sarakhs or Meshed on the Persian border, with free access to Merv, and he urged the British government to send arms and officers to assist the Turcomans, views that were reinforced by W. T. Thomson, the British minister at Teheran.[73] But in London, Salisbury did not share the aggressive notions of Lytton and feared that Britain might become embroiled in some affair over a worthless bit of desert.[74] This was particularly important given that a war had just broken out between Russia and Turkey in Europe.

Russians at the Gates of India?

In July 1877, three months after the outbreak of war between Russia and Turkey, the British Cabinet decided that a Russian attack on Constantinople would constitute a *casus belli*. When the Russians broke through in the Balkans and reached the outskirts of the city, the Royal Navy moved to within striking distance. The Russians had already considered what action to take in the event of British intervention. Miliutin had suggested diversionary action in central Asia, and at a special council hosted by the tsar, several officers proposed an attack on Herat. Nevertheless, the Governor-General of Turkestan, General Kaufman, believed that sending troops to the Oxus and to Merv, whilst concluding an agreement with Sher Ali of Afghanistan, would be sufficient to persuade the British not to go to war with Russia. Miliutin agreed and aimed to keep Persia neutral, in case the British retaliated through Persia into the Caucasus.[75] He ordered that Kaufman send troops to Merv to win over the local population in case larger formations had to move through the area in the future. In addition, the garrison of Turkestan would be reinforced and Kaufman was to prepare a force of 20,000 men to move on to the Afghan border. The most important measure was to be the despatch of a diplomatic mission to Kabul. Major-General N. G. Stolietov, the former commander of the first Russian garrison on the eastern shore of the Caspian, was given orders by Kaufman to encourage the Afghan amir 'to further resistance to their [the English] attempts to establish themselves in Afghanistan'. Stolietov was authorised to offer gold and was instructed to obtain the free passage of Russian troops through the country.[76]

Stolietov exceeded these instructions, sending despatches to Kaufman that suggested Sher Ali wanted Afghanistan to become a Russian protectorate. He offered military support, including a force of 30,000 men, in a treaty of friendship signed on 21 August 1878.[77] In India, news of the lavish reception given to the Russian envoy was greeted with dismay. Lytton was informed of what the Russian mission was doing by newswriters and he decided to send his own resident to Kabul to counteract the Russian presence. The India Office in London simply did not believe that the Russians had sent a mission at all. Montgomery, an official at the IO, wrote: 'I should like to know through what medium the Cabul news in received. The Intelligence I have seen for the last two years is the utmost rubbish ... manufactured from bazaar gossip ... in Peshawar.'[78] Captain Clarke of the Intelligence Division felt confident that the British government would be able to prevent a Russo-Afghan 'coalition'.[79] But the Asian newswriters were right, prompting Lytton to call ever more urgently for a British resident at Kabul. Lord

Cranbrook, the Secretary of State for India, and the Cabinet, reluctantly concurred, believing that a 'British Resident on the frontier would be of great use, as we get the most unreliable information at present when we get any at all.'[80]

On 7 July 1878, there seemed to be further evidence of Russian aggression and intrigue.[81] The British chargé d'affaires at Teheran reported that, according to an agent at Astarabad, Russian troops had landed on the eastern coast of the Caspian. Two weeks later, intelligence suggested that the Russians were about to seize the Akhal oasis on the Persian border, perhaps prior to a move on Herat. George Napier's conclusion, as he travelled about the region, was that Persian officials were actually preparing to support a Russian advance through Trans-Caspia with supplies.[82] Thomson urged the Persian government to protest against the Russian actions, but it refused, arguing that the British had failed to support Persia in previous years.[83]

Nevertheless, the Persian government did prevent supplies reaching the Russian General Lomakin who was at that moment being recalled by the more cautious government in St Petersburg. As the Russians fell back, the Tekke-Turcoman tribesmen, who had been the first target of Lomakin's advance, were emboldened to raid the Russian fort at Chat. Thomson felt his cajoling in Teheran had compelled the Persians to co-operate, but the news that Lomakin was pulling back did not reach him until September, illustrating how fragile the intelligence network there was. Essentially Thomson was dependent on just two consuls at Resht and Tabriz. The Indian Foreign Department also had representatives at Bushire 'and other places', but they reported to Calcutta, not London.[84] Captain Collen, presiding over the Central Section of the Intelligence Division in London, believed that there would be merit in sending Indian intelligence officers to Persia alongside the Foreign Office appointees like Thomson, in order to 'beef up' intelligence efforts there. He stated that the 'Indian Intelligence Branch will have special agents for the collection of information', but Thomson was concerned lest this channel of information interfered with his own exclusive communication with the Government of India.[85]

In Afghanistan, Sher Ali was advised by Stolietov not to accept any British mission, and Kaufman, believing that a conflict in Afghanistan was imminent, prepared his invasion force – the largest ever gathered in central Asia. However, when Stolietov arrived back in Tashkent on 17 September 1878, Kaufman sent him on to the tsar. By the time he arrived, the situation in Europe had changed. The Congress of Berlin had averted a war in the Balkans and there was no longer any need to risk a clash in central Asia. Kaufman was ordered to call off the invasion. Miliutin saw no reason to provoke Britain into an attack on Afghanistan, but Kaufman protested. He felt that with an Afghan protectorate, 'we could do everything . . . we could dominate England and oblige her to execute the will of the [Russian] sovereign' and he was worried that Russia's prestige in central Asia would suffer if the tsar's forces did not back the Afghans as they had promised.[86] But it was Razgonov, Stolietov's successor, who kept up the pressure in Kabul through the summer of 1878, urging the amir to resist the British, even though he knew there could be no military support.

The Viceroy of India was utterly convinced that Russia intended to take Afghanistan and the reports of Burnaby, Napier and MacGregor enhanced these anxieties. Lytton told the India Council in London that:

> According to modern notions of military science, India could only be defended against an enemy advancing from the west by the British occupation of the whole mountain mass of Afghanistan, that is, by securing the western passes leading into the valley of the Oxus, as well as those debouching on India.[87]

This ambition, fostered by MacGregor and the QMG, Colonel Frederick Roberts, was challenged by Evelyn Baring of the London Intelligence Division. Baring argued that a Russian attack on India was unlikely to succeed and he questioned the ability of Russia, engaged in operations in Turkey, to mount any large-scale campaign in central Asia.[88] But Roberts and the Indian Intelligence Branch vehemently disagreed in their analysis, producing a report of their own which stressed the need for offensive operations beyond the Hindu Kush.[89]

Consequently, when the amir refused to accept a British mission to Kabul, Lytton used the opportunity to issue an ultimatum. The Second Afghan War, which began on 20 November 1878, forced Kabul to accept a British resident, the loss of the Khyber Pass and Kurram valley, and British control of Afghan foreign policy.[90]

Yet no sooner had the new resident, Sir Louis Cavagnari, and his small escort of Guides been installed in a compound in the capital, than disgruntled regiments from Herat arrived demanding arrears of pay.[91] Soon, rioting broke out and the British residency became the focus of the mutineers' bitter attention. The whole party of seventy-nine British and Indian men was wiped out after several hours of resistance. News of the attack on the residency was conveyed by Jelaladin Ghilzai, one of the men in 'Sir Louis Cavagnari's secret service', who had left the residency at noon on the day of the attack and arrived at Alikhel, thirty miles away, the next day.[92] The message was passed on by telegraph to Roberts, now an acting major-general, who acted quickly to mount a relief expedition.

As Roberts marched on to Kabul, Lytton informed him that he was to offer generous payments to informants who could identify the mutineers who attacked the residency.[93] However, further messages confirmed the worst: Cavagnari and his men had been killed and their mutilated remains tossed onto the city's rubbish heap. The viceroy told Roberts to punish the Kabulis and to 'keep the Ameer under careful surveillance'. Lytton then proposed that Afghanistan be broken up into more compliant parts.[94] However, despite the swift recapture of the capital, resistance to the British occupation increased. Roberts was unable to gather all the intelligence he needed on this developing threat, and he later admitted: 'My intelligence was most defective; neither the nature of the country nor the attitude of the people admitted of extended reconnaissances, and I was almost entirely dependent for information on Afghan sources.'[95] For field intelligence Roberts made use of his own sepoys and local chiefs: 'Some of the Afghan soldiers in our ranks aided me to the best of their ability, but, by the *sirdars* [guides], notably Wali Mohammed Khan, I was, either wilfully or from ignorance, grossly misinformed as to the formidable character of the rising.'[96] However, by cross-checking the information he received, Roberts created a more accurate if bleak picture. He noted: 'that there was serious trouble ahead was plain enough when the conflicting reports had been carefully sifted'. After some preliminary fighting for a week outside Kabul, Roberts decided to fall back on the Sherpur cantonment.

Roberts took several precautions, using 'spies who managed to pass to and from the city [of Kabul] under cover of [the] night'.[97] From these sources Roberts learned of the construction of scaling ladders on 22 December 1879, and that the mullahs were appealing to the people to make one gigantic effort to wipe out the infidels. The final piece of intelligence he gathered was the most crucial: he discovered that Mushk-i-Alam, the leader of the resistance, was to light a beacon on the night of the 23rd as a signal to begin the assault on Sherpur. When the attack came, by perhaps as many as 100,000 Afghans according to the British estimate, the Indian troops were able to drive them off with heavy losses in an engagement lasting six hours.[98]

Yet the defeat and potential fragmentation of Afghanistan carried the risk that the Russians would be able to annex outlying lands. The opportune arrival of Abdur Rahman, a claimant to the throne, offered a solution. It was felt that he could preserve the country's territorial integrity and even act as a client ruler. Afghanistan was thus soon handed to Abdur Rahman intact.[99] However, it was never entirely secure. The ruthless absolutism, secret surveillance and sheer cruelty of the 'Iron Amir' fuelled the hatred of his people. Kabulis were so keen on revenge by the time of his death, that they lined his proposed funeral route in order to attack his corpse.[100] However, for the Government of India the alternatives to Abdur Rahman – civil war, anarchy, or partition into small and weak hill states – could only offer opportunities for Russian intervention.[101] Sir Henry Mortimer Durand, the Foreign Secretary of the Government of India, later wrote:

> The Amir is a troublesome and unsatisfactory ally, and there is no doubt he is thoroughly detested throughout the country. His cruelties are horrible, and one feels reluctant to support him in power, especially as he shows the utmost jealousy of ourselves. If it were not for the fact that his fall would throw everything into disorder and give Russia an opening, I should not be sorry to see him driven out of the country.[102]

An Uncertain Future

The consequences of the Second Afghan War certainly interested the Intelligence Division in London. Indeed, its recommendations and conclusions pointed to the potential that, in the future, this body might form the nucleus of a general staff, a far cry from the group that had begun collecting maps and newspaper cuttings. Before the war, it had already been decided where the jurisdiction of the London and Simla intelligence branches lay. Responsibility for Russia, Turkey, Siam, China, Japan, Egypt, and Africa was with London, whilst Arabia, Baluchistan, Afghanistan, India, Kashmir, Nepal, Burma, Malaya, Ceylon and the non-British colonies in the Indian Ocean were in the sphere of Simla. Persia was to be in Simla's hands, too, but the Foreign Office continued to have its own men there and central Asia was to be split into western and southern zones.[103] Moreover, the Intelligence Branch in India was expanded to 'three officers, three draughtsmen, a Persian Moonshee [sic], and a certain number of guides, . . . [a few] draftees and 4 peons'.[104] Crucially the intelligence departments offered advice about the future border of India, and recommended the annexation of Quetta and Pishin on the North-West Frontier to control the approaches to India.[105]

The Intelligence Division in London was nevertheless very critical of native reports which were sent to London. This was mainly because they were sent, unedited and unfiltered, to the India Office, and few of them actually reached the War Office where the military Intelligence Division was based.[106] Finding discrepancies in the maps put together by Napier, and concerned by his Russo-phobic reports, Major-General Archibald Alison, the head of the Intelligence Division, warned Salisbury they were not to be trusted. In a spirit of co-operation developing between the Foreign Office and the Intelligence Division, Salisbury responded to Alison's request for information from the British consul at Tiflis (an FO agent), with a bundle of confidential prints and the promise of a regular exchange of information.[107] In other words, the basis of a Foreign Office intelligence service had been founded too.

The solution to the difficulty of gathering intelligence, which had been the root of the Afghan War, was not to be in the expensive permanent occupation of Afghanistan but in the establishment of a screen of consuls through Asia Minor, Persia and Afghanistan. The Intelligence Branch was to be responsible for setting up posts at Girishk and Bamian, two outposts of Kandahar and Kabul. These would, according to an Intelligence Division officer, provide protection from a Russian *coup de main*:

> . . . strong in her security from surprise . . . England might then afford for the present to look on, calmly awaiting the further development of the events affecting the safety of her Asiatic possessions.[108]

But it was not to last.

Chapter 8

An Intelligence Screen

Border Security, 1880–1885

By the 1880s, as the frontiers of Russia drew across central Asia and closer to India, the rivalry between the two powers reached a new level of intensity. The remaining territory that lay between Afghanistan and the Russian frontier was the subject of diplomatic debate. Whilst the tsar's official line followed its usual assurances that no military operations were planned in the area, A. G. Jomini, the Senior Counsellor of the Ministry of Foreign Affairs, told Lord Dufferin, the British Ambassador in St Petersburg (and later the Viceroy of India), that:

> Although we do not intend to do anything which may be interpreted as a menace to England, you must not deceive yourselves, for the result of our present proceedings [in the region] will be to furnish us with a base of operations against England hereafter, should the British Government by the occupation of Herat threaten our position in Central Asia.[1]

In the following months the fate of Merv, an ancient settlement on the Murghab river, became a source of suspicion between the two powers. For the British, the Murghab was a vital water supply and therefore the axis of advance that, in Russian hands, would furnish an army moving on Herat, and from there, perhaps, to India. For the Russians, British interference with the local tribesmen appeared to be just the beginning of an attempt to win over the peoples of Central Asia against the tsar's dominion.

In the first half of 1879, Ronald Thomson, who had become the British minister at Teheran, had been trying to persuade the shah not to support the Russians as they approached the northern border of Persia. The shah demanded an alliance with Britain, with promises of military support, but Thomson could only insist that as a 'friendly power', Persia should not assist the tsar's forces, and thus help them to annex territory *en route* to Herat and the Afghan border. The Persians, disappointed that the British would not commit themselves to defend Teheran as they had Constantinople, took the view that co-operation with Russia was the only guarantee of survival. But both Thomson and the shah perhaps overestimated Russia's strength.[2] In September, General Lomakin had tried to advance on Geok Tepe, the stronghold of the Tekke-Turcomans that lay close to the Persian frontier, but he was quickly outnumbered by the fast-moving desert nomads and fought to a standstill during a wearying battle in intense heat. Moreover, his transport was decimated by a lack of water; half of the 4,000 camels died, and his exhausted troops were forced to withdraw.[3] Nevertheless, Russian attempts to move closer to Afghanistan prompted the idea in the British Cabinet that, in the interests of India's security, Herat might, in fact, be given to Persia.[4] When the proposal was made to the shah, Britain insisted on closer military and commercial ties, and demanded that the Persians re-present their historic claims to Merv to the Russians. However, just at the moment when the shah approved, a Liberal government came to power in Britain and withdrew the proposal for an alliance.

From an intelligence perspective, the departments in London and Simla were in agreement about the need for a screen of agents or consuls across Persia and Afghanistan. General Alison reminded Salisbury that: 'Early and reliable information with regard to Russian or other military movements near the Northern Border of Persia therefore appears to be the most important, and this information can only be satisfactorily obtained on the spot.'[5] He argued that the monitoring of Russian troop movements was the surest way to gauge Russian plans in central Asia. The Intelligence Division recommended a consul at Astarabad and another at Meshed:

> If we were kept accurately informed about the state of affairs in those regions the government would be at once able to dispel the discreditable state of alarm into which this country is periodically thrown ... If knowledge is power, ignorance is weakness, and this weakness we constantly show by the undignified fear displayed at every report or threat of Russian movements.[6]

It was also suggested that an officer be sent to travel along the northern border, but without attracting the sort of attention that Napier or MacGregor had done in 1874–5. Earl Granville at the Foreign Office disapproved of the idea.[7] The Liberal government at home informed the Government of India that, in its view, the movements of Russia in central Asia simply did not merit anxiety about an invasion of India.[8]

Emboldened by the British government's attempts to return to a policy of 'masterly inactivity', effectively washing its hands of central Asia altogether, the Russian Army drew up new 'forward' plans. Colonel Pozharov, the Chief of Staff of the 21st Infantry Division of the Army of the Caucasus, was typical in his proposals that the occupation of Akhal and Merv should be the first step in an advance against India. Once the Russians were on the Indian border, Pozharov estimated that 200 million Indians would rise up against the British.[9] However, the Chief of the General Staff, Count Heiden, disagreed, believing that railway construction was the chief priority. In fact, Russia was simply too poor to mount any large-scale military operations, and, at home, anarchist terrorism was growing. The Minister of Finance, Adjutant-General Greig, insisted that internal disorder in Russia must be quietened before any large-scale military operations. But Miliutin, the War Minister, deliberately exaggerated the menace posed by Britain to Russian Central Asia and he persuaded the tsar to send General Skobelev against the Turcomans whilst I. A. Zinoviev, the Russian minister in Teheran, launched a diplomatic offensive on the Persians. Under Zinoviev's direction, Russian officers in civilian clothes purchased supplies and camels from Khorassan province in northern Persia.[10] Generous bribes also assisted in keeping Persian officials quiet.

To discover what the Russians were planning, Lieutenant-Colonel Charles Stewart, 5th Punjab Infantry, made a reconnaissance, apparently without official authorisation and in the disguise of an Armenian horse trader, across the Persian border. He reached Mohsinabad, which was to be his listening post, on 25 November 1880, maintaining his cover by purchasing horses and making contacts in the bazaar. Whilst there, he met Edward O'Donovan, a special correspondent of the *Daily News*, but he did not reveal his identity and O'Donovan did not penetrate Stewart's disguise.

In November 1880, Skobelev laid siege to Geok Tepe, and on 24 January 1881, the stronghold of the Turcomans was stormed. Some 6,500 were killed in the fortress and 8,000 'of both sexes' were butchered as they fled across the desert. O'Donovan was able to witness the slaughter and wrote a graphic account of the episode.[11] Stewart, meanwhile, lost no time in relaying the information to the British Legation at Teheran, where he reported personally a few days later. The value of this timely and accurate reporting was certainly recognised by the Foreign Office and Stewart was later posted to Meshed to set up a permanent 'listening post' there.[12]

The defeat of the Tekke-Turcomans was greeted in St Petersburg as a triumph, removing a scourge of civilisation and restoring Russian military prestige. In central Asia, as news spread of the severity of Skobelev's attack, a widespread fear of Russian forces developed. In Persia, the effect was immediate. The shah responded quickly to Zinoviev's demand that a new border agreement be drawn up. Negotiations were to be conducted in secret and would exclude the British. Yet the tsar's announcement on 18 May 1881 that the Tekke lands were now part of the Russian Empire made it obvious to the British that some new border delimitation would take place.[13] Lord Hartington, the patrician Secretary of State for India, suggested that a British officer should accompany any Russo-Persian boundary commission as an observer.[14] The Government of India, already alarmed by a Russian reconnaissance to Herat, went further and urged London to obtain from the Russians a treaty that recognised the independence of Afghanistan. However, initial negotiations proved fruitless as the Russian Foreign Ministry refused to give assurances that it would not make further annexations in central Asia.[15] The Liberals continued with the withdrawal from Afghanistan, still hoping that direct negotiations between London and St Petersburg would be sufficient safeguard against a clash in central Asia between the two powers.

Captain Biddulph and the Gilgit Agency

In 1878, the easternmost part of the planned 'intelligence screen' had been established at Gilgit in the western Himalayas. The officer who manned this post was Captain John Biddulph, an officer of the Bengal Cavalry and ADC to Lord Northbrook. Biddulph was one of the more authoritative and less flamboyant Great Game agents who, with respect for secrecy, did not leave much material on his secret explorations. He travelled extensively in the mountains to the north of

India, taking part in the mission with Sir Douglas Forsyth to Sinkiang across the Karakoram in 1873, before striking out from Kashgar into the Taklamakan Desert – the first European to do so since Marco Polo and Benedict de Goes. In 1874, he explored the southern Pamirs and the Wakhan Valley, and scouted some of the passes across the Hindu Kush. In the next four years, he continued to travel the mountains and he was the first European into both Hunza and Chitral, which he recognised as strategically significant.[16] Biddulph also remarked how the Hindu Kush valleys were more difficult to reach from the south because they tended to drain through narrow defiles. The central sections had wider valley floors that could support agriculture and hence their remote populations. From the north, the mountain states were accessible only via high-altitude passes, or so it was thought.

The Hayward explorations of 1870 and Forsyth's mission had uncovered disturbing information that some of the passes across the Hindu Kush were easily crossed by parties of men or horses, if not by artillery. The Ishkoman and Killik passes were thought especially vulnerable if unguarded. Their conclusions about the Pamirs were that even field guns could traverse the wide valleys and reach the Wakhan without difficulty, provided they travelled at the right time of the year. The result was that the northern flank of India, apparently secure, was in fact open and exposed. News of the fall of Khokand in 1876, and the demise of Britain's erstwhile 'ally' Yakub Beg in Kashgaria in 1877, seemed to represent a new threat to India.

The solution was to send Biddulph to see if it was possible to extend Kashmiri authority up to the Hindu Kush and persuade local troops to man the passes. In addition, he was ordered to find any other strategic passes that had been previously missed. As he made his way north, he received an invitation to meet Ghazan Khan, the Mir of Hunza. Suspecting treachery, Biddulph insisted that the mir's son be submitted as a hostage at Gilgit.[17] It took six patient weeks of negotiations to persuade the mir to agree, but he relented. So, at last, Biddulph, with an escort of six sepoys, scaled the 'path' (at places, little more than a perilous ledge in a river gorge) into Hunza. On the way he passed two important forts at Chaprot and Chalt, held by the neighbours and rivals of the Hunza tribesmen. Biddulph noted that, in the hands of the Kashmiris, this was just the sort of location to control potential invasion routes.

Ghazan Khan was a ruler with a grossly inflated sense of his own importance, but he soon saw through Biddulph's cover of 'sportsman' on a 'hunting expedition' and demanded concessions from the British. He wanted the fort at Chalt and he held Biddulph as a prisoner, but the lone officer refused to give in and after four days he was released to make his way back to Gilgit. Biddulph's report recommended that Hunza and the forts to the south should be annexed, and much was later made of the nominal 'tribute' that the hill state paid to Kashmir, as well as raiding and slavery, to justify military action. However, there can be little doubt that the real reason for the subsequent operations was to secure the passes of the Hindu Kush.

Yet this was in the future, because Biddulph had yet to complete the reconnaissance of the passes that he had begun two years before. As he explored, it was clear that glaciers could advance and recede across the high passes and valleys, effectively blocking them, but, from a military point of view, he calculated that it was relatively easy for small groups of men to hold off British or Indian forces from the south. What was needed was reliable men to hold the passes, and, after a number of confrontations with tribesmen from Yasin, it was clear that the strategic routes into India from the north were in the hands of the wrong men. The solution, in the long term, was to advance the Kashmiri cause up to the watershed of the Hindu Kush, even though few in India had much faith in the prowess of Kashmiri troops. In the short term, Biddulph believed that the establishment of a permanent agency at Gilgit, as a conduit for intelligence and a channel for communication with the Dard tribesmen of Gilgit (an idea first put forward by Forsyth), was the best way to keep the passes under observation. Thus, in 1878, the Gilgit Agency was established.

Biddulph's chances of winning over the Dards, and, eventually, the Chitralis, to accept Kashmiri authority were pretty slim. First, the tribesmen were fiercely independent and resented all interference from outside. Second, as Muslims, they had no love for the Hindus of Kashmir, as the conflict in that state since 1947 has amply illustrated. Biddulph's position was made more difficult by the problem of communications. There was no telegraph and he was dependent on dak runners being able to traverse the 200-odd miles of mountain valleys to Srinagar. Nevertheless, he recruited a network of agents whose work extended through the mountains and into Russian Central Asia. His reports were submitted, as usual, to the Foreign Department of the Government of India and known as the Gilgit Diary. However, the unexpected obstacle was the Kashmiri government. The Maharaja of Kashmir had accepted four field guns, rifles and ammunition as a concession in return for permission to set up the agency, but the Kashmiri governor of Gilgit was actively plotting to have Biddulph removed. Worse, the viceroy (at that time Lord Lytton) discovered in 1879 that the maharaja was in secret communication with the Russians and the Afghans.[18] Yet the value of the agency was clear: the despatch of one of Kaufman's three columns in May 1878 against India during the Eastern Crisis was aimed against Gilgit and Hunza. It had foundered in the snows of the Alai plateau before it reached the Hindu Kush and was recalled.

In late 1878, Biddulph reached Chitral in order to negotiate the suzerainty of Kashmir, in accordance with the original plan to bring all the northern hill states under British influence. After gifts had been handed over, the mehtar, Aman-ul-Mulk, was presented with Biddulph's terms. But the mehtar was after a better deal, and he insisted on a direct agreement with Britain. Unable to offer any concessions, Biddulph withdrew to Gilgit only to learn that Aman-ul-Mulk had reopened negotiations with Kabul in the hope of subsidies from there. Biddulph recommended that Chitral could not be incorporated into a scheme of British–Kashmiri defence. Meanwhile the ruler of Yasin, Pahlwan, who was eager to distance himself from Kashmir and Chitral, sought an alliance with the British through Biddulph. The British officer seized upon the chance to have the passes closed using these allies, with British troops stationed at Gilgit as reinforcements. When Biddulph returned to India, leaving another officer, Dr Scully, in charge, he learned of Kashmir's secret negotiations with Kabul. It had therefore been decided in Simla that Kashmir too was not to be trusted with control of any of the northern states.

With this news, Biddulph returned to Gilgit in June 1880 to begin negotiations once again with the Dards and to maintain his watch on the northern approaches. However, soon after his arrival, rumours of an alliance between Hunza, Nagar and Yasin, with possible Chilasis sympathy, against the Kashmiri Dogras at Chaprot, Chalt and Gilgit, were picked up. It seemed that all the hill states had decided to confront the Kashmiris and wrest control of the area by seizing the strategic forts. On 27 October 1880, the anticipated attack began. Chaprot was invested, and Biddulph was forced to take shelter with a skeleton force of Kashmiris in Gilgit. With the first snows closing the passes, Biddulph's position seemed hopeless, but an opportune advance by the Chitralis against Yasin caused the Dard confederates to pull back. It is unclear if Aman-ul-Mulk was acting in his own interests, namely to recover Yasin, or whether he was anxious to assist the British in the hope of greater reward. The whole affair certainly gave the Maharaja of Kashmir the excuse to demand an end to meddling by a British agent. When Biddulph recommended a punitive expedition to crush the Dards, Lord Ripon, the new Liberal Viceroy of India, refused and ordered Biddulph to return to India. Eager to restore the close border policy, Ripon believed that the disturbance in the northern states exemplified precisely the reason to avoid interference there. He was anxious to avoid unnecessary expense, and to hold India by evidence of good government. He therefore promptly closed the Gilgit Agency in 1881.

William McNair and Syed Shah

Against this background of official disapproval for any missions, William Watts McNair and a pundit surveyor known as 'The Syed' (Syed Shah) made a journey into the northern states apparently for private purposes. The two had worked together during survey operations at the end of the Second Afghan War, and it was perhaps not unusual for them to be granted a years' leave. However, McNair, whilst denying any official connection, later confessed to having joined Syed Shah for the journey to the north. This suggests, perhaps, that 'The Syed' was indeed on an official clandestine survey. McNair never explained his reasons for making the journey, but it was standard practice for native agents not to travel with Europeans because of the risk of being compromised (the exception being Forsyth's more overt mission in 1873).

McNair disguised himself as a Pathan doctor called 'Mir Mohammed', and, using 'a weak solution of caustic and walnut juice' to stain his hands and head, he set out from Nowshera in April 1883 with the Syed. Concealing two compasses, McNair also cannibalised the inside of an Islamic text on medicine in order to conceal other instruments and used the cover that he was a recent Muslim convert. The Syed and McNair then set out on the most direct route to Chitral, surveying the routes and passes whilst pretending to collect herbs and medicinal roots. At times McNair came close to being discovered, but his skills at impersonating the local people, and perhaps the fact he was accompanied by the 'real thing', seem to have been highly effective.[19] However, rumours began to circulate, and although the Khan of Dir denied they were British officers in disguise, news of the approach of spies circulated as far as Chitral and Kafiristan. Nevertheless, McNair pressed on over the Lowari Pass, and, hurrying into Chitral, he decided to let honesty be his best protection. He let Aman-ul-Mulk know his and the Syed's true identity.

It was a wise policy, but the mehtar insisted that the Syed and McNair had to take with them a Chitrali guide if they intended to make any journeys beyond his kingdom. They accepted the conditions and marched on to Kafiristan, noting along the way that the Dorah Pass, which they did not actually cross, was 'the easiest of all the routes leading north from Chitral'.[20] Confirming previous pundit reports, it revealed yet another breach in the ramparts of the Hindu Kush. Leaving the Syed and the Chitralis behind, McNair then followed a Kafir guide into the heart of Kafiristan, but he stayed only a couple of days. Recalled by the Government of India, first to Chitral, and then back to India itself, he returned to an official censure. Although he was able to present his findings to the Royal Geographical Society, where he received the accolade of the Murchison Award, the Government of India ensured he took no further part in exploration in the north. However, he did submit a confidential report to the Government of India.[21] Indeed, he returned to official employment in the subcontinent, and, like so many hard-working servants of Empire, he died in 1889 from a fever whilst surveying in Baluchistan.

What McNair, the Syed and Biddulph had achieved, in terms of geographical information, looked pretty small. Moreover, the suspicions of the hill state rulers had been aroused, perhaps contributing to the destabilisation of the region. But these men had demonstrated that, despite all the surveys so far completed, the complex of mountains, valleys and passes to the north of India was still relatively unknown. In the minds of the Indian Army's commanders, what made the need for further exploration so pressing was the steady advance of Russian troops and their surveyors across Trans-Caspia, Turkestan, and the Pamirs towards the sub-continent. Given the attitude of the Liberal government in London, and the mild-mannered viceroy, Lord Ripon, in Calcutta, the army's commanders felt that opportunities were slipping away. Lord Lytton captured the mood by arguing that, if the Liberals were to create two new departments of the Foreign Office and War Office devoted to the 'careful preparation of measures to be taken only when it's too late', they would be the most active in Downing Street.[22] Nevertheless, Gladstone's administration put its faith in a clear and unambiguous understanding with St Petersburg, believing that it was only the Russian generals who talked of aggression against India.[23]

The Fall of Merv and the Penjdeh Incident

In February 1882, Lieutenant Alikhanov, a Daghestani in Russian service, accompanied by another officer, joined a caravan of Turcomans *en route* to Merv. In disguise, the two men entered the oasis at night and made contact with a group of tribesmen sympathetic to Russia. Using the pretence of opening trade negotiations, they carried out a survey of the defences and continued to play on the factional divisions of the elders in the settlement. It took two years to win over sufficient numbers of Merv tribesmen, and the positioning of a substantial force just eighty miles to the west, before Alikhanov felt confident enough to ride into the oasis with an armed escort and demand submission to the tsar. The immediate cause had been a raid by Turcomans in October 1883, although it seems this had little to do with the Mervites.[24] Russian troops quickly took possession of a fortress and Alikhanov announced that the tribesmen had taken an oath of allegiance, 'conscious of their inability to govern themselves'.[25] Although the British government was informed through its ambassador at St Petersburg, Asian agents, probably working under Stewart, had supplied the details of the Russian intrigues and reported that they followed a premeditated plan.[26] Stewart and Thomson were also aware of Russian survey activities.[27] Stewart revealed that the local Russian troops at Merv had told the tribesmen: 'All they wanted was the road to India'.[28]

The British government was therefore not surprised by the announcement. The Duke of Argyll, the former Secretary of State for India (1868–74), thought the Russian move inevitable, perhaps even justified, because of the Turcoman habit of raiding caravans, and most of the Cabinet agreed with him.[29] Reactions by the Conservatives and the Anglo-Indians were not so restrained. Edward Stanhope remarked in the House of Commons that it was the Liberal insistence on the evacuation of Kandahar in 1880 that had emboldened Russia. Salisbury believed that the loss of Merv was due to inactivity and warned that 'the prestige of the power coming against you is greater than your own'. With a hint at the unrest this would cause in India, he added: 'it will undermine your sway, it will dissolve the loyalty and patriotism of those you rule', and suggested that the loss of this settlement could not be viewed as 'not on the route to anywhere in particular – the event must be looked on in a graver light than that'.[30] The Liberal government was even more incensed by the publication of *The Defence of India: A strategical study* by Sir Charles Metcalfe MacGregor, Quartermaster-General of the Indian Army 1881–5, who was closely connected to the Intelligence Branch at Simla. Although it was confidential (and dependent on Intelligence Branch sources), it was leaked to the press and eventually a copy made its way to Russia where it was regarded as official British policy.[31] MacGregor argued that settlement of the 'Central Asian Question' would only be achieved when Russia was 'driven out of the Caucasus and Turkestan'.[32] The report was disowned and MacGregor forced to issue disclaimers that it was his own personal view. Nevertheless, as a precaution, Ripon was ordered by the British government to recommence work on the Quetta railway, a project that would enable British and Indian troops to race for Kandahar, but which had been abandoned due to the expense in 1881.[33]

However, if the Liberals thought they could solve the matter in the capitals, events on the frontier took on their own momentum. Newswriters in Afghanistan reported that Abdur Rahman was unconvinced by the platitudes of the British government, or by the subsidy of 12 lakhs of rupees he had been given in June 1883, to ignore the Russian threat. Without consulting the Government of India he sent troops across the Oxus into Roshan, a province of the Pamirs. When the Russians protested that this brought the Afghans into territory owned by their ally Bokhara, Sir Edward Thornton in St Petersburg demanded to know why a force of 500 Russian troops had just crossed into Wakhan, a recognised 'Afghan' province.

Alexander Vlangaly, Assistant of the Russian Foreign Ministry, argued that the party in Wakhan were merely 'Russian gentlemen' touring for pleasure with an armed escort. It was unconvincing.

On 6 June 1883, Abdur Rahman had accepted an Asian agent of the Government of India, Afzal Khan, as an intermediary, hoping that the British would assist him against the 'aggressive, grabbing and pushy' Russians.[34] Ripon clung to a policy of 'inactivity', trying to dissuade the amir from visiting India to explain his concerns.[35] He opposed all the defence schemes of the British generals and wanted to avoid installing a British resident in Herat for fear of alienating the Afghans.[36] Abdur Rahman therefore decided to act unilaterally. He pushed troops up the Murghab to Penjdeh in August 1884 and by October he took over Shignan on the Oxus. Sir Henry Rawlinson then issued two memoranda which showed that the old frontier line on the Oxus, established by the treaty of 1873, was inaccurate and that Afghan claims did, indeed, cross the Oxus to the north.[37] Thornton then passed on a map, declared unofficial but clearly drawn up by the Imperial Russian cartographers, that showed the Russian border to be far further south than ever envisaged in 1873.[38] Indeed, the Russian charts seemed to indicate they intended to extend their authority to the mountains overlooking Herat – now widely regarded as the 'key to India'. The only solution was to establish precisely the border between Afghan and Russian claims with a boundary commission.

Even as the proposal was being discussed – and the Russian Foreign Ministry debated every detail of the commission to delay its despatch – Russian troops were making their way southwards down the Murghab to Penjdeh, and to Sarakhs on the Persian border.[39] Asian agents working for the Kabul newswriter reported that attempts were being made to persuade the Saryk Turcoman tribesmen at Penjdeh to accept the authority of Merv, which was increasingly under Russian influence.[40] The Afghan amir stated that Russian spies were being sent amongst his tribesmen. This was particularly important because it appeared the loyalties of the Saryks were in doubt. A merchant called Azizuddin, who had travelled extensively in the area, helpfully reported to Mr Lambert, the Deputy Commissioner of Police in Calcutta, details of the attitudes of the various Saryk clans around Penjdeh.[41] Stewart investigated and discovered that the Russians were indeed scouting the Murghab and the surrounding area: a Russian had been challenged by the Afghan picquets and responded by claiming he had 'lost his way'.[42]

The Afghan Boundary Commission was a grand affair, designed to impress as much as to settle a border line.[43] But it was also an opportunity to carry out surveys and extend the intelligence picture of central Asia. The Intelligence Branch sent Captains Barrow, Yate, Maitland, Peacocke, Holdich, and the Hon. M. G. Talbot to work under the command of Major-General Sir Peter Lumsden and his second-in-command, Colonel West Ridgeway. Whilst the commission members were forced to wait until their Russian counterparts arrived, they set to work mapping the area. However, to the alarm of the Liberal government, Lumsden sent back only sketchy despatches (which, given the distance from the nearest telegraph in Persia, was entirely understandable) and did not reveal what advice he was offering to the Afghan garrison at Penjdeh.[44] Ridgeway, with the political officer, W. R. H. Merk, was busy establishing an intelligence network amongst the locals.[45] Impatient with Lumsden's unwillingness to support the Afghans openly, Ridgeway ordered a consignment of 8,000 Snider rifles for the defence of Herat.[46]

In fact, the Indian Army officers on the commission were clearly pursuing a different agenda from that envisaged by the Foreign Office in London. On the ground, the feeling was that the Afghan claim was legitimate and had to be upheld if Herat was not to be compromised and thus the way to India left open. The officers, a third of whom also had the status of special correspondents with British and Indian newspapers, were 'sowing' the press with information before it was being despatched to the British government. Condie Stephen, the Foreign Office representative at Teheran, reported that the Indian Government had given permission for the officers to represent newspapers, but even the clerk of Calcutta's confidential archive was a 'special correspondent'.[47]

Apart from the risk to security this proliferation of sources threatened, the sheer volume of material flowing in seemed to engulf the tiny Intelligence Branch at Simla. Unable to filter the information fast enough, the Government of India simply passed the whole lot on to the India Office or the Foreign Office, or both, in London. There was simply no time to check and verify the intelligence, and yet it was all typed up and sent as a monthly despatch.[48] By the time it arrived in Britain, and with events moving so quickly in central Asia, it was often out of date. On 5 January 1885, for example, a Foreign Office official wrote on the bundle, 'These are very old'.[49] Some reports were marked with an 'X', which suggests they were not read. Other reports were dismissed as 'Gossip from Kandahar' or with the line 'Not much of interest – see one or two passages'. From a situation in the 1830s where the British in India had no idea of what was going on in central Asia and Afghanistan, it was now a case of simply knowing too much.

The task of processing data from India and from Teheran for the Foreign Office fell to the new head of the Intelligence Division in London, Colonel Aylmer Cameron.[50] He was eager to obtain an assessment of Russia's likely moves from the Intelligence Branch at Simla, but, other than the opinions of Sir Charles MacGregor or General Roberts, who clung to the idea of a race to Herat regardless of Afghan sensibilities, he could get no report.[51] However, the Indian Branch was able to provide some information on Russian strengths in the region. Initial reports about the numbers crossing the Caspian from the Caucasus were supplied by Sardar Muhammed Afzal Khan and corroborated by the British military attaché at St Petersburg.[52] Nevertheless, not everyone was impressed with the intelligence *assessment* coming from Simla. Colonel Cameron and Major L. A. Gregson took the view that MacGregor's ideas for an offensive in central Asia by the Indian Army were unsound, challenging, in particular, the indifference to logistical and transport problems and the difficulties of operating without telegraph.[53] Roberts disagreed, although he later modified his views about going on the offensive in central Asia in favour of a defensive posture along the line of the Hindu Kush, the so-called 'scientific frontier'.[54]

In March 1885, the Russians drove in the Afghan picquets and routed their garrison in the 'Penjdeh Incident'.[55] It was a grave development. The news was immediately relayed by the Boundary Commission to Teheran and on to London and India. A direct attack on Afghanistan, an ally of Britain, confirmed the fears of the Anglo-Indian community that the tsar's armies were intent on gaining a foothold with which to harass the subcontinent. Few believed that Russia would, or even could, actually invade India; it was rather that the near approach of Russian forces would so unsettle the Indian people as to put British rule in jeopardy. In fact, Indians rallied to the Raj in its hour of need.[56] In Britain too, the Penjdeh Incident was widely regarded as a challenge to the British Empire. Gladstone's government struggled to settle the issue, and for a brief period even the Grand Old Man himself, stung by accusations that he had recently let Gordon die in the Sudan and faced with Russian aggression, considered military action.[57] The militia were called out and plans for naval operations drawn up. Some 18,000 breech-loaders were sent to India along with railway building materials and extra troops. Plans were created for the strengthening of the port defences of India against Russian cruisers. Port Hamilton was occupied off the coast of Korea in readiness for an attack on Vladivostok. Ships were refitted for war, new ship orders made out and recruits for the army were given a short emergency course of instruction. In short, these were the largest war preparations since the Crimea, and, given the deployment of an army already in the Sudan, the armed forces were operating at full stretch. Russian preparations were no less intensive, if less publicised.[58]

Essentially, three sources of information on the Russian mobilisation were available: the embassy in St Petersburg, the glimpses offered by the Russian boulevard press, and the intelligence agents inside Central Asia. In March and April, Asian agents operating out of Meshed (and with the Boundary Commission which had withdrawn into northern Persia) were able to report that the Russians had augmented their strength in Turkestan by 10,000 men.[59] This brought the total to 48,000 infantry, 12,000 cavalry and 145 guns of which some 30,000 could be concentrated at Sarakhs, north of Herat, by the end of March. Troop movements to Kerki on the Oxus were also monitored by agents, including the 'newswriter at Samarkand'.[60] A further 25,000 troops were apparently sent from St Petersburg, the news being picked up by Syed Abdullah, the Afghan agent in Bokhara, and Haji Muhammed Azim in Samarkand.[61] Troops also moved to the northern border of Persia, whilst new steamers appeared on the Caspian and the lower Oxus. Russian railways were being laid at a rate of one mile a day. All this, and information on improvements to the supply of water and forage, were gathered by Asian agents operating inside Russian Central Asia. But this was not all. British newspapers like *The Observer* and *The Times* reported that Russian agents were trying to purchase ships in the United States, and that two Russian warships were heading towards the Suez Canal and Gibraltar.[62] A British captain on a steamer at Batoum on the Black Sea also reported on Russian preparations there.[63]

Yet, as before, there was some difficulty in sifting fact from rumour. This explains the frustration of the Foreign Office with the sheer volume of unedited material, peppered as it was with unfamiliar names and locations. By contrast, faced with a Liberal government at home that seemed reluctant to stand up to

Russia and hold strategic positions, the Indian Intelligence Branch tended to promote a more 'active' defence and devoted much time to drawing up papers or plans with which to persuade the politicians. There was a general feeling that those back in Britain simply did not understand the nature of the threat to India: they dismissed too readily the potential for unrest in the subcontinent and did not realise the importance of places like Herat or Kandahar. Whatever the interpretations, the Foreign Department of the Government of India continued to act as the repository for information flowing in from Afghanistan, Meshed, the Boundary Commission and the government of the Punjab. The Political and Secret Department processed some of the information, but it was impossible to verify everything. Nevertheless, it was clear that by the 1880s, British intelligence had come a long way and the aspiration to create a 'screen' across central Asia was almost realised.[64]

Lockhart's Mission to the Northern States

With Russian troops apparently poised to attack Herat, it was still unclear if the Russian action at Penjdeh was a localised incident, or part of a larger drive to the south. The Boundary Commission kept watch from the ramparts of the Paropamisus and Hindu Kush mountains, and consuls maintained a watch on the ports of the Caspian and Black Seas, but India's northern approaches were unobserved. Colonel William Lockhart the DQMG of the Intelligence Branch therefore set out from Srinagar in June 1885, aiming to answer several questions, specifically: was it possible for the British to use the route from Peshawar to Chitral to hold the mountain passes; could the pagan peoples of Kafiristan be persuaded to assist in the defence of India; was the Dorah Pass a viable route for Russian troops; and were there other passes like this as yet undiscovered?[65] Moreover, it was still unclear whether Aman ul Mulk, the Mehtar of Chitral, could be persuaded to join the British in order to protect the Dorah Pass. Colonel Biddulph had found him hostile, but the mehtar was aware of Russian reconnaissances to the Pamirs and he had reported the presence of Russian 'explorers' in Shignan and Wakhan. Aman ul Mulk claimed that the Russians had made an offer for the Ludkho Valley, which leads southwards from the Dorah Pass, but the mehtar had contacted Ripon, and offered to kill them, capture them, or send them to him.[66] In the past, the Government of India had found the mehtar too untrustworthy to deal with. But after the Penjdeh Incident, the aim was to secure Chitral as a friend and ally at all costs, such was the importance attached to the Dorah Pass. The mission was also designated secret, partly to avoid the suspicions of the Amir of Afghanistan, but also to avoid press coverage, and, therefore, a Russian response.[67]

Lockhart arrived in Chitral in July 1885, along with Dr Giles, the expedition's medical officer, Colonel Woodthorpe, the mission's surveyor, and Captain Barrow, the intelligence officer.[68] The officers were supported by five Asian surveyors, a company of Sikhs, and 300 mules. Amongst the baggage were gifts of beads and breech-loaders for the mehtar. Once again the aim was to impress the Chitralis with the wealth and prestige of the Raj, and to convince the tribesmen of the material benefits of alliance with India. Yet logistics were to prove a significant problem for the expedition, as mules were really unsuited to the terrain that the mission would have to cross. Lockhart lost a mule carrying the expedition's 4,000 rupees of silver over a precipice on the first day, and this must have seemed especially ironic, as he had just exchanged 240 mules for 200 porters at Gilgit because of the difficulties experienced on the approach march.

The first surveys were carried out by Woodthorpe and Barrow, while Lockhart continued up to the Shandur Pass which marked the border between the hill states of Chitral and Hunza. Woodthorpe confirmed Biddulph's observations that the Baroghil Pass at the watershed of the Hindu Kush range was easily crossed. But from the pass, it would be necessary for an invader to cross the Darkot Pass, and the Darkot Glacier, into Yasin or, alternatively, descend via other glaciers into Chitral. When Woodthorpe tried both these routes, his party was severely frostbitten and delayed, even in the mild month of August. The conclusion they reached was that no Russian invasion force of the size envisaged by MacGregor could use this route, but infiltration by a small Russian party was still a possible threat. By contrast, the Shandur Pass presented no such difficulties to Lockhart's party, and he referred to it as a 'plateau'. It was a serious obstacle in winter as Indian troops found out in 1895 when the pass was choked with deep drifts. Nevertheless, in summer, this was a route that could connect Gilgit and Chitral, and ultimately provide the British with the means to dominate both states. The reconnaissance complete and reunited with Woodthorpe on 2 September 1885, Lockhart covered the sixty miles to Chitral in just eight days and concluded a detailed survey of the valley.

The mehtar greeted the mission with great ceremony, and the mission responded with the grandeur of a durbar. Tents formed an avenue, which was lined with Sikhs in scarlet tunics. Officers in their dress uniforms stood at one end, flags fluttering overhead. It was all designed to impress the 'Oriental mind' – the mission was making its presence felt in order to reassure the mehtar that the British meant to support him against the 'Power in the North'. Lockhart's aim was to persuade the Chitralis to hold the passes and defiles against any Russian party that might make its way across the Hindu Kush and he sincerely believed he had achieved this. The mehtar expressed his desire to 'pass on his territories to his heirs intact' which implied agreement. Yet Aman ul Mulk also had an eye for business, and he knew what the British wanted. To hold passes against the Russians would mean new responsibilities, and, therefore, an increase of his existing 16,500-rupee subsidy from Kashmir. Lockhart's gifts had already been presented (an assortment of Snider rifles, revolvers, tools, and trinkets) but it was not in his power to make offers of subsidies. Nevertheless, Lockhart believed that, as a result of the durbar, Chitral was effectively under British control. However, even when the subsidy question was resolved, the mehtar still regarded himself as fully independent.[69]

Lockhart was keen to exploit the opportunity to travel within Chitral and wrote optimistically, 'It would be great to get hold of Dir as we now have hold of Chitral.'[70] Dir was the most direct route to Chitral from the south, the one recommended by McNair, and, if the British controlled it, it would mean they had, but for a small section of upper Malakand, complete access to the passes of the

Hindu Kush in the north. In the event, Lockhart did not get as far as Dir, only reaching Drosh on the northern side of the Lowari Pass, and he did not get 'control' of either.

During the winter, Lockhart put together a defence plan based on the possession of the hill states but which excluded Kashmir.[71] This may have been in deference to the recommendations of George Hayward and John Biddulph that Kashmiris were not to be trusted. It may also have been the result of a rumour that he had been pursued by Mulk Aman, an assassin who had been sponsored by the Kashmiri governor in Gilgit. Alternatively, it may just have been that Lockhart realised that Kashmir exercised no real control over Chitral and Yasin. In fact, Kashmir was no longer necessary in the defence of India, except perhaps for the supervision of the Kilik and Shimshal passes. A separate deal had been concluded with Chitral that actually bordered the strategic passes. As for Gilgit, Lockhart declared it virtually annexed, even though the agency had not yet been reconstituted. He wanted nineteen British officers to command a mountain battery and twelve companies of infantry there, and a nominated agent was to have wide powers of administration and revenue collection. His report concluded that fears about the insecurity of the Baroghil Pass were exaggerated, but the Pamirs might still prove a viable route for a Russian force which was supporting a major thrust towards the Khyber and Bolan Passes. He believed that, in winter, the Pamirs could not be crossed, and, in summer, the rivers denied any easy passage, so it was only in spring or autumn that the mountains could be traversed by small parties intending to infiltrate and disrupt lines of communication.[72]

The Frontier: Porous or Sealed?

The missions of the early 1880s, by Colonel Stewart, Captain Biddulph, Syed Shah and Colonel Lockhart were part of a broad attempt to ascertain Russian intentions and movements, and the detailed topography of their likely routes through central Asia. Their work was given an added urgency by the aggressive designs of the Russian Army, supported, as it was, by the Asiatic Department of the Foreign Ministry. Urgency meant less time to train and deploy Asian personnel, but they still assisted. At Penjdeh in 1885, the clash between the Russians and the Afghans marked a turning point. For several months it appeared that a war might break out between Britain and Russia. The crucial intelligence needed at that time was: were the Russians moving on to Herat, and therefore towards India? This thoroughly tested the existing intelligence arrangements. What the British found was that it was difficult to be certain of exactly how many Russian troops were massing in Central Asia through the existing networks of agents and newswriters from St Petersburg to the Pamirs. It was clear that what was needed was a more comprehensive intelligence screen and more efficient procedures for the filtering of information. Fresh deployments were therefore made, and a new, more sophisticated, system of intelligence-gathering was now established.

Chapter 9

On Her Majesty's Secret Service

Espionage on the Frontiers, 1885–1886

Ney Elias at Kashgar and in the Pamirs

Whilst wintering in Gilgit, Lockhart had received reports of an English explorer arriving in Shignan having crossed the Oxus from the north with an Indian medical assistant, a Chinese interpreter, a munshi and a cook. No British exploration had been carried out there since the expedition of Colonel Biddulph and Colonel T. E. Gordon in 1874, but now the mysterious British explorer and committed Great Game player, Mr Ney Elias, had been across the Pamirs at the height of the central Asian winter. He had covered 2,000 miles, crossed five mountain systems, had confirmed the source of the Oxus, and had explored most of Badakshan.[1] He possessed incredible endurance, and seemed to prefer the austerity of lone exploration to the complex protocols of Victorian society. In 1868, he had surveyed the mouth of the Yellow River. Four years later, and at his own expense, he made a solo crossing of the Gobi Desert and Mongolia, part of a journey from Beijing to Moscow for which he earned the Royal Geographical Society's gold medal. As a former president of the RGS, Sir Henry Rawlinson was impressed with Elias's achievements and he recommended that Elias should become a government agent, although he did not wish to see him suffer the fate of George Hayward. As a result, in 1875 Elias was a member of a mission that crossed Burma into China, and in 1876 he became the British representative in Leh. Whilst there, he made two journeys across the Himalayas to Sinkiang province, although Tibet had really been his goal. In short, Elias was one of Britain's pre-eminent explorers.

In 1885, faced with an urgent need for intelligence on Russian movements after the Penjdeh incident, Henry Mortimer Durand of the Foreign Department of the Government of India envisaged Elias moving through Kashgar and the Pamirs, eventually linking up with the Afghan Boundary Commission. Elias was a trusted agent and an observant traveller. Nevertheless, Durand did not always get on with him, claiming, somewhat cryptically, 'he would not learn the work of the Department'. Elias's biographer, Gerald Morgan, described him as a 'man of contradictions'.[2] He was immensely self-critical and his high expectations made him as critical of others. Colleagues found him difficult to work with. This attitude could be explained by his frequent illnesses, including dyspepsia and anaemia, as well as the usual scourge of travellers who are invariably exposed to contaminated water: amoebic dysentery. Yet his records reveal little of his physical state, regardless of the extreme conditions.[3] He believed only that, given the scarcity of supplies and resources, exploration parties had to be small and fast, a factor which suited his restless energy.[4]

Above all, Elias had an expert's grasp of the problems of defending India and he was a firm believer in the forward policy. Thus, at the height of the Penjdeh crisis, Elias returned from sick leave to go to Kashgar and the Pamirs. The authorities would have preferred another large and impressive party, but concurred with Elias's view that only a small expedition could be supplied in such a remote and inhospitable region. Chinese sensitivity about the Pamirs might also create difficulties, and it would be easier to block the passage of a large group. Elias therefore left from the Dovedale Hotel in Simla on 29 May 1885, taking 6,000 rupees for the journey's expenses, and a further 2,000 rupees for 'secret service' work: an anticipation of his use of locals as observers and spies. In his private journal, the 6,000 rupees are meticulously accounted for, but there are no records of the 'secret service vouchers' mentioned by Durand and so we have little idea who received the money.[5] A number of names are introduced, then, somewhat enigmatically, they disappear, but the dates of the journal entries suggest several men were employed as agents by Elias, especially in the Badakshan area.

His official objectives were, first, to improve trading and political relations with the Chinese in Sinkiang and, in particular, to remove the trading restrictions which were killing off Indian trade. Second, he was to explore the Upper Oxus and Pamirs with special reference to the territorial status of the region and any routes and passes which led into India. Most important of all, he was to monitor Russian movements around the Pamirs.[6] In secret instructions from Durand, Elias was told:

> It is unnecessary to give you any detailed instructions. You will of course maintain friendly relations with the Russian Consul at Kashgar; but it will be your endeavour to gain all possible information about Russian strengths to the north and west of Chinese Turkistan; about the relations between Russia and China; about any military movements on the part of the former to the south and west; and generally all matters which may seem likely to prove of interest to the Government of India in the present condition of affairs . . . I am to request that you act in this manner with all possible caution.[7]

There is little doubt that, during the mission, the Chinese interpreter, Tseng S. Laisen, gathered useful information in Kashgar. Moreover Niaj Muhammed, a Yarkandi trader, acted as a courier for a confidential Special Branch report that was sent to Elias from the Punjab. Elias probably established a network of observers in Roshan and Shignan, and there is evidence that the Russians imprisoned a local chief for two years on suspicion of spying for the British.[8] Elias recorded the action against potential spies at the time. He reported, for example, that three parties of Shikarpur Hindus were accused of espionage and 'roughly handled', before being obliged to leave Russian territory.[9]

That Sinkiang was under Chinese authority at all had come as a shock to the

British, since Kashgaria, under the freebooter Yakub Beg, seemed to be a more tightly controlled state than China, which many regarded as an empire in decline. Nevertheless, when all the central Asian states from Khokand to Khiva had fallen to the Russians, it was anticipated that Yakub Beg's lands would also fall to 'the power in the north'. In fact, when Yakub Beg died in 1877, the Chinese had resumed their control of Chinese Turkestan and renamed it Sinkiang (New Dominion). Britain had backed Yakub Beg, and consequently the Chinese were in no mood to negotiate with the British, whereas the Russians had remained uncommitted in the conflict and reaped the benefits of closer relations with Beijing. Furthermore, the Leh–Yarkand trade flow had all but died out in favour of commerce with Russia following the Treaty of St Petersburg (1 February 1881), which had prompted Elias's mission. Dufferin calculated that cheap Russian goods were only accepted because there was no effective competition, and he was concerned that Russian influence might spread through China, unless there was some balance in the region.[10]

Elias faced a difficult situation when he arrived in Kashgar as he had no official 'position'. The Indian government, no doubt concerned that a commercial or political mission would merely provoke a Russian one, pointed out to Beijing that he was 'travelling for pleasure'.[11] Despite the claims made by his biographer, namely that the British chargé d'affaires and the Indian government failed to secure the right type of passport, the letters between Durand (the Foreign Secretary), Cunningham (the Permanent Under-Secretary), and N. R. O'Conor (the chargé d'affaires in Beijing), all indicate that they tried to obtain for Elias the status of consul as a first step to securing a permanent residence in Kashgar to match a Russian consulate established there in 1882.[12] The Chinese authorities were embarrassed by the fact that Andrew Dalgleish, a British trader struggling to develop the Kashgar–India trade route, had been operating in Chinese Turkestan without a passport for some time and the trade with India that already existed had never been officially recognised.[13] Although the *tsungli yamen* (governor) was prepared to permit Elias to travel, there was a reluctance to anger the Russians who enjoyed a monopoly of trade. The Chinese authorities placed great store on diplomatic protocol and they were suspicious of any 'unofficial' attempts to promote commerce with India. They claimed the volume of trade to Yarkand from Leh was too small to be given the status of a specific treaty anyway. Consequently, they refused even to meet Elias to discuss the political situation, and stopped him at Yarkand. Since Elias also had no rank, he was regarded with contempt by the Chinese authorities. Moreover, the Russian consulate in Kashgar, led by Colonel Nikolai Petrovsky, had gained considerable influence. Petrovsky reminded the Chinese that any obstruction of Russian interests could mean the despatch of the tsar's troops who were stationed just across the border.[14]

Lord Kimberley, the Secretary of State for India, had argued that Britain should enjoy the same influence as Russia. He wrote:

> A British Consul ought to be as safe at Kashgar as a Russian, and the position seems to me to be one of some importance for the observation of Russian

movements on the northern frontier of Afghanistan and Chitral, and for the promotion of our trade.[15]

In the absence of a permanent consulate, men like Dalgleish were useful observers, but Petrovsky eventually succeeded in removing Dalgleish from Kashgar by pressing the Chinese authorities. Dalgleish was thus dismissed on the grounds that he 'had no passport' which had been conveniently ignored for many years. As he pulled out of Chinese territory, he was murdered on the Karakoram Pass in 1888 by Daud Mohammed, an Afghan who may not have been acting purely on his own initiative.[16]

The decline of Indian trade in Chinese Turkestan was a concern, but it was a secondary one and really no more than a cover for the business of observation. The real aim was to establish a permanent consulate with the man regarded as the authority on China: Ney Elias. Elias was under no illusions about his instructions:

> The main object of the proposed agency would in fact be to watch Russian movements in Central Asia; and it need not be pointed out that the proceedings of Russia may at any time prove a source of danger to Chinese Turkistan as well as to other countries.[17]

Elias was also in Sinkiang to see if the Chinese were likely to work with the British, and, if the Russians invaded the province, perhaps even accept British officers as military advisers in the style of General 'Chinese' Gordon. However, Elias did not rate the fighting performance of the Chinese troops sent to meet him at Yarkand.[18] They were poorly armed and ill disciplined, and, in Elias's assessment, no match for the Russians. Moreover, it was clear that the Chinese were unlikely to accept local arrangements for military assistance without the approval of Beijing, or of Petrovsky.

For the rest of the mission, Elias was more fortunate. The Chinese permitted him to leave Sinkiang via the Pamirs which he did on 30 September 1885. He took two months to cross the Pamirs from Yangi Hissar in Sinkiang to Zebak in Badakshan, surveying twelve passes over 3,900 metres (13,000 feet), and discovering the 7,546-metre (24,748-feet) high Mustagh Ata to the north of Tash Kurgan, which he called Mount Dufferin. The crossing in winter was a severe challenge: temperatures fell so far below freezing that the mercury froze in his thermometer. The combination of intense cold, poor diet and older, long-term illnesses began to take its toll and he stumbled out of the mountains on 8 January 1886 in a poor physical state.

It took two and half months for a letter to reach him from Simla telling him that Lockhart was in winter quarters in Gilgit, which prompted a desperate message from Elias requesting medicine and news.[19] He then appealed to Ridgeway, now the commander of the Afghan Boundary Commission, to send a doctor. Ridgeway, possibly unaware of Elias's condition, and restricted by his Afghan attaché, replied that Elias should cross northern Afghanistan to join the Boundary Commission if he wanted help. Durand was also eager for Elias to link up with Ridgeway and thus close the gap in the surveys between the Pamirs and Chinese territory.[20]

When Elias eventually reached the Boundary Commission, describing himself as 'too old and too broken' to do any more work, he brought reassuring news. He believed that he had found a common boundary between the Chinese and the Afghans, and thus no opening for the Russians to reach the Indian frontier. From his intelligence-gathering, he had learned that Abdur Rahman's annexation of Shignan across the Oxus in 1883 had compelled the Chinese to assert their own rule up to the river Murghab. This was achieved by rounding up all the Khirgiz nomads and preventing them from straying any further down the river than Ak Tash, a point recognised locally as the *de facto* 'border'.[21] Therefore, in 1885, the existence of Afghan rule in the western Pamir provinces of Roshan, Darwaz and Shignan, and the existence of Chinese authority as far as Ak Tash seemed to indicate that the Pamirs were closed to Russian encroachments.[22] Elias also reassured the commission that there had been no new advances by the Russians in the Pamirs. Nonetheless, the Russians, for their part, were concerned by the secretive exploration of the Pamirs, and suspicious of the enquiries amongst the Kirghiz herders as to their allegiances.

Despite his assurances, Elias was unable to offer any easy solution on how the Pamirs could be controlled in the future. An area of 40,000 square miles was inhabited by a handful of independent nomads in a wild complex of mountains and valleys. There was a confusion of streams which defied a border settlement of the question of the source of the Oxus and there were no distinct watersheds. The only solution Elias could offer was the demarcation of the ground based on where the nomads secured their supplies.[23] The Intelligence Branch in London believed that a clear border line was a necessity if a creeping approach to India was to be prevented, 'or we shall find Russian troops occupying the passes of the Hindu Kush before we have made up our minds at what point a Russian advance must be checked'.[24] Lord Salisbury disagreed, stating that changes of government would lead to inconsistent responses and that a line was superfluous if Afghanistan was to be the theatre of war anyway. Above all, and somewhat ominously, Salisbury argued:

> Does not the idea of a frontier line ignore the character which our struggle must assume whenever it comes? It will be a war not of battles but of devastation. Our security will not be to defeat them but to make it impossible for them to live within reach of us. And that will imply not a frontier line but a frontier region.[25]

The Indian government had supported the Afghan claims to Roshan and Shignan in the Pamirs in 1873, believing they were all south of the Oxus, but Elias confirmed what the pundits had discovered in the 1870s: the Afghan claims seemed to extend right across to the Chinese territories on the banks of the Murghab-Aksu. If true, this closed the gap, covered the Hindu Kush, and looked as if it might bring to an end the vulnerability of the northern states of Gilgit, Hunza and Chitral. However, the use of local allegiances was not consistently applied across the frontier as a measure of authority. Around Lake Rangkul and the Murghab there was largely indifference to Afghan rule, but by Lake Karakul, in 'Russian' territory, the locals declared themselves for the amir. Ironically, in Wakhan and Shignan, amongst the settled populations with greater contact with

Afghanistan, there was sheer hatred for the amir.[26] Nevertheless, Elias advocated that Afghan garrisons should be established across the region. From a proponent of the forward policy, perhaps one would expect no other suggestion. Rawlinson's line of 1872 had been on the Oxus; exploration in 1873 by Sir Douglas T. Forsyth put the boundary thirty miles across the river; and now Elias had 'extended' the claims 100 miles to the north, as well as east, since the Kirghiz seemed to show a vague allegiance to Shignan, and therefore, in British eyes at least, to Kabul.

However, the clash of claims to the Pamirs would lead to fresh disputes in the next decade. The Russians believed that the northern Pamirs belonged to them, based on a vague Kirghiz recognition of Kokendi authority. The Chinese too, regarded the Kirghiz as their subjects. The Amir of Afghanistan was just as determined to uphold his own claims and he grew impatient with the British in early 1886; he was particularly anxious that the Russians and British might co-operate in order to partition his country. Just at that point, Colonel Lockhart crossed into Wakhan without diplomatic approval. Lockhart had intended to complete negotiations with the hill men of Hunza and to survey the remaining passes between Chitral and northern Afghanistan. After considerable hardships in crossing the Hindu Kush, Lockhart's men reached Badakshan, but Abdur Rahman was highly sensitive about the loyalty of his northern territories and he brought the Boundary Commission to a halt. Anglo-Afghan relations were tense. Aman ul Mulk of Chitral, having supported the British, now feared a clash with Afghan-istan, but when Lockhart retraced his steps, it was clear that the old Chitrali ruler was in poor health, and a succession struggle was likely to begin at any moment. This might have seemed immaterial to India, but, because of the presence of the strategic Dorah Pass (the only easily traversed pass in that part of the Hindu Kush), Chitral appeared to be the keystone of the defence of the north. Indeed it was to assume even greater importance in the years to come.

Durand felt that Lockhart's expedition had been a success. Every major pass in the north had been surveyed and, in some cases, successfully crossed. It had been established that only the Dorah Pass could be used by large bodies of troops, and firm agreements had been secured from all the major rulers and tribes in the region. However, relations with Afghanistan had suffered.[27] Abdur Rahman was alert to anything he perceived as a forward move by the British on his eastern border. He was determined to resist any territorial expansion and any future interference with his authority. The Kafirs were disappointed, since they had no assurances of security against the Afghans. Furthermore, the Nagaris were alienated by Lockhart's new agreement with their traditional rivals in Hunza, whilst the Chitralis' friendship rested on future material gains that might be wrung from the Raj, even if the old mehtar lived. From an intelligence point of view, Lockhart had secured valuable information, but he had damaged political arrangements in the process.

Elias reached different conclusions on how India was to be defended. Having completed six weeks' convalescence with the Boundary Commission in Afghan-istan, he was fit to take the field again in May 1886. Durand ordered the Boundary Commission to continue to Badakshan, and Ridgeway thought Elias was now under his command. He made a series of requests for Elias to gather supplies, since the commission consumed a vast amount of resources every day, including half a ton of firewood, a ton of grain, two tons of hay and five hundredweight of flour. Elias resented these duties, and criticised Ridgeway, who, he believed, wanted to be the first authority to survey the remainder of the Afghan border.[28] However, Elias himself was not above the rivalry he detected in others. Detaching himself to explore Badakhshan, he followed Lockhart's route towards India, claiming that it was not as easily traversed as the DQMG had implied. He also disagreed with Lockhart's recommendation to support the Mehtar of Chitral, whom he saw as 'avaricious, unscrupulous, and deceitful to an uncommon degree'. Since he was 'an irresponsible barbarian', Elias argued, he could not be entrusted with the defence of the passes.[29] Elias recommended that Chitral should be intimidated into submission by the garrisoning of British troops. Nevertheless, the partial garrisoning of Chitral that followed proved ineffective in preventing an uprising in 1895, and it may even have created a focus for local resistance. Indeed, Elias had also advocated that a road should be built from Peshawar, through Dir, to Chitral. This idea was actually taken up, but, in the short term, it too worsened relations with the tribes in the areas through which it passed.

The Government of India was eager for men of Elias's calibre to remain *en poste*, but his refusal to stay and work with the Boundary Commission meant that, when it withdrew a few weeks later, Elias was not in the area to continue his exploration of the southern Pamirs, although there is no evidence that the amir would have let him stay anyway. Durand wanted him to do so, but, by the time Elias received instructions to that effect, he was already nearing India. Yet, whatever the short-comings of his recommendations, Elias had contributed a great deal to the British intelligence effort in central Asia. In a remarkable feat of endurance, he had covered a grand total of 3,000 miles and traversed some of the world's harshest mountains in a period of seventeen months. He was made a Commander of the Order of the Indian Empire, but, ever critical of the organisation he served, he returned the award, earning universal disapproval.[30]

Lockhart's and Elias's were not the only expeditions to the hill states to the north and west of India in light of the Penjdeh crisis. Dr G. W. Leitner was also despatched to compile as much information as possible about Hunza and Nagar, with a view to future influence there.[31] He was, like Lockhart, a firm disciple of the forward policy with a long and varied career in exploration, and he was convinced that Russian advances were the product of adventurous Russian soldiers, where 'the devil finds work for idle hands'. He speculated on the likelihood of small parties crossing the northern mountains, and, prophetically, predicted that the first crossing of the Pamirs after the British expeditions of 1885 would be by Russian parties heading south. Another similar expedition set out in May 1885, led by Dr A. D. Carey of the Indian Civil Service, but Carey's task, like other explorers in the region, was a geographical study of the Chinese Turkestan frontier, rather than an intelligence mission. Of course, to the Russians, this distinction was lost. They believed the British were trying to win over the tribesmen against the tsar – and they were now prepared to act decisively.

Developments in the Intelligence Division in London

Whilst Elias was completing his surveys of the Pamirs, looking for the advance of Russian columns, the Intelligence Division in London was focussed on the city of Herat. Using information from India, the conclusion was that Herat could not hold out for long, and would probably fall before British and Indian troops could render effectual support.[32] Cameron, the Intelligence Division's new chief, explained to the Foreign Office that the news coming in to the British Embassy at St Petersburg, that Russian troop movements were 'paltry', was being manufactured to mislead the government. Intelligence from Central Asia clearly indicated that the build-up of Russian troops was substantial, if not so large as to indicate an all-out attack on India.[33] However, the situation was still grave. An intelligence assessment by Major J. S. Rothwell showed that a Russian attack on Herat with 50,000 men would successfully tie up the entire Indian Army, leaving only the Royal Navy and about 36,000 troops in the United Kingdom as a counter-offensive force. Any idea of blockading Kronstadt would be useless, Rothwell argued, and the Russian defences around St Petersburg were stronger than they had been in the Crimean War.[34]

Captain James Wolfe Murray, another Intelligence Division officer, examined the possibilities of an attack through the Caucasus to save India. An offensive here, providing Turkish co-operation could be secured, would sever the Russian lines of communication to Trans-Caspia and force the tsar's troops to make the far more difficult journey from Orenburg to Turkestan. However, he concluded that secrecy was almost impossible to maintain in the region, thus negating the element of surprise. This would mean: 'It would be almost useless to undertake the operations without having a force most fully equipped for an immediate advance upon landing.'[35] Instead, he considered the transmission of false telegraph messages that might tie up Russian forces for some time – an early example of deception using 'signals intelligence'.

The fall of the Liberal government in June 1885 saw the return of Lord Salisbury, now in the capacity of Prime Minister and Foreign Secretary. He immediately resurrected the idea of extending the intelligence screen from central Asia through the Caucasus.[36] A close watch was now kept on the development of Russian railways and the logistical procurements of the Russian Army which gave a good indication of the shifting strengths of the garrison in Turkestan.[37] In addition, there was an attempt to synergise the work of the intelligence departments in London and Simla. The Government of India recommended that Major George Napier should be transferred from the Intelligence Branch to London where he would set up a new 'India' section.[38] In fact, Napier was unsuitable as he did not speak Russian, and Sir Henry Brackenbury explained to Roberts: 'The one point in which this office is useful to the India Office is in our study of information from Russian sources'.[39] Like so many intelligence staff, Captain Grierson, the Russian scholar then with the Division in London, was eager to return to active service and so Brackenbury asked Roberts to send Captain A. F. Barrow who had been on the Afghan Boundary Commission and who also spoke Russian.[40] Roberts agreed and the Intelligence Division continued to make itself useful by offering the government departments, and the Cabinet, estimates of Russian capabilities and the nature of the threat to the British Empire.[41]

Before long, the London Intelligence Division was proving to be the focus of a more centralised system. On the ground, a network of informers, consuls and roving agents was able to supply a stream of information. This information was passed through a number of centres, including Teheran, the Government of the Punjab and newswriters in Afghanistan. Not all of it was reliable, but the exchange of intelligence between London, the embassy in St Petersburg and Simla or Calcutta was the beginning of a more sophisticated system in which intelligence could be cross-checked. Compared with the previous forty years, the British were now far better informed on Russian movements, strengths and capabilities. Moreover, they had a clearer picture of the topography, the routes that an advancing army might use, and the complexities of central Asian politics. In relative terms, the system was not yet as effective as it would be in the twentieth century, but British secret intelligence was certainly not as amateurish as it has so often been portrayed. The difficulties of gathering reliable intelligence on the frontier were far from small and many Asian agents put their lives at risk. But the stakes were high, and nowhere is this clearer than in the work of the consulate at Meshed.

The Consulate at Meshed

The Indian Intelligence Branch was concerned by tribal unrest on the frontiers, the shifting politics of Afghanistan and Persia, and the movements of the Russians in Central Asia. On the North-West Frontier, for example, the British kept themselves informed of the Wahabi 'Hindustani Fanatics', an anti-British Muslim sect, and, following intelligence on their movements in 1871, they suppressed them. The disappointing 'revivals' of the Wahabi movement in 1888 and 1891 were also swiftly dealt with.[42] But the combination of religious fanaticism and political grievances was a cause for concern in many of the North-West Frontier campaigns, particularly as any military reverse might contribute to unrest in the subcontinent. There was some relief when the Indian people ignored the setbacks of the Second Afghan War, and expressed their loyalty during the Penjdeh crisis of 1885.[43] Therefore, whilst India was secure and the frontier disturbances, if monitored, could be contained, the only threat was the combination of a Russian thrust with widespread rebellion in India. If small groups penetrated the passes, or fomented sedition from a base within Afghanistan, then, it was feared, the British would be unable to hold South Asia.[44]

A massive increase in India's military forces to garrison districts which might revolt was ruled out on financial grounds, although large sums were spent on vital communications, roads and railways. It was anticipated that there would be significant problems in reinforcing the British forces in India, and in getting troops to the frontier, or beyond it, in time to stem a Russian advance.[45] Once again, the real problem was one of information. There was an urgent need to detect any Russian troop concentrations early, and to gather information on the movements of Russian forces, especially within their territories in Central Asia. Consequently, there was a determination to locate all the passes into India from the north, estimate the possible numbers of Russian troops that could use them, and to determine, and counter, the influence of Russian agents.

However, there were problems in relying on untrained Asian personnel. Colonel C. E. Callwell, the author of a handbook on colonial warfare, commented disparagingly on the risks of field intelligence:

> The difficulty in dealing with Orientals and savages, whether as informers or spies, is referred to in many textbooks and works of reference on reconnaissance and intelligence duties. The ordinary native found in theatres of war peopled by coloured races lies simply for the love of the thing and his ideas of time, numbers, and distances are of the vaguest, even when he is trying to speak the truth ... But that this difficulty can be overcome has often been proved in actual campaigns.[46]

The same sentiments were echoed by Colonel Lockhart:

> The information derived from these Native Agents is often misleading, and a tendency to exaggerate was found in them all ... even when dealing with intelligent natives it is always difficult to make them understand what we want to know, especially concerning roads, passes and approaches thereto.[47]

Richard Popplewell believed that the topographical contribution of both the British and Asian agents was 'debatable', and he described their intelligence efforts as 'makeshift', or dependent on the 'initiatives of individual members'.[48] The Indian Intelligence Branch realised these limitations at the time. In July 1883, Major-General MacGregor complained to General Donald Stewart, the Commander-in-Chief, that they were living in a 'fool's paradise':

> We are ... burying our heads in the sand, in fact. The steps we should take at once are, in my opinion, to send an officer to the Caucasus to report on what is going on there – i.e. on the distribution of troops, the facilities for moving reinforcements by rail, and for embarkation and disembarkation on the east coast of the Caspian. Another officer should go to Askhabad, and go about as much as he could along the east coast, and make good arrangements for getting early information of what is going on ... I know we have Stewart at Khaf, and at all events he is doing no harm; but we want more officers than him.[49]

MacGregor, in fact, echoed the feelings of Colonel Stewart, the British consul at Meshed (a post which had been established in 1874), that there ought to be a permanent British presence with a more extensive espionage screen. D. R. Peacock, the consul in the Caucasus, and Colonel Chenevix-Trench, the British military attaché at St Petersburg, were directed to make enquiries about the crossings of the Caspian, but there was still a role for an enterprising intelligence officer in northern Persia. Therefore, in March 1884, Stewart had expanded the spy network at Meshed. He was assisted by Abbas Khan, a Persian recruited by the Intelligence Branch, and an important continuity figure when Stewart was either temporarily incapacitated by poor health or when he was travelling about the northern provinces.

Having enlisted a few agents to gather information within Persia's borders, family members of these paid observers were employed and despatched to Dereghez, Merv and Sarakhs inside Russian territory.[50] However, initially there were doubts about the effectiveness of the network. News of the fall of Merv in January 1884 was transmitted first from a Russian newspaper via Teheran, not from the tiny band of agents at all. Nevertheless, with the arrival of A. Condie Stephens, a member of the Foreign Office who had served with the Afghan Boundary Commission in 1885, and the establishment of a vital telegraph link to London, the status of the operation at Meshed was raised.[51] Funds increased from £300 to £480 p.a., the consulate was placed on a permanent footing, and Colonel C. S. McClean, formerly of the Punjab Cavalry and Indian Political Service, was appointed as its head. When he arrived in July 1885 there was a significant improvement in the volume of information collected. The task of intelligence-gathering 'behind enemy lines' was a constant struggle, and despite the sparseness of the records that have survived, it is possible to get a glimpse of the bitter and dangerous activities conducted by the agents in northern Persia and Russian Central Asia.

The consulate at Meshed was clearly designed to resist Russian covert operations and diplomatic intrigue in the Persian province of Khorassan. Although the first efforts exposed the inexperience of the personnel, the aim was to deny the growth of Russian influence, to counter Russian propaganda, and, if necessary, spread disinformation in northern Persia. It had a responsibility for a long frontier some 500 miles in length, but Meshed was selected because it lay close to the Russian lines of communication between Krasnovodsk and the rest of Trans-Caspia. Moreover, the city was specifically mentioned in Russian military plans intercepted in 1885. General Kuropatkin had stated in his scheme for the thrust against British India that Meshed was strategically important. According to the Russian general, the mullahs of this sacred city were to be won over, and with them the people of the region, so as to secure the right flank of operations against Afghanistan. He wrote: 'Here the holy plain of Meshed will play a great role in our advance, for Meshed is the key to our affairs in Central Asia, and of our moral success amongst the Mussulmans.'[52]

The British consulate at Meshed is a clear example of the important role played by Asian agents in British intelligence, particularly in areas where Europeans could not operate without detection. Selection and training were difficult, but Colonel Maclean, who had served in both the Mutiny and the Second Afghan War, seemed an ideal choice for the command and co-ordination of espionage. His orders were issued in India, in co-ordination with the Foreign Office.[53] His detailed objectives were, first, to establish good relations with all local inhabitants, which was especially important given that the governor of Khorassan province, Asaf Ud'Dowlah, was hostile to the British; second, to gather information, particularly with regard to Russian troop movements; and third, to keep a close watch on members of Sher Ali's family, led by the pretender to the Afghan throne, Ayub

Khan. This threat could not be underestimated. There was a danger that, backed by
the Russians, Ayub Khan would attempt once again to take Herat, as he had in
1880, prior to a *coup d'état* in Kabul itself.[54]

Maclean's agents were recruited on the prospect of good and regular pay, and
the consulate expenses in 1886 averaged some 2,500 rupees a month (*circa* £190).[55]
At first, Maclean had to rely on a scattered field, but, on his return from the Afghan
Boundary Commission in September 1886, a series of coded spy 'rings' was established. In October, the registered agents were 'the Turkmen of Andkhoi' operated
by Colonel Ridgeway, Hazim Ali Shah, Kizil Bash (also known as 'The Merchant'),
Mullah Marmin Sartip (also known as 'Mohammed Nazar'), and the Wali of
Maimena. All these men were Afghans and were useful not just on the frontier with
Turkestan, but also in monitoring the movements of Ayub Khan's men, usually
listed euphemistically as 'the Afghan Refugees'.[56] In addition, Maclean was able to
recruit Turcoman Saryks, such as Kaji Mohammed Hussein, with 'compensation'
payments of 1,500 krans (approximately £10) each for losses of property at Penjdeh.
They were given the cover of suppliers for the Boundary Commission. One of these
agents, known only as Razei, performed the dangerous mission of crossing the
southern Karabil Desert from Chaharjui to Meshed, via Merv, on a secret
reconnaissance.

By January 1887, the network had begun to acquire some systemisation.
Maclean recorded that he had newswriters at Sarakhs, Penjdeh, Yulatan, Merv,
Chaharjui (on the Oxus), Bokhara and Samarkand, although he noted all were 'on
probation'. A separate agent was deployed to the Caspian coast.[57] Without training,
the agency struggled at first. On 18 February 1887, Maclean wrote that:

> [The network] is not yet a great success. Either owing to snow, or treachery,
> or fear of discovery, they have not yet acted up to their agreements. They
> will be kept for a month and discharged if no improvement. I am trying
> messengers especially selected.[58]

The problems were considerable. Maclean's house was under close observation
from agents the Russians had themselves selected.[59] Raza Beg, formerly a hand on
a Caspian steamer, and a 'promising man', who had the added attraction of being
able to speak Russian, was a suspected double agent. Said Hakim was a 'useful
correspondent, but talkative'. The Merv messenger disappeared leaving a 'family
anxious about him'. Even Abbas Khan, through fault or design, failed to pay the
agents regularly, so that, at times, posts were abandoned, and it was later
discovered that a report on Russian troop trains submitted by one of the agents in
January 1887 was fabricated for a cash reward. Maclean himself valued the efforts
of the agents, but he was sceptical about their ability to estimate accurately the
sizes of Russian forces, or the distances they had travelled, 'our news-agents being
utterly unreliable in the question of numbers'.[60]

However, there were also some successes. Sardar Abdullah Khan was a close
adviser to Ayub Khan, and by paying him, and buying him a house, Maclean
hoped indirectly to influence the renegade pretender. General Laj, a violent and
ambitious officer, also accepted Maclean's pay. The postmaster-general of Meshed

was an ally, as was a shrine official who could eavesdrop on Afghan exiles' conversations. Beyond Persia itself, an agent was despatched to the Caucasus and, by the end of February 1887, Maclean could note with satisfaction that the Askhabad and Merv agents were doing well disguised as merchants.[61] The expansion of the operation can be estimated through the accounts, as expenditure increased from 3,139 krans in January 1887, to 22,530 krans just six months later.

Maclean was able to pass on useful intelligence about Russian intrigues in northern Persia too. In June 1887, he learned that the Russians had deputed an agent to 'spread Russian influence' only to discover he was 'an enemy of Russia', which resulted in the agent's exile to the Caucasus. Maclean's greatest successes came with the employment of the Meshed telegraph clerk, who passed on any sensitive material to the British consulate, and the information of Mirza Jahir who, via a mysterious 'agent number 5', reported on the Russian consular office. Even more surprising was the employment of Mirza Ali Khan, an actual employee of the Russian consulate. This man had no knowledge of 'number 5' – an excellent way to corroborate the intelligence they were both providing. By the end of 1887, Maclean had established circles A (Askhabad), B ('northern Persia', Bujmund, Kuchan, and even, for a time, Krasnovodsk on the Caspian), C (Sarakhs, Penjdeh, Yulatan, Merv, Chaharjui, Bokhara and Samarkand), D (Askhabad, Sarakhs, Merv) and E (Meshed, Kelat). As the consulate became more efficient, it was able to contract, so although intelligence operations extended, the number of agents was reduced from thirteen to seven in August 1887. Correspondingly the budget was reduced to 8,687 krans in the same period.[62]

The value of Maclean's agency was sometimes doubted, but the first report of Ishaq Khan's rebellion against Abdur Rahman in 1888 was transmitted by Maclean from Meshed shortly before the amir's own despatch to the Government of India.[63] In addition, Maclean gave warning of the Russian Army's attitude to the prospect of a Russo-Afghan boundary revision in 1887: 'If our news-agents reports can be credited, the occupation of Herat in the near future is openly spoken about by Russian officers.' To which he added: 'The targets at which the troops practice are made to represent British soldiers!'[64] Maclean continued that the Russians might use their Muslim officers to assist the tribesmen on the North-West Frontier of India to resist British punitive expeditions. He therefore recommended the extension of British suzerainty over the whole of Afghanistan.[65] Significantly, it was Maclean who relayed details of a secret meeting between General Kuropatkin and the Afghan Governor of Herat in 1891.[66]

Russian efforts to detect the agents operating in Central Asia were unceasing. On 1 August 1887, two couriers were captured in Merv by Colonel Alikhanov, the Russian governor of that oasis. He later released them through lack of evidence. The following month, agents 'I' and 'J' were compromised and therefore discharged. The Dereghez agency was closed down, and Maclean recorded with despondency that it was becoming more difficult 'to get a trustworthy man'.[67] Similarly, only one agent remained at Ashkabad since 'no eligible men have come forward due to the dangerous nature of the duty'.[68] An agent in ring C, Sihat Bai, went missing in November 1888, after being dispatched to get 'photos of Russian guns, troops and barracks at Old Sarakhs and Pul i Khatun', and Maclean later recorded that Alikhanov was threatening Sihat Bai's brother.[69] In July 1890, Penjdeh was completely sealed off, ring C was 'under threat', and two agents sent to Samarkand in October 1890 had failed to reach the city. Worse still, systematic searching of mules and muleteers on the border by Russian troops in March 1891 resulted in the arrest of two agents from ring B. Agent Ozam Adak also went missing, and, despite precautions, such as invisible ink messages, nothing had been heard from the Penjdeh agent for weeks.[70]

Maclean was temporarily relieved in the winter of 1888 by Ronald Thomson, and again in the summer of 1889 by Colonel Stewart, before Ney Elias took over as his replacement on 1 January 1892.[71] However, the 'agency' which was redesignated as a 'consulate-general' in 1889, underwent some more fundamental changes than just its title or personnel. From 1889, the posture was increasingly defensive and operations were restricted to intelligence-gathering inside Persia, rather than in Turkestan.[72] Attempts were made to establish A as Bokhara, B as Ashkabad, C as Merv and D as Penjdeh, but the B cell of three agents was rounded up in March 1891 (there is no record of their fate). When Lieutenant-Colonel C. E. Yate took over, having run his own intelligence section during the Afghan Boundary Commission of 1885–6, he frequently operated from Seistan, the so-called 'open flank' of the approaches to India, because Meshed had become untenable.[73] Nevertheless, Maclean, his British successors and the Asian agents managed to establish a forward 'listening post' which contributed a steady stream of information, some valuable, some mere rumour.[74] On balance, it would be fair to say that a surprise *coup de main* on the Persian border was less likely given the existence of the Meshed consulate.

Intelligence on the Frontiers

Apart from Meshed, the Government of India's other main agencies were based at Peshawar and Kabul. Peshawar relied on a collection of itinerant travellers and Afghan dissidents, as well as its own paid agents who were disguised as merchants, trading everything from walnut wood to carpets. Despite the frequent assertion that Victorian intelligence was an amateur affair, it is interesting to note that the Peshawar diaries are full of detailed information from Kabul and Kandahar, and they can still be found in both the India Office and Foreign Office records.[75] The Amir Abdur Rahman's own newswriter at Kabul, Mirza Muhamed Yusuf Khan, was, in fact, in British pay and received between 12 and 20 tomans (c. £2–£4) a month. Unfortunately he was compromised in the autumn of 1889.[76] However, the British were not reliant on just one agent in the Afghan capital. The instructions from H. M. Durand, the Foreign Secretary of the Government of India, to Sardar Mohammed Afzal Khan, the British agent in Kabul, were to befriend the amir and to watch for Russian spies or envoys. However, he was not favourably received and complained of Afghan intrigues against him.[77] In Herat, the (British) newswriter was Khan Bahadur Mirza Yakub Ali Khan. His information contributed to the Peshawar confidential diaries and seems to have included, amongst its more prestigious successes, an intercept of a copy of a letter to General Kuropatkin.[78] At Kandahar, the newswriter was Khan Bahadur Mirza

Mohammed Taki Khan, and he communicated via Colonel John Biddulph as the agent for Baluchistan, and thence on to the Government of India's Foreign Department.[79]

From the Foreign Office records of these 'confidential diaries' it is clear that, whilst the Intelligence Division in the War Office closely observed the Russian press, this was only part of the intelligence gathered. The Indian Intelligence Branch passed on its information from both established newswriters, and less well established agencies, such as Balkh, via the Government of India. Although there was a great deal of rumour, with frequent war scares in Herat about border violations or an impending Russian invasion, occasionally there were more useful pieces of counter-intelligence. For example, Peshawar reported that the amir had a spy, Mustan Shah, at Simla in August 1888, and he was consequently put under close observation.[80]

The Meshed consulate was considered to be India's most strategic listening post for the monitoring of Russian movements across the border. After Maclean, it was commanded successively by Elias, Yate and even H. M. Durand himself. However, in 1895, Lieutenant-Colonel H. Picot, the British military attaché at Teheran, reflected on the 'advisability of extending our Agency system of espionage in Central Asia and the Caucasus'. In a confidential memorandum, he pointed out that:

> During the war scare of 1885 about the only information we had regarding the movements of Russian troops into Trans-Caspia was from the telegrams and reports of Mr Peacocke, the Consul at Batoum. Since then the Consulate-General at Meshed has been established, and a watch is kept on the various cantonments of Trans-Caspia as far north as Samarkand.[81]

Picot demanded more agencies, particularly along the Caspian coast, because he concluded that:

> We now expend a large sum of money on a system which may fail at the most critical time. It supplies doubtful, if useful, information regarding the present development of Russian resources in Central Asia, but can give no indication of those preparatory movements of which it is vital to us to have the earliest information.[82]

What Picot acknowledged was that the British were able to monitor the Russian garrisons, but they were unable to keep a track of reinforcements. With the extension of Russian railways in the region, it was vital to be able to observe both the Caucasus and the Caspian routes, and thus buy time for the mobilisation of forces within India.

British intelligence in central Asia was thus extensive and expanding in the last decades of the nineteenth century. Until now there has been a tendency to examine the elements of British intelligence in isolation, either focussing only on the limited developments in Britain or on the work of European personnel in India. In fact, co-operation between agencies in Britain and the subcontinent was improving. The networks in Asia were supplemented by observations in St Petersburg, and Foreign

Office or military attachés' reports in the European capitals. Colonel Chenevix Trench, the military attaché to the British Embassy in St Petersburg, for example, sent the Foreign Office a detailed breakdown of all the troops in Turkestan and the Caucasus, their transport and artillery.[83] These details were shared with the Intelligence Division in London and passed on to India. There were still many problems in filtering and transferring information, however, and a fresh round of Russian annexations (which brought them to the very border of India) in the 1890s was to be the catalyst for greater centralisation and co-ordination.

Chapter 10

Closing the Gap

Espionage in the Pamirs and Hindu Kush, 1887–1895

New threats to the British Empire from Great Power rivals evolved in the last decade of the nineteenth century, in Africa, on the world's oceans and in east Asia. Old problems continued to fester, too. Afghanistan was rocked by periodic rebellions, although the 'Iron Amir' crushed the insurgents ruthlessly before any Russian intervention could be organised. In the Pamirs, small Cossack detachments made contact with the hill states to the north of India, and intercepted Russian military plans revealed that the passes of the Hindu Kush and the northern plains of Persia were the ultimate objectives of the tsar's armies. The British Empire could not be strong everywhere. It required a centralised intelligence service that could properly collate and co-ordinate the information it received and pass it on to the right authorities in a 'timely and accurate' fashion. The chief difficulty was that the Indian Intelligence Branch and Government of India saw things very differently from London. To those at Simla, the theatre of operations had to be Afghanistan. The Royal Navy could defend the United Kingdom and the colonies, but the British Empire's greatest land frontier was the one that lay across the Himalaya and Hindu Kush. It was here, they reasoned, that Russia could throw its vast army and seek to turn the Indian population against the British.

Henry Brackenbury, who had joined the Intelligence Division in London in 1886, had long been impressed with the potential of intelligence work. In 1870, whilst serving with a British hospital unit during the Franco-Prussian War, he was able to observe the workings of the Prussian General Staff. From a spell teaching at the Royal Military College at Woolwich, he went on to serve Sir Garnet Wolseley as military secretary with intelligence responsibilities in the Ashanti campaign in West Africa in 1873. Wolseley described him as a 'profound reasoner with a strong will and logical mind'.[1] After service in Cyprus, Zululand and the Sudan, Brackenbury became the first Director of Military Intelligence, the head of the Intelligence Division. His first duty in 1886 was combating Irish nationalist bomb attacks in Britain and Ireland. But, eager to maintain his reputation in military intelligence, he arranged for Edward Jenkinson, a Mutiny veteran with plenty of espionage experience, to take over the handling of 'the dynamite war'.[2] In fact, 'Brack', as he was known, was an 'empire builder' with his own ideas of how the British Army should be managed. The young Edward (later Lord) Gleichen recalled how, whilst attending a dinner as a young Intelligence Division officer, the Duke of Cambridge had confided in him that Brackenbury was 'a very dangerous man'.[3] Other than this reference to his reforming zeal, there were several officers who distrusted the chief of Military Intelligence. Sir George White, the Commander-in-Chief of the Indian Army in the 1890s, complained that Brackenbury often tried to 'turn everything to his own credit' and was an 'intriguer'.[4]

Brackenbury was indeed determined to make the Intelligence Division in London 'not only the eyes and ears of the army, but a most valuable Department to the State'.[5] He was pro-active in making the Intelligence Division useful to the Foreign Office by providing assessments of threats to the empire. In September 1886, with Russia poised to strike against Bulgaria, Brackenbury examined how the tsar might use the opportunity to launch a *coup de main* against the Ottoman Empire through the Caucasus. Gathering intelligence from Batoum and Asia Minor, Brackenbury was able to report on the shipbuilding programme at Sevastopol, the acceleration in the construction of a trans-Caucasus railway, and the decrepit state of the Turkish Army.[6]

The acquisition by the British minister in Teheran of General Kuropatkin's plans in 1886 was another intelligence coup with implications for the Near East. The Russians aimed to advance against India in three stages, and the first phase was to bring their frontier up to Afghanistan and Herat. Having spent three years in consolidation, the next objective was to annex Kashgar, Kabul and Kandahar. British influence would then be threatened by a combination of unrest in India and Russian troops on the borders. In consequence of all this, Kuropatkin anticipated an easy advance upon Constantinople. To ascertain the nature of this threat, Brackenbury sent two intelligence officers to the Russian ports on the Black Sea, while he went to Constantinople to see Sir William White, the British ambassador. The two officers, Captains Beaufort and Surtees, were able to obtain some useful information, but Surtees wrote about their travels for the *Globe* and *Daily News*, which earned a severe reprimand from the Army and the Foreign Office. Beaufort was arrested and the Russians were hardly convinced by his 'travelling for pleasure' cover story.[7]

The consul-general at Odessa reported Russian troop concentrations on the border of Bulgaria in 1886, but the Intelligence Division was dismissive of any idea of an imminent attack.[8] Once again, the intelligence screen functioned successfully, even when those that received the information failed to acknowledge its importance. There were three men, Harford, Stevens and Perry, at Odessa, whilst another Foreign Office official, Peacock, served at Batoum. In addition, Captain Wolfe Murray travelled through Odessa counting the number of tents, and the rifles piled outside each one, to estimate the strength of Russian forces in the area. His conclusion was that, without command of the Black Sea, the enlarged garrison at Odessa could not launch a strike against Constantinople. He accompanied Stevens to check rumours that steamers were being kept in readiness as troopships, and confirmed his view that no attack was imminent.[9]

Brackenbury then considered the problem of how Britain would strike at Russia.

Naval operations against Vladivostok could hardly affect the outcome of a major war, and any British campaign in the Black Sea or Caucasus needed Turkish co-operation (which was less likely after the British occupation of Egypt, a former Ottoman dominion, in 1882).[10] Like the Indian Intelligence Branch, his assessment was that the prospect of being able to launch offensive operations through central Asia seemed less likely with each passing year. The Turkestan railways were making logistical arrangements for the Russians easier, internal assessments of British mobilisation strengths made gloomy reading and the Government of India was told it could expect no reinforcements in the event of a war with Russia.[11]

There were still occasional border incidents that kept the intelligence agents on the frontiers busy, and the politicians in the capitals anxious for news. In 1887, a skirmish between Afghans and Russians resulted in a boundary revision, but it was to northern Persia that attention now shifted, particularly in light of Kuropatkin's secret plans concerning Meshed.[12] The Foreign Office believed that railway construction might offer the chance for Persia to develop and be less susceptible to the commercial temptations offered by Russia. A railway link from Teheran down to the Persian Gulf would, it was reasoned, tie Persia more closely to the maritime trade of Britain and India. The head of the Intelligence Branch at Simla, Colonel Mark Sever Bell, concurred enthusiastically with this assessment.[13] He went to visit Sir Henry Drummond Wolff, the minister at Teheran, and suggested that a line might also link Quetta, the forward base of the Indian Army, with Seistan in Persia.[14] Salisbury was lukewarm and, after further enquiries, the Foreign Office realised that the volume of Russian trade and the development of Russian roads and railways were exaggerated.[15] Nevertheless, Prince Dolgorouky, the Russian consul at Teheran was, at that moment, trying to persuade the shah to grant railway concessions from the Caspian and from Sarakhs to western Afghanistan – in accordance with Kuropatkin's plans.

The Intelligence Division in London believed that any British-backed railway in Persia would provoke the Russians into actually building a rival line towards northern Afghanistan. Given the cost of building railways, Brackenbury thought it a prohibitive burden to India's budget.[16] But Drummond Wolff took the view that the Russian railway project was an inevitability. Moreover, it would raise the prestige of Russia in the eyes of the Persians. Only the construction of a British railway, partly funded by Baron Reuters, offered the opportunity of a strategic balance of power.[17]

The December 1888 edition of the Indian Intelligence Branch report noted that Russian agents were active in Persia, Afghanistan and China.[18] Brackenbury thought this alarmist, but the Russians were pressing the shah for an answer on their railway schemes and Drummond Wolff was anxious that Britain was losing its influence over northern Persia, perhaps even the whole country.[19] In fact, the Intelligence Division believed it was already a lost cause. Brackenbury did not think 'the advance of a single line of railway to a remote corner of Persia would make our influence in that country equal to that of Russia', which virtually 'controlled' Persia anyway. Bell, the intelligence chief in India, was dismissed as a 'dangerous enthusiast' and Brackenbury thought that Major-General Chapman, the Quartermaster-General of the Indian Army, had a better idea of developing Baluchistan as a base of operations whilst winning over the local tribesmen there.[20] Nevertheless, Salisbury urged Wolff to block the Russian railway schemes and ensure that any concessions to the Russians in the north were balanced by concessions to the British south of Teheran.[21] In the end, Butzow, a new Russian minister to Persia, concluded an agreement to ban all railway development for ten years, much to everyone's relief. Sir Robert Morier, the ambassador to St Petersburg, revealed that the Russians had been just as fearful of a British railway into the heart of Persia and added, with some feeling: 'we are quit of the question'.[22] Yet as the curtain fell on this sensitive theatre of operations, a new drama was about to unfold further to the east.

Francis Younghusband on the Hindu Kush

In the late nineteenth century, France was as much an imperial rival of Great Britain as Russia, particularly in Africa and south-east Asia, so the arrival of Gabriel Bonvalot and two other French explorers in May 1887 below the Baroghil Pass was regarded as an unwelcome and suspicious trespass. It was that fact that they had proved it was *possible* to traverse the Pamirs from Russian to British territory which really alarmed the authorities.[23] However, they had not been able to do so without detection, and the British could draw some satisfaction that they had been alerted to the presence of these foreigners by their Chitrali allies in the north. Dufferin interviewed the small French party about their experiences, but he was privately delighted that, from a strategic point of view, the Pamirs were difficult in the extreme, especially in winter.

However, in 1888, Captain Grombtchevsky and a party of Cossacks also made the crossing of the Pamirs and Hindu Kush, and arrived to a cordial welcome from the new Mir of Hunza, Safdar Ali.[24] Safdar Ali had murdered the previous ruler, Ghazan Khan, and proceeded to invite the Russians to establish a post in return for military support against Gilgit (where the British had reopened their agency after a period of seven years). Money and arms were supplied.[25] However, like his predecessor, Safdar Ali also claimed to be an outlying dependency of the Chinese, which prompted some forthright correspondence with Beijing.[26] The British Gilgit agent, Colonel Algernon Durand, knew he had to outbid the Russians before their next visit when the winter snows that blocked the high passes had melted. Algernon's brother, H. M. Durand of the Foreign Department, had already decided that the only way to secure the northern passes was by the presence of reliable rulers and a military road up to the Hindu Kush.[27] He arranged for subsidies to be paid to Safdar Ali in return for a cessation of raiding on local caravans, and the free passage of British officers through the states of Hunza and Nagar. Nevertheless, Safdar Ali and Rajah Uzr Khan, the Thum of Nagar, concluded an agreement in 1890 to resist the development of the road that the British were building to Chalt.[28] Moreover, Uzr Khan recommenced raiding the area to the north of Chalt and then murdered his brothers in May 1891 for collaborating with the British. Eventually, war parties gathered and marched towards Chaprot and Chalt, intending to capture the two forts there. Algernon Durand moved quickly north with just 200 men and reinforced the forts ahead of the tribesmen, so, after just an angry demonstration, they withdrew.[29] The British agency at Gilgit was reinforced too, but Safdar Ali was haughty and defiant; a conflict for supremacy in the Hindu Kush was likely.[30]

However, there was just as much interest in events to the north of Hunza's border. Grombtchevsky's reconnaissance had demonstrated that, in the words of historian Gerald Alder:

> It was obvious that no amount of activity south of the Hindu Kush could in itself prevent Russian infiltration down to the northern slopes of the range. And so, since the territories to the north of the mountains were beyond the range of effective Indian influence, diplomacy had to be employed to achieve what was impossible by any other means.[31]

The first test of that diplomacy occurred in 1888, for in that year Safdar Ali revived a tradition of raiding the Ladakh–Sinkiang caravan highway. The victims were Kirghiz who appealed first to Chinese and then British authorities for protection. The Ladakh agent passed on the information, and the Foreign Department wondered how it was that the Hunza raiders were able to reach the region between the Kun Lun and Karakoram across impenetrable mountains. It could only mean there were more passes that had not been discovered in previous missions. In fact, Dufferin was concerned that the gap between the Pamirs and the Karakoram had still not been closed, and that it was possible that the Russians might try to take up the intervening regions.[32] Russian reconnaissances had been conducted by the explorer Grum Grjimailo to the north and west Pamirs in 1885, and in the same year by Grombtchevsky to Kashgar, Yarkand and Khotan, in order to assess Chinese strengths. In 1886, another explorer, Potanin, completed a three-year survey of north and western China, and Captain Pokotilo toured the western Pamirs, even entering Darwaz and advancing claims that the area belonged to Bokhara. The following summer, Grum Grjimailo surveyed the southern Pamirs accompanied by his brother, a lieutenant in the Imperial Guard Artillery.

Dufferin's viceroyalty came to end in December 1888, and it was Lord Lansdowne who gave authority for a new expedition, planned by Algernon Durand, to draw Safdar Ali back into the British camp as a first step in the consolidation of the north.[33] The means to do this was a vastly increased subsidy. The Government of India had avoided Lockhart's plan to annex Gilgit, but it accepted that Russian pressure was now about to fall on the eastern Pamirs, and even beyond. The arrival of Grombtchevsky's mission in Hunza appeared to be confirmation of that intent.[34]

The next step was to mount an expedition that would survey the 'missing' passes. The candidate selected was Captain Francis Younghusband, already an accomplished mountaineer and traveller who had explored northern Manchuria with Colonel Sever Bell, before setting out across the Gobi in April 1887.[35] He had reached Kashgar at the end of August that same year, carefully noting any military details as he had been ordered to do. But Petrovsky had Cossacks 'escort' the young officer on to Yarkand. He had then crossed the 5,700-metre (19,000-foot)

Mustagh Pass in September, an epic of courage and endurance, before staggering back into India.[36] The combination of Younghusband's 'forward policy' views, his endurance and his enthusiasm for the Great Game were crucial factors in his selection for the important mission of 1889.

Younghusband's fears of Russian espionage were no doubt enhanced by the discovery of Nikolai Notovich, a Russian adventurer, on the Zoji Pass in Upper Baltistan in 1887. Notovich was a colourful character. A report by Donald Mackenzie Wallace noted that this young Russian was originally a correspondent of the *Novoe Vremya* who was ready to sell the secrets of his country, but he also seemed eager to make his name as an expert on India, perhaps as the means to climb the social ladder in Russia. He was not above clandestine surveying, but, having crossed the northern mountains, he then approached the British for permission to travel across the deserts and hills of Baluchistan. He perceived the British would not wish to let any Russian march across such a sensitive frontier region, so he offered to do so blindfold, just so that he could say that he had done it. Even if this had not aroused suspicion, his contradictions exposed him as a fraud. He seemed keen for Russia to expand, but was very quick to criticise his own military, probably because his Pan-Slavist tendencies made him resentful of the 'German' officers in the Russian Army's hierarchy. He had been in Constantinople during the 1885 crisis, and had applied to become the Russian consul at Meshed – but now he seemed eager to work for British intelligence. He implied that he could act as a courier since Prince Dolgorouky and Count Kleinmichael were willing to supply sensitive information, but he provided no evidence. He was shown the door. H. M. Durand warned that his presence on the frontier was dangerous only in that he might try to engineer an 'incident' in Kashmir.[37]

However, the mission for which Younghusband had been selected was not simply one of exploration, as he would also have to negotiate with the Mir of Hunza and win him over, in order to block any Russian moves made in the direction of Hunza by Grombtchevsky, Notovich, or others. Younghusband had been interviewed by General Roberts, who impressed on him the importance of the mission. He had read MacGregor's *Defence of India*, and, by chance, *en route* to Simla, he had met Ney Elias too, so he was regarded as the only Great Game player who could resolve the situation in the north.

Younghusband thus set out in July 1889 with six Gurkhas, seventeen Kashmiri sepoys, two Balti guides, his cook from the Mustagh crossing, an interpreter, and a surveyor of the 11th Bengal Lancers called Shahzad Mir. He was given 4,000 rupees for 'political purposes', which was double the amount Elias had had for his secret service work.[38] He marched first through northern Ladakh, in an attempt to reassure the Kirghiz who had appealed for help, but also to forestall any Russian overtures. He crossed the Karakoram Pass, apparently without difficulty, and established contact with Turdi Kol, the chief of the Kirghiz, who was keen to get British protection. Younghusband also arranged a ceremony to hand over 900 rupees, a revolver, and the promise that Kashmiri sentries would defend them. In fact, these moves were later to prove ineffectual. The Kashmiris were withdrawn, the raiders took the money, and Turdi Kol was arrested by the Chinese. It proved that, without the ability to reinforce a protectorate, such assurances were meaningless.[39]

Younghusband pressed on, narrowly avoiding an avalanche in his exploration of the Saltoro Pass, before reaching the Shimshal Pass and the Chong Jangal Valley, high in the Hindu Kush. Whilst he was awaiting supplies from his new allies, the Kirghiz, the Foreign Department informed him that Algernon Durand, the Gilgit agent, had received a hostile reception from the Mir of Hunza. But Younghusband was undeterred and approached the Hunza raiders' fort at Darwaz boldly, despite the risk of being shot below its walls. Fortunately, the negotiations with the fort's defenders were successful, and they let him proceed to Hunza unmolested.[40]

Before Younghusband set off for the capital of the defiant hill state, news arrived from Simla warning that a Russian party was operating in the area which might seek to re-establish contact with Safdar Ali. To his surprise, the commander of the Russian mission, Colonel Grombtchevsky, contacted Younghusband himself, and invited him to a dinner party at Khaian Aksai, which, as a gentleman, he duly attended.[41] It was a strange meeting between agents who should, in fact, have been avoiding each other. Yet this was an age where protocol and good form were perhaps more important than the cold-blooded behaviour of spies in the twentieth century.

Nonetheless, even though they could each pass themselves off as an envoy of their respective governments, they were still playing the Great Game. Grombtchevsky was accompanied by a Cossack escort and at one point he called on his men, asking how much would they like to invade India: he was greeted with a 'rousing cheer'. Indeed, Grombtchevsky boasted that the hardy Cossacks did not need supplies to cross the mountains into India. In a counter to this bluff, Younghusband impressed the Russians with a drill performance of great precision by the Gurkhas, as if to indicate that, supplies or not, the Cossacks would have to face the firepower of the Indian Army at the end of their journey.[42]

Although this was the first meeting of two Great Game agents, it was not the first time that British and Russian officers had parleyed in central Asia. Captain Yate of the Indian Intelligence Branch had sat down to dine with Colonel Alikhanov, the governor of Merv, before the Penjdeh Incident, and the Afghan Boundary Commission had established a regular dining routine in 1886. Neither side had wished to appear the meaner and so caviar and champagne were common. However, Patrick French believes that Younghusband was less charitable on his departure, suggesting to Grombtchevsky that he follow a route that was, in his private opinion, 'impossible'.[43] It was such a difficult route that Grombtchevsky and his frostbitten troops were forced to retreat to Shahidulla in Chinese Turkestan. Younghusband knew that Grombtchevsky was well equipped, but he was eager to ensure that the Russians did not steal a march on him or discover too much about the passes he had recently traversed. He was playing for any advantage.

In Tashkurgan, Younghusband met two British officers, Major Cumberland and Lieutenant Bower. These men were officially on a 'hunting expedition' but really engaged on the same observation work as Younghusband. They had crossed the Kilian Pass, escorting the French explorer Dauvergne away from the Indian border, but they then turned westwards to discover Colonel Pietsov with twenty-five Cossacks making a circuit of the southern Pamirs. Cumberland had apparently explored the Tisnaf Valley alone, and reported on its difficulties, before tracking down Grombtchevsky.[44] What information they exchanged at Tashkurgan remains unknown, but Younghusband did not delay for long. He passed on to survey the Khunjerab Pass on the Hindu Kush before proceeding to Hunza, making maps the whole way. At Mintaka Aksai he was stopped by two Kashgari officials, sent by the Chinese *taotai* (governor), to investigate the reason for the arrival of a British officer in Chinese territory. Younghusband managed to persuade the officials that his stay in Taghdumbash Pamir (on the Chinese side of the Hindu Kush) was brief, but it proved that the Chinese were just as keen as before to see off the British.

Younghusband finally surveyed the Mintaka Pass, which he found to be easily traversed, before crossing into Hunza. There, at last, he met Safdar Ali. However, negotiations failed to impress the mir, who demanded compensation if he promised to end his raiding. Younghusband tried to overawe the mir with a demonstration of firepower, and he attempted to explain that Hunza was really an ally of India through Kashmir, and bound to keep out the Russians, but Safdar Ali was more interested in acquiring the contents of Younghusband's baggage.[45] He did not kill him, even though he could easily have done so, but when Young-husband left, Safdar Ali continued raiding, and, in 1891, he threatened that any other British political officers sent into Hunza would be executed. The unreliability of this 'ally' prompted Younghusband's final recommendation: a military expedition to conquer Hunza and Nagar. The hill states were defeated in just one month of fighting that same year.[46]

The Foreign Department regarded Younghusband's mission as successful. He received the prestigious Founder's Medal of the Royal Geographical Society and his maps and report, completed in April 1890, added considerably to the Indian government's knowledge of the borders, the buffer states, and all the passes. But the very existence of Russian survey parties with armed escorts suggested that the tsar intended to make further territorial acquisitions. The sense of urgency was the result of Russian railway construction, a massive increase in forces stationed in Turkestan, and continued Russian exploration.[47] Before long, Younghusband was again ordered to investigate the possibility that the Russians were exploiting a gap between Afghan and Chinese territories on the Pamirs which would give them access to the passes of the Hindu Kush.

The danger posed by the expanding Russian rail network in Turkestan promp-ted another, less official, intelligence-gathering expedition. George Curzon MP, the future Viceroy of India who had developed a considerable interest in central Asia, made a railway journey across Turkestan in 1888. He did so with the approval of the Russian government, along the very lines the Russians would use to reinforce their operations against Afghanistan, Persia, or even China in the event of war. He travelled as far as Tashkent, making observations about the efficiency and strengths of the Russian Army in the region. It was not surprising that information was difficult to obtain, since the Russians knew why he was there. However, he visited Geok Tepe and Merv, noting how the Turcomans wore the uniforms of the

Russian Army. He observed that conscription was not imposed on Central Asians – the prospect of employment and loot was attractive enough to induce a ready supply of volunteers. He also visited the Emir of Bokhara, the puppet ruler of the Russian satellite state, and terminated his railway journey at Samarkand, at that time the furthest point on the line from the Caspian. Later, he returned to London to write that, although Russian rule had brought development to Central Asia, the railway was still a threat, particularly to Persia, since it would keep the shah compliant. The solution was to be as prepared as the Russians: a state of military readiness to discourage any opportunism. Conquest was not the Russian aim, he argued, but an invasion 'feint' to absorb the British Army in order to focus on the real objective, namely Constantinople. Russian policy was: 'To keep England quiet in Europe by keeping her employed in Asia.'[48] Later, Curzon was to be associated with the forward policy, but typically he condemned that idea in forthright terms, calling it 'infatuated nonsense'. Instead, he advocated reciprocal advances on the British side if the Russians advanced from theirs. He believed, rightly as it turned out, that the Russians were unlikely to risk war. Above all, it was necessary to be well-informed so as to take prompt action.

The Pamirs Crises, 1891–5

On the mission to the Pamirs in 1891 to establish where the limits of Afghan and Chinese territory lay, Younghusband was accompanied by a young officer called George Macartney. Although Macartney was officially only 'an interpreter' in the Political Department, he was, in fact, an agent in his own right. His mixed English and Chinese parentage made him an ideal candidate for work in Chinese central Asia, and he was destined to become the permanent British resident at Kashgar. However, the territory between the occupied areas of Chinese Sinkiang and Afghan territories north of the Oxus seemed to have attracted interest from Russian surveyors too. The question was: what had been the purpose of the missions of Grombtchevsky and Notovich?[49] Was it, as some in India feared, to exploit a gap between the settled areas in order to establish a military outpost? The development of Russian railways across Turkestan pointed to military preparations. It was difficult to appreciate that, for Russia, the railways were the only guarantee that they could flood troops into the region should it be affected by tribal rebellion, and it seemed likely that British agents, who now appeared in virtually every settlement, would incite such disturbances.

Younghusband and Macartney reached Yarkand and, whilst they proceeded to map the Alichur Pamir, they discovered that the Chinese now claimed an area to the west, previously thought to be Afghan.[50] Whilst the Chinese had formerly accepted that the Alichur Pamir lay outside their dominions, they had subsequently built forts at Gumbaz and Somatash.[51] To gauge the extent of Chinese authority, the two British officers made a circuit of the southern Pamirs before returning to Sinkiang in November for the winter, but they came across no Russian expeditions.[52]

Something of the dual tasks that British 'politicals' carried out is evident in their next move. Not only were they expected to survey and to observe Russian move-

ments, but they also carried out the tasks of diplomatic envoys. Younghusband
made a second attempt at establishing better relations with the Chinese in
Sinkiang, and hoped to find some agreement with them over the status of the
Wakhan Valley, but he was taken to task by the taotai for the expulsion of Chinese
subjects from a fort at Somatash by Afghan troops, that is, Britain's allies.[53] The
Chinese stated that they would only negotiate if the British induced the Afghans to
withdraw, and furthermore they demanded that the British make arrangements for
the security of Somatash themselves. Faced with this uncompromising line, and
conscious of his brief to establish closer relations with the Chinese, Younghusband
actually accepted this Chinese demand, which prompted an angry letter from
Abdur Rahman to Simla.[54] The British were in a difficult position. Afghanistan had
to be supported, but, if its friendship was more important than securing Chinese
co-operation, then there was a danger that the Chinese would rely on Russian
support to a greater extent. Younghusband hoped that there might be room for
compromise, with the Chinese taking up the Wakhan Valley, and the Afghans being
established further west.[55]

Petrovsky discussed the Chinese situation with Younghusband, but the Russian
consul had a clear advantage. His knowledge of the region, his closer relations with
the taotai, and, given the proximity of Russian troops, his ability to threaten the
Chinese, gave him the edge in diplomacy. Younghusband, by contrast, was less
experienced and he could not count on military support. He had to wait four
months for instructions from Simla and his letters, carried by dak runners, were
intercepted by Petrovsky. Younghusband seems to have been unbelievably naive in
the respect of his mail, describing his 'indebtedness' to the Russian consul for being
'most obliging in forwarding our letters through his couriers to Russian
Turkestan'.[56] The Russian consul had taken the precaution of sending agents out to
follow the British officers when they had crossed the Pamirs, even though Younghusband was unaware of this throughout his stay in Kashgar.[57] However, it is not
clear if the Russians had always managed this. Lennard and Beech, two British
officers 'on a sporting expedition', arrived at Kashgar sometime in 1891. Details of
their mission are a mystery, but Lennard subsequently took part in the
Hunza–Nagar expedition as a political officer, and it is possible that both these men
were engaged on the same observation task as Younghusband and Macartney.
Another officer, Lieutenant Davison, also joined Younghusband in June 1891. The
explanation for his presence was given as 'picking up information for the Government of India'.[58] It was clear that every effort was being made to get early warning
of events in the Pamirs.

Intelligence about Russian troops moving south through the mountains actually
came from two sources. On 15 July 1891, Hatzfeldt, Germany's Foreign Minister,
had told Salisbury that the Russians intended 'to seize a number of forts which
protected the passes penetrating the mountains into India'.[59] Sceptical though he
was, Salisbury informed the viceroy, Lord Lansdowne, in India. The Chinese had
already sent their own detachment to Somatash, anticipating that the Russians
would try to occupy the area. That month, Younghusband too left Kashgar to
investigate, leaving Macartney as sole agent. Back in London, Brackenbury had

also received reports of Russian intentions from the Germans. On 27 July, he passed the details on to Salisbury. Just three days later, the Russian Under-Secretary for Foreign Affairs, Chichkine, flatly denied that any Russian force had entered the Pamirs.[60] But then, on 5 August, Foreign Minister Giers issued a statement to the effect that a Russian detachment of eighty infantrymen *had* been permitted to move into the undefined territory of the Pamirs if only to 'practice shooting' in a 'hunting party'. Nevertheless, he admitted that their purpose was also to observe Afghan and Chinese forces in the region. Giers assured Salisbury that his aim had always been to 'furnish your Lordship [with] full details', but the British knew this was another smokescreen.

Events were moving quickly in central Asia. Younghusband had sent Davison to Somatash to keep watch, while he himself had marched on into the heart of the southern Pamirs.[61] On 10 August 1891 he reached a windswept valley called Bozai Gumbaz and there, as he expected, he discovered a small Cossack detachment. Initially, he wrote home that he felt the idea of a Russian 'advance' had been exaggerated and that 'the whole thing was a piece of brag'.[62] Nevertheless, this was a premature judgement. A portion of the Russian force had already crossed the Hindu Kush into Chitral via the Darkot and Baroghil Passes, and then withdrawn. What the British officer could see was merely a detachment. Younghusband was still encamped when another, larger body of Cossacks arrived. This was led by Colonel Yanov, a decorated officer who explained quite openly that his objective was to annex large sections of the Pamirs, including those parts claimed by Afghanistan.[63] He even showed Younghusband a map to that effect, with an area shaded green as far as the Baroghil Pass and the Hindu Kush.[64] Younghusband remarked on their:

> ... gross ignorance of India, and their deeply rooted desire to attack us there ... The officers of Colonel Yonoff's party displayed their ignorance of the situation by talking of advancing on Afghanistan and India with three or four hundred thousand men, ignoring all the difficulties in the way of transport and supplies which would prevent their marching anything like such a number towards our frontier. Imagining that the natives of India loathe and detest us and would rise up as one man to welcome the Russians and only thinking of the loot, the shower of decorations and the promotion which would follow on a successful campaign in India.[65]

Yanov's party then moved off, to the north, to continue their reconnaissance, whilst Younghusband waited for Davison to arrive. But three days later, Yanov returned with thirty Cossacks, and demanded politely, but firmly, that Young-husband leave Russian territory. Younghusband disputed that it was Russian at all, but Yanov insisted with a threat that force would be used.[66] With no means to resist, Younghusband pointed out that he would inform his government of Yanov's high-handedness, and then, in a demonstration of good manners, he promptly invited the colonel and the other Russian officers to supper. Yanov accepted, and, in the meantime, drew up a document in French, detailing the route Younghusband should take to return to Chinese territory. He was not to be permitted to return to

India via any of twenty-one named passes, and therefore would not get in the way of Russian military movements. In fact, Yanov appears to have had instructions to see Younghusband off the Pamirs by escorting him the whole way, but Yanov, as much a gentleman as Younghusband, apologised for having to behave like a 'police official'.[67] Younghusband left on 17 August, having accepted further apologies and a haunch of Marco Polo sheep (*Ovis poli*) from Yanov, but, as soon as he was out of sight, he sent a dak runner to Gilgit. News of Younghusband's dramatic 'arrest' reached London on 3 September 1891.[68]

The Government of India reacted quickly. Lansdowne had interpreted Younghusband's despatch of 10 August to mean that a considerable force was moving towards the Hindu Kush. He approved of the advice given to the Gilgit agency that:

> If Russians cross Hindu Kush into Chitral or Hunza territory, they should be called upon to withdraw. No Russian parties [are] to be permitted to descend the Ishkoman, Yasin or Chalt valleys; the Russian officer commanding such party on meeting our detachment [is] to be called upon to retire, and warned that if he attempts force he does so at his peril.[69]

General Roberts remarked privately, 'Now's the time to go for the Russians. We are ready and they are not.'[70] Ever alert to the long-awaited Russian advance, and concerned that this might be a prelude to the annexation of the Pamirs and a clash with Afghanistan, he mobilised the Quetta Division, a portion of the two corps he had organised for the purpose after 1885. Early mobilisation would give the British the chance to reach the passes of the Hindu Kush before the Russians disgorged their divisions from the railways. Indeed, it seemed no coincidence to Roberts that the Russian lines had just reached the edge of the Pamirs that year. Having taken these early precautions, the Government of India sought advice from the Foreign Office, but there was some confusion over the location of Bozai Gombaz, where Younghusband had been arrested, and no one could say what had happened to Younghusband. He seemed to have disappeared.[71]

The Indian press was full of rumours that a British officer had been killed by Cossacks in the mountains.[72] Had Younghusband joined Moorcroft, Hayward and Dalgleish in becoming another victim of the Great Game? Whatever his fate, E. F. Knight, a correspondent in Ladakh, was vociferous in his condemnation of the Russians' actions, which were tantamount to 'a declaration of war'.[73] The Government of India despatched Lieutenant Stewart with a party of Gurkhas to find the missing officer.

Younghusband was, in fact, alive and well at the Wakhijrui Pass opposite the Kilik Pass on the Hindu Kush, deliberately ignoring the route the Russians had dictated for him. He was convinced that the Russians intended to push south of the Oxus into Afghanistan, but he believed he had to maintain a watch on the passes that led towards India and he sent out spies to watch and report on Russian movements.[74] The agents that were despatched followed the practice of all Great Game espionage: hill men disguised as traders, itinerant holy men or herders. Younghusband explained that they all wrote small messages in Hindustani with an

English alphabet, and wrapped and stored their messages in the lining of clothes, hats and boots.[75]

First reports suggested that Davison had also been captured, but then Young-husband learned that Yanov had withdrawn from Bozai Gumbaz. On 4 October 1891, Davison managed to rejoin Younghusband, having been 'frog marched' from the Alichur Pamir to 'Chinese territory' by a Cossack detachment, a move Salisbury condemned as 'lawless violence'.[76] With a degree of irony, Salisbury pointed out to the Russians that Yanov seemed to have been acting without authority, and the Russian government should endeavour to give firmer instructions to its subord-inates.[77] Ambassador Morier at St Petersburg was more direct and demanded an explanation from de Staal, the Russian foreign minister. The tsar's minister tried to excuse Yanov's actions as being 'without the knowledge of the Russian government or of the emperor'. Morier was prepared to swallow St Petersburg's line, offered in a private note from Giers: 'Je ne puis que vous reiterer que nous reconnaisons que l'expulsion du Captain Younghusband et Lieutenant Davison n'était pas légale en elle-même et que nous la regrettons.' Morier enjoyed good personal relations with Giers, and both viewed Russia's acquisition of Central Asia as a great achievement, not a threat.[78]

Salisbury did not share the belligerence of the Anglo-Indian press either, and felt that the idea of military action to avenge the humiliation of Younghusband was pointless, advising the Government of India to ignore the offence. Morier hoped that the preservation of good relations would lead to a satisfactory delimitation of the Pamirs, and avoid the crisis that had arisen at Penjdeh. Yet Salisbury put little faith in a definitive boundary, and he urged the Chinese to take up their claims in the Pamirs.[79] The fact that Yanov had orders from the Russian War Ministry via the governor-general in Turkestan was overlooked, in case it provoked a 'newspaper war' or tempted the tsar to feel that his honour was being challenged.[80] In contrast, the Russian press saw Younghusband, not Yanov, as the military threat, believing that he had been sent to incite the Chinese and Afghans against Russia.[81] The Caucasus governor's own newspaper, *Kavkaz*, hoped that the advance in the Pamirs meant that 'the dream of an advance to India' was about to be realised.[82]

The Foreign Office eventually concurred with the Government of India that a border settlement was desirable sooner rather than later. However, buffer zones could only work where some kind of authority already existed, and the sparse population of the Pamirs offered none. Moreover, existing satellite states, like Afghanistan, Hunza, Kashmir and Chitral, were only successful where British forces could impose their will and where large subsidies kept their rulers in power, and no such situation existed in the Pamirs. But, as Russia aligned itself with France in the early 1890s, anglophobia in both countries increased, especially among the military. Correspondingly, Russian intrigue on the frontiers continued to develop, despite 'the official line'. Giers, for example, tried to play down the espionage activities of General Kuropatkin in Trans-Caspia and northern Persia.

Salisbury, however, saw the Pamirs crisis as a new opening to work with the Russians and settle the issue peacefully by boundary delimitation, since conditions had become 'somewhat critical'.[83] At the same time, the Government of India seized the opportunity to improve the security of the subcontinent. Lansdowne authorised 'the bringing of Hunza and Nagar under complete control', thus extending British authority up to the rim of the Hindu Kush and all the northern passes. With the onset of fresh disturbances there, the Gilgit agency was reinforced with more Gurkhas.[84] However, the extent to which either the language of diplomacy or the threat of force could persuade the Russians to rein in their ambitions was about to be tested again.

Withdrawing to India for the winter of 1891–2, Younghusband enjoyed a warm reception, and both Roberts and Lansdowne questioned him at length. However, the Foreign Office, prompted by the Intelligence Division in London, viewed Younghusband's telegrams as unnecessarily troublesome.[85] They believed the Pamirs were irrelevant to the defence of India. The government wanted to see the peaceful delimitation of the Russo-Afghan border, but the India Office warned that fresh Russian advances would be made in the spring of 1892. Fortunately, the Russians also wanted a resolution to the Pamirs question. Yet, once again, they feared British officers would encourage Afghan resistance. General Vrevsky, a senior officer in Turkestan, summed up the frustration caused by espionage:

> The one thing I will not stand is that political adventurers should go careering over territory which we call, for the sake of argument, doubtful. I consider the said territory Russian, therefore I arrest these gentlemen. If you consider it British, you should support the view officially, and not by the intrigues of young officers. The matter is one which can only be treated by the two governments, and neither by me nor Captain Younghusband.[86]

British intelligence met with mixed success in the Pamirs in 1892. At Kashgar, Macartney filed some useful information on Russian troop concentrations. It is not clear how he obtained his information, but he was able to report in February and March that a large number of cavalry had mustered at Osh.[87] Using his spies, Algernon Durand in Gilgit relayed intelligence on the Russians' moves towards the Afghan outposts. Initially it was thought they were in three detachments numbering 2,000 in all.[88] Some of this information had been obtained from an unidentified 'news-agent' at Tashkurgan on 25 July. The same agent reported a skirmish between the Afghans and the Russians at Somatash on 12 August in which the Afghans claimed to have been attacked. They had killed five Russians and captured the rest of a party of twenty-five. Attempts to have them released had evidently failed.[89] From the report given by Lieutenant Davison in December 1891, Russian intentions were now fairly clear. During his brief captivity the Russians had told the young officer where they thought their frontier lay and their troop movements seemed to indicate that they now meant to enforce their occupation of the Pamirs.[90]

Russian newspapers kept up the pretence that their forces in the Pamirs were 'sporting groups', and they all excused their troops' aggression. Even Morier's patience had its limits. He felt St Petersburg's explanations to the British were the product of 'a character of arrogance, superficiality, contempt for facts, and offensive self-assertion which we might expect to meet in a missive of the tsar to the

Amir of Bokhara'.[91] When Rosebery took office as prime minister in August 1892, he reiterated his call for the delimitation of the Pamirs by a boundary commission, but the Russian foreign minister still demanded that, if a commission was to proceed, it must accept the Oxus as the extent of Afghan claims and the 'Afghan' territories of Roshan and Shignan must be given up.[92] Rosebery rejected the Russian demands on 19 September, arguing that the Russian proposals had the object of 'menacing our Indian possessions', but then he took a softer line, aware that it was impossible to reinforce British interests with troops as readily as the Russians could. Nevertheless, he declared that Bozai Gumbaz, in Wakhan, was the 'Gibraltar of the Hindu Kush', a term which appeared similar to the label for Herat as 'the key to India'.[93] It was a belligerent statement, and probably designed to arouse support amongst his party, the Liberal Imperialists, but he knew that simultaneously restraining the amir and fighting the Russians in the Pamirs was strategically impossible.

Until September 1892 Lansdowne had clung to the idea that British influence could be exercised north of the Hindu Kush, including the Pamirs, but now news of growing discontent in the northern hill states filtered back to Simla, and Lansdowne grew less certain of how Britain could maintain control of the vital passes. There was further fighting on the 'Roof of the World' in 1894 at Roshkol. Shooting broke out between Russian and Afghan picquets, which threatened to involve more troops deployed across the region. Ironically, it was the winter weather that drove back the detachments of both sides and prevented a wider conflict.

However, by June of that year, the conquest of Hunza and Nagar persuaded Lansdowne that no routes east of Bozai Gumbaz could be used by the Russians for an attack on India.[94] In addition, Younghusband was established as a permanent political agent at Chitral where he was able to keep watch for Russian detachments, through agents, on the whole Hindu Kush watershed. Furthermore, negotiations between H. M. Durand and the Amir of Afghanistan in 1893 had established the Wakhan 'corridor'. This strip of territory, only a few miles wide, effectively sealed India off from the Russian Pamirs. The violation of this boundary would clearly constitute a *casus belli*. However, even if there was a war, any fighting could only take place between relatively small forces on the margins of the Hindu Kush, in passes that the British had surveyed and could defend, against Russians who would have over-stretched lines of communication, and a limited campaign season. At last, in February 1895, the Russians relented and the delimitation of the Pamirs began, despite continued uncertainty about Britain's relations with Russia.[95]

An Intelligence 'System'?

Reviewing the conduct of British intelligence officers and the organisation of military intelligence before 1900, the initial impression is that the system, if indeed it can be called a 'system', lacked professionalism. Christopher Andrew believed the Intelligence Division had 'relatively little to do with secret intelligence'.[96] Intelligence officers in London spent most of their time collating information from foreign newspapers and journals. Staff work appealed to some officers, but there was a universal preference for field command. When there was a chance of seeing action, as in the Egyptian campaign of 1882, officers at the Intelligence Division rushed out to the theatre of war. Moreover, most British officers adopted an air of indifference to peacetime training and preparation, preferring a range of social and leisure pursuits. Social conversation on military matters was certainly frowned upon, and being too much of an expert, or too 'bookish', was thought to be a handicap to good character. Younghusband noted that the aim of every officer was simply to be regarded as a 'good fellow'.[97] It has been suggested that this apparent cult of the amateur was, in fact, a good cover from accusations that the British were running spy rings.[98]

There can be no doubt that, in the late nineteenth century, the difference between political envoy, 'handler' and secret agent was purposely vague. Most British officers on 'special duty' in central Asia enjoyed their excursions from regimental routine on the languid plains of India, and if their cover was some *shikar* (hunting), then they certainly enjoyed that too. Moreover, if the boundaries between British officers' duties were sometimes indistinct, then that was also true of the Asian personnel. Clerks, translators, and couriers could just as easily be employed as informers, observers, and spies. In Kashgar, some of the Indian personnel engaged in espionage lived with their families in or around the British consulate, mixing freely with the local population. Senior merchants who had *bona fide* businesses were perfect agents because of their need to travel and their ability to pick up all the news in the bazaar. These *aksakals* (elders) could pass information to the consul and sometimes received requests for specific information. In 1919, but clearly in a long-established tradition, the British consul-general of Kashgar told the merchants to 'watch for enemy agents and propaganda'.[99]

Despite many difficulties, British consuls and political officers were able to maintain a network of agents in overlapping rings right across central Asia, from the Black Sea and the Caucasus, through northern Persia, Afghanistan, Chinese central Asia and on to Gilgit. They collected the intelligence and sent it by 'diplomatic baggage' to the nearest government agency, ranging from Constantinople, Teheran, Peshawar, Bombay and Simla. From there it was eventually sent to London where some sort of intelligence picture could be drawn. But the division of the military intelligence effort across the world between London and Simla was itself made more complex by the coexistence of the Foreign Office consulates. British personnel might find themselves reporting to either the Foreign Office or the Government of India's Foreign Department, or directly to either the British or Indian Army. This complexity necessitated close co-operation at some central point. Furthermore the fragile nature of the networks, and the need for cross-checking of information, added to the problems of collation and interpretation. For these reasons, Brackenbury sought to centralise the whole effort under the Intelligence Division. He confided to a successor that the key was 'having the complete friendship and hearty cooperation of the Foreign Office. So long as you have that, as I had, you can command the use of all their staff at home and abroad.'[100]

In addition to the agents, friendly foreign governments, returning explorers and travellers (who were interviewed by the Government of India), and military attachés (a post created after the Crimean War) all contributed towards the intelligence picture. Nevertheless, it is evident that a large amount of information gathered 'on the ground' was provided by Asian personnel. Not all of it was reliable or accurate. One *canard* that reached the Intelligence Division in London from an agent on the northern border of Afghanistan in 1889 reported: 'Afghanis have advanced towards Kerki and Panjdeh, and have killed two or three hundred Russians . . .'[101] But the result of these deficiencies in the system of the 1890s was that more British officers were engaged in intelligence work, and, at the turn of the century, the British approach to intelligence as a whole was about to change.

Chapter 11

Pulling the Bear's Teeth

Intelligence and Defence Planning, 1895–1914

The information that agents gathered was not simply to track the movements of Russian troops or to locate the passes that they might take into India. The Intelligence Branch at Simla and the Intelligence Division in London filtered and processed the agents' observations in order to create, to use modern terminology, an 'intelligence product'. The 'consumers' of that product were the offices of the British Government, but also the leading generals of the day, including Lord Roberts (former C-in-C India) and Sir Garnet Wolseley (Commander-in-Chief of the British Army). The assessment of topography, Russian strengths and movements identified the problem. It was up to these 'consumers' to provide the solution, but inevitably, there were disagreements. Even the nature of the threat was a source of dispute. The eminent military historian, Brian Bond, summed up the tsarist army:

> Its officer corps had little cohesion or sense of professionalism. Nor was modern organisation and training helped by Russia's poverty, vast sparsely populated country with poor communications and lack of a substantial armaments industry ... [but] despite clumsy mobilisation, weak logistical arrangements, a divided command and obsolete tactics [it] did not destroy her awesome reputation as the 'steamroller'.[1]

It was the sheer size of the Russian Army that caused the British concern. The mobilised strength of the Russian Army was 1,928,510 men, but in Central Asia, War Office calculations in 1889 estimated that there would be no more than 30,000 to strike against Afghanistan.[2]

Roberts and the Scientific Frontier

Roberts was convinced that Russian agents and sympathisers would prepare the way with campaigns of sedition, and he knew that the British Army could never hold down the Indian people in revolt at the same time as stemming a Russian invasion. The aim was to keep Russia at arm's length by securing the Hindu Kush passes in Afghanistan.[3] Herat was the lynchpin of the plan, both for its strategic and geographical position, and the way it would 'check the advance of Russia towards India from the southern shores of the Caspian, and the lower valley of the Oxus'. However, Roberts warned of the dangers of subversion. The Russian 'explorers' he deemed:

> The inevitable fore runners of every Russian advance ... will endeavour by
> all means in their powers to gain influence amongst the tribes, and if they
> can accomplish this, we are certain to have trouble in the neighbourhood of
> Punjab and Peshawar.[4]

Lord Salisbury agreed with Roberts and commented: 'The scientific frontier
doctrine, which was so much derided some years ago, is master of the field now.'[5]

Roberts had offered a neat solution: 'We must advance nearer to Kabul. If Russia
advanced on Balkh and established posts at Bamian, and a railway, we would not
be close enough [to get there first]'.[6] However, the DMI, Brackenbury, criticised
Roberts's growing pessimism about Russian capabilities. He wrote a note to James
Grierson in the Intelligence Branch at Simla, which strongly suggests *he* believed
the Russians' main focus was not in central Asia, but in south-east Europe:

> Your Memorandum strengthened my hands greatly against those in this
> country, and there are many, who live in a constant state of apprehension of
> Russian aggression against India, an apprehension they never disguise,
> which they communicate to a timorous press, and thus play the very game
> of Russia, which is, as you and I have always agreed, to paralyse the whole
> Army of India by threats of aggression along its northern frontier.[7]

In 1890, Brackenbury expressed his dissatisfaction with Roberts and his
influence over the Indian Intelligence Branch. He accused him of giving 'an
exaggerated estimate of the Russian situation in Central Asia, and of Russian
readiness for war ...'[8] He was sceptical of the value of the Russian railways in
Turkestan, which the Intelligence Branch regarded with some anxiety. But the root
of the criticism was not simply a difference of interpretation. Brackenbury was
eager to bring the Indian Intelligence Branch under the control of the Intelligence
Division at the War Office, and therefore under his own command.

Sir George White, who succeeded Roberts in 1893 as Commander-in-Chief in
India, expressed concern that Brackenbury was ambitious for more authority.[9] The
reforms in the Indian Intelligence Branch under Brackenbury from 1891 were
designed to limit intelligence activities to information-gathering, rather than
providing analysis and solutions to Russian invasion plans. The Intelligence
Division in London concerned itself with the compilation of reports which could be
used by the army or the government offices, but Brackenbury did not want rival
analyses to interfere with an overall army intelligence assessment.[10] Under
Brackenbury, the Intelligence Division was divided into sections responsible for a
geographical area as before. But now D section covered Russia, Persia, central Asia,
the Far East and India, as well as Burma and Afghanistan. Intelligence-gathering
itself was also more clearly defined. Brackenbury opposed clandestine operations,
but encouraged foreign travel so that 'intelligencers' could familiarise themselves
with their areas of responsibility. Covert espionage was ruled out, but officers were
expected to 'use their initiative'. Whilst these reforms appeared to temper the
'alarmist' attitudes of the Indian Intelligence Branch, in reality they changed little.
British officers still manned the consulates through central Asia, and occasionally

roamed the mountains and deserts engaged on undercover missions, most of which were not recognised as 'official'. Asian agents were still employed, and some still operated inside Russian Turkestan.

Ultimately, the Indian Intelligence Branch had rarely developed its own plans for the defence of India anyway. It had, in fact, informed the ideas drawn up by the commanders-in-chief. Nothing was done about that until the formation of a general staff in 1905, but it is likely that the ambitious Brackenbury was working towards the creation of just such a body, albeit in a centralised form, from the very beginning.

The plan British India ended up with was, in fact, the best one of all, following a natural political and defensive line. The North-West Frontier followed a range of mountains and arid hills from Baluchistan to the Hindu Kush. It was cleft by several large passes but its proximity to India meant that it was possible to maintain a watch over them and even garrison key positions like Quetta and Peshawar. However, concerns about internal security meant that offensive action was still thought preferable to waiting on this natural frontier. The chief problem was that the border lay astride a belt of tribal territory where the people were intensely suspicious of feringhees. Roberts believed there was a need for closer relations with the tribesmen to thwart Russian intrigue. He explained the Russian tactics:

> Their emissaries [once Afghanistan has fallen] would be busy everywhere, rousing the restless, discontented spirits which are to be found in every province of India, and tampering with the loyalty of our native soldiers ... Our troops would be harassed by incessant raids from one end of the country to the other. .... by remaining on the defensive, we might drive the Afghans, and the frontier tribes, into the arms of Russia, while we should run a very serious risk, not only of seeing our fellow subjects turn against us but of losing the service of our native soldiers.[11]

The solution proposed was threefold. First, 'to have such a hold over the Afghans and the warlike tribes of the frontier as would ensure their throwing their lot in with us'. Second, 'command of the approaches from Afghanistan to India' (namely the key passes in tribal territory). Third, 'the front contracted to such a length to make it defended [*sic*] by a reasonably sized army'. He urged a policy which would 'improve relations with all the frontier tribes from Gilgit to Seistan' based on respect for British power: 'We live by prestige, and we cannot afford to let our Native troops or the people of India doubt the maintenance of our supremacy.'[12] But he acknowledged that in some areas, this would be an uphill struggle. The Afridis were especially important, for not only were they the most likely, in Roberts's view, to side with the Russians, but they lived astride the strategic Khyber Pass. No less vital was the need to prevent any uprisings amongst the Baluchis in the south, which might be exploited, letting the Russians outflank them, and which, ultimately, 'would make the defence of Afghanistan untenable'. Roberts warned that the existence of the vast Baluchistan deserts was no bar to the Russians, who had marched considerable forces across similar wastes in central

Asia in 1873.[13] Roberts's 'scientific frontier' doctrine was therefore more than just a race to the passes of the Hindu Kush inside Afghanistan. On the North-West Frontier it involved road construction, new rail links, the deployment of political agents, subsidies, and operations to pacify the recalcitrant tribes. There were even military campaigns in Wana (1894) and Chitral (1895) to secure the approaches to India. Nevertheless, in 1897–8, a serious uprising by the frontier tribes in Swat, Malakand, Buner and Kohat was a surprise to the Indian Army and it required the deployment of over 30,000 men to crush it. By the turn of the century, the frontier was closely garrisoned and monitored for any signs of disturbance or sedition, but the tribesmen remained an intractable element in the security of India.

Intrigue in Persia

One problem the Victorian intelligence agencies had not yet solved was whose job it was to verify incoming data. The Intelligence Division in London, despite its criticisms of the assessments provided by the Intelligence Branch at Simla, clearly believed that it should be sent processed information rather than the bulky raw data picked up in bazaars across central Asia. Referring to Meshed, one of the officers of the Intelligence Division warned the Government of India about Colonel Maclean's 'very bad habit of telegraphing any rumour that reaches him without verifying it'.[14] It is difficult to see quite how Maclean was supposed to do this when he was reliant solely on the agents in the field and he had no access to the sources the Intelligence Division enjoyed in London, such as the reports of the military attaché in St Petersburg, or the observations of the consuls by the Black Sea. Indeed, the Intelligence Division called for more observers to augment its own sources. It wanted a man stationed at Tiflis in the Caucasus and it wanted to get British and Indian Army officers to study in Russia.[15] It advocated that officers trained in the Intelligence Division should take over as military attachés and when the existing officer at St Petersburg, Herbert, was caught by the Russians receiving military plans from Colonel Schmidt in 1890, there was just such an opening. With news of fresh Russian interest in the northern Persian frontier, the Intelligence Division also urged a delimitation of the Perso-Afghan border.[16]

By May 1888 the ID believed Russia was in a stronger position from which to threaten Afghanistan and northern Persia than in any previous period. Wolfe Murray produced a cogent memorandum on the ability of the Russian Army to concentrate in Central Asia but also the difficulties it would face in trying to advance as far as Teheran.[17] He concluded that Russia could take Herat and Afghan Turkestan but it was not yet in a position to 'menace British India'. Nevertheless, he added, 'after carrying out certain measures, which are by no means impracticable, she will stand in a far more formidable position than at present'.[18] This was a reference to the improvements being made in Russia's transport network across Central Asia. Like the tentacles of some gigantic octopus, Russian railway lines continued to advance southwards towards Persia and Afghanistan. Before the construction of the railways, it had taken 50–60 days to make the journey from Orenburg to Tashkent, but by 1900 it was possible to move troops in a matter of hours along the new lines from Krasnovodsk on the Caspian to Merv (1885),

Samarkand (1888) and Kushk on the Afghan border (1900). Another line reached Tashkent from Orenburg in 1898 and branches pushed into the Pamirs and to the Oxus at Kerki. Despite successful revisions of the Afghan boundary in 1887 and in 1893, and the settlement of the Pamirs dispute in 1895, the Intelligence Division remained unconvinced that this new co-operation was 'détente'. It concluded, 'symptoms had not been wanting in that Russia was desirous of strengthening her political influence in those regions [on her borders], as affording a possible line of advance towards Afghanistan and India'.[19]

However, when Brackenbury came to the end of his tenure as Director of Military Intelligence he was posted to India to become the military member of the viceroy's council. Salisbury wrote in support of the decision, and noted how much he respected his 'ability and clearness of judgement'.[20] With Major-General Edward Chapman appointed the new DMI, and an old colleague from the Intelligence Division, John Ardagh, as the viceroy's secretary, Brackenbury established a closer communication between London and Simla. New procedures for intelligence-gathering were proposed.[21] Chapman noted that: 'Our means of communication, through newswriters reporting to our agents in Persia, and in Peshawar and Quetta, is an old and worn-out arrangement.'[22] Brackenbury told Lord Lansdowne: 'The reports of our newswriters are the cause of much unnecessary alarm in this country.' Referring to the British handlers, he added: 'When I was at the War Office I had repeatedly to call attention to the reckless way in which they accepted the news-writers' reports as Gospel.'[23] He insisted that the Intelligence Branch at Simla must only gather information and avoid political missions. There were to be four sections each with a paid attaché, although unpaid officers could join the branch for specific duties. The Foreign Department of the Government of India was to have control of the publication of any reports and would, in return, grant a budget of 10,000 rupees. A weekly exchange of views was then established between Colonel E. R. Elles, head of the Intelligence Branch, and Chapman in London, but, given the contrasts in perspectives and priorities between India and London, there were still differences of opinion.[24]

By 1898, the focus of Anglo-Russian rivalry had shifted once again to Persia's Khorassan province, regarded as an avenue of advance against western Afghanistan and the 'left flank' of India. Throughout the 1890s, efforts to maintain a network of 'newswriters' continued at Meshed. H. M. Durand was posted to Teheran at the end of 1894 to replace Sir Frank Lascelles, the British minister there, and Ney Elias took over in May 1895. The consul-general was served by three Europeans: the vice-consul, E. C. Ringer Thomson, an assistant, Fraser, and Dr Woolbert, a surgeon. Amongst his Asian staff were Khan Bahadur Moula Baiksh (an interpreter and advisor on Persian affairs), five men of the Corps of Guides, seven Persian soldiers and 22 Turcoman *sowars* (cavalry troopers).

However, at the time Elias arrived, the British intelligence effort at Meshed was on the back foot. It seems that there was probably only one Asian agent still operating in Trans-Caspia and he was deemed unreliable, although new men were despatched to observe and report on rumours of troop movements that summer. They were known only by their code letters. One of these met and spoke with

Russian officers, which suggests that he held some rank, but another was shadowed and almost intercepted with letters for the consul. The agents reported on a number of military exercises and made unverified claims about the extension of the Trans-Caspian railway. Some information arrived quite unexpectedly, as in the case of a Japanese colonel who had crossed Siberia. The colonel informed Elias that the railway at Charharjui on the Oxus was in poor repair since all Russia's railway construction was being concentrated on the Trans-Siberian route. It is likely that the colonel was another agent assessing Russia's military capacity. Less encouraging was the dismissal of Mirza Hassan Ali Khan, the consulate assistant who had served Maclean. No charges were made but Gerald Morgan suspects he had fallen to 'Russian blandishments'.

Russian attempts to get greater influence in Persian affairs were certainly driven by ambitious men like Petr Mikhailovich Vlasov, the consul-general. His efforts to undermine the Persian governors by complaints to the shah were a part of Russian intrigue that threatened to destabilise the country. British intelligence efforts to thwart these moves met with some success. Lieutenant Coningham was secretly despatched to the Russo-Persian border in 1891 when the Meshed consulate had received rumours that the Russians were trying to press the Persians to relinquish the village of Firuzah. His route was carefully planned to avoid telegraph offices or Russian informants. On arrival, Coningham discovered the village commanded a remote pass into Persia with well-irrigated pastures that could supply troops and horses. His information was passed to the shah and the Persians, for a time, successfully resisted Russian demands.[25]

But there were many other attempts by the Russians to gain more influence. The Cossack brigade in the capital was reformed into an effective fighting force that could put pressure on the Persian government. This extraordinary unit had been set up in 1879 when the shah, struck by the bearing of a Cossack escort on a visit to Europe, decided to have his own version. The Russian officers sent to train the force were of a poor calibre and it was badly managed until 1894 when V. A. Kosogovsky took command. However, throughout its existence, the Russian commander of the brigade was always invited to form part of the governing circle in Teheran, giving the Russians direct access to the Persian court. Elsewhere, the pressure on the Persian authorities was just as relentless. In Meshed, the tsar's agents spread rumours of a bread shortage, and accused the Khorasan governor of hoarding vital supplies. Unsurprisingly, the volatile crowds in the bazaar made violent protests which quickly degenerated into rioting. The Khorasan governor was then offered Russian 'protection', and there were rumours that the tsar's troops would march in to 'restore order'. The British consul only discovered the conspiratorial nature of the affair when the wives at the Russian consulate inadvertently admitted that they had known about the bread 'shortage' some days before and had made appropriate preparations to meet it.[26]

In another incident, the Afghans captured a Russian agent disguised as a Turcoman who had been despatched by Vlasov. When Vlasov complained and demanded the release of this 'innocent Russian subject', the British consulate replied using the Russian's real name, indicating it knew about the whole charade.

It was due to the Asian agents that key information on the Russian's identity and pay was known to the British. Moreover, copies of Vlasov's letters were being passed to Thomson, the vice-consul, by Persians working for the British so that details of Russian intrigues against the Vizier of Meshed and the British-owned bank there were revealed. The vizier was naturally delighted by the support he received from the British. Supporting the local elites turned out to be vital when, in 1896, the shah was assassinated and there was a danger the country might collapse.

Vlasov was undeterred. He turned his attention to Seistan, the region of Persia beyond the semi-arid and mountainous Afghan border, which lay on the direct route to India. In the early years of the twentieth century, the possibility of a railway to this point became as critical as the Russian threat to Herat had been in the 1880s. Russian consular agents were established at Birjand and Seistan in 1893, which seemed to fit into a pattern of increased clandestine intelligence-gathering and survey activity.[27] In fact the first consuls were withdrawn the same year, because, despite initial assurances, it was discovered that they were not Russian nationals. However, hearing of a Perso-Afghan boundary commission in Seistan, Vlasov informed Ney Elias he intended to send a doctor there to study yellow fever. Elias, wise to the game, suggested South America was a better location for the study of the disease. When Vlasov pressed his desire to send a man, Elias pointed out that there was no yellow fever in Seistan – 'only in the Russian army'. He then added that the commission had finished its work, and so, unsurprisingly, Vlasov lost interest.[28] Nevertheless, a Russian consulate was eventually established there in 1899, followed by a stronger Russian agency in 1900.

The decay of Persian central authority fuelled the rivalry of British and Russian officials. When, in 1898, Teheran decided to sell off customs revenue to raise capital for the near-bankrupt Persian government, it provided an opening for foreign interference.[29] Joseph Rabino, the manager of the British-owned Imperial Bank of Persia, pointed out that a proposed road from the Gulf to Teheran had been abandoned as the £80,000 allocated from British sources had been insufficient. By contrast, Russia had spent £250,000 on a road from Resht to Teheran.[30] Kosogovsky, commander of the Cossack brigade, believed that it was the British who were predatory, whilst his own side was 'inactive'. However, the Commercial Bank of St Petersburg was eager to loan money to Persia in return for control of all Persia's customs revenues to manage debt repayments. This would mean, in effect, that the whole country, including southern Persia, would fall under Russian influence. Durand tried to block it, and suggested a joint Anglo-Russian loan.[31] The Russians rejected the idea and continued to make inroads in the north: mine concessions were obtained, and port taxes were payable to the Russian government at Enzeli.

Hostility towards Britain was also more overt, both among officials and in Russian newspapers, reaching a crescendo during the South African War (1899–1902). There was considerable resentment of British commercial power and the Royal Navy's presence in southern Persia and the Gulf.[32] Aggressively promoting their loan, the Russians put forward monopolistic terms which included the total exclusion of the British from Persian railway concessions. Firuz Kazem-zedah noted that the British saw loans in a commercial sense (asking themselves whether the Persians could repay the amount), but the Russians subordinated economic interests to political ones: they simply intended to gain a monopoly of influence over Persia. As far as commerce was concerned, that could be developed after they had secured control.[33] For this reason they sought to avoid expensive railways which would lead to more British goods flooding Persian markets. Durand, for one, regarded the Russian loan issue as a defeat for Britain.

The hostile atmosphere created a new crop of Russian plans to attack the British in Asia. Captain V. Lebedev of the Russian Imperial Guard published just such a plan for the invasion of India in 1898.[34] Anti-British sentiments in the press and academia were especially fuelled by British setbacks in South Africa in December 1899. In January 1900, by when an even larger part of the British Army was committed to the conflict with the Boers, Count Muraviev, the Russian Minister for Foreign Affairs, urged the tsar to authorise a more determined effort to penetrate Persia and block British influence there. Above all he wanted to maintain the freedom to push Russian influence further south at some point in the future. Consequently he encouraged Russian commerce in the region, the construction of roads that linked Persia to Russian territory, the development of trans-Caspian shipping, and postal and telegraphic links.[35] Others at the Russian court advised caution and stressed the far greater importance of reaching the Bosporus. The final decision rested with the tsar who, according to General Kuropatkin,

> ... had grandiose plans in his head: to take Manchuria for Russia, to move toward the annexation of Korea to Russia. He dreams of taking under his orb Tibet too. He wants to take Persia, to seize not only the Bosporus but the Dardanelles as well.[36]

Yet caution prevailed in St Petersburg and there was no dash for the Persian Gulf. Troop concentrations on the Afghan border, although numbering some 60,000 men, were little more than demonstrations.[37] Nevertheless, news of greater ammunition production in the Russian Kolomna and Mytishchi factories and the increased troop transport traffic on the Caspian were carefully monitored.

Lord Curzon, the new Viceroy of India, was deeply alarmed by these developments and by fresh Russian demands to open diplomatic relations with Afghanistan, which suggested a desire to interfere in India. Moreover, he believed that Persia was in such a state of decay that it could not be revived. He believed it was particularly vulnerable to Russian imperialism. As a solution, he proposed a partition of the country with consulates in every quarter, high-profile visits to the Gulf by the Royal Navy and urgent improvements to the telegraph system so as to provide early warning of a Russian *coup de main*. Ever critical of the snail's pace of officialdom, he was soon frustrated by the sheer inactivity of the government at home. Curzon privately warned:

> One day the crash will come, and then my Despatches will be published and in my grave I shall be justified. Not that I care for that. But I long to see prescience, some width of view, some ability to forecast the evil of tomorrow, instead of bungling over the evil of today.[38]

The establishment of Russian consuls, and their monopolistic loan, merely convinced the Foreign Office of the futility of trying to influence northern Persia. In short, the British government was unable to stop the fall of Persia and its financial collapse seemed to be fast approaching. Reminders were sent to the Persians that customs in southern ports must not be handed over, but Curzon was more belligerent. He advocated reciprocal moves, including the landing of troops along the southern coast if the Russians seized the northern provinces. The Russians also began to believe that the disintegration of Persia into satellite zones was the best policy, avoiding any firm boundary that might give the British reason to block future development or expansion in the region.

Intelligence Failure and the Invasion of Tibet

Curzon was deeply anxious about Tibet. Although the mountain chain of the Himalayas provided an effective curtain wall in northern India's defences, the prospect of this province falling under Russian influence, as seemed to be happening to Persia, filled Curzon with dread. The Tibetans themselves were not a threat at all. In 1888, the British had found it easy enough to throw back a Tibetan force which had occupied the Chumbi Valley. The main problem was in the weakness of Tibet's Chinese overlords. Defeated by the Japanese in the war of 1894–5, paralysed by a rebellion in its north-western provinces, and thrown into confusion by a far more serious anti-foreign and revolutionary uprising by the Society of Harmonious Fists in 1900, the Chinese Empire was clearly on the wane. Moreover, the construction of the Russian Trans-Siberian railway suggested a more vigorous policy from St Petersburg in east Asia, which might fill the vacuum of power left by the Chinese. The British ambassador had already been informed by Count Witte, Russia's economics minister, that the tsar's railways would eventually penetrate Sinkiang province.[39] Meanwhile Curzon was unable to get the Tibetans to carry out the terms of an agreed trade treaty of 1893. They even tore down boundary markers in defiance of a settlement and refused to demarcate the rest of the border. Letters to the Dalai Lama were returned unopened or undelivered. News then arrived from the chargé d'affaires in St Petersburg, reporting that Aharamba Agyan Dorjiev, apparently an emissary of the Dalai Lama, had been granted an audience with the tsar in September 1900. To Curzon, it seemed that the Russians were indeed beginning their penetration of Tibet.

British intelligence on Tibet, not including that from St Petersburg, was gathered from three sources. The Government of Bengal forwarded reports from its frontier posts at Darjeeling, Kalimpong and in Sikkim. Like much trans-border news elicited from traders, the majority was bazaar gossip and rumour. It was, like the newswriters' material further west, simply transmitted without any attempt at editing or verification. The second source of information was the British minister in Beijing. He, in turn was dependent on consulates inside China, and on the reports of missionaries deep in the interior, but still hundreds of miles from Tibet itself. The third source was Colonel Ravenshaw, the British resident at Kathmandu who used the Nepalese government's information to complete useful reports, even though the material itself was often obscure and difficult to interpret. Names of

Tibetans proved particularly problematic because of the variety of transliteration techniques. Dates too were complex since the Nepalese, Chinese and Tibetan calendars were all different. Tibetan suspicions about all outsiders, and their strict desire to prevent anyone reaching Lhasa, made the penetration of Tibet by agents almost impossible. There was consequently no way of verifying the rumours that a party of Russians had reached Lhasa in 1900.[40] What was clear was that Dorjiev was back in Russia that year, and it appeared he was, as a Buryat Mongol, a Russian citizen acting as an intermediary between Lhasa and St Petersburg.[41]

In 1902, the British minister in Beijing, Sir Ernest Satow, passed on an extract from the *China Times* which suggested a secret agreement had been concluded between China and Russia over Tibet.[42] The Russian government denied the existence of any treaty, but after years of similar protestations over central Asia, which had been followed by military action, the Foreign Office regarded the assurances as valueless. In fact, as Major Bower of the Intelligence Division in London had pointed out, a Russian invasion of India through Tibet would be impossible. The altitude, lack of supplies, natural barriers of mountains and rivers, not to mention the distance (it was a thousandmiles from Lhasa to the nearest Russian military post) ruled out any attack. However, it was subversion and the political dominance of Tibet that the British feared. If Tibet became a Russian protectorate, there was a chance tsarist agents could stir up trouble on India's north-east frontier. Nor were such fears far-fetched. In the aftermath of the Boxer Rebellion in China, Russia occupied and retained Mongolia, an enormous province of the Chinese Empire: was Tibet next?

Curzon's first attempt to get the Tibetans to negotiate on a proper footing was to send Francis Younghusband at the head of a well-armed boundary commission as far as Khamba Jong, a few miles inside Tibetan territory. The Tibetans refused to discuss the border and Younghusband had to remain inactive for five months. He seized upon every scrap of information and sent it to Delhi. Rumours of Cossacks entering Tibet, sinister emissaries by the names of Tsybikov and Norzanov (the latter deported from Darjeeling in 1900) and an elusive spymaster in Mongolia called von Grot seemed to support the need for firmer military action. The Government of India duly passed it all on to London where Younghusband was beginning to be seen as somewhat unreliable. Younghusband protested, but there was little he could do to verify intelligence whilst he was stuck on the frontier.[43]

The log-jam was broken by the arrest of two Asian agents by the Tibetans in August 1903. Major Frederick O'Connor had been running agents recruited from Lachung village (inside Sikkim but not far from Khamba Jong) to gather intelligence on the strategically important Shigatse, home of the Pachen Lama and the gateway to western Tibet, but two had been caught. Demanding their release, the mission seized Tibetan livestock and Younghusband informed the viceroy. Letters from the families also demanded their release and Lachung villagers feared the men would be tortured and executed (for which the Tibetans certainly had a reputation). Curzon, convinced the men had been killed, wrote to the Secretary of State for India on 5 November that the seizure of the men on a 'trading mission' was the last in a series of episodes of defiance to the British Empire. Their arrest provoked a new military phase to the mission, and over 1,200 British and Indian troops fought their way to Lhasa. For a year the fate of the agents remained unknown. In fact, they were taken to the capital and kept in solitary confinement underground for twelve months until released under the terms of Younghusband's treaty. Despite an initial beating they had been fed and cared for.

The flight of the Dalai Lama and the absence of any authority in Lhasa made it difficult for Younghusband to make an agreement that would last. Moreover, it could not be concealed that there was no evidence of Russian influence at the capital at all. Balfour's government hoped that some indemnity might be secured and considered destroying part of Lhasa as a punitive measure but the Tibetans argued the British should pay an indemnity for their invasion, knowing, perhaps, that the winter and scarce supplies would eventually force the British out. In the end, Younghusband managed to extract his treaty, but the British Government disapproved of its terms which included a permanent resident, a trade deal favourable to British India and the exclusion of all foreign agents.

At first, the British Government had approved enthusiastically of Younghusband's achievements, but they disowned all the arrangements after strong protests from China and Russia. Although Russia was at that moment engaged in a war with Japan, the movement of its troops to the border of Afghanistan and the extension of the railway network seemed to threaten Britain with a war it did not want over central Asia. Under the terms of the alliance of 1902 with Japan, Britain would be honour-bound to assist its east Asian partner if another country was involved.[44] Russia's military ally was France and the last thing that Balfour's government wanted was to ruin the rapprochement then developing with Paris. Moreover, extending British influence over Tibet carried the risk that a dispute might arise with Russia in the future, committing British troops to the defence of a remote, worthless region. The agreement, which Younghusband had so painstakingly acquired, was thus repudiated.[45] St John Brodrick, moved from the War Office to replace George Hamilton as Secretary of State for India, ensured that Younghusband became the scapegoat for the mission's failure, but he was just as determined to rein in Curzon and the whole independence of the foreign policy of the Government of India too.[46] Gripped by an overwhelming sense of imperial insecurity, the Cabinet wanted to bring Curzon under their close direction. In fact, Curzon resigned in a storm of controversy ostensibly over the control of the Indian Army and its reform in 1905. Kitchener, the Commander-in-Chief in India, played on his contacts back in London to outmanoeuvre the headstrong viceroy; Curzon played into his enemies' hands by clinging stubbornly to his view that he should control policy in India, rather than the Secretary of State or the Commander-in-Chief.[47]

German Intrigue in Persia

The defeat of the tsar's armies and fleets in the Russo-Japanese War (1904–5) and the Revolution in Russia in 1905 marked a turning point in the Great Game. The combination of external defeat of its land and naval forces with widespread internal unrest graphically demonstrated Russia's weaknesses. Financially, too,

Russia lagged far behind the powers of Western Europe, and lacked the industrial capacity of Britain and Germany. The logic of Britain's Entente Cordiale with France was now to settle the differences with France's ally, and, in just two years, the British government concluded the Anglo-Russian Convention of 31 August 1907. Two spheres of influence were defined in Persia, the north to Russia and the south to Britain with a neutral strip between, although the Persians were not consulted about the arrangement. The territorial integrity of Afghanistan and Tibet were guaranteed by both sides and Russia also obtained Britain's approval for the eventual Russian occupation of the Bosporus, provided other powers agreed.[48] The decision was certainly influenced by the joint statement of the Military and Naval Intelligence Divisions' finding that the Russian Navy could only be tackled 'across the ruins of the French fleet', and that the Eastern Mediterranean could no longer be considered a 'British lake'.[49] However, there can be little doubt that it was the new aggression of Germany that finally persuaded the British government of the need to bring to an end disputes it could not resolve by other means.

The sincerity of the Convention of 1907 may not have been questioned in London, but in India the old suspicions remained. Intrigues in Persia did not abate and the Russians seemed just as active in trying to extend their influence throughout the country. However, it was the arrival of German consuls in the region and their blatant attempts to win over the Muslim world to further their own territorial ambitions that tended to draw the British and Russians into some semblance of co-operation.

In the 1890s, a new climate of aggressive expansionism had developed in Germany which, to some extent, reflected the ambitions and anxieties of the new Kaiser, Wilhelm II. Von Bülow, the State Secretary of the Foreign Ministry, echoed the Kaiser's sentiments when, in 1899, he stated the end of the century would bring about a 'redistribution of empires and power' – and Germany would have to choose whether it was going to be the 'hammer or the anvil of world politics'.[50] Clustered around the imperial court were a number of extreme right-wing pressure groups variously demanding developments in the German armed forces, protection of the landed elites and colonialism. One of these groups, the Naval League, predicted that unless Germany was able to expand it would either be 'choked in its [present] narrow territory or it will be squashed by the major world powers to which it will moreover have to send millions and millions of emigrants'.[51] Admiral Müller, the Kaiser's chief naval aide, asked von Tirpitz, the grand designer of the German High Seas Fleet, what should be done if the expansion of the German Navy provoked a war with Britain and provided his own reply: 'Our answer must be . . . a world war which will lead our armies into India and Egypt.'[52] Max von Oppenheim, known to the British as 'the spy', persuaded the Kaiser that the Middle East offered considerable potential for Germany. Believing that the Ottoman Empire would eventually be eclipsed, Oppenheim envisaged a *Drang nach Osten* with colonial *Lebensraum* stretching from the Bosporus to British India. The concept of an empire across the ancient civilisations of the Middle East appealed to Wilhelm's vanity, and seemed to offer an outlet for the right wing's expansionist energies.

Courting Abdul Hamid, the Sultan, in 1896 in spite of widespread European condemnation of the Turkish massacres of Armenians, the Kaiser was soon invited on a state visit to Jerusalem and Constantinople. Many in the British administration ridiculed Wilhelm's histrionics, but there was some unease at his attempts to win over Muslims given that such a large number of them lived under British rule. This unease was reinforced by the Kaiser's support for the Boers, the German seizure of Tsingtao in China and a rapid naval building programme – all of which seemed designed to threaten the British Empire. In Persia and the Ottoman Empire, German agents were sent on 'archaeological expeditions' to gather intelligence and visit the oilfields, and a number of German banks and businesses appeared offering low rates of interest to undercut the Imperial Bank of Persia. The idea of a railway from Berlin to Baghdad also raised the possibility that commerce would be drawn away from the coasts to the interior. Such a railway might also provide a strategic route for the deployment of German troops deep within the Middle East. Curzon had made a high profile visit to the Persian Gulf and persuaded the Foreign Office to declare the region a British sphere of influence, but the government seemed reluctant to do anything which might jeopardise the Anglo-Russian convention. The Government of India therefore sent Major Percy Cox, a former Indian Army officer in the Political Service, to southern Persia to monitor German intrigue and to befriend the local Persian elites. At the same time, Wilhelm Wassmuss, a protégé of Oppenheim, was busily engaged in fraternising with the Tangistani tribesmen in the same area; he was to be most persistent thorn in the side of British forces in the region in the years to come, but, ironically, his mistakes would ultimately lead to Britain's most important intelligence coup of the Great War.

In fact, Germany's Middle East policy was in tatters before the outbreak of the war in 1914. The Young Turk revolt in 1908 and the exile of the Sultan the following year was initially accompanied by anti-foreign sentiment and open criticism of reactionary Germany. The German ambassador, Konrad von Wangenheim, was able to back a right-wing coup by Enver Pasha, a Turkish officer trained by the German Army, on 23 January 1913 in order to restore some German influence. However, the appointment of Liman von Sanders to high command in Constantinople in October that year was the subject of an international dispute. The Turks had requested German assistance in the reform of the army after their stinging defeats in the two Balkan Wars (1911–13). Wangenheim described this as a unique opportunity to 'imbue the Turkish people with the German spirit' and the Kaiser despatched General Sanders in order to effect the 'Germanisation of the Turkish Army' and make Germany dominant in Turkish foreign policy.[53] Russia objected in the strongest terms and was supported by France and Britain, forcing Sanders to be moved to a new appointment within the Turkish Army. The climb-down was unpopular in Germany, giving rise to a sense of desperation in Berlin. Referring to the demise of Napoleon, the Kaiser remarked: 'Either the German flag will fly over the fortifications of the Bosporus or I shall suffer the same sad fate as the great exile on the island of St Helena.'[54] The reality was that Germany was simply unable to create the exclusive economic bloc envisaged in *Mitteleuropa*, and the Berlin–Baghdad railway terminated in the mountains of Turkey. Most significant of all was the continued mistaken belief that the Germans could create a united pan-Islamic empire under the Kaiser's leadership.[55] It was a dangerous delusion in keeping with the notion that Wilhelm II was a beloved *Volkskaiser* (people's emperor) presiding over a nation that must either expand territorially or perish.

The Formation of the British Secret Service

The Secret Service Bureau, the forerunner of the Secret Intelligence Service (SIS), was not established until 1909, but there were already several converging strands of development thanks to the emergence of a German threat. Alongside the Army's Intelligence Division (which worked closely with the Foreign and Colonial Offices) the Royal Navy had been persuaded to set up a Naval Intelligence Division by Lord Salisbury in 1886 to monitor first the development of the French and later the German fleets. At home, a Secret Service Department in the police had existed briefly in 1867–8 to deal with Irish terrorism, but a more permanent Special Branch of the Metropolitan Police was set up in 1887 (the staff of which were drawn in part from the Irish Special Branch set up at Scotland Yard in 1883). The role of the Special Branch was to deal with political crime, but apart from the arrest of a handful of anarchists, it had little work to do until the German spy scares of the Edwardian era.

Military Intelligence was still the most advanced of all the agencies at the turn of the century. The War Office Library, representing the distillation of foreign periodicals and journals, as well as a wide range of military literature, provided a wealth of information that could be passed on to field commanders. This proved useful in the campaign in South Africa at the turn of the century, but not all appreciated the effort: General Sir Redvers Buller returned his Intelligence Division handbook believing he knew all there was to know about Southern Africa. Unfortunately this knowledge did not save him from a serious check at Colenso in 1899.[56] Successive governments were also eager to limit the budget of the Intelligence Division. Lord Edward Gleichen explained how the 'secret service funds' did not cover the expenses of his missions overseas. However, it should be remembered that all army officers were expected to depend partly on their private means during their service lives so there was nothing unusual in this arrangement. The Government of India was far more generous in its budgeting, but Gleichen used his numerous social contacts across Europe, including the King of Spain, to facilitate his travel and accommodation anyway.[57]

Robert Baden Powell, who spent his leave 'spying' on the North-West Frontier in the 1880s, believed the absence of payment was a way of ensuring that only men with conviction played the game:

> The best spies are unpaid men who are doing it for the love of the thing ...
> and though the "agent", if caught, may "go under", unhonoured and
> unsung, he knows in his heart of hearts that he has done his "bit" for his
> country as fully as his comrade who falls in battle.[58]

Baden Powell demonstrated his typical ingenuity whilst sketching foreign fortresses in the Mediterranean. Spending a few days collecting butterflies with a giant net to establish the idea he was just a 'mad Englishman', he would then sit down to paint his specimens with a water-colour set. Only close observation would reveal that the delicate patterns of the wings were in fact the plan outline of walls, ditches and gun emplacements.[59] Sir John Ardagh, DMI 1896–1901, knew that collating material from periodicals and the reports of informers on the ground, such as the head of the Persian telegraph network or British railway officials, was a key aspect of intelligence labour, but ID officers were permitted to travel, and, like Baden Powell, were encouraged to 'use their initiative'. He remarked: 'It was not often that a secret agent discovered anything of importance, but it sometimes did happen.'[60]

The chief problem was that the Intelligence Division, staffed by just eighteen officers in 1900, seemed to be too small to provide coverage for the entire British Empire. Although sections were responsible for different parts of the world, the periodic missions of the ID officers provided only a small proportion of the intelligence gathered. Captain Wallscourt Waters, head of Section D covering Russia and Asia, stated that 'underground intelligence really amounts to very little, nothing to worry about in my opinion'.[61] Nevertheless, such sentiments really conceal the enormous network that spanned across the Empire. Given the sheer scale of Britain's colonies, and the abundance of naval stations and patrolling vessels, the British were remarkably well informed about events around the globe in an age before satellite communications. As the voluminous archives of the Indian Office Library indicate, a vast amount of detailed intelligence was transmitted to Britain from consuls, postmasters, newswriters, planters, merchants and travellers via the Indian government.

Gathering intelligence through local sources was also certainly common practice in the penumbra of colonial wars of the Victorian period and suggests a typicality in the activities of the Great Game. Moreover, in the summer of 1899, the ID sent ten 'special officers' to South Africa as the nucleus of a new Field Intelligence Department to gather information of tactical significance. Baden Powell and a handful of other officers had been in South Africa since 1896, posing as 'civilian travellers' and they collected information on topography and Boer strengths. However, it was not until the arrival of Lord Roberts in January 1900, three months after the outbreak of the South African War, that the Field Intelligence Department was expanded, and improvements were made to the provision of accurate maps and the skills of reconnaissance. Eventually even small sub-units found themselves accompanied by an intelligence officer. Under Kitchener in the second half of the war, Lieutenant-Colonel David Henderson (DMI in South Africa) created a sophisticated system to track the movements of guerrilla forces. Four broad zones were subdivided and each section manned by an intelligence officer. The officers maintained regular reports, liaised with commanders of field units, and submitted intelligence summaries at fixed times each day. By the end of the war in May 1902, there were 132 officers, 2,321 white civilian staff and 'several thousand' African agents or couriers.[62] The only problem seemed to be the inexperience of many officers in their duties and field commanders therefore frequently dismissed their advice or the information given as unreliable. However, Henderson's manual for intelligence officers was later published in 1904 as 'Regulations for Intelligence Duties in the Field' and his ideas formed the basis of the Intelligence Corps that was founded on the outbreak of the First World War.[63]

There were other reforms at the turn of the century. In 1899, a new Section H of the Intelligence Division was set up to deal with censorship, counter-intelligence and 'secret service'. In 1901, Section H was replaced by Subdivision 13 of which Section A was concerned with 'secret service' work. Its task was to watch the continent of Europe for the despatch of arms and ammunition bound for the Boers in South Africa. Colonel J. K. Trotter, head of 13, argued that, when the South African War was over, a permanent staff would enable the army to run agents whose reliability could be ensured over a long period. This would do away with the method of picking up people casually for specific tasks, only to find they had absconded with their payments. Trotter was, in fact, advocating a system that had been used for years on the Persian, Afghan and Indian border. In March 1903, the Committee of Enquiry believed there was really no need for such an organisation in Europe and 13A was disbanded. Nevertheless, a year later, during substantial army reforms, Major-General James Grierson was appointed Director of Military Operations and Intelligence (DMO & I), thus bringing together intelligence-gathering and operational planning. Grierson made a tour of inspection of the Franco-Belgian frontier, urged preparations for war with Germany and held secret talks with the French Army.

The years before the First World War were characterised by widespread anxiety in Britain about the growth of the German Navy and the threat of German invasion, concerns that were to open a new phase of the Great Game. The revolutionary new design of the *Dreadnought* type of battleship, laid down in 1905, gave the Germans the opportunity to expand their own fleet with similar designs at the same rate as the British. The Kaiser, and the architect of the German High Seas Fleet, Admiral von Tirpitz, did not believe they could invade Britain, but they did feel that a decisive battle in the North Sea would force the British to be more compliant and accede to German demands for more colonies. Across Britain and the Empire there was a universal concern that the Germans intended to usurp the power of the Royal Navy. This would appear irrational and meaningless in light of Germany's ultimate defeat in 1918, but to a nation that had grown used to the idea that its commerce, its worldwide empire and its wealth were based on naval supremacy, there was a genuine fear for the future. This made the far-fetched speculations about secret German invasion plans, or the fear that Britain was overrun with Teutonic spies already, all the more believable.

In 1907, Major Edmonds, the head of MO5 (Military Operations, Section 5 or the 'Special Section'), was tasked to establish a secret agent network in Germany to find out just what preparations Germany had in hand. The brewers Courage offered one Mr Rue to collect information, but all he provided was news of a generalised political nature. Yet, the following year, British Naval Intelligence was running four spies jointly with MO5. In 1909 R. B. Haldane, the Secretary of State for War, set up a subcommittee of the Committee of Imperial Defence to examine the nature and extent of the German espionage threat within Britain and its recommendation was to establish a Secret Service Bureau. The first Secret Service chief was Captain Vernon Kell, an officer of the South Staffordshire Regiment who had studied languages and lived in both Russia and China where he had had the chance to see the effect of revolutionary subversion at first hand. After just twelve months, the Bureau was subdivided into a home section (later MI5) and an overseas section (later MI6) and established a close working relationship with Special Branch at Scotland Yard – now also on the look-out for suspicious behaviour amongst Germans.

Gustav Steinhauser, the German naval intelligence chief, had indeed sent several German agents to Britain to spy on British dockyards, but the British greatly exaggerated the numbers they believed were operating across the country. One of the genuine agents was Dr Max Schultz. He entertained naval staff at Plymouth and tried consistently to turn the conversation to naval matters. He was promised information by a local solicitor called Mr Duff, but Duff reported Schultz to the police. The German was arrested and found to be in possession of codebooks and messages from his intelligence superiors: he was sentenced to twenty-one months' imprisonment. A new security law was introduced in 1911 in time for the trial of the second German agent, Heinrich Grosse, caught trying to purchase information on Portsmouth and Southampton. Nevertheless, the Germans succeeded in recruiting a member of the Royal Navy, George Parrott, by black-mailing him over an affair. He was paid to provide information on torpedoes, but Karl Hentschel, his German handler, eventually betrayed him and he was appre-hended. Wilhelm Klauer was also quickly arrested by the police when he attempted to recruit a German Jewish colleague in Portsmouth. However, Frederick Schröder, alias Gould, was far more successful at interrogating naval personnel near Chatham. He was uncovered by Kell after extensive investigation lasting a year. Kell achieved his greatest coup in 1911. An overheard conversation in a railway carriage led to the recovery of a list of all twenty-two members of a German spy ring. For the three years prior to the outbreak of war, Kell and the police carefully monitored all the men. On 4 August 1914, they were rounded up and interned, depriving the Germans of vital wartime intelligence.

But, if counter-espionage had been a great success, the overseas section of the Secret Service Bureau, whilst acquiring some useful intelligence, fell far short of expectations. Its first chief was Commander Mansfield George Smith-Cumming, affectionately known as 'C'.[64] He himself had taken part in 'special duties' abroad in the ten years before his appointment and he occasionally continued his covert missions using his many disguises. Cumming did not speak German, but relied on the assistance of Kurt Hahn, a German-Jewish Oxford graduate, and friends in Germany. Fascinated by technology and gadgets, the bearded and jocular Cumming inspired confidence and respect amongst his subordinates, and sustained them through the tedium of trying to scour German and foreign periodicals for snippets on the German fleet. Cumming also ran a number of 'casual agents' who lived or worked in German dockyards and Zeppelin hangars. One engineer, named Hippsich, was handled by Max Schultz, a Southampton ship owner (not to be confused with the agent working for German naval intelligence captured in Britain). Two British officers were nevertheless captured by the German authorities in 1910 when they tried to gather intelligence on North Sea coastal defences.[65] Another was easily trapped when he eagerly snapped up an offer of information.

In Russia, Cumming ran perhaps the most colourful agent of them all: Sidney Reilly. Reilly was born Sigmund Georgievich Rosemblum in Russian Poland, and despite the wild claims of his abilities as an expert assassin and spy, he was really a charismatic confidence trickster prone to mental delusions. He may have provided some information on the Russian Far Eastern Fleet in 1904 (although one of his biographers believes the same information was passed to the Japanese for whom he may also have been working).[66] He certainly set himself up as a commissioning agent for several firms in Russia and claimed to have passed on manifest details of German shipping. Reilly, for all his faults, was called upon to provide further espionage work during the Great War. But, by then, the British were desperate to contain German intrigue across the globe, and entirely new strategies would be needed to contain the threat to the Empire.

Imperial Defence

Military plans for the defence of India were to a large extent shaped by the findings of intelligence personnel. At the beginning of the twentieth century, many Indian Army officers were convinced that a war between Britain and Russia was inevitable. Given the threat of widespread insurrection in India during a conflict, the aim was to hold the Russians on the 'scientific frontier' of India, that is, deep inside Afghanistan along the Hindu Kush. Major-General Henry Brackenbury, the first Director of Military Intelligence, had agreed with these conclusions, but he was exasperated by methods of intelligence-gathering in India. He had been particularly concerned by the lack of filtering of information and the failures of verification which tended to foster war scares in India. He had begun to centralise intelligence-gathering across the whole Empire, and had tried to prevent the despatch of British agents whose arrest or interception might lead to political embarrassment.

There was no let up in the intrigue of British and Russian consuls in Persia despite the Anglo-Russian convention of 1907. The effect was to destabilise Persia at a time when central authority was already deteriorating. This was to have serious implications later. By contrast, Tibet was, in a sense, more fortunate. It was the lack of reliable intelligence on what was really going on in Tibet that prompted the invasion of 1904, but the fear of Russian expansionism that lay beneath it was brought to an abrupt end by the unexpected defeat of the tsar's armies in the Russo-Japanese War. The neutralisation of the Russian threat caused a change in priorities, for it coincided with the emergence of a new menace in the form of Wilhelmine Germany. The domestic challenge of German espionage led to the creation of the Secret Service Bureau and this agency soon turned its attention to the global and imperial dimensions of the new threat.

It is all too easy to dismiss British intelligence before the First World War as a failure. Its agents appear amateur and somewhat inept. Its intelligence assessments for the defence of India seem unrealistic, and unnecessarily alarmist. However, until now, there has been no attempt to tie together an analysis of intelligence-gathering in central Asia with either the development of the Secret Service in Britain or the formulation of defence plans for India and the Empire. Yet, taken as a whole, it is clear that there was a transfer of ideas and personnel, and frequently a frank exchange of views, between London and Simla. Crucially there was a change in the way that agents were run by their handlers. Much greater emphasis was placed on keeping reliable men over longer periods. In the dark days of the war ahead, this would be a crucial development.

Chapter 12

War and Revolution, 1914–1919

The Forging of Counter-Espionage

The First World War was the catalyst for revolutionary change in British intelligence. It brought about the development of signals intelligence, counter-espionage and code-breaking, the last having been abandoned in 1844. The war also proved that British intelligence, whilst often appearing amateur and unprofessional by later standards, was able to defeat German espionage in the Middle East. The Indian intelligence system, which was extended beyond its purely military interests, expanded into a global network able to monitor German gun-running in the East Indies and China, and track the activities of Indian revolutionaries as far as the Pacific coast of the United States of America. At the other end of the spectrum, the British continued to recruit Asian agents on a casual basis as informers, and they began to perfect their ability to run more permanent agents and even infiltrate revolutionary cells. By 1918 British intelligence had been forced to adapt to an entirely new ideological enemy in the shape of Communist Russia. All the skills and ingenuity developed in wartime were soon put to the test in a new phase of the Great Game. In essence, there can be little doubt that the First World War marked the coming of age of the British Secret Service.

Counter-espionage in Persia and Afghanistan

The German Zimmermann Plan of 1914, named after the Kaiser's Under-Secretary for Foreign Affairs, was a plot to raise a pan-Islamic jihad across the Middle East.[1] Using their Turkish allies to broadcast the rallying cry of holy war, the Germans hoped to foment rebellion through Russian Central Asia and British India, thus throwing the Entente powers into confusion. Zimmermann calculated that the Allies would be forced to commit thousands of troops to contain the outbreaks. The *coup d'état* of generalissimo Enver Pasha on 2 August 1914 ensured a pro-German lobby was already established in Turkey, and, with the British decision to impound Turkish ships being built in Britain causing further resentment, Enver steered the Ottoman Empire into the conflict. Under German command, the Turkish fleet (including the German ships *Goeben* and *Breslau*) bombarded Odessa in October that year and the following month Turkey was at war with Britain and France.

The first phase of the plan, namely to get Turkey into the war, was thus complete. The Sultan, as the spokesman of Muslims everywhere, dutifully declared a jihad on Turkey's enemies. Specially prepared inflammatory literature was then sent from Germany and Turkey, and Ottoman agitators, primarily radical preachers and scholars, set out for the east. The second phase of the German plan was for a joint Turco-German mission to enter Persia and then Afghanistan, stirring up the local tribes and persuading the rulers of the two states to declare holy war on the British and Russians.[2]

The Government of India was naturally concerned that the nominal head of the Islamic faith, the Sultan of Turkey, had declared a holy war which might affect the loyalty of Muslim sepoys or radical elements inside British India. Militant clerics had never had much difficulty in raising thousands of tribesmen on the volatile North-West Frontier of India, but the last thing the British wanted was to be tied down in frontier campaigns when there was an acute manpower shortage in Europe and Africa. The Government of India therefore moved quickly to persuade the Muslim princes of India to make declarations of loyalty to the Raj.[3] General Sir Edmund Barrow, the military secretary on the viceroy's council, proposed that strong action against Turkey in Mesopotamia, where a decisive defeat could be inflicted, would also neutralise the jihad's appeal. The 6th Division of the Indian Army was thus hastily despatched to the Gulf, local tribal leaders being forewarned by consuls and politicals in the region.[4]

Nevertheless, the predictions of Major-General Sir Percy Cox (the resident and chief political officer of southern Persia who had first been sent to the area in 1904), namely that Arabs would welcome British intervention against the Turks, proved disappointingly inaccurate. Many simply remained neutral, and a few actively assisted the Turks. As a result, it proved more difficult to get information on the strength of Turkish forces facing the British and Indian advance on Baghdad than expected. Worse, German 'consuls' (without any recognised status from the government at Teheran but accompanied by heavily armed escorts), poured into Persia. Wilhelm Wassmuss, who had an intimate knowledge of southern Persia, was originally detailed to lead the German mission, but detaching himself from the main body after disagreements with his second-in-command, Oskar von Niedermayer, he proceeded towards the Gulf coast.

British intelligence knew Wassmuss was on his way. He was ambushed and briefly captured on 5 March 1915 by Persian tribesmen working for Major Sir Frederick O'Connor, the consul at Shiraz. O'Connor's men had been tipped off by a network of Persian informers paid by Sir Percy Cox. Wassmuss gave his captors the slip before he could be handed to the British, but he lost all his propaganda literature, and, concealed within his baggage, a diplomatic codebook.[5] Although no one knew of it at the time, this vital piece of intelligence was inadvertently shipped to London and stored in the archive of the India Office until retrieved by Admiral Sir Reginald Hall of Naval Intelligence in 1917.[6]

Werner Otto von Hentig, the head of the mission to Afghanistan, set out in May 1915, accompanied by German troops, Indian Army deserters, a Muslim radical called Mohammed Baraktullah and Raja Kunwar Mahendra Pratap, an anti-British prince who had spent years in exile in Switzerland and who entertained fantasies about becoming India's next head of state.[7] Fortunately, Turkish raids on Persian territory enabled British agents to foster an anti-Turkish and thus an anti-German sentiment on Persia's western border. There was some co-operation with neutral consuls within Turkey, too, particularly the Italians (who joined the war on the Allied side on 23 May 1915) and Americans, who kept British intelligence informed of the German mission's progress.[8] Wireless intercepts from Turkey also gave clues to the disagreements within the German mission as well as the identities of its personnel. Local Persian agents, and vigilance by the British themselves, had already helped to apprehend a German agent spying on the Royal Navy in the Gulf in Bahrein in November 1914.[9] A raid on the agent's quarters produced a wealth of compromising material which led to the arrest of several other German spies. However, it was a different matter with Wassmuss. Re-establishing his old contacts with the tribesmen of southern Persia and distributing gold, Wassmuss was able to recruit a quasi-nationalist guerrilla force that made raids on isolated posts. An attack on the British residency at Bushire was beaten off when the garrison received intelligence from local Persian sources, but, despite warnings to O'Connor at Shiraz, Wassmuss was able to surprise and capture the British soldiers and civilians there in November 1915.[10] The women were sent to Bushire but Tangistani tribesmen under Wassmuss's command held all the men for nine months.

O'Connor was nevertheless a resourceful officer with a background in intelligence work. Using a letter he knew Wassmuss would transmit to the British at Bushire, he composed a message in invisible ink using alum dissolved in water. He then persuaded an Indian carpenter to accept a tiny scroll alerting the recipient of the letter to its secret contents. The carpenter's plane was drilled, the scroll inserted and the small hole sealed with wax and sawdust. In addition, knowing that Wassmuss did not speak Italian, O'Connor requested three books that he could read to wile away the time in captivity. The titles he asked for were: *Rascaldate sul Fuoco*, *La Parta Bianca*, and *Di Questa Lettera*. In other words, instructions to: 'heat the white part of the letter over a flame'. Intelligence officers at Bushire clearly understood. They sent O'Connor a packet of biscuits with a compass sealed inside to assist in any escape attempt. Warned of the hostages' location, British politicals also began negotiations with the Tangistani tribesmen, eventually persuading them to hand over all the prisoners on 10 August 1916, despite Wassmuss's protests.[11] In the end, after months of guerrilla resistance, and short of funds to sustain his support, Wassmuss was no longer able to continue the struggle. He was arrested by the Persians in 1918 and deported.

Whilst Wassmuss was engaged in his campaign in the south, Niedermayer and Hentig made a punishing ride across central Persia. Alerted by Cox's network of Persian agents, the Viceroy Lord Hardinge urged the key consulates at Meshed and Kirman to use 'secret service' money liberally in order to track and obstruct the German mission. Meanwhile, British Indian troops set up the East Persian Cordon to prevent the Germans from reaching neutral Afghanistan.[12] The German party moved so quickly it was difficult to obtain information and process it in time to block them, however. One of the armed Persians accompanying the German party intended to abscond to the British after their crossing of the Kavir Desert, but he was caught and shot on Niedermayer's orders.[13] Leaving false trails and sowing misinformation to locals, the Germans successfully slipped past the East Persian Cordon and reached Afghanistan on 26 September 1915 – accompanied by news of the stalemate at Gallipoli, the bottling up of a British and Indian Force at Kut el Amara in Mesopotamia, the assassination of British officials in Persia and the robberies of seven out of seventeen British banks in that country. The outlook seemed bleak indeed. However, Hardinge believed that the Afghans could be relied upon to resist German inducements to support the Kaiser. In the meantime, further efforts were made to strengthen the cordon and to discover the whereabouts of other German parties.[14] In particular, the aim was to prevent any large-scale forces arriving in Afghanistan.

These efforts were rewarded. Lieutenants Zugmayer and Griesinger claimed to be the official German consuls in Kirman but they used bribes and assassinations to seize control of the town through their Persian allies. They really had no recognised status at all and the British persuaded the Persians to insist that they raised no flags and transmitted all their telegraphic correspondence *en clair*. The messages were subsequently passed to the British and a network of agents kept the Germans under close observation. Nevertheless, the Germans were successful in recruiting the Swedish-trained gendarmerie as a force with which to harass the British. When Zugmayer and Griesinger left Kirman, they were found to be making their way to Baluchistan. There, unable to rouse the tribes to join a holy war (although the Baluchis were more than willing to relieve them of their funds), the two Germans grew disillusioned. Information about them was regularly passed to Quetta by British sympathisers until Brigadier-General Reginald Dyer was sent out with just 100 men to take on the Germans and the men they had recruited. After Dyer carefully spread the idea that his force was just the advance guard of a whole brigade, a war party of 2,000 Baluchi tribesmen declined to fight him and the Germans were forced back towards Kirman to avoid capture.

Meanwhile another German officer, Lieutenant Seiler, formerly the German consul at Isfahan, had tried to lead a second force into Afghanistan. A Persian working for the British was caught attempting to report the position of Seiler's advance party, but he escaped and managed to warn a fifty-strong Indian cavalry patrol from the East Persian Cordon. After a long pursuit and four casualties amongst the Germans' escort, Seiler escaped eastwards. Calling for reinforcements, the British cavalry patrol then set up an ambush for the main body which they expected at any moment, but, forced to turn back because of a shortage of supplies further east, the bulk of the German forces failed to materialise.

In fact the German conspiracy was falling apart. Seiler and Zugmayer both tried to link up with Wassmuss, but they were attacked by Persian brigands and then captured by a British force called the South Persia Rifles set up by Sir Percy Sykes.[15] The German captives were taken to Isfahan (the Russians had just seized the German base) and paraded in chains in the manner of war criminals. Meanwhile, in Kirman, the local Persian governor had tired of the overbearing Germans and the anarchy they had created. He actively assisted Sykes in the restoration of law and order.[16] Indeed, all over Persia, the German efforts to raise a holy war were beginning to unravel. Isolated at Qum, the Germans declared that there had been a revolution and the shah was overthrown. For a while, attacks on British and Russian posts took place, but they died away when the truth was revealed. The defeat of the German plan to raise a jihad was achieved in the nick of time, for the fall of the British and Indian garrison at Kut el Amara was interpreted as a blow to prestige which may have encouraged Muslims to resist the Empire, although news of the disaster was skilfully concealed at the time.[17]

However, the presence of Niedermayer's mission in Kabul was still a cause for concern in Delhi. Amir Habibullah deliberately delayed and probed his guests in an effort to avoid any commitment that might elicit a military response from the British and the Russians. It was difficult for the British to be sure what was actually happening in Kabul. Indian intelligence was still reliant on the official Muslim envoy and a handful of newswriters; Sir George Roos-Keppel, Chief Commissioner of the North-West Frontier Province, admitted that: 'News from Afghanistan is scanty.'[18] The situation improved slightly with the despatch of an Indian agent known only as 'X'.[19] But the amir eventually disclosed the truth. Transmitting secret correspondence to the viceroy through trusted couriers, he indicated that he had no wish to jeopardise his relationship with (or his generous subsidy from) the British.

To strengthen the amir's hand against anti-British factions who would have willingly accepted German support, Sir Charles Cleveland, the head of Indian intelligence, suggested that a letter from George V, congratulating the amir for his loyalty and neutrality in the war, and written in the king's own hand, would provide a useful counterweight to the expressions of friendship now being proffered by the Kaiser's agents. The letter was eventually delivered to the Afghan border with great ceremony and the amir was delighted. Nevertheless, there was still a strong possibility that the amir would be overthrown by more radical elements. Encouraged by Baraktullah's taunts that Amir Habibullah was not defending Islam, there were many Afghans who would have been only too willing to fight the British. However, a coded message from the Germans that was intended for their minister at Teheran, concerning a coup against the amir, was despatched by a courier who had formerly been in Russian service. He took the message to the Russian consulate in Meshed, and the Russians passed a copy to the British ambassador at St Petersburg, Sir George Buchanan. Unaware of the intercept, the Germans mistakenly believed they had 1,000 armed men on their way from Teheran. The amir was forewarned, and the coup was thwarted.

Even though Afghanistan had so far resisted the temptation to join a German-inspired holy war against Britain, the threat to India through subversion remained. In October 1915, Maulvi Obeidullah, a radical Muslim, had made his way to Afghanistan in secret with a group of loyal followers. Joining Pratap and Baraktullah, the three men formed an Indian 'government in exile'.[20] They declared the formation of an 'Army of God', and, encouraged by news of a mutiny by the 5th Light Infantry at Singapore, and by stories of desertions from some British frontier units, they expected thousands of Pathans from the North-West Frontier to join it.[21] Acting on intelligence about the formation of the 'government in exile', Colonel Roos-Keppel called together 3,000 tribal leaders from across the frontier. In the presence of thousands of onlookers, he announced an increase of subsidies to all the tribes.[22] Then, to the astonishment of the tribesmen, the Royal Flying Corps gave a demonstration of how accurately it could bomb and strafe targets from the air. This timely display of force had a salutary effect and the tribal districts were quiet for months. A militant Islamic faction called the 'Hindustani Fanatics' was also kept under close observation after the interception of two letters written on yellow silk that announced a revolution, and twenty of its leaders were arrested in 1916.[23] However, just as the crises seemed to have passed, an entirely new threat, inspired by the Germans, emerged within India which meant there was still a possibility that unrest could spread from Afghanistan.

Neutralisation of the Indian Revolutionary Threat

The Germans had hoped that serious unrest in Persia, Afghanistan and India could be achieved with just a handful of troops and a generous supply of money. The bulk of the fighting would have to be done by the Asians themselves, but the Germans at least recognised that weapons would need to be smuggled into each area. In Persia, this was simply a case of crossing a long and poorly supervised border with the Ottoman Empire. Afghanistan was more problematic because of the vast distances involved, but India was the most remote. The solution here lay in smuggling arms to the coast, preferably using neutral vessels to avoid suspicion.

Before the war, terrorist activity by nationalists in India had become more frequent. Although there had been widespread unrest in Bengal during the partition of the province in 1905, the agitators were usually well known to the British authorities through the police and their informers. In 1904, the Government of India had established the Department of Central Intelligence (DCI) to monitor extremist activity, with a staff of twenty-six and a budget of just 12,000 rupees.[24] However, two bomb attacks in 1907 on Sir Andrew Fraser, the lieutenant-governor of Bengal, a series of mysterious armed robberies in 1908 and a bomb attack against the viceroy, Lord Minto, in 1909 were, it seemed, being directed by an unseen hand. To meet this new threat, the DCI was expanded.[25] Successively, Sir Harold Stuart, Charles Stevenson-Moore and Sir Charles Cleveland led the DCI and a close working relationship was established with the criminal investigation departments of the Indian Police.[26] The discovery of a printed terrorist manual and smuggled weapons fuelled suspicions that the campaign was being orchestrated from outside India. The DCI requested permission to send its operatives into countries not under British rule, a move that coincided with the formation of the Secret Service Bureau in Britain. Then, in the summer of 1909, the assassination in Britain of Sir William Curzon-Wylie, an aide to the Secretary of State for India, revealed that a cell of Indian revolutionaries was operating from London.[27] Wylie's killer was a Punjabi called Dhingra and he had been trained at India House, a hostelry for students, by Vinayak Savarkar.

Savarkar had written a one-sided and extremist account of the Indian Mutiny as an expression of his passionate anti-British sentiments and, whilst studying law, he had founded a terror cell amongst Indian students in London to turn words into deeds.[28] Training them in the use of firearms (they used a local pistol range) and revolutionary philosophy, Savarkar planned to send a stream of activists back into India to disrupt and eventually overthrow the British. Scotland Yard, which had no files on Indian revolutionaries, got a retired Indian Police officer to assist them in the infiltration of India House using informers. One of these who risked his life to spy on the seditionists was Sajan Ranjan Banerjea, alias Sukasagar Dutt.[29] In January 1910, Savarkar fled to Paris, but when he returned in the spring of that year, he was arrested and imprisoned on the Andaman Islands.

One of Savarkar's protégés, Har Dayal, had also made his way to Paris where he mixed with Russian revolutionaries.[30] Convinced that assassination and terrorism were not enough to overthrow regimes like the Raj, Dayal came to believe that a whole army was required. When he moved to the United States in 1911, ostensibly to escape the attentions of British intelligence, he found a disaffected Sikh population and thus many potential recruits. The only British agent operating in the United States from 1905 was F. Cunliffe Owen, but even before Dayal's arrival he had acquired useful information on Indian extremists either by infiltrating meetings himself or through trusted newspaper reporters.[31] This information was passed on to the Government of India. However, despite Cunliffe Owen's efforts, his intelligence was difficult to verify. Rumours in 1908 that Mauser pistols were being shipped from the United States to the Persian Gulf, prior to being transferred by land to India, caused some anxiety until the British consul at Smyrna discovered the ship under suspicion was carrying bicarbonate of soda.[32]

In 1910, hoping to throw off British surveillance, the Indians excluded all non-Asians from their meetings at the New York Club. This prompted a plea from the Home Office for 'at least one native agent' to be sent from India to penetrate the organisation.[33] Sir William Lee Warner, the senior member of the Council of India, reiterated this demand to the India Office, and suggested that a man from India might be able to win the confidence of Indians in the United States by first infiltrating India House in London. At first, however, the DCI relied on relatives of Indians in the United States to gauge the sentiments of those who had left India's shores. An actual informer, Mohamed Hussain, proved totally unreliable and was later arrested for shooting at passers-by in Chicago, but, in 1910, a second agent proved much more useful and provided details of names and locations of seditious groups. However, it was a British official working for the Canadian Immigration Service who would produce the breakthrough in intelligence on Indian terrorists. William Hopkinson, who had lived in India and spoke Punjabi fluently, offered information about Sikh activists in Vancouver. Whilst remaining in the Immigration Service, he provided a steady stream of information on arms purchases, publications and other activities by Indians who opposed British rule. Travelling into the western United States, he learned from his American counterparts in the Immigration Department that Indian students had contacts in Bengal and possessed a good grasp of handling explosives.[34] On his own initiative, he offered to protect a local Indian priest from a seditionist's hit squad, and was repaid with a loyal contact at the very heart of the Indian community of the Pacific coast.

When there was an attempt to murder the viceroy, Lord Hardinge, on 23 December 1912 at a durbar in Dehli, the Indian intelligence service stepped up its efforts to reveal the link between Indians in America and terrorists in the Raj. Hopkinson soon realised that Har Dayal was having a significant effect on the Indian students in America. In 1913, Dayal named his expanding movement *Ghadr* (revolt) and despatched a revolutionary paper by the same name to India. Attending a series of meetings and lectures by prominent revolutionary spokesmen to glean more information on the movement, Hopkinson was pro-active in developing contacts both amongst Indians and the American Immigration Department, which, by now, was convinced Dayal was a dangerous anarchist. The San Francisco post office allowed Hopkinson to intercept Dayal's letters, and, using these with other evidence, Hopkinson persuaded the American government to agree either to deport or detain leading Ghadrites. New cells were discovered in China, Burma, Malaya and Japan and there had clearly been some contact with the German Embassy. The German Consul to the United States even attended a meeting of Indian revolutionaries on 31 December 1913. However, when German newspapers leaked stories of Indian terrorists working from the United States in February 1914, Dayal was arrested then released on bail. Sikh extremists wreaked their revenge by murdering several of Hopkinson's informers. Hopkinson himself was shot dead by a revolutionary called Mewa Singh outside a courthouse at Victoria in Canada in October 1914.[35]

The Indian government had come to depend on Hopkinson's information, and there had been warnings that to rely solely on one man was too great a risk if something should happen to him.[36] Nevertheless, although Hopkinson was murdered, his contacts passed on the crucial information that, now a war had broken out, large numbers of Sikhs and revolutionaries were making their way back to India. This intelligence gave the British in India time to prepare a reception for Ghadr activists and seriously disrupt their plans.

Of the 8,000 immigrants returning to India, many were merely concerned to make their way home at the outbreak of the war and others sought to join in the Indian war effort. Ghadr activists hoped to slip unnoticed through this human stream but, as they came ashore, a screening process by British immigration officials led to the internment of 400 and the close police observation of 2,560 more. A number of loyal Sikhs also helped as informers in the Punjab itself. The revolutionaries were thus deprived of many of their key personnel, and they also found procuring arms difficult. Acting on British intelligence, one German ship full of weapons bound for the east was impounded by the Italians.

However, there were some serious disturbances within the Punjab, with gun battles, assassinations and terrorism against those who 'collaborated' with the British.[37] The Ghadrites were led by Rash Behari Bhose, the extremist who had masterminded the bombing of Lord Hardinge in 1912. Bhose's attempts to get Punjabi regiments to mutiny was thwarted by the prompt action of Michael O'Dwyer, Governor of the Punjab. But the terrorists were not content to stir up just one region of India. Punjabi conspirators also made contact with Bengali revolutionaries, and set 21 February 1915 as the date for a general uprising. They hoped this would spark a conflagration across the entire subcontinent. Information about the plot was intercepted in the United States and Canada, and passed on to the British in India, but it was the courageous efforts of Kirpal Singh, a police agent posing as a revolutionary at the heart of the organisation, which uncovered the fine details of the conspiracy. Kirpal also discovered that the revolutionaries, sensing the British had learned of the plot, had brought forward the date of the rising to 19 February. Already under suspicion, Kirpal was caught and imprisoned by the would-be rebels but, managing to get to the roof of the revolutionaries' head-quarters where he was being held (under the pretence of wanting to relieve himself), he waved to the undercover officers who had the building under surveillance. Immediately the police stormed the building, arrested the conspirators and turned the place upside down to locate further information. It worked. Armed with full details of the plot, British sentries were placed at strategic points and patrols were stepped up in Calcutta and beyond. There were a number of arrests. Bhose was forced to flee to Japan (where, in the 1940s, he assisted the Japanese Army to raise another force against British rule). In total, 175 conspirators were tried, and, of these, eighteen were sentenced to death. In March 1915, the Indian Defence of the Realm Act gave British administrators the power to intern without trial, and to try cases of sedition and terrorism without juries.

The failure of the Ghadr revolt proved that, without substantial external support, the revolutionaries would be unable to overthrow the Raj by force. That is not to say that the threat could be dismissed as unimportant. As Richard Popple-well points out: 'The British were able to defeat the Indian revolutionaries only by developing a complex intelligence network on a global scale.'[38] The need for that worldwide network was demonstrated by the emergence, in 1915, of an entirely new threat: the Indian Revolutionary Committee in Berlin.

The aim of the Indian Revolutionary Committee was to co-ordinate the preparation of a major revolt in India that would be fully supported by German arms and gold. The so-called Christmas Day Plot would begin with the dynamiting of railway junctions and bridges, the cutting of telegraph wires and the covert deployment of armed revolutionaries to key parts of Calcutta. Sprung from training camps on the Siam–Burma border and equipped with rifles and machine guns shipped secretly to the coast, the revolutionaries would be joined by their pre-war leaders, who would have been liberated by an attack on the Andaman Islands just a few days earlier. Moreover, if all went to plan, the revolutionaries would hear that Afghanistan and Persia had declared a jihad on the British, thus enabling thousands of Muslim tribesmen to join hands across the subcontinent and throw the British into the sea.

With the 'government in exile' already in Afghanistan, and with a bogus firm called Harry and Sons set up ready to receive rifles, explosives and machine guns from Germany, all that was required was for the Germans now to send the weapons and skill-at-arms instructors. The German consul in the United States, Franz von Papen (later the Weimar Chancellor who was instrumental in the appointment of Adolf Hitler), arranged the purchase of firearms which were to be transferred, via the Caribbean, across the Pacific to the Dutch East Indies. From there, via small craft, there were to be sent to the coast of India.[39] By chance, the German vessels in the Caribbean missed their rendezvous and the Americans arrested the weapons ship with all its cargo. Yet other weapons supplies were being sought in China. Once again, British informers were able to detect the purchases and they even discovered what vessel the Germans intended to use to transfer them to India, although at the eleventh hour the Germans switched to overland routes to reach the subcontinent. Meanwhile, Indian revolutionaries established secret training camps in the remote areas to the east of Calcutta and began recruiting volunteers through 'front' shops and businesses. It was here the revolutionaries' security was most vulnerable. To engineer a popular uprising clearly requires mass support, but in trying to advertise the cause, the revolutionary movement was in danger of being detected and infiltrated. However, to assist in the recruitment process, propaganda leaflets had been prepared by the Germans and these were carried by men like Wassmuss and Hentig in their crossings of Persia, some of them making their way into the hands of frontier officials. In addition, British residents attached to the princely states of India also began to intercept German letters calling for their support in a holy war.

Up to this point, the details of a German-backed revolt were hazy, but the breakthrough came when the authorities in the Dutch East Indies gave the British a tip off about a German officer arriving in Singapore. Code-named by the British as 'Agent X', the German officer was quickly picked up, was interrogated and confessed that his mission was to get arms to Bengal. He had in his possession maps of the proposed landing points, codebooks and the means to communicate with Berlin. It seemed that the unfortunate man, whose real name was Vincent Kraft, had fallen foul of the German Army on the Western Front and had been offered the chance to redeem himself by taking part in a dangerous mission, although he may have intended to act as a double agent, having already tried to contact British intelligence in the Netherlands.[40] Pretending that his cover had not been blown, he was able to prove the authenticity of his story to the British by transmitting messages to his contacts and giving vital details of the movements of arms in the region.[41] Whatever his original motives, he had effectively been 'turned'.

Immediately Royal Naval patrols were stepped up around the coasts of India and one German arms ship was reported as 'having gone down in a storm', which may have been a euphemism for 'blown out of the water'. Consuls were alerted to the new threat and known conspirators were simply shadowed to build up a picture of their network. The Dutch provided another tip-off about the arrival of a ship carrying arms from the Philippines and it was intercepted. Interrogations of the crew revealed the whereabouts of the training camps on the Siam–Burma border and the German plans to send weapons instructors there. The Siamese authorities were soon persuaded to move in and arrest the members of the camps. On 15 December 1915, with a complete picture of the conspiracy, the British rounded up all the Indian revolutionaries.[42] The threat was neutralised.

Although the British government was eager to have the Germans in Afghanistan arrested too, the viceroy knew that the Afghan amir should be allowed to take that decision. His trust was rewarded. Having effectively delayed any deal with the Germans, Habibullah concluded a vacuous Treaty of Friendship with Hentig and then promptly refused to ratify it. The Germans at last realised they had been deceived. Hentig decided to strike out for Kashgar, hoping to raise Muslim guerrillas there to tie up British and Russian troops. After much wrangling, the British and Russian consuls managed to persuade the Chinese to arrest him and he was eventually repatriated. Niedermayer wanted to return to Persia to stir up anti-Russian feeling, but he was attacked by Turcoman bandits and was forced to return to Germany as a beggar. The main body of the German mission under Lieutenant Wagner was attacked by guerrillas as it withdrew past the East Persian Cordon and many of its personnel were taken prisoner. They were subsequently handed over to the Russians in the north. It marked the collapse of the German intelligence effort in the Middle East.

The defeat of the Germans in Persia was accompanied by greater success against the Turks too. The Russians had already smashed Enver's army in the Caucasus and taken Erzerum, whilst in the south, the loss of Kut el Amara was later avenged by an Indian Army offensive in Mesopotamia under General Maude, and General Allenby made a painstaking advance through Palestine. More encouraging still, but outside the scope of this narrative, was the precipitation of the Arab Revolt, encouraged by a number of British officers from the Cairo Bureau (which was seen as a rival organisation in Delhi), including T. E. Lawrence.[43] The greatest coup of them all was Admiral Hall's use of the diplomatic codebook, found in the baggage taken from Wilhelm Wassmuss in southern Persia.[44] Although the Germans had made use of a new variant, the special wartime cryptographic department, known as 'Room 40' (later ID25), was able to translate the bulk of a telegram from German Foreign Minister Arthur Zimmermann to the German Embassy in Mexico. The telegraph message, which passed on submarine cables tapped by the Admiralty, revealed a German plan to embroil Mexico and Japan in the event of the United States declaring war on Germany. Against a background of unrestricted U-boat warfare and with President Wilson already angered over the sinking of the *Lusitania* in 1915, the revelation was enough to push the United States into the First World War on the Allied side. It was the turn of the tide.

British Missions during the Russian Revolutions

At the outbreak of the First World War, Vernon Kell's counter-espionage department had quickly rounded up Germany's spies in Britain. At the time it was not clear whether any more German agents were at large, or whether new ones would enter the country through neutral states, but Kell's department (which changed its title from MO5 to MI5 in 1916) did not underestimate the threat of subversion or sabotage. German efforts to raise a jihad in India, Persia and Afghanistan had provided ample evidence of how determined the Kaiser's agents could be. Consequently, when the people of Russia overthrew Tsar Nicholas II and a new Provisional Government was set up in March 1917, the information that a group of Bolshevik revolutionaries was plotting to take Russia out of the war immediately raised suspicions about a German connection. Indeed, it seems that Lenin had accepted German funds and the offer of a sealed train journey through Europe to reach Russia that spring on the understanding that the Bolsheviks opposed any further conflict with Germany and possibly would arrange to release German prisoners of war.[45] Members of the Russian Provisional Government certainly believed that Lenin was a German spy and raids on the Bolshevik head-quarters in the late summer of 1917 apparently produced compromising documents.[46] The opening of the Soviet archives from 1990 has revealed that, in fact, millions of German marks were made available to the Bolshevik Party in order to promote peace-making propaganda and support its newspapers. Lenin of course believed that, in time, Germany too would be overthrown and the matter of funding would be immaterial. In Lenin's mind the success of Bolshevism in Russia was but a prelude to a worldwide revolution. He predicted that the industrialised nations, including Britain, would be the first to be consumed by Communist insurrection.

In Britain, the threat posed by the far left before 1917 was thought to be minimal. In 1916, Special Branch and MI5 were only concerned by left-leaning 'peace cranks' of the No-Conscription League, but they were easily contained in the patriotic atmosphere of the war.[47] It was not until 1918 that the Secret Service was troubled by more militant labour unrest and by the expressions of support for the 'workers' revolution' amongst some trade unionists.

However, the more immediate concern of 1917 was keeping Russia in the war against Germany. It was imperative that the Russians tie down troops that might otherwise overwhelm the British and French Armies on the Western Front before the Americans could arrive in strength. But, even before the revolution, the Russian Army had been reluctant to co-operate with the British military mission, even though British intelligence agents offered assistance with the interception of German wireless communications. Moreover, Russian intelligence had been a chaotic affair, with separate and rival agencies serving General Headquarters, the different army groups, the Orthodox Church and the royal court. Samuel Hoare, a British intelligence officer in MI1c (Communications), described despondently the confusion and rivalry within the Russian Army to 'C' (Cumming) back in London.[48]

Gradually it became clear that Kerensky's Provisional Government was doomed and the Bolsheviks staged a *coup d'état* to overthrow it in October 1917. Consequently, another agent, Robert Bruce Lockhart, was sent to work with the new Bolshevik authorities and encourage them to sustain the war effort against Germany. It was a hopeless mission. Lockhart, a former consul to Moscow in 1912, was simply unable to persuade the Bolsheviks to fight the Germans, and by the spring of 1918 he was in contact with an anti-Bolshevik underground movement led by Boris Savinkov. Other agents were also sent by Cumming but they failed to gather much information of significance except to pick up on continued German funding of the Bolsheviks. However, in order to understand what made the Bolsheviks tick, Sidney Reilly was sent (under the code-name ST1) to find out more about Lenin. Unable to get close to the Russian leader, Reilly also made contact with anti-Bolsheviks, as did his colleague Captain G. A. Hill. In an attempt to foster some spirit of co-operation, Hill later claimed to have assisted the Bolsheviks in setting up their own intelligence service, soon to develop into the feared Cheka, but this was probably an exaggeration.[49] He did manage to organise a courier network, but admitted the 'results were poor'. His attempts to form a sabotage gang were also limited, but he did carry out some work of this nature against the Bolsheviks.

Felix Dzerzhinsky, the Jesuit-educated former tsarist secret policeman who became the head of the Cheka, was as brutal as he was efficient. He was the dedicated enemy of the bourgeoisie. He infamously summed up his view of justice: 'the Cheka does not judge – it strikes!'[50] Setting up three *agents provocateurs*, Colonel Eduard Berzin, Jan Buikis and Ian Sprogis, Dzerzhinsky fed Lockhart, Reilly and Captain Cromie, the British naval attaché, false information. When Reilly made available 1.2 million roubles to Berzin for anti-Bolshevik purposes, Berzin simply passed it on to his Communist superiors.[51] Having exposed the true sympathies of the British agents, the Communists were even more incensed at their support for the Whites in Russia's tragic civil war. Moreover, the arrival of an Allied intervention force at Archangel in the summer of 1918 caused a sharp deterioration in relations between the British and the Bolsheviks. An 'intelligence war' developed. Two teams of Russian agents recruited by the British were arrested by the Communists and imprisoned. An anti-Bolshevik seizure of power in Archangel was probably assisted by Colonel C. J. M. Thornhill, a MI1c agent serving the expeditionary force commander, Major-General Frederick Poole. However, Poole's replacement, Major-General Edmund Ironside, complained that British agents spent too much time involved in intrigue and not enough time collecting useful field intelligence for his force.[52]

The attempted assassination of Lenin by the Socialist Revolutionary Fanya Kaplan on 30 August 1918 led to a massive witch-hunt for counter-revolutionaries and something of a spy-mania amongst the Communists. In Petrograd, 500 political prisoners were executed in a fortnight. Across Russia, many hundreds of captives were slaughtered. Captain Cromie was killed in a firefight when Red Guards stormed the British Embassy in Petrograd. Lockhart and Boyce, the MI1c station head in Russia, were picked up and Berzin tried to entrap Reilly by suggesting another assassination attempt. After the arrest of one of his mistresses, Reilly was smuggled out the country. Lockhart and Boyce were subsequently released in return for Soviet officials being held in London, but they were lucky to escape with their lives. Eighteen couriers who had worked for the British were executed. In a political gesture, the Moscow Supreme Revolutionary Council sentenced Lockhart and Reilly to death *in absentia*.

In the Caucasus, the collapse of tsarist authority in the spring of 1917 had led to a temporary unity between former rivals – Russians and Caucasians, Christians and Muslims. But it proved impossible to sustain that co-operation in the face of a possible Turkish invasion. The defeat of Enver Pasha by the tsarist army two years before had temporarily checked Turkish expansion in the region but, as the summer of 1917 drew on, it appeared that a counter-attack was imminent. Furthermore, the Germans were also winning the war on the Eastern Front and they were able steadily to drive the Russians back. The Georgians, with historic connections to the German peoples in the west, were eager for the Kaiser's troops to reach the Caucasus to provide some balance against the Muslims of the region.

However, the Armenians, whose lands lay astride the mountains, were more concerned to fight the Turks and avenge the terrible massacres perpetrated by Enver's troops in 1915. Further east, the Azerbaijani Muslims would have welcomed Turkish support and they resented the last vestiges of Russian influence.

Amidst this confusion of peoples and ambitions, the British were eager to provide some sort of front against the Turks and the Germans. They considered it vital to prevent the precious oilfields of Baku from falling into the enemy's hands. Moreover, it was possible that the thousands of German and Austrian prisoners of war, who had been held in tsarist prisoner of war camps across Turkestan, might be able to join hands with the advance of the Central Powers. As Russian resistance collapsed, the potential for the Germans and Turks to march virtually unopposed across central Asia towards India looked as if it might just be realised. There was also the chance that, encouraged by this apparent victory, the peoples of Persia, Afghanistan and India might begin to doubt the ability of the British to win the war. Already there were signs of severe unrest in Persia. Sir Percy Sykes' South Persia Rifles, for example, mutinied and nationalist disturbances spread across the country in the spring of 1918.[53]

Until more troops could be spared to reach Baku, Major Aeneas Ranald MacDonnell (a Foreign Office consul who was given a temporary military rank) was sent to persuade the motley collection of forces in the region to hold the Turks back. When he arrived, MacDonnell found that the situation was deteriorating rapidly. Each of the different groups refused to work with the others although all were eager to obtain British financial support. MacDonnell found himself smuggling roubles to the Armenians, the only group really prepared to resist the Turks, but this became impossible once the Azerbaijanis had seized part of the vital railway line from Tiflis. MacDonnell was only able to get back to Baku when the Bolsheviks smashed their way through with armoured trains. In the town, the provisional government collapsed and was replaced by an Armenian Bolshevik, Stepan Shaumian, and his Communist clique. MacDonnell was unable to persuade the Bolsheviks that the Turks posed a threat, and Communist reinforcements from Astrakhan numbered barely 1,000 men. The Turks were thought to number 14,000.

In February 1918, Captain Edward Noel was sent to the Caucasus to report on what levels of resistance were likely to be offered against the Turks. Noel had always been something of a daredevil. Having served on the North-West Frontier, his passion for exploration led him to make a clandestine journey into Persia without official permission whilst on leave. He was detected by Sir Percy Cox's Persian spy network and Cox gave the young officer a 'dressing down', but he also recommended his transfer to the Indian Political Service. An intrepid sportsman, Noel had got to know the Middle East by bicycling to India in 1909 and again in 1910. Now, in the Caucasus, he quickly made contact with MacDonnell and got a full appreciation of the situation which he intended to relay to Major-General Lionel Dunsterville, the commander of a British force being assembled at Hamadan and destined for Baku. However, as he returned to Enzeli on the Caspian coast he was captured by Persian Jungali guerrillas. Unknown to Noel, a massacre of Azerbaijani Muslims in Baku was blamed on foreign interventionists, and the

Bolsheviks had tipped off the Jungalis. Noel managed to destroy his codebooks by throwing them into a fire just as his captors arrived, but other documentation on his person revealed his mission and identity. At first, the Jungalis threatened to shoot him in order to get a confession, but Noel refused to crack. He was taken to a remote prison, escaped, was recaptured and was eventually released months later after military action against the Jungalis by General Dunsterville's force.

However, Noel's compromising correspondence was passed to the Bolsheviks in Baku and Shaumian used it to confront MacDonnell. MacDonnell explained that his mission was to persuade the Bolsheviks to hold Baku, but Shaumian was convinced that the Turks would not attack and that any British force would be sent only to colonise the region. When MacDonnell tried to get Shaumian to accept the assistance of a British force, the Bolshevik leader insisted that it would have to serve under a Communist committee and be subject to Red Army regulations. At the time this meant that British soldiers and NCOs would be able to elect their own officers and would be subject to the indoctrination of political commissars. MacDonnell rejected this blatant attempt to spread revolutionary ideology to the British Army and he remained immune to Shaumian's endless Communist rhetoric over the next few months. He was also under no illusion that Shaumian was having him shadowed, and, when Shaumian insisted that MacDonnell should send all his wireless messages *en clair*, he had rapidly to warn his contacts in Persia not to send any compromising transmissions. MacDonnell also had to avoid being trapped by *agents provocateurs* and this made him cautious when a woman called Marie Nikolaievena approached him asking for assistance in an anti-Bolshevik coup. In fact, she and a large number of other young women were genuine counter-revolutionaries and they acted as couriers for MacDonnell over several weeks.

Whilst MacDonnell continued negotiations at Baku, Major-General Wilfred Malleson, a Military Intelligence officer, was sent to Meshed at the head of a military mission. His task was to keep abreast of developments in Trans-Caspia and Turkestan, and to resist the attacks of any Turco-German forces in the area. In the event of the Turks breaking through at Baku, he was to advance and cut the railway lines across Trans-Caspia.[54] It seems that MacDonnell also had a contingency plan, namely to destroy the oil wells and sabotage the docks at Baku if the Turks took over. However, in July 1918 Malleson had little real idea of what was happening across the Caspian or of how close the Turks had now got. He therefore sent Captain Reginald Teague Jones, disguised as an Armenian, to link up with MacDonnell and inform him that he was to join forces with any anti-Bolsheviks so that, with Shaumian out of the way, British troops could land at the threatened port.

Teague Jones had been educated at St Petersburg and was an excellent linguist, which, combined with his experience of frontier intelligence and police work in India before the war, made him an ideal candidate for intelligence operations.[55] Since 1914 he had been in Military Intelligence in the Gulf, so he was fully aware of the overall regional situation. Making his way to Baku, he crossed the Caspian to Krasnovodsk and found German agents frantically trying to purchase cotton, a vital resource for explosives. The impoverished Bolsheviks were just as eager to sell it. Teague Jones considered setting fire to the stocks in the port, but, using funds he had concealed in his jacket lining, he persuaded the port's radio mechanic (an anti-Bolshevik) to transmit a false message supposedly from Bolshevik regional head-quarters in Astrakhan about unloading the ships.[56] The mechanic agreed and then secretly sabotaged the radio transmitter to prevent the ruse being discovered. The ships were duly unloaded and sent away, thus thwarting the Germans' plans. Teague Jones then continued along the Trans-Caspian railway, looking for vulner-able bridges and culverts that might be blown in an emergency. At Kaakha, he made a startling discovery. On 12 July 1918, the Bolsheviks at Askhabad had been overthrown. Workers angry at the draconian treatment the Communists were meting out had seized power and a new Socialist Revolutionary group was in charge. Teague Jones knew this information was of vital importance and he made an incredible ride over seventy miles of harsh desert terrain in just forty-eight hours to inform General Malleson at Meshed.[57]

In Baku, MacDonnell was now contacted by a number of ex-tsarist officers who were eager to get rid of the Bolsheviks. As Shaumian would not allow British troops to assist in the defence of the town, MacDonnell pursued some of these counter-revolutionary contacts and learned of a conspiracy to overthrow the Communists, and he offered considerable funds. However, despite careful preparations and good security, the plot was betrayed at the eleventh hour and the conspirators arrested. As Bolshevik agents closed in on MacDonnell, looking for evidence of his complicity in the plot, a group of anti-Bolsheviks provided him with an alibi and a lawyer the night before his arrest. When a show trial was staged, MacDonnell was able to use the 'evidence' he had been given to discredit his accusers. The Baku police chief was then given a generous payment to cover his gambling debts to ensure MacDonnell's escape to Enzeli.

When MacDonnell had left, news that the Turks were pressing closer prompted a fresh attempt to overthrow Shaumian on 31 July. This time it was successful and a government calling itself the Centro-Caspian Dictatorship was established. Bolsheviks who tried to flee were captured and imprisoned, and urgent appeals were sent to the British. General Dunsterville and his 'Dunsterforce' had fought their way through the Jungalis and they immediately set sail for Baku. By the time they arrived the Turks were already close to the line of hills that surrounded the town and Dunsterville knew that his small force could do little without the active support of the locals. Despite taking the brunt of the Turkish attacks, and suffering heavy casualties, the British troops were too heavily outnumbered to hold Baku and they fell back to Enzeli. Without the British, resistance collapsed and Turkish irregulars poured into the port, massacring men, women and children in revenge for the destruction of their co-religionists months before. The fall of Baku meant there was now nothing to stop the Turks crossing the Caspian.

Teague Jones had worked for a short time as Dunsterville's intelligence officer, but he was recalled to Krasnovodsk by General Malleson to assess the defences there against a Turkish landing. Whilst engaged in this survey, he learned that the British position was even more exposed than initially feared. A British force under Colonel Denis Knollys was engaged in a battle with Bolsheviks who were trying to retake Askhabad from the east. The significance of the event was not lost to him or the other British officers: Indian sepoys had finally clashed with the Russian Army in central Asia, just as so many had predicted for so long. Hurrying to the east, Teague Jones had the opportunity to see Knollys drive off a second Bolshevik attack at Kaakha. In fact, although an anachronism of modern warfare, it was an Indian bayonet charge that settled this action. The Bolsheviks, accompanied by Austrian ex-prisoners of war, had mounted a determined assault, but, at the critical moment, a company of the 16th Punjabis had hurled themselves at the assaulting troops intending to close in hand-to-hand fighting. It had proved too much for the Russians, who pulled back. British officers had a pretty low opinion of their adversaries in this engagement. Some Bolsheviks had pretended to surrender and appealed to the Indians to kill their own officers. The sepoys responded robustly by opening fire on the Communists.

Within weeks, despite being heavily outnumbered, the British and Indian force had driven the Bolsheviks out of Dushak and occupied Merv. Ever alert to the importance of propaganda, the Communists explained this defeat by multiplying the number of men in Knollys's command from 400 to 4,000.[58] However, to hold the region, which was now threatened from the east *and* the west, Malleson knew he needed more troops. Given the fierce fighting raging in Western Europe and Palestine, he was unlikely to get them and his requests to pursue the Bolsheviks across central Asia were refused by the Government of India. The situation was still in the balance.

Teague Jones had been wounded in the battle at Kaakha by a stray bullet and he was taken to Askhabad where he learned that Shaumian and twenty-five other Bolsheviks from Baku were to be executed by Russian counter-revolutionaries. The shooting of the twenty-six commissars was later blamed on the British Secret Service and Teague Jones in particular, but, as Peter Hopkirk points out, it was clearly a decision taken by the Askhabad Socialist Revolutionary Tribunal and not the British.[59] For decades the Communists created an elaborate mythology about the martyrdom of the Baku commissars at the hands of 'British Intelligence' so that Teague Jones was forced to take on a new identity as Ronald Sinclair to avoid Communist vengeance.[60] As early as July 1918, Josef Stalin, who appointed himself head of the North Caucasian Military Area, had ordered that all foreign officers were to be arrested and imprisoned as fears about espionage developed. When Stalin became more powerful, his capacity for executing his opponents grew to monstrous proportions. Indeed, throughout Soviet historiography, British intelligence was blamed for a series of attempts to overthrow Communist rule, but with the exception perhaps of Reilly, there was really only indirect assistance to anti-Bolshevik groups, and, in contrast to the Soviet Secret Service, no evidence of assassination.[61]

New Ideological Threats

By the autumn of 1918, the Central Powers were collapsing. Bulgaria pulled out of the war, leaving Turkey's northern flank exposed. In Palestine and Mesopotamia, the Allies had broken the Turkish armies, and the failure of Ludendorff's last offensive in France meant that the German Army was being pushed back towards its own frontiers. On 4 November 1918, the Kaiser abdicated, and a week later the armistice brought the Great War to an end. The defeat of Germany and Turkey meant the termination of the threat to India and it also meant there was no further need to shore up the Russians. In February 1919, Malleson was ordered to pull out of central Asia.

The war had thrown up three separate threats to the British Empire in south Asia. The first, namely German attempts to raise religious revolutionaries, had failed thanks to the expansion of the British intelligence networks in Persia and the co-operation of their Afghan and Persian allies. The second threat, posed by Indian revolutionaries, had also been contained thanks to the Indian police, resourceful officers like Hopkinson and Kirpal Singh, and the sophisticated monitoring of extremists by the Indian intelligence service, the DCI. This supervision was on a global scale, stretching from China to the United States, and it was to prove a vital component in the defence of India long after the war. The third threat was the uncertain direction of central Asian politics. In the latter stages of the war, it was unclear whether Turkish, Socialist Revolutionary or Bolshevik forces would triumph. For a time the distinction between a Bolshevik and German threat was nebulous, but Germany's defeat in November 1918 made it apparent that Communism was an independent phenomenon. Thus, the British intelligence effort in revolutionary Russia did not end with the termination of Allied inter- vention. Indeed, a whole new chapter of the Great Game was opening and the need for resourceful individual agents, both British and Asian, was just as pressing as it had ever been.

Chapter 13

Recessional

Ideology, Intelligence and Independence, 1919–1947

In December 1917 Lenin had announced that all the workers of Asia should follow the example of the Bolsheviks and throw off their oppressors. He believed that the momentum of 'world revolution' would come from the industrialised nations of Europe, but he saw that there could only be advantages for Russia if the Great Powers were deprived of their colonies. He had described imperialism as an 'abscess' that provided the bourgeoisie with funds with which to 'bribe certain sections of the workers'.[1] If colonies were swept away, Lenin argued, then the workers would be able to bring down the weakened capitalist states. However, despite this fiery rhetoric, the British only gradually became aware of the Bolsheviks' intentions the following year. Initially, Britain's policy was to keep the Russians in the war against Germany, but when the Bolsheviks concluded the Treaty of Brest Litovsk with Germany in March 1918 and began to espouse the doctrine of revolution beyond Russia's borders, attitudes towards the Russians changed dramatically.

Given the new threat, the British government decided in 1919 that the wartime cryptographic unit, known as ID25, should not be abolished. Its purpose was to send intercepted cipher communications to the foreign secretary who would pass the most relevant ones to the Cabinet. It was given the new title of Government Code and Cypher School (GC&CS) and was supported enthusiastically by Lord Curzon, the former viceroy. The Foreign Office took over full control of GC&CS from the Admiralty in 1922 but its first chief, Alastair Denniston, remained in charge. Although GC&CS was interested in monitoring the transmissions of several major powers, thanks to Curzon's concern for the defence of India and the insecurity of Bolshevik communications, the greatest focus was on Russia. The Russians relied either on old tsarist codes, which the British had access to, or they used simplistic encryption systems, which were easily broken. Their dependence on former tsarist signallers also meant that they could not avoid defections. As a result, GC&CS gave the British the ability to thwart Bolshevik subversion against India and the United Kingdom.

In 1920 Lloyd George made clear to the Bolsheviks the conditions under which Britain would resume normal trading relations with Russia and these included a complete end to hostile propaganda that was being transmitted into India from

Central Asia, recognition of Russia's pre-war debts and a prisoner exchange. Chicherin, the Soviet Commissar for Foreign Affairs, had no idea that his messages to the Soviet delegation in London were being intercepted. He had urged the delegation to take an uncompromising line with the British, stating: 'The situation that has been created in the East is a difficult one for England. In Persia they are almost helpless in the face of the revolution. Disloyalty is increasing amongst the Indian troops.'[2]

In the belief that a world revolution was imminent, the Russians had precious stones smuggled into Britain to support Communist sympathisers and to fund the *Daily Herald*, a left-wing newspaper. In August 1920, the Communist Party of Great Britain (CPGB) was established. Special Branch was able to identify Russian gems from the distinctive manner in which they were cut, and through 'sigint' (signals intelligence) was fully aware of the Soviets' activities. Signal intercepts also provided the British Secret Service with details of the CPGB's aim to set up an armed revolutionary force through subversion, namely: 'systematic propaganda and agitation in the armed forces, and the organisation of Communist cells in every military unit'. This was not a remote threat. When some soldiers went on strike due to frustrations with the speed of demobilisation, red flags had appeared. Amongst the citizen soldiers of 1919–20, there was also widespread disgust at the suggestion they could be sent to fight the Bolsheviks. This was an understandable response from men who felt they had done their bit against the Kaiser. All they wanted was to go home, but the government was concerned that Communist agitators might exploit the unrest. Moreover, there were serious disturbances in the Punjab and in Ireland which elicited a harsh response from British troops and police. Their commanders were convinced that, unless prompt and severe action was taken, the situation could degenerate into anarchy and revolution. Brigadier-General Dyer, the man who had saved Baluchistan, found himself censured for ordering his men to open fire on an unarmed crowd at Amritsar in 1919.[3] He claimed he had intended to 'make a wide impression' on what he saw as a revolutionary mob, and, whilst there can be little defence for the shootings, there is no doubt that the Ghadr disturbances of 1915 were in his mind at the time.[4]

The CG&CS intercepts seemed to confirm that the Bolsheviks were making unceasing efforts to win over sympathisers in India. Curzon, now Foreign Secretary, read that Soviet delegates were 'constantly in the company of notorious agitators . . . behind much of the trouble in India'. Moreover, the Russians were 'pressing on the Amir of Afghanistan a treaty aimed directly at our Indian Empire'. He believed they had already 'plunged Northern Persia into peril and anarchy'.[5] Anger at continued trade negotiations with the Russians prompted a GC&CS member to leak details of Soviet funding of the *Daily Herald* and the CPGB to the *Daily Mail* and the *Morning Post* in September 1920. There were some arrests of leading Communists in light of more labour unrest and one Comintern (Communist International) courier was caught with sensitive documents about the Communist movement in Britain. One of the items he carried was in a code GC&CS had cracked and so the complete portfolio could be scrutinised. Further arrests followed and by 1921 it seemed the Communist threat to Britain had been temporarily contained.

However, Curzon told his Cabinet colleagues: 'The Russian menace in the East is incomparably greater than anything else that has happened in any time to the British Empire.' Lord Montagu, the Secretary of State for India, agreed, arguing that the subcontinent was 'the main objective of Bolshevik foreign policy'. He was convinced that Mahatma Gandhi's activists were the product of 'undiscovered ramifications of international revolutionaries'.[6] Sigint was again the medium used to unearth the Communist connection. Radio intercepts from Soviet Central Asia were picked up at a special listening station in Constantinople and relayed to the Government of India. The enquiry into the Amritsar shootings also mentioned the possibility that the unrest in the Punjab, which preceded the incident, was somehow pre-planned and carefully orchestrated, perhaps even with external connections. An attack on the Amritsar railway station was thought to be a deliberate attempt to prevent the arrival of British reinforcements, although it is more likely the station was attacked simply because it was a symbol of British power. Indeed, the rioting was in fact largely a spontaneous reaction to the arrest of two prominent men in the city.

Older methods of humint had not been neglected. Between 1919 and 1924, the head of the intelligence effort in India, known as the Delhi Intelligence Bureau (DIB) was Colonel Cecil Kaye. Kaye set up and ran a huge network of Asian informers and arranged for the interception of mail between known subversives. He also exchanged information with Indian Political Intelligence (IPI), the London office for the supervision of extremists set up in light of the India House conspiracy.[7] It was to prove an effective link.[8]

There was certainly a connection between some Indian nationalists and the Communists.[9] Following Germany's defeat in the First World War, the Indian revolutionaries who had been working in Berlin had made their way to Moscow, led by Manabendra Nath Roy. Roy had joined an anti-British terror gang before the war and took part in the German-inspired Christmas Day Plot. After the failure of the conspiracy he had fled through east Asia to the United States, and then on to Mexico. In Mexico he met Mikhail Borodin who had converted him to Communism before inviting him to Moscow in April 1920.

In May 1921, the Raj's most committed adversary, Chattopadhyaya, brought more Indian revolutionaries to the Russian capital. These men, watched by Cumming's agents, were instructed by Lenin to create the nucleus of a communist revolutionary movement in India, but Roy regarded Chattopadhyaya's followers as rivals and he tried to convince Lenin they were nationalists rather than Communists. Sir David Petrie, who succeeded Kaye as head of the DIB (and later led MI5), gathered intelligence on these activities in Moscow and learned that the task of 'intensified propaganda in India' had been entrusted to Roy.[10] Roy nevertheless disapproved of the crude performance staged in Baku in September 1920 by Gregori Zinoviev and Bela Kun. Here, the Soviets had invited 1,800 delegates from across central Asia and the Middle East where, after prolonged oratory, they demanded a jihad for the liberation of the region. There was an enthusiastic response from all but the Central Asian representatives. This group was in fact critical of the lack of freedoms offered by the Bolsheviks who ruled them, but the propagandists made sure these feelings were omitted from the official report of the congress. Asian agents working for Indian intelligence attended the meeting in secret, so the British were well informed and somewhat relieved by the outcome. Despite all the rhetoric, the whole event proved singularly ineffective. No coherent, long-term strategy was evolved, and there seemed little chance of a marriage between Islamic fundamentalism and Russian Communism.

Nevertheless, Lenin gave his approval for the formation of an 'Army of God' that would carry the revolution across central Asia and into India. By the winter of 1920, weapons, ammunition, radios, dismantled aircraft and supplies were being concentrated at Tashkent. Firing ranges and training camps were established. It was intended to make overtures to the Afghans, where some 30,000 Muslim exiles from India were now stranded, in order to set up more training camps for terrorists and paramilitaries. With a curious parallel to the situation in 2001, many of the fighters that the 'Army of God' would appeal to were Pathans from the North-West Frontier. However, information about these preparations reached the Indian traders in the bazaar of Tashkent despite tight security. One man who lived amongst the revolutionary volunteers, known as Maulana, was shadowed whilst making contact with the Indian traders, and, when arrested, he was found to be in possession of Indian rupees. Two other volunteers were also caught with Indian currency, which suggested Maulana was a British-Indian spy trying to 'turn' some of the activists. M. N. Roy gave the order for him to be shot, but the whole affair was kept secret lest the other Indian volunteers changed their mind about the Communists. According to Hopkirk, Maulana may have been working for the British consulate in Kashgar under Colonel Etherton. The British consul later admitted trying to establish an intelligence agency in Tashkent.[11]

Sending Asian agents into central Asia to infiltrate the Communist camps was only one of the measures being adopted to combat this new threat to India's frontiers. The passes were under constant surveillance along the whole border.[12] Inside India itself, the interception of mail, infiltration of pressure groups that appeared to be sympathetic to Communism, and the banning of the rouble to make the transfer of Soviet funds more difficult, were all designed to thwart Soviet intrigue. Some of Roy's agents were picked up as they entered the country. Even the climate had a curious part to play: invisible ink messages tended to become legible because of the intense heat in the subcontinent.[13] British intelligence sent details of Communist doctrine to the DIB, too, so that black propaganda could be used to discredit Soviet ideas. Articles also appeared in *The Times*, describing the Bolsheviks' aims in central Asia. Whether these were deliberately leaked by the Bolsheviks to put pressure on the British government, or whether they were released by the British Secret Service to demonstrate the evil designs of Communists, is unknown.

Cumming's department, known from February 1921 as the Secret Intelligence Service or SIS, continued to provide information on the link between Soviet espionage and the Indian revolutionaries to DIB throughout the 1920s. For a few months, changes in the Russians' encoding methods prevented British intelligence from reading its intercepts but, by April 1921, GC&CS was once again able to decrypt telegrams between Moscow and its officers in the Middle East. However, when Curzon challenged the Soviets on their subversion and propaganda (using intercepts from Berlin so as to protect his GC&CS sources), the Russians claimed that the communications were all forgeries from an anti-Bolshevik organisation called *Ostinformation* based in Germany. Since it was impossible to prove that the intercepts were completely safe from forgery, Curzon regarded the SIS 'with dismay' over the 'entire history of this case'.[14] To verify sources, a new grading system of reliability was introduced, but it was clear that, if British intelligence was going to outwit the Soviets, greater care and scrutiny in handling sigint intercepts was essential.[15]

Intelligence Operations inside Russia and Central Asia

As the authority of the Russian Provisional Government collapsed, Lieutenant-Colonel Frederick Bailey of the Indian Political Department was selected to travel into central Asia to gather intelligence on the situation there. Bailey had been a Tibetan-speaking interpreter on Younghusband's expedition to Lhasa in 1904 and an accomplished explorer before the First World War.[16] He had twice been wounded in action, once at Gallipoli and then in Flanders, before being posted to Persia. There, as an intelligence officer, he had joined the effort to hunt down the German guerrilla leader Wilhelm Wassmuss. In July 1918 he was ordered to lead a mission to Tashkent, despite considerable reservations in the Foreign Office.[17] It was clear that, with a civil war raging across Russia, there were grave risks to British and Indian personnel. Should the officer get into difficulties, there was no way that he could be extracted and British prestige could be damaged by accusations of espionage deep inside Russia. As if to underline the risks involved, an officer called Marshall who was tasked at the same time as Bailey, was compromised at Najaf in Mesopotamia and murdered by the Arabs.

Assisted by Stewart Blacker, an ex-Royal Flying Corps officer who had travelled undercover to Tashkent before the war, and the former tsarist consul of Kashgar, Stephanovich, Bailey led his small party across the Russian border via China's Sinkiang Province. They found Turkestan in turmoil. Thousands of central Asian Muslims had expected liberation after the revolutions in Russia, but the Bolsheviks of Tashkent refused to make any concessions. Beating off an attempt to overthrow them, the Bolsheviks launched a counter-attack that spread into the Ferghana Valley and Khokand. Despite the assistance of Kirghiz tribesmen, Khokand fell to the Bolsheviks and was sacked. Thousands died in the massacre that followed and in the subsequent Communist reign of terror across the region. Only Bokhara managed to throw out the Bolsheviks and defeat an attempt to retake the city. It was to remain independent until 1920. If the fighting was not hazardous enough, Bailey and Blacker were interrogated the moment they arrived in Tashkent.[18] The local commissar for foreign affairs, Damagatsky, challenged them to explain why British-Indian forces had fired on the Bolsheviks at Askhabad a few days before. Bailey bluffed his way through, arguing that the Indian troops were mercenaries employed by the Afghans. The deception worked and the two British officers were allowed to remain in the city. Bailey observed that the thousands of Austrian and

German prisoners of war were managing to survive the new conditions. Some enlisted in the Red Army to obtain food or to escape the appalling conditions in the camps. He also came across a German officer called Lieutenant Zimmermann who tried to recruit a military force of his own in order to prevent the prisoners joining the Bolsheviks.[19]

However, in August 1918 Bailey was accused of espionage. His interrogator was Kolesov, known as the 'butcher of Khokand' for his ruthlessness in suppressing resistance, who demanded to know why British forces had landed at Archangel. Bailey, who had been joined by the outgoing British consul of Kashgar, Sir George Macartney, suggested the landings (of which they had no knowledge) must be directed against Germany and once again the Communists were temporarily satisfied. As the situation in Central Asia was so precarious, Macartney and Blacker decided to withdraw to Kashgar, but Bailey stayed on. In a sense they escaped in the nick of time, as news of the attempt to assassinate Lenin (and the suspicion that the British agent Robert Lockhart was involved) led to renewed fears of espionage in Bolshevik ranks. Bailey managed to obtain a message for himself from the Bolsheviks' own wireless office to the effect that his mission had been terminated. However, it was now impossible simply to journey out of Turkestan. Indeed, he anticipated his arrest by the feared Cheka and created a set of false documents, being careful to destroy the authentic observations he had made to date.[20]

Bailey was picked up by the Cheka on 15 October 1918 and, when accused of funding anti-Bolshevik forces, he referred to the documents he had created which blamed such activities on the Germans. Without evidence against him, the Cheka released him, but they maintained a close surveillance. This was so clumsily carried out that Bailey was able to give his shadows the slip on 20 October. He disguised himself as an Austrian prisoner of war, and, using the assistance of a Serb called Manditch, he entered one house, slipped out the back and left by another house, before the Bolsheviks realised what had happened. Whilst Bailey made for the hills beyond the city, a former Communist commissar and his associates seized power for themselves. The rising of Osipov, the so-called 'January Events', was crushed with great brutality and thousands of Tashkent civilians were killed.[21] Bailey, who had broken his leg in an accident in the mountains, tried to return to the city. Much time was taken up carefully evading Red Army patrols and the secret police who were looking for fugitives.

If the Bolsheviks had lost track of Bailey, so had British intelligence. Lieutenant-Colonel Ernest Redl, the consul at Meshed, was able to eavesdrop on Russian radio transmissions but there was no news of the agent. Colonel Percy Etherton, the consul at Kashgar, and Sir Wilfred Malleson, in command of the British intelligence effort in northern Persia, had a network of agents, many of them Indian traders and moneylenders, on the look out for Bailey too. Malleson even offered the Bolsheviks three hostages in exchange for Bailey and other consuls thought to be languishing in gaols in Tashkent, but the plan failed when the three Russian men, fearing the consequences of revolutionary judgement, claimed asylum from the British.

In fact, Bailey was being hidden in Tashkent by sympathisers. Changing his identity and appearance several times to avoid being traced, Bailey took careful note of developments within the city. His main objective seemed to be making an assessment of the level of resistance Malleson could expect if he led British and Indian troops as far west as Tashkent (his troops having taken Merv). What Bailey did not know was that Malleson had, in fact, been ordered to withdraw from central Asia. He was also unaware that most of his messages, sent by couriers, were not reaching Etherton in Kashgar as he had hoped. One of Bailey's men was actually caught and shot and Etherton reported to India that several of his own men were missing. Nevertheless, Bailey was able to pass on funds from Etherton to Nazarov, a counter-revolutionary leader. He also hoped to be able to contact the local Muslim fighters, the Basmachi. Unfortunately, his injuries, snow-blocked passes and a Red Army offensive prevented him from making any links. The Basmachi were driven into the Pamirs where they fought a guerrilla war until 1923. Incredibly, Enver Pasha, the former Turkish war leader, was sent by Moscow to recruit an anti-Basmachi force amongst Central Asian Muslims. Enver simply changed sides at the first opportunity and captured Dushanbe before being cornered and killed in the mountains.[22]

Bailey finally managed to get one faded invisible ink message through to Etherton on 6 July 1919, confirming that Indian revolutionaries, including Baraktullah who had accompanied Niedermayer and Hentig to Afghanistan during the war, had set up their headquarters in Tashkent. His report stated that propaganda literature was being printed in several languages. He identified a Bolshevik called Bravin as the Russian liaison with the Indians and he noted that the Soviet envoy to Kabul had been sent to prepare the way for an insurrection across the border.[23] In February, the moderate Amir Habibullah had been assassinated and his third son, Amanullah had taken power. He had launched the Afghans and their Pathan tribal allies into a precipitate war against the British.[24] However, the Afghans' intelligence that India was on the verge of revolution and the British were weak was very wide of the mark. By contrast, using a network of frontier officials and allies, the British knew the Afghans were coming.[25] In a series of actions that were greatly assisted by the Royal Air Force, the British bundled the Afghans back across the border. Amanullah was chastened but the British tried to ensure his co-operation in the future by not imposing any terms. Indeed, Britain actually recognised Afghanistan's full independence.

Malleson was able to use intercepted signals between Kabul and Tashkent to sabotage relations between the Afghans and the Soviets.[26] With agents in both camps, Malleson kept himself informed of what both sides secretly intended to do with the other.[27] He leaked to the Bolsheviks information that the Afghans had sent emissaries to the Ferghana Basmachi rebels, and he also informed the Communists of an Afghan incursion as far as Merv. Resurrecting claims from the 1880s, the Afghans and Bolsheviks clashed near the oasis. This damaged the achievements of an Afghan delegation that had secured from Moscow the promise of arms, ammunition, gold and, most important of all, aircraft, with which to shoot down the RAF's fighters. The Russians cancelled the deal, fearing it would be used to support some pan-Islamic jihad in Central Asia. Signals intelligence had once again proved its worth. However, there can be little doubt that humint, namely the Asian and Russian agents that Malleson employed, had effectively destroyed Moscow's first attempt to spread unrest across the frontiers into India. Nevertheless, it has to be said that the Afghan defeat in the war of 1919 made Kabul's full co-operation extremely unlikely too.

Bailey's ability to gather intelligence whilst the Cheka continued to make intensive searches for him was due to his skill and good fortune, but his escape from Soviet Central Asia was simply miraculous. The routes through the mountains to Kashgar or across the deserts to Persia were both difficult and dangerous. Nonetheless, through his Serbian contact, Bailey heard that the Bolsheviks wanted volunteers to infiltrate Bokhara. Fifteen Communist agents had attempted to get into the city and had been killed, so Bailey (disguised as an Albanian army clerk), had little trouble being accepted for a suicidal mission. He was enrolled into the Cheka and despatched on 15 October 1919, accompanied by the Serbian and his wife. At Kagan, just a few miles from Bokhara, Bailey discovered the extremist Mehandra Pratap and was able to interview him without being compromised. Bailey thought him a fantasist.[28]

Just as he and his friends were about to set out for Bokhara, Bailey (alias Josef Kastamuni) was ordered by the Cheka to look out for a British agent called Colonel Bailey. Struck by the irony of the situation, Bailey reported that the British officer had been seen making his way from Afghanistan to Ferghana. Bolshevik suspicions about the Afghans were thus reinforced. With the Bolsheviks looking in the wrong place, Bailey ditched his disguise and removed secret letters of introduction from his watch and a box of matches before setting out for the last few miles to Bokhara. He was favourably received by the Bokharans and initially considered running a network of agents from the city. Malleson advised him to leave but this meant crossing the desert in winter. Nevertheless, within days it was clear that it was simply too dangerous to remain in Bokhara. After an arduous journey, Bailey's party reached the Persian border on 6 January 1920, but they were spotted by a Bolshevik patrol just as they drew close to the river Tejend. An Indian Army NCO called Kalbi Mohammed managed to reconnoitre a crossing, and he gave warning of an ambush by Bolshevik troops. So, under fire, they galloped across the Tejend and escaped without loss.[29] Cheated of their prey, the Bolsheviks claimed Bailey had been shot dead on the border, but he got a hero's welcome back in Britain.

The volume of information British agents brought out of Russia and central Asia seems painfully small when contrasted with the information gathered by signals intercepts, when, of course, the British were able to break Russian codes. Nevertheless, the real mine of information was the network of Asian agents operating across central Asia and to a lesser extent amongst anti-Bolsheviks in Russia. Malleson and Etherton managed to maintain links with a settled community of Indians in Turkestan, but both also ran agents in the same way as their Victorian and Edwardian forebears.

Etherton was so successful at this the Soviets put a price on his head. This enterprising officer was no stranger to hardship. He had worked as an Australian gold miner before enlisting in Kitchener's Fighting Scouts during the Boer War. He had been commissioned into the Garwhal Rifles of the Indian Army and then, in

1918, took up the post of consul-general in Kashgar. Served by a wireless operator, clerks and his Chinese staff, Etherton was protected by a platoon of sepoys and a British officer.

However, it was his agents who were his eyes and ears, and he established a network that crossed the Tien Shan range into Soviet Turkestan. He managed to monitor troop movements, track Communist agents in Sinkiang province, and he thwarted Russian attempts to establish a consulate in Kashgar. He intercepted and burned inflammatory propaganda bound for India, and persuaded the Chinese to tighten the 'stop and search' procedures on the border. This yielded results. The Chinese caught and executed at least one Soviet spy. The Indian Pratap even reappeared leading a 'trade mission', but that was turned back. The majority of Indians in Central Asia had no wish to see their trading and capitalist enterprises abolished by the Bolsheviks, so they had good reason to co-operate with anti-Bolsheviks, and it was thanks to them, and the courageous individuals who acted as runners across the mountains, that Etherton really owed his success.

Subversion against the Raj and British Counter-espionage

Great Britain agreed to recognise the Soviet Union in March 1921 at the conclusion of an Anglo-Soviet Trade Agreement. The Russians were desperately short of machine tools and other materials required for reconstruction after the Civil War, and their desire to secure the trade agreement tended to moderate their revolutionary zeal. Lenin gave the British government assurances that the Soviet preparations for war against India would cease and that their training camps would close. Some of the Indian volunteers were, in fact, simply transferred to Moscow but the rest were dispersed. Of these, many drifted back over the frontier where they were either intercepted by border patrols or surrendered. A few simply abandoned their weapons and returned to civilian life in India. However, whilst plans for an invasion of India by a Muslim army were abandoned, the training of subversives and terrorists was not. The Pan-Hindu Revolutionary Committee in Tashkent simply changed its premises and its name. British intelligence also learned that a Dr Abdul Hafiz was running a bomb-making factory in Afghanistan. When Stalin took over M. N. Roy's department in Moscow, he ordered the Indian Communists to seize control of the Indian nationalist movement, even though Roy insisted that Gandhi was a reactionary who would force nationalists to abandon any campaign the moment it turned to violence. Indeed, fear of being associated with Communist extremists had the effect of making some nationalist activists more moderate. Nonetheless, Roy's agents travelled to India to begin their campaign. The DIB picked up the first group of ten, and then subsequent groups thanks to the interception of Roy's mail and the interrogation of prisoners. Faced with the prospect of at least five years' imprisonment with hard labour, and with their cover compromised, some of the agents proved useful sources of intelligence.

In 1922, the Foreign Office continued to receive intercepts from GC&CS about Indian revolutionaries' activities in Moscow. It was learned that, despite assurances from Foreign Minister Chicherin that anti-British espionage had stopped, a group of Indian activists had been offered 'full support'. Cross checking the information with SIS, the IPI and the intercepts of traffic between Moscow and its agents in Persia and Afghanistan, Curzon felt he had irrefutable proof of Soviet espionage against India. A measure of how grave the British considered the threat to India is that further evidence was collected and shared by the Interdepartmental Committee on Eastern Unrest, a body made up of representatives from MI5, Special Branch, the Indian, Colonial, Foreign and War Offices, as well as SIS and IPI. On 8 May 1923, armed with a mass of evidence, the 'Curzon Ultimatum' was presented to the Soviets accusing them of sponsoring subversion and anti-British propaganda and it demanded a reply in just ten days. It was decided the case was so serious that text from the intercepts was included in the ultimatum, revealing the ability of the British government to read Soviet transmissions. Curzon referred to dates and times of actual communications so that the Soviets could not simply deny their activities. In fact, Moscow claimed the bulk of the accusations were 'inventions' and that the rest had been 'manipulated'. Nevertheless, anxious to preserve the trade agreement with Britain, the Soviets once again promised not to support agencies 'whose aim was to spread discontent or foment rebellion in any part of the British Empire'.[30] Raskolnikov, the Soviet envoy at Kabul, who had been distributing weapons, ammunition, propaganda and money to anti-British nationalists, was recalled. Curzon thought it a triumph, but Raskolnikov was about to be transferred anyway.

There were two significant changes to the British intelligence system in 1923. The Foreign Office handed over control of GC&CS to an Inter-Services Directorate Committee (made up of the three armed services' intelligence departments) so as to place code-breaking back into an operational and strategic sphere. In June that same year, just before he died, Cumming handed over command of SIS to his successor, Rear-Admiral Hugh 'Quex' Sinclair. Sinclair was also tasked with the management of the GC&CS although the day-to-day running remained with A. G. Denniston. Sinclair was known to his colleagues as a 'terrific anti-Bolshevik' and he took a keen interest in the Soviets' compliance with the Curzon ultimatum.[31] GC&CS learned that, in Teheran, the Soviet envoy had informed his consular agents that political activities with their secret agents had to cease and at the end of the year, Chicherin reminded his Kabul representatives to avoid support for revolutionary and nationalist organisations. However, now alerted to the ability of the British to break their codes, the Soviets changed their encryption methods. The intercepts could no longer be read.

In 1924, intercepted Comintern materials suggested that a new propaganda offensive against the British Empire was underway. SIS revealed that the Soviets were to 'play down' the Communist element of their propaganda in favour of a nationalist line, 'as an unconscious means of furthering Communist aims'.[32] At the same moment, Soviet agitation recommenced on the North-West Frontier of India. The Politburo aimed to create a 'united empire of Muslim-India and Afghanistan ... which should liberate millions of Indians from under the foreign yoke'. Furthermore, they aimed to make available almost unlimited funds to M. N. Roy, and, on 24 August 1924, the campaign was unleashed.[33] Controversy was raging in Britain over the Zinoviev Letter, which promised support for the CPGB to subvert

Britain. Coming four days before an election, the publication of the letter supported the insinuation by Conservatives that the Labour Party was in sympathy with the Soviets. Although denounced as a forgery, Christopher Andrew has shown that the letter was typical of the Soviet instructions being issued at the time, and it *did* coincide with a deliberate attempt to target labour organisations in Britain.[34] Coming on the back of a new propaganda offensive in central Asia, there seems to be more to the Zinoviev letter than mere 'conspiracy theory'. Both SIS and the Indian intelligence services intercepted a large number of documents of a similar nature in 1924 and MI5 had at least one agent in the CPGB who passed on this sort of material via 'agent runners'.[35]

Increasing militancy amongst miners and other industrial workers in Britain in the mid-1920s, as well as open expressions of support for Lenin, coincided with more intensive Comintern activity. There was deepening concern at the 'Red Menace' and the Conservative government believed that much of the unrest that led to the General Strike of 1926 was directed, or at least guided, by the hidden hand of foreign Communists. Mikhail Borodin, for example, was arrested by Special Branch in Glasgow, having entered Britain without a passport in an attempt to strengthen the CPGB. He was deported. In 1925 SIS and MI5 learned of renewed attempts to subvert the British armed forces. The following year the activists of the CPGB were told by the Comintern: 'Upon the success of the revolutionary movement in England now depends the whole course of the international socialist revolution. Only a well-organised mass strike movement can prepare the way for active revolutionary struggle.' This new emphasis on Britain was reflected in the Soviet Politburo's decision to place the direction of agitation in India not in the hands of M. N. Roy, but in the care of the British CPGB. Roy complained that the decision smacked of 'imperialism', but this attitude did little to help his case. The CPGB established its own 'Colonial Department' and sent agents to India to organise an Indian Communist Party.[36]

Their agents were again outmatched by the British intelligence services. Percy Glading (alias R. Cochrane) was the CPGB's first agent and arrived in India in February 1925. His mission was to encourage Bolshevism amongst Indian industrial workers and set up a Labour Party with agitators highly placed within its hierarchy. But Glading failed to find any suitable candidates, and, on his return, he reported that India was not yet ready for revolution. M. N. Roy was dismissive and claimed Glading's visit had been too short to get a full understanding of Indian labour relations and politics.[37] The following year, another CPGB member, George Allison (alias Donald Campbell), reached India to convert the Indian trade union movement to Communism. An intercepted letter from Roy exposed his purpose to the Indian secret service and he was arrested in January 1927 for using a false passport.[38] The third CPGB agent fared no better than his colleagues thanks to the close supervision of the secret service. Philip Spratt was a disaffected Cambridge graduate who, the Comintern thought, was unknown to the police. In fact, Spratt was tailed and when he arrived in India to open a booksellers (which was, in fact, a means of receiving and distributing Soviet funds) in 1926, he was kept under close surveillance.

Very few Indians were drawn to the Communist Party of India (CPI) but the intelligence services decided to infiltrate the organisation with a police spy. A defector, Boris Bajanov, who was picked up on the Persian border on 1 January 1928 and rushed to Simla for questioning, also provided crucial information. Frederick Isemonger, the head of the Indian Intelligence Bureau, was his interrogator. Bajanov revealed that, with war considered inevitable between the USSR and the British state at some date in the future, Moscow intended to weaken the British Empire from within.[39] Consequently, at the third CPI meeting in Bombay in March 1929, Spratt was arrested along with thirty-two other Indian Communists. Their trial, known as the Meerut Conspiracy Trial, lasted four and half years, involved 300 witnesses and over 3,000 documents. Ironically it provided a good advert for the Communists who lost no opportunity for expressing their revolutionary opinions. Nationalists were not, however, interested in these extremists. The CPI failed to get established because, as Jawarhalal Nehru remarked, despite the initial attraction of its principles: 'Communists often irritated me by their dictatorial ways, their aggressive and rather vulgar methods, [and] their habit of denouncing everybody who did not agree with them.'[40]

If the internal threat of subversion was relatively easy to contain, it was a different matter beyond the North-West Frontier of India. Having established the Turkestan Soviet Republics, the Soviets were eager to spread their influence to the south. Sir David Petrie, the head of the DIB, reported that: 'Afghanistan was being insidiously penetrated'.[41] The aim appeared to be to unite the republics with 'racially allied elements across the border', a process that would eventually carry them across the frontier of India. The completion of the Trans-Caspian railway to Termez, just forty-five miles from the Afghan city of Balkh, suggested that Soviet troops might be used to carry out a *coup de main*. In December 1925, the Political Department noted: 'Intelligence reports show that the ... railway is a military work and that its completion portends an attack on Afghanistan.'[42] However, Petrie believed that, despite the Communists' efforts, they were making limited headway in Kabul. He estimated that, whilst significant sums had been spent on propaganda and corrupt agents, the Soviet threat could be contained. The Foreign Office agreed. It believed that the Red Army was in no state to fight a major war. The War Office was less confident. Not only was the Indian Army vastly outnumbered by the eighty divisions of the Red Army that might be deployed in central Asia, but the Soviet Union also possessed air power that could strike across the mountain belt that had traditionally protected India.[43] The Interdepartmental Committee on Eastern Unrest reported that India was the main focus for the Soviet Union's foreign policy in Asia.[44] Lord Birkenhead, the Secretary of State for India, concluded that this policy was to prepare for 'an external attack synchronising with, or consequent upon, internal disruption'. In March 1927, the Defence of India Subcommittee was established to consider how best to resist this new threat, but between 1927 and 1939 there were almost no decrypts of Soviet communications which left British planners in the dark about the Russians' intentions.

British intelligence in India was therefore dependent on other means to detect the hidden hand of Soviet espionage. CPGB members, using Comintern funds, had set up several political parties which coalesced into an All-India Workers and Peasants Party in 1927. Special Branch and the DIB now traced the funds from Britain, intercepted correspondence and deciphered the various methods used to conceal the contents, from invisible ink to cryptic writing. The Communists referred to their own party as the 'YMCA', the Indian parties as the 'Methodists', and money as 'MSS'. By inverting 'send' and 'receive' and making creative use of this cryptic text, messages could be made to appear as innocuous exchanges between religious groups.

Once again, Asian agents were deployed to infiltrate the Communists' meetings. Tragically, Masood Ali, who had been tasked to attend the Sixth Comintern Congress in Moscow in July 1928, was compromised and arrested by the secret police. He was executed soon after.

Nevertheless, the arrests of the CPGB members and the leading Indian Communists in 1929, intelligence on the subsequent bitter internal rivalry in the CPI, and the news that M. N. Roy had been expelled from the Comintern for embezzling Soviet funds (in order to support his champagne lifestyle in Paris), seemed to reduce the threat. Roy made his way to India, but after seven months on the run, he was arrested in Bombay. Indian Communists, who were rivals of the Moscow clique, had betrayed him and he was sentenced to six years' imprisonment. Furthermore enquiries into the Soviet munitions industry revealed it too was weak and probably unable to sustain a long war. Moreover, Communist influence in Afghanistan was on the wane as the Afghans tired of Soviet intrigue.[45]

However, in Kashgar, a new threat emerged. Major George Gillan had replaced Etherton as the British consul-general in 1922, and for several years he had reported that the Soviets had managed to get Chinese permission for consulates across Sinkiang. From these, they had tried various means to gain more influence. Bribery, the interception of mail and a whispering campaign against the Chinese *taoyin* (governor) were all employed with more or less success. Gillan was concerned that a coup was being planned and he obtained the permission of the Chinese to augment his garrison, although he also asked India to provide more agents using the cover of traders. There was already a precedent for Soviet coup attempts in China. In February 1927, Mikhail Borodin had tried to seize power in Canton, but it had been crushed by the Chinese Kuomintang forces. Borodin was recalled to Moscow, forced to confess his failures and was later liquidated in one of the *gulags* on Stalin's orders. A second coup attempt in December that year, carried out on Stalin's instructions, also failed disastrously.

In the revolutionary atmosphere of the 1920s, it came as no surprise that Kashgar was also affected by unrest. The taoyin was assassinated by a rival but his successor was so unpopular that he provoked an uprising led by Ma Chung Yin, a local Muslim Tungan. Concerned by rumours that Ma Chung Yin was being supported by the Japanese and might spread a pan-Islamic jihad into Soviet Central Asia, Stalin sent 2,000 troops with armoured cars and air support into Sinkiang in December 1933. Ma Chung Yin was defeated and the Soviets withdrew, but left behind military advisors in large numbers. It was clear Stalin intended to retain his influence in the region, perhaps as a counterweight to the

Japanese in Manchuria (although this was an unlikely rationale given the distances involved).

In Europe, the new threat posed by Nazi Germany in the mid-1930s seemed to indicate the need for a rapprochement between Stalinist Russia and Britain. For a time, it did seem that relations would improve, but Stalin calculated that a conflict in Western Europe would allow him to dictate the peace. Mindful of the damage the purges of the Great Terror had done to the Soviet Union, Stalin concluded a non-aggression pact with the Nazis in August 1939. The world was stunned.

As the British armed forces found themselves driven back to the English Channel in the summer of 1940 by Hitler's Panzers, and occupied by a campaign against the Italians in North Africa, a new threat to India emerged. In 1937, the Italians had tried to arrange the overthrow of the pro-British Afghan Amir Zahur Shah, seeking to replace him with the deposed Amanullah. Amanullah had been living in Fascist Italy for years and had even taken an Italian mistress, but British-Indian intelligence was aware of the intrigue. They also uncovered attempts by the Italian consul in Kabul, Pietro Quanoni, to make contact with the radical Islamic leader, the Faqir of Ipi, who had fought a campaign against the British in Waziristan in 1936–7. The British knew that this was doomed to failure since the faqir was unlikely to seek an alliance with infidel Fascists. But the Nazis also attempted to use unrest on the North-West Frontier to harass the British. Operation Tiger involved the despatch of two agents, Lieutenant Dietrich Winckel and another, code-named 'Rassmuss', to Kabul where they would contact disaffected tribesmen. In the event, two German agents did attempt to travel overland to the Pathans, but they were intercepted by Afghan troops.[46] The Germans and the Italians also recruited Indian prisoners of war, but there was little chance of them serving against the British in India. Hitler was dismissive of the Indian nationalist movement. He had hinted before the war that the British ought to shoot Gandhi and other Congress leaders to assert their authority.[47] This did not dissuade Subhas Chandra Bose from advocating a revolutionary political movement based on Communism and Fascism. Rejected by the Soviets, Bose acted as a recruiting sergeant for the Free India Legion in Germany and broadcast anti-British propaganda on Goebbels's *Azad Hind* radio.

Nevertheless, the Nazi invasion of Russia on 22 June 1941 thrust Russia and Britain together as unexpected allies. Russia, it seemed, would be the buffer against any German threat to the subcontinent, even when the Germans drew dangerously close to the Caucasus oilfields. Nevertheless, as a precaution, British troops occupied Iran. Then, on 7 December 1941, the Japanese launched a surprise attack on the United States and the British in south-east Asia, and a dangerous second front was opened against India.

Britain was over-stretched by the war. There were only four divisions in Malaya and six in Burma. India was protected by an army of 250,000 men – less than half the size of pre-war Belgium's. With demands for men and materials in Britain and Egypt, the south-east Asian garrisons had to make do with obsolete ships and inadequate aircraft. Many rated the Japanese air forces at 'the same level as the Italians', an assessment designed to put everyone at ease because the Italians had effectively been defeated by 1941.[48] But British complacency and a surprise attack by the Japanese proved a deadly cocktail.

One historian notes that for the British the 'lack of information about their foes was almost total'.[49] But in fact British intelligence had known about the Japanese threat for some ten years before the war.[50] There were 7,000 Japanese residents in Malaya amongst whom Japanese agents could hide, and there was a steady stream of commercial traffic through Malaya, although some Japanese officers were more blatant in their observations. When the Straits Settlement Police recommended a reduction in Japanese labour, the governor ignored them, as he was afraid of a diplomatic incident. Similar attitudes prevented the colony being put into a proper state of defence. To make matters worse, there was a lack of co-ordination of the British intelligence effort in the region and there was a shortage of local agents and virtually no influence over the civil and military authorities. For example, RAF intelligence had acquired information about the new Japanese Zero fighter after the Chinese, who had shot one down in May 1941, passed the details of the aircraft to London. This vital intelligence, and the full order of battle of the Japanese Army, was ignored at the highest level.

The cause of complacency lay in attitudes towards the intelligence service in Singapore. Despite the fact that FECB (Far East Command Bureau) was supposed to act as the co-ordinating agency for the intelligence wings of the three armed services, and for some SIS reports, its main role was that of a simple collecting station for sigint which it then passed on to Britain. This secondary status meant that it was not respected. However, there were other organisational problems. There was some rivalry between MI5 and the Defence Security Officer, Colonel Hayley Bell, who represented the services. The police were also fragmented, and they refused to share intelligence because they feared to do so would be a breach of institutional security. Furthermore, the Singapore defences were vulnerable in two other vital respects. Firstly, Captain Patrick Heenan, a mole working for the Japanese, had almost certainly passed on details of all RAF airfields in the region before he was arrested. Secondly, the Germans obtained a full secret appreciation of the vulnerabilities of Singapore when they captured the *Automedon* in November 1940, and they passed them to the Japanese prior to their offensive. When the Japanese attacked in December 1941, they knew precisely where Singapore's weaknesses lay.

Hong Kong, Singapore, Malaya and Burma fell in short order. By April 1942, the situation looked bleak as Japanese fighters and bombers attacked the Royal Navy in the Bay of Bengal and their armies reached the border of Assam. Here was the greatest irony. After years looking for the enemy across the North-West Frontier of India, it was from the North-East Frontier that the greatest challenge had come and for the first few months there was an almost complete lack of intelligence about the threat.

The Second World War proved victorious for the British Empire, but it was a victory from which it never recovered. Many Indian people stuck to the British during the war but the nationalists insisted it was only on the condition that independence would be granted at the peace. In May 1942, thanks to the interception of an Indian Communist's letters, the viceroy learned that Gandhi was preparing to launch a massive non-cooperation campaign to force the British out.[51] The police were reinforced and many were armed. Troops were also alerted to the coming disturbances which included deliberate acts of sabotage. Unlike the Mutiny of 1857, Lawrence James notes: 'This time it [the Raj] knew what to expect and was ready, thanks to its intelligence services.'[52] The violent 'Quit India' campaign of 1942 tied down some troops, although it did not really hasten the process of *swaraj* (home rule).[53] What it did do was cause the erosion of the Raj's internal intelligence network. The governor of Bihar reported that he had 'had very poor reports of the ordinary constabulary and in some places of the armed police: their hearts are not in the job'.[54]

Concerned by the risk of the Indian Army also falling into decay, military intelligence decided to monitor the mood of the soldiers. There were remarkably few grievances of a political nature, but to combat Japanese propaganda, a special psychological warfare unit was set up to encourage 'Josh' (a positive mental attitude). During training, Indian troops were given information on how the Japanese intended to run India and how their terrible record of atrocities was affecting the areas they occupied. The courageous exploits of Indian soldiers were also widely disseminated. Among the Indian soldiers there was total contempt for the traitorous Indian National Army, which had been formed by the Japanese from prisoners of war, deserters and extremists. Some 1,200 INA activists were put ashore in India by the Japanese to act as a 'fifth column' but they were quickly rounded up – several even changed sides. Those INA on the front line were so demoralised by Japanese mistreatment that hundreds deserted to the British. Delivered by U-boat, Bose arrived in Asia too late to turn the tide. Agent 1198, a British spy inside the INA, kept British intelligence informed of Bose's movements and his attempts to rally nationalists or obtain further support from the Japanese.

The Indian Army gradually got the measure of the Japanese. They pushed them back through the sweating jungles of Burma, whilst the Americans assaulted the Pacific Islands until they got within bomber range of the Japanese mainland. Bose was killed when his plane crashed shortly after the Japanese surrender in August 1945. Britain and her allies had won, but, bankrupted by war, the British had not the will to hang on to India against the wishes of its people. The British had always relied on the 'informal' support of Indians at every level of society. Now there was no one left available to 'spy for the empire'. As co-operation with the British administration evaporated in 1946, it was just a matter of time before the Raj was wound up for good.[55] In 1947, the last British regiment left India, and the Great Game, for the British at least, was over.

Chapter 14

The Great Game Reassessed

A Retrospect

The accepted view of British intelligence before the twentieth century is of a limited, amateur organisation. Before 1800, it is difficult to identify any permanent secret service organisation, and the Victorians were hostile to any agency that smacked of 'secret police' work. Consequently, even the military intelligence departments in the United Kingdom were under-funded for much of the nineteenth century. The closure of the cryptographic unit in the 1840s, the naivety of British politicians, and the inept espionage of a few untrained British officers in Europe are all evidence of how the British saw secret intelligence. These factors help to explain why Rudyard Kipling's *Kim* or John Buchan's *Greenmantle* are regarded as exaggerations as befitting a novel. Perhaps they are merely the inventions of a novelist's mind.

However, there are many problems with this traditional view. First, many studies have focussed only on the history of the secret services in the United Kingdom. Whilst this has revealed episodes of intelligence work before 1909, particularly with reference to Irish terrorism, it has obscured the development of intelligence beyond Britain, that is to say out in the Empire. If intelligence work develops as a result of the emergence of a specific threat, then it follows that the British Isles were relatively secure during 'the long peace' of 1815–1914. Threats to Britain's imperial possessions were a different matter.

The British intelligence services have long regarded secrecy in their work as paramount. Indeed, it was only after the Cold War had ended that the importance of the efforts of Station X, the intelligence headquarters at Bletchley Park in the Second World War, was fully understood. Moreover, public discussion of British intelligence was discouraged until relatively recently. It was not until 1989, for example, that the Security Services Act laid down legal procedures for the operations of MI5. And it was not until the appointment of Stella Rimington as the first female head of MI5 in 1992 that the security services were placed in the media spotlight. This tradition of secrecy can be traced right back into the history of the service. Before the Second World War, spying was thought of as an 'ungentlemanly' business and the British establishment carefully avoided references to it. This attitude can be detected in the nineteenth century personnel too. British officers engaged on spying missions referred to their work as 'special duty', and they called themselves 'players', not spies.

It is not only in British historiography that problems arise. In India, work on intelligence in this period is conspicuous by its absence. Richard Popplewell believes this is due to the emphasis that Indian historians have placed on the success story of Indian nationalism after 1919. The early revolutionaries who failed are simply less attractive than the likes of Subhas Chandra Bose or other 'freedom fighters' of the 1930s and 1940s. Moreover, the emphasis of Indian historiography of the twentieth century is on the actions of the Asian activists, and not on the British responses to it. In some ways this focus is understandable, but a deliberate historical amnesia about the British creates an entirely false picture of the Indian nationalist movement. All too often in the history of the British Empire, caricature replaces sound historical analysis.

The greatest problem though lies in the issue of co-operation, or collaboration with the British Empire.[1] It is too easy to explain away the 300 years of British occupation in the subcontinent purely in terms of military force. It is widely acknowledged that the British conquest of India's states, which took place over an extended period, was the result of a combination of military power, alliances, and skilful diplomacy. In other words, without Indian co-operation with the British and internal divisions between the rival states, the development of the Company Raj would have been very unlikely. Furthermore, we now know that, rather than always acting from a position of strength, some of the episodes of British aggression were the result of apparent weakness. Put another way, the British sometimes conquered because they believed they were under threat. Taken into the nineteenth century, this same mentality can be seen working itself out in Afghanistan, the Punjab and even in Persia.

Another problem with existing histories of the British secret services has been the very definition of intelligence. A conventional interpretation would identify the gathering and analysis of secret information by clandestine means, and its use in some strategically valuable way. The difficulty is how we define 'information'. In military intelligence, for example, acquiring knowledge of the strengths and dispositions of an enemy is clearly vital from a tactical point of view, but, in a strategic sense, knowledge of the resources, transport network, organisation, replenishment systems, or command and control apparatus is also essential. From a political perspective, the intentions as well as the capabilities of an adversary are just as important. The attitudes of neighbouring or allied powers are also crucial. Consequently it is important to widen the definition of intelligence beyond the realm of tactical information to include a range of political, diplomatic, and geographical criteria. If we do this, the Great Game becomes far more intelligible. The 'players' who set out across central Asia were not simply envoys of the Indian political service engaged in open diplomatic missions – they were part of the fabric of intelligence-gathering. Indeed, the agents' tasks did not stop here. They had also to persuade the people of central Asia to side with the British. In order to construct spheres of influence, it was vital to acquire the friendship of local rulers. Often this required the offer of material gain as a subsidy, salary, or gift. Alternatively the threat, or even application, of considerable military force could be employed.

What of the charge of amateurism? One can only make a rather ineffective relativist judgement if one compares the intelligence work of the early 1800s with that of the later twentieth century. It has to be said that there was little training for most men engaged in espionage, but even in the mid-nineteenth century clandestine surveyors were receiving some instruction at Dehra Dun and Roorkee. There were certainly improvements in training before the First World War for British personnel, and, at Meshed, Asian agents were getting some instruction on the use of photography, invisible inks and disguises. But in order to answer this charge more fully, some overall analysis of the personnel, their failures and their achievements needs to be addressed.

There were several types of agent, either British, Eurasian and Asian, engaged in the Great Game. The first European personnel, men like William Moorcroft, were perhaps no more than envoys picking up information but whose interests nevertheless indicate the closeness of commercial and military intelligence. By the 1830s, the technique of employing local Asian agents, which had been used in the subcontinent for years, was being extended beyond the Indian frontier. Towards the end of the nineteenth century, the practice of European officers acting as handlers for a number of agents was well established. An intelligence screen was erected centred on Teheran, Meshed, Kashgar, Gilgit and Chitral. Asian personnel were used as newswriters in Kabul, Kandahar, and, from time to time, in Herat. But Europeans also manned consulates across Asia, from the Black Sea and Mediterranean coast to China. By the twentieth century, there were not only agents inside Russian Central Asia, but also in Canada and the United States, the last deployed to monitor Indian revolutionaries.

Until now, the focus has been on British agents, but it is important to acknowledge the hidden role played by the Asian newswriters, couriers and observers. There can be little doubt that the work of the British consuls would have been less successful but for the contribution of local men. A steady stream of information was passed to London, the government of the Punjab and to Simla, and, whilst it was an imperfect system, it meant that Russian (and German) preparations for war, or even limited operations, could not go undetected. The establishment of the consulate at Meshed enabled the British, through their rings of Asian agents, to observe vital Russian lines of communications in Trans-Caspia, and keep watch on Russian intrigues in Khorassan. Thus any moves against Persia's northern province, which would have great strategic significance in any war with Afghanistan, could have been countered from India. Moreover, whilst it was difficult to obtain reliable information on Afghanistan throughout the period (since the safety of European personnel could not be guaranteed), the neighbouring agencies at Chitral, Gilgit and Kashgar extended espionage rings that supervised the Hindu Kush and Pamirs. These, and political officers amongst the tribesmen of the North-West Frontier, made it difficult for any power to infiltrate India's borders.

The cover stories used by British and Asian agents were surprisingly similar, but commercial travellers, horse traders and holy men were always the best explanation for strangers on the caravan routes of central Asia. If exploration was made without a disguise, the British could always claim to be indulging in sporting activities such as mountaineering or hunting.

There was clearly a wide range of personalities engaged in the work of the Great Game and this, perhaps more than anything else, makes the Victorian secret services appear amateurish. There were enthusiasts like Robert Baden-Powell who pretended to be a butterfly collector to cover his spying, through to Frederick Bailey, the master of disguises who was, ironically, a genuine butterfly enthusiast. The visionary William Moorcroft disguised himself as a holy man, whilst Sir Francis Younghusband never recovered from his exposure to Eastern religions and became something of a mystic in later life, forming the World Congress of Faiths in the 1930s. In sum, the men of the Great Game could probably be categorised between bad, mad, intelligent or courageous – perhaps even a combination of all these.

Too many of the agents paid the ultimate price for their part in the game. Captain Grant was murdered in 1810, Lieutenant Christie was killed in action against the Russians in 1812, Moorcroft and Mir Izzet Ullah died in Afghanistan in 1825. Alexander Burnes was hacked to pieces a few years later in Kabul. Connolly and Stoddart were beheaded in the lonely square of Bokhara. George Hayward fulfilled his own prophesy about feeling 'cold steel across his throat' in the Hindu Kush and Andrew Dalgleish was similarly cut down in 1888. After much useful work in the United States, William Hopkinson was shot dead by a Sikh revolutionary in Canada in 1914. Many of the Asian personnel in British intelligence were reported missing, including those who worked for Colonel Maclean at Meshed, Colonel Etherton at Kashgar and Frederick Bailey at Tashkent. Maulana, who may or may not have been working for the British, was executed in Soviet Turkestan for trying to 'turn' Indian Communist volunteers in the 1920s. How many died in the service of the British Empire will probably never be known.

Did these men die in vain? It was thanks to the agents that the British acquired a vast store of knowledge on the topography of central Asia, information on its rulers, military strengths, the location and nature of strategic passes, the most likely avenues that an invading force might take, and the resources on these routes. The British also obtained information on the wars and revolts of the region, enabling the governments in India and Britain to adapt their policies. In short, it was intelligence, however incomplete, that ensured Britain could defend India.

In 2001, there was much media speculation that the intelligence services in the United States and Great Britain had failed to pick up Al Qaeda's plot to attack the World Trade Center and the Pentagon. The criticism has been repeated after subsequent terror attacks in Bali and the Middle East. However, it was Stella Rimington who pointed out that: 'There is no such thing as 100 per cent intelligence.'[2] She admitted there could only be 'snippets of intelligence which you have to piece together'. If this is true of the twenty-first century, with its global and satellite communications, then it is an even more appropriate assessment of the previous 300 years. The fact is that British intelligence made mistakes. This was not always in the gathering of information. Misreading and misunderstanding were common and in processing intelligence there was sometimes unnecessary duplication of effort.

However, for all its supposed amateurism, by the first years of the twentieth century there was a well-established Military Intelligence Department with its own sub-branch in India. There was also an embryo of an Intelligence Corps. There was a General Staff to carry out strategic planning. There was a Secret Service Bureau for counter-espionage in Britain, and a Special Branch in the police force for detection of crimes that threatened the state. In India, the Department of Central Intelligence worked with the police criminal investigation departments to combat subversion and terrorism. In London, the Indian Political Intelligence department monitored British-based subversion and the Committee on Eastern Unrest brought together government and intelligence agencies in a co-ordinated fashion. Along with the work of the Government Code and Cypher School after the First World War, British intelligence was a force to be reckoned with.

Tsarist Russian Army officers perhaps overestimated the threat or effect of British intelligence, but they were convinced that Britain intended to subvert the tribesmen of Central Asia and undermine their authority. The Russian authorities certainly had reason to fear widespread insurrection, as the events of 1905 and 1917 proved, and most of the vast Russian Army was deployed on internal security duties. In Persia and Chinese Sinkiang Province, the Russians complained of British intrigue, as much as the British criticised tsarist subterfuge. However, the greatest successes of British intelligence were undoubtedly in thwarting the efforts of German, Soviet Russian and Indian Communist subversion. It could be argued that, in each case, Britain's adversaries were rather inept, but the fact was that these threats were identified, monitored and then countered successfully. Richard Popplewell notes that 'victory was not lightly won'. He argues that the British were only able to defeat the Indian revolutionaries 'by developing a complex intelligence network on a global scale'.[3] Moreover, as Christopher Andrew remarked: 'In their secret war against Soviet subversion . . . the intelligence services were not simply tilting at windmills.'[4]

British and south Asian agents thus fulfilled many objectives. Before the First World War they provided information on Russian deployments, avenues of advance, terrain, and the attitudes of local rulers, their allies and their enemies. They generally fulfilled the underlying principle of good intelligence, that of accurate and timely information, even if they lacked the sophistication of twentieth-century organisation and technology. In addition, agents enabled the British and Indian governments to conduct influential diplomacy with small states, denying access to their Russian counterparts, and, in some cases, even enabled local troops to perform the tasks of watching the passes on their behalf at a fraction of the cost of British forces. British agents, or their Asian employees, were able to keep Russian military movements under observation throughout the period. During the Great War, and in the wake of the revolutions in Russia, British and Asian agents were able to keep enemy agents under surveillance, intercept their communications, and, thanks to a few exceptionally brave individuals, infiltrate their organisations.

Inevitably there were setbacks and failures. In the nineteenth century, some of the intelligence missions destabilised the areas in which they operated. In the 1890s, the British were on the defensive in Persia and they were excluded from

Afghanistan. They were forced to impose their will by force of arms in the northern states of India as they judged the magnitude of the Russian threat to be greater than the reliability of the local rulers. Military action was also deemed necessary to hold the mountain tribes in check although recruitment into the ranks of the Indian Army and increasing regional prosperity did as much, if not more, to quieten the area. But military action did not always guarantee a compliant satellite state. Afghanistan was invaded twice to bring it within the British-Indian sphere of influence, and large sums of money were used to ensure its continued co-operation, but it was never absorbed into the Raj. Until the establishment of permanent consulates or posts in the states beyond British jurisdiction (such as Persia and Sinkiang), information was often intermittent. Agents were vulnerable, and the British were not always able to maintain a presence where it was needed. The alternative was to despatch periodic missions, but here too it was difficult to ensure the safety of British personnel.

The greatest failures of intelligence were those surrounding Tibet in 1904 and south-east Asia in 1941. They provide an interesting contrast. In the case of Tibet, Curzon grossly overestimated the threat Russia posed to India. It was not that he believed that Russia could invade India, but that Russian intrigue would make it possible to turn Tibet into a Russian satellite, and thus, eventually, tsarist emissaries would be able to subvert sections of the Indian population. Given his expertise on Persia, it is easy to see why Curzon fell into this way of thinking. In 1941, the situation was reversed. British authorities in India were too complacent about the limited intelligence they were receiving about the Japanese threat, even though, before the war, defence planners saw Japan as a naval power of some note. Again, the prevailing attitude can be explained. The British Empire's defences were already stretched by campaigns in Europe and the Mediterranean, and the defences of south-east Asia had been run down by years of defence cuts. But misreading intelligence was not the only disaster. In the intelligence war with the British Empire in the 1930s, Soviet recruiters focussed on vulnerable and idealistic members of the establishment, men like Philip Spratt from Cambridge. For a long time, this outflanked the British Secret Service and the traitors caused immense damage to British security.

The verdict on the Great Game needs a rethink. It is clearly misleading to suggest that British intelligence in this period was amateur and ineffective. Any judgement based only on the existence of British institutions and the relatively small numbers of British personnel involved is flawed. Intelligence gathering was concerned with far more than the acquisition of tactical information, and even military intelligence officers were interested in political and diplomatic information. With a broader definition of intelligence, a better understanding of the role and achievements of the Great Game players will be possible. Indeed, post-colonial scholars, who are deeply interested in the use of knowledge, have reminded historians of the value and purpose of acquiring information in the Empire. Whilst their definitions might only be seen as serving a limited agenda of assessing where power lay in the British–colonial encounter, they do highlight the way that, in Western historiography at least, the Asian personnel have for too long been the hidden 'other'. The employment of thousands of Asian personnel and the expenditure of the Government of India on secret service needs to be acknowledged if the true dimensions of British intelligence are to be assessed. This study has attempted to show that the close co-operation of British and Asian personnel was just one part of a typical Imperial phenomenon. Asians were an integral part of the fabric of the British Empire. Their co-operation was vital to the functioning of it. Their roles may have been 'subordinate' but they were no less important for that.

In this book, the wider connections of the Indian intelligence services, stretching from the United States to China, and from the beginnings of the Company Raj to Britain's retreat from Empire in 1947, indicate that the British possessed a far more sophisticated and extensive system of secret service than we have previously realised. It is for this reason perhaps that the individual British and Asian agents, who risked so much, deserve a more fitting epitaph in the pages of history.

Notes

Chapter 1. The Great Game (*pp. 21–35*)

1. HD 2/1 p. 34, PRO (Public Record Office).
2. HD 2/1 pp. 23 and 55. Entry for March 1889. PRO.
3. HD2/1 pp. 97–8, 107 and 109. PRO.
4. Rudyard Kipling, *Kim* (London, 1901; repub. Oxford, 1987) p. 118.
5. Kipling, *Kim*, p. 3.
6. Kipling, *Kim*, p. 22.
7. Andrew Lycett, *Rudyard Kipling* (London, 1999) p. 107.
8. Peter Hopkirk, *The Great Game* (Oxford, 1990); Derek Waller, *The Pundits* (Kentucky, 1990).
9. Richard J. Popplewell, *Intelligence and Imperial Defence: British Intelligence and the Defence of the Indian Empire, 1904–1924* (London, 1995) p. 10.
10. Popplewell, *Intelligence and Imperial Defence*, p. 28–9.
11. Lawrence James, *Raj: The Making and Unmaking of British India* (London, 1997) p. 145.
12. P. Fritz, 'The anti-Jacobite intelligence system of the English ministers, 1715–1745', *Historical Journal* xvi (1973): pp. 265–89.
13. Christopher M. Andrew, *Secret Service* (London, 1985) p. 2.
14. The Post Office Secret Office was closed down after a diplomatic incident during the tsar's state visit to Britain. HD 3/3. PRO.
15. KV1/2 PRO.
16. Mark Urban, *The Man Who Broke Napoleon's Codes: The Story of George Scovell* (London, 2001) p. 199.
17. Elizabeth Sparrow, *Secret Service: British Agents in France, 1792–1815* (Woodbridge, Suffolk, 1999) p. 413; David Hamilton-Williams, *Waterloo: New Perspectives* (London, 1999) p. 87–8.
18. Andrew, *Secret Service*, p. 23.
19. 'Secret Service', Treasury Records, TI 11689/25183 PRO.
20. HD 5/27/701 PRO.
21. John Zephaniah Holwell, *A Genuine Narrative of the Deplorable Deaths of the English Gentlemen and others who were suffocated in the Black Hole* (London, 1758) BL (British Library) 1093. E.59.
22. When Omichund expected a huge financial reward, Robert Clive balked at the sum and turned to 'art and policy, warrantable in defeating the purposes of such a villain'. A fake treaty was created suggesting Mir Jaffa would pay the reward, effectively denying Omichund any payment at all. C. A. Bayly, *The Raj, India and the British, 1600–1947* (London, 1990) p. 96.
23. See for example, John Keay, *Where Men and Mountains Meet* (Oxford 1975) and Peter Hopkirk, *Trespassers on the Roof of the World: The Race for Lhasa* (Oxford, 1992).
24. Gerald Morgan, 'Myth and Reality in the Great Game', in *Asian Affairs* 60 (1973) p. 55.
25. Morgan, 'Myth and Reality', pp. 57–9.
26. Peter Hopkirk, *The Quest for Kim* (London, 1996) pp. 15 and 33.

27. Morgan, 'Myth and Reality', p. 59.
28. N. A. Khalfin, *Politika Rossii v Sredney Azii, 1857–1868* (Moscow, 1960); translated by H. Evans as *Russian Policy in Central Asia, 1857–1868* (Central Asian Research Centre, London, 1964).
29. Captain Rollo Burslem, *A Peep into Toorkisthan* (Hampshire, 1846).
30. Morgan, 'Myth and Reality', p. 64.
31. Morgan, 'Myth and Reality', p. 59 and Khalfin, *Politika Rossii*.
32. Hopkirk, *Great Game*, pp. 153–62; Moshe Gammer, *Muslim Resistance to the Tsar: Shamil and the Conquest of Chechnia and Daghestan* (London, 1994).
33. Andrew, *Secret Service*, p. 12; Adrian Preston, ed., *The South African Journal of Sir Garnet Wolseley* (Cape Town, 1973). Entry for 11 July 1875.
34. Susan, Countess of Malmesbury, *The Life of Major General Sir John Ardagh* (London, 1909) p. 269. Ardagh Papers, PRO 30/40/2.
35. C. E. Callwell, *Small Wars, Their Principles and Practice* (London, 3rd edn., 1906) p. 51.
36. Callwell, *Small Wars*, p. 54.
37. Norman Polmar and Thomas B. Allen, *The Spy Book: The Encyclopaedia of Espionage* (London, 1996) p. xviii.
38. Polmar and Allen, *Spy Book*, p. xi.
39. Bayly, *Raj*, p. 254.
40. Bayly, *Raj*, p. 257.
41. D. Arnold, *Police Power and Colonial Rule, Madras, 1859–1947* (Delhi, 1986) p. 138.

Chapter 2. Agents of Empire *(pp. 36–50)*

1. C. A. Bayly, *Empire and Information. Intelligence Gathering and Social Communication in India, 1780–1870* (Cambridge, 1996) pp. 87–8.
2. James J. Morier, *Journey through Persia* (London, 1812) p. 33.
3. Morgan, 'Myth and Reality', p. 56.
4. A. R. Wellesley, The Second Duke of Wellington, ed., *Despatches, Correspondence and Memoranda of Field Marshal Arthur Duke of Wellington, K.G., from 1818 to 1832* (London, 1867–80) I, pp. 286 and 432. Percy Sykes, *A History of Persia* (London, 1921) ii, pp. 298ff.
5. George Pottinger, *The Afghan Connection* (Edinburgh, 1983) p. 15.
6. R. Pasley, *'Send Malcolm!': The Life of Major General Sir John Malcolm, 1769–1833* (London, 1982).
7. Pottinger, *The Afghan Connection*, p. 16.
8. For Malcolm's mission to Persia in 1808, see V/23/202 (Index) 1624. OIOC.
9. Morgan, 'Myth and Reality', p. 58; H. W. C. Davis, 'The Great Game in Asia', *Proceedings of the British Academy* (1926), p. 9.
10. Grant's mission is recorded in *Transactions of the Royal Asiatic Society* V, pp. 328ff.
11. Lt Henry Pottinger, *Travels in Baloochistan and Sinde* (London, 1816).
12. Pottinger, *Travels in Baloochistan and Sinde*.
13. Lieutenant-General William Montieth, *Kars and Ezeroum, with the campaigns of Prince Paskiewich in 1823 and 1829, and an account of the conquests of Russia beyond the Caucasus* (London, 1856).
14. See the Political and Secret Department records, OIOC. Macdonald-Kinneir later dropped the last name to become Sir John Macdonald.
15. Sir Robert Wilson, *A Sketch of the Military and Political Power of Russia in the year 1817* (London, 1817), cited in Hopkirk, *The Great Game*, pp. 59–62.
16. M. Glover, *A Very Slippery Fellow: The Life of Sir Robert Wilson, 1777–1849* (Oxford, 1977).
17. Elphinstone, 18 May 1810, in Moorcroft to Metcalfe, 'Death of Mir Izzet Ollah Khan and pension to his family', 2 December 1824, Board's Collections 1038/28641. OIOC; for further descriptions of Mir Izzet Ullah see C. Elliot to Swinton, 8 September 1824, Home Miscellaneous Series 664.
18. Mir Izzet Ullah, 'Travels beyond the Himalaya', journal republished in *JRAS* 4 (1837) pp. 283–340.
19. Davis, 'Great Game', p. 32. Hearsey's narrative of his expeditions with Moorcroft are cited in John Snelling, *The Sacred Mountain: The Complete Guide to Tibet's Mount Kailas* (London, 1990).

20. *Bengal Despatches*, 65, p. 760. OIOC.
21. William Moorcroft and George Trebeck, edited by H. H. Wilson, *Travels in Himalayan Provinces, etc* (London, 1841).
22. *Bengal Despatches*, 68, p. 123. OIOC.
23. Moorcroft tried to revive the Tibetan trade idea by persuading a merchant from Patna to establish a link in 1818, but the Tibetans blocked it. *Bengal Despatches*, 80, p. 730. OIOC.
24. G. Alder, *Beyond Bokhara: The Life of William Moorcroft, Asian Explorer and Pioneer Veterinary Surgeon, 1767–1825* (London, 1985).
25. Keay, *Men and Mountains*, p. 28.
26. K. Meyer and S. Brysac, *Tournament of Shadows: The Great Game and the Race for Empire in Asia* (London edn., 2001) p. 49.
27. Moorcroft papers, f.28, Mss Eur D.250. OIOC; Bayly, *Empire and Information*, pp. 135–6. Merchants continued to be important to intelligence-gathering. Mirza Mullah Rahmat of Kashgar arrived in Peshawar in 1878 and passed on information about local politics. See L/P&S/7/19, 16 August 1878.
28. Keay, *Men and Mountains*, p. 46.
29. In a bizarre footnote to the story of Moorcroft's death, William Fraser, a British political officer who accompanied Mountstuart Elphinstone to Kabul in 1808, tried to collate all the information about the final stages of the expedition and interviewed subsequent travellers to the region. His habit was to adopt an Asian style of dress and mix with respected Indians, but he was murdered by an unknown assassin before he could publish the results of his investigations. Keay, *Men and Mountains*, pp. 44, 77–8.
30. Davis, 'Great Game', p. 6.
31. John Howes Gleason, *The Genesis of Russophobia* (Cambridge, Mass., 1950; repub. New York, 1972) p. 27.
32. Gleason, *Russophobia*, p. 31.
33. One of the earliest reference to a threat to India, albeit one that would manifest itself in the future, was in the *Edinburgh Review*, October 1815, XXV, cited in Gleason, *Russophobia*, p. 421.
34. Dietrich Geyer, *Russian Imperialism* translated by Bruce Little (Leamington Spa, first pub. 1977, this edn., 1987) p. 5.
35. Geyer, *Russian Imperialism*, p. 10.
36. Geyer, *Russian Imperialism*, pp. 97–100.
37. Geyer, *Russian Imperialism*, p. 90.
38. John Darwin, 'Imperialism and the Victorians: The Dynamics of Territorial Expansion', *English Historical Review* 447, CXII (1997) pp. 624–5.
39. Robert Johnson, *British Imperialism* (London, 2002) pp. 40–58.
40. Davis, 'Great Game', p. 10.
41. Morgan, 'Myth and Reality', p. 65.
42. Bayly, *Empire and Information*, p. 100.
43. Home Miscellaneous series 664 and 645.
44. Adam to Gardner, 25 April 1815, Home Miscellaneous series 653.
45. Bayly, *Empire and Information*, p. 104.
46. Bayly, *Empire and Information*, p. 116.
47. David Ochterlony, Ludhiana, to Adam, 9 July 1814, Home Miscellaneous series 644.
48. Morgan, 'Myth and Reality', p. 58.
49. Davis, 'Great Game', p. 16.
50. Elphinstone's report in Ms, Home Miscellaneous 658, ff. 209–11 and 383.

Chapter 3. Misreading Intelligence *(pp. 51–67)*

1. In fact, although Sir John Kaye picked up on the expression in his work, *Lives of Indian Officers* (2nd edn., 1904), the phrase had been current long before then. Other than the famous use by Kipling in *Kim*, Francis Younghusband, that redoubtable Great Gamer in the 1890s, commented: 'We and the Russians *are* rivals ... We are both playing at a big game, and we should not be one jot better off for trying to conceal the fac''. Francis

Younghusband, *The Heart of a Continent* (London, 1896) p. 272. Henry Creswicke Rawlinson went on to become a director of the East India Company and then a member of the Council of India, serving until his death in 1895. He was British minister in Persia (1859–60), a leading Assyriologist, and president of the Royal Geographical Society (1871–3, 1874–6) and the Asiatic Society (1878–81). See G. Rawlinson, *Memoir of Henry Creswicke Rawlinson* (London, 1898).

2. Lieutenant Arthur Connolly, *Report of a Journey Overland from Tabreez to the North of India* (Bengal, 1830) p. 1. F/4/1385. OIOC.

3. Morgan, 'Myth and Reality', p. 55.

4. The quote was by (later Field Marshal) Sir Neville Chamberlain (1820–1902), cited in Charles Allen, *Soldier Sahibs: The Men Who Made the North-West Frontier* (London, 2000) p. 11.

5. Lieutenant Arthur Connolly, *Journey to the North of India, Overland from England, Through Russia, Persia and Affghaunistaun* [sic], 2 vols (London, 1834).

6. *India and Bengal Despatches*, I, pp. 783–5. OIOC.

7. Nancy Tapper, 'Abdur Rahman's North-West Frontier: The Pushtun Colonisation of Afghan Turkistan', in Richard Tapper, ed., *The Conflict of Tribe and State in Iran and Afghanistan* (London, 1983) p. 233–5.

8. Connolly, *Report of a Journey Overland from Tabreez*, pp. 9 and 34.

9. Davis, 'The Great Game', p. 20.

10. Connolly, *Journey to the North of India*.

11. Michael Edwardes, *Playing the Great Game* (London, 1975) p. 33.

12. *General Kuropatkin's Scheme for a Russian Advance Upon India*. June 1886. CID 7 CAB 6/1. PRO.

13. George de Lacy Evans, *On the Designs of Russia* (London, 1828) and *On the Practicability of an Invasion of India* (London, 1829).

14. Ellenborough to Wellington, 22 August 1829, in Wellesley, *Despatches of Wellington*, VI p. 100.

15. Ellenborough, *Political Journal*, 30 October 1829 and 16 December 1829, II pp. 122–5 and 149–50. OIOC.

16. Edward Ingram, *The Beginnings of the Great Game in Asia, 1828–34* (Oxford, 1979) pp. 50–84, cited in C. J. Bartlett, *Defence and Diplomacy: Britain and the Great Powers, 1815–1914* (Manchester, 1993) p. 27.

17. David Gilliard, *The Struggle for Asia: A study in British and Russian Imperialism* (London, 1977) pp. 30–3.

18. Gillard, *Struggle for Asia*, p. 32.

19. James Lunt, *Bokhara Burnes* (London, 1969) p. 208.

20. Davis, 'Great Game', p. 23, note 2. The original report is in the Political and Secret Department records.

21. Cited in Hopkirk, *The Great Game*, p. 134.

22. Donald Featherstone, *Victorian Colonial Warfare: India* (London, 1992) p. 39. See also Fauja Singh Bajwa, *The Military System of the Sikhs during the period 1799–1849* (Delhi, 1964).

23. Hopkirk, *Great Game*, p. 143.

24. L/P& S/19/42–44. OIOC.

25. L/Mil/17/22. OIOC.

26. Alexander Burnes, *Travels into Bokhara: Being the Account of a Journey from India to Cabool* [sic], *Tartary and Persia* (London, 1834) II, pp. 26–7.

27. Burnes, *Travels*, II, pp. 379–81.

28. n.a. [Dr Gerard, ed.], 'Continuation of the Route of Lieutenant A. Burnes and Dr Gerard from Peshawar to Bokhara', *Journal of the Asiatic Society of Bengal*, II (1833) pp. 1–22, ST 472 OIOC; Keay, *Men and Mountains*, p. 135.

29. India Office MSS book, 1833 (80).

30. Mohan Lal, *Journal of a Tour through the Punjab, Afghanistan, Turkestan, Khorassan and parts of Persia, 1834*. IOL T5289. OIOC.

31. Keay, *Men and Mountains*, p. 136.

32. Keay, *Men and Mountains*, p. 141.
33. Davis, 'Great Game', p. 25.
34. Charles Masson, *Narrative of Various Journeys in Balochistan, Afghanistan and the Punjab, etc* (London, 1842); see Gordon Whitteridge, *Charles Masson of Afghanistan: Explorer, Archaeologist and Intelligence Agent* (London, 2003).
35. Keay, *Men and Mountains*, p. 146.
36. J. Wood, *Journey to the Source of the Oxus* (London, 2nd edn., 1872).
37. Sir John McNeill (published anonymously), *Progress and Present Position of Russia in the East* (London, 1836). OIOC.
38. Pottinger, MS Journal, cited in Pottinger, *The Afghan Connection*, p. 38.
39. H. Pottinger, Account of the Defence of Herat. L/MIL/17/14/22; Pottinger, *Afghan Connection*, p. 42; Kaye, *Lives of Indian Officers*, ii.
40. Pottinger, *Afghan Connection*, p. 44.
41. G. J. Alder, 'The Key to India? Britain and the Herat Problem, 1830–63', in *Middle East Studies*, 10 (1974) p. 306.
42. Anon. [G. R. Elsmie], *Epitome of Correspondence regarding our relations with Afghanistan and Herat* (Government Press, Lahore, 1863) p. 50. OIOC.
43. Charles John, 1st Earl Canning, to Vernon Smith, 7 December 1856. Can/32 no. 44. Disraeli later put it even more succinctly, telling the House of Lords that the 'key of India is not Herat and Candahar. The key of India is London', suggesting diplomacy between the capitals was the best form of defence. 'The Persian Empire', *The Westminster Review* (1881) p. 414.
44. Auckland, 12 May 1838, Enclosure in Bengal Secret Letters. OIOC.
45. Patrick Macrory, *Signal Catastrophe: The Retreat from Kabul, 1842* (London, 1966) pp. 68–9.
46. Pottinger, *Afghan Connection*, p. 63.
47. Macrory, *Signal Catastrophe*, p. 114.
48. Victoria Schofield, *Every Rock, Every Hill: A Plain Tale of the North-West Frontier and Afghanistan* (London, 1984) p. 73.
49. Macrory, *Signal Catastrophe*, p. 133.
50. Linda Colley, *Captives: Britain, Empire and the World, 1600–1850* (London, 2002) p. 349.
51. Meyer and Brysac, *Tournament of Shadows*, p. 107–8.
52. Morgan, 'Myth and Reality', pp. 58–9.

Chapter 4. Internal Insecurity *(pp. 68–82)*

1. K. N. Chaudhuri, *The Trading World of Asia and the English East India Company, 1600–1760* (Cambridge, 1978) p. 243.
2. Mohammed Reza Khan was descended from a Persian family of physicians and he argued that British justice should be moderate and accessible, but he opposed the promotion of Hindus in an attempt to preserve Muslim hegemony.
3. P. Saran, *Persian Documents, being written, letters, newsletters and kindred documents pertaining to the several states existing in India in the last quarter of the eighteenth century from the Oriental Collection of the National Archives of India* (London, 1966).
4. S. C. Nandy, *Life and Times of Cantoo Baboo, the Banian of Warren Hastings* (Calcutta, 1981) pp. 234–69, cited in Bayly, *Empire and Information*, p. 50.
5. Bayly, *Empire and Information*, p. 79. Families seeking British service, Boards Collections, 1402/55500 OIOC.
6. J. Grant, 'Political Survey of the Deccan', 1782, Hastings Papers, Add Mss 29,209 and 29,383ff, British Library.
7. Bayly, *Empire and Information*, p. 51.
8. Major O. T. Burne, response to a lecture by Captain F. Trench, 'The Central Asian Question', 12 February 1873, *Journal of the Royal United Services Institute* (1873) p. 206.
9. Bayly, *Empire and Information*, p. 55.
10. J. Rennell, *Memoir of a Map of Hindoostan or the Moghul Empire* (London, 1788; reprinted Calcutta, 1976) pp. iv–xiv, xxvi; R. Phillimore, *Historical Records of the Survey of India, I, The Eighteenth Century* (Dehra Dun, 1945) pp. 1–6.

11. Bayly, *Empire and Information*, pp. 71–2.
12. 'Captain Fullarton's Hircarrahs', Home Miscellaneous Series 84, folio 913. OIOC.
13. W. J. Wilson, *History of the Madras Army* (Madras, 1882) II, pp. 86–93.
14. Wilson, *Madras Army* I, pp. 336 and 367.
15. J. Gurwood, ed., *The Despatches of Field Marshal the Duke of Wellington, KG* (London, 1837–9) I, pp. 390–3.
16. 'Reports of Transactions at Vellore for the last month', Lord Clive to Governor-General, 9 June 1801. Home Miscellaneous papers 564.
17. Brigadier Alexander Walker Mss 13,665, pp. 2–48, National Library of Scotland, cited in James, *Raj*, p. 146.
18. Major Birom, *A Narrative of the Campaign in India which terminated the War with Tipoo Sultan in 1792* (1793) pp. 87–8.
19. L/MIL/3/56, 598 D; Jac Weller, *Wellington in India* (London, 1972) p. 177.
20. Weller, *Wellington in India*, p. 195.
21. J. Young, 'The Siege of the Fort of Deeg, 9 December to 26 December 1804', D. O. Khanse and T. R. Tandon, eds., *Journal for the Society of Army Historical Research* LXIII, p. 43.
22. Mountstuart Elphinstone to the Marquess of Hastings, Governor-General, 23 March 1817. L/MIL/5/364.
23. Carnac to Governor of Bombay, 23 March and 10 April 1812. L/MIL/5/363; V. Blacker, *Memoirs of the British Army in India During the Mahratta War of 1817, 1818 and 1819* (London, 1821) p. 110.
24. Lieutenant-General Sir Francis Tuker, *The Yellow Scarf* (London, 1961) p. 14. The first Indian reference to the stranglers appeared in Zia Udbarni's *History of Firoz Shah* (*c*. 1356), which noted that, in 1290, a gang had been captured and then released.
25. Bayly, *Empire and Information*, p. 175.
26. James, *Raj*, p. 196.
27. Bayly, *Empire and Information*, p. 176; S. Gordon, 'Scarf and Sword: Thugs, marauders and state-formation in eighteenth century Malwa', *Indian Economic and Social History Review* VI, 4 (1969) pp. 403–29.
28. Bodies were always subsequently punctured to avoid secret graves being disturbed.
29. Tuker, *Yellow Scarf*, p. 39.
30. 28 were hanged and 70 were transported.
31. Tuker, *Yellow Scarf*, p. 61.
32. James, *Raj*, p. 198.
33. Tuker, *Yellow Scarf*, p. 114.
34. Tuker, *Yellow Scarf*, p. 115.
35. Bayly, *Empire and Information*, p. 173.
36. Tuker, *Yellow Scarf*, p. 38.
37. Tuker, *Yellow Scarf*, p. 124.
38. The *Delhi Gazette* of 2 February 1842 and 20 June 1842 reported that Muslim sermons called for the defeat of the British.
39. Saul David, *The Indian Mutiny, 1857* (London, 2002) p. 37.
40. Robert Montgomery, Punjab Administration Report, 1857–8 in *Selections from the Public Correspondence of the Administration of the Affairs of the Punjab* (Lahore, 1859) p. 190, in Montgomery Papers, Mss Eur D1019/3 OIOC.
41. Bayly, *Empire and Information*, pp. 322–3.
42. James, *Raj*, p. 236.
43. James, *Raj*, p. 236.
44. E. A. Reade, Acting Lieutenant-Governor of the North-West Provinces, to John Kaye, 10 March 1864, Reade papers, Mss Eur E124, 223. OIOC.
45. Mark Thornhill, *The Personal Adventures and Experiences of a Magistrate during the Rise, Progress and Suppression of the Indian Mutiny* (London, 1884) p. 3; David, *Mutiny*, pp. 65–6.
46. T. Rice-Holmes, *History of the Indian Mutiny* (London, 1904) p. 90; Sir John Kaye, *History of the Sepoy War* (London, 1864–7) I, pp. 632–9; Sir Syed Ahmed Khan, *An Essay on the Causes of the Indian Revolt* (Calcutta, 1860) p. 3.

47. Kaye, *Sepoy War*, II, pp. 244–5.
48. Rice-Holmes, *Mutiny*, p. 101.
49. Rice-Holmes, *Mutiny*, p. 106.
50. Montgomery, *Punjab Administration*, p. 2, Mss Eur D1019/3. OIOC.
51. Robert Montgomery, 'Memorandum of events since we first heard of the Mutiny in Meerut', f. 59, 3, Mss Eur D1019/3. OIOC.
52. Montgomery, *Punjab Administration*, p. 23, Mss Eur D1019/3. OIOC.
53. Montgomery, *Punjab Administration*, p. 86, Mss Eur D1019/3. OIOC.
54. Home Miscellaneous Series 725, pp. 390–1. OIOC.
55. Thornhill, *Personal Adventures*, pp. 10, 20, 68 and 71.
56. Home Miscellaneous Series 725, pp. 615–16. OIOC
57. M. Gubbins, *An account of the Mutinies in the Oudh and the Siege of the Lucknow Residency* (London, 1858) pp. 102–3; Correspondence of Lieutenant-Colonel Herbert Bruce, Add Mss 44,003, p. 113. BL.
58. Anon., *Mutiny Correspondence*, I, (Lahore, 1911) p. 193.
59. W. Muir, *Records of the Intelligence Department of the Government of the North West Provinces of India* (Edinburgh, 1902) I, pp. 16–17.
60. Muir, *Records of the Intelligence Department*, I, p. 24.
61. Muir, *Records of the Intelligence Department*, I, p. 97.
62. *Press Lists of the Punjab Civil Secretariat (XX): 1859 to 1868, Political Department* (Lahore, 1928) p. 122. OIOC. Also in Delhi was Raja Nahar Singh, the ruler of Ballabargh, who himself controlled a network of agents throughout the city. He paid his men ten rupees a day for their information on British strengths, cash supplies and morale.
63. Bayly, *Empire and Information*, p. 326, n. 59.
64. Bayly, *Empire and Information*, p. 327.
65. 'Statement of Khagesoor', 23 September 1857, Bruce papers, Add. Mss 43,996 f.172. BL.
66. James, *Raj*, p. 264.
67. Colonel Thomas Pierce, papers, Add. Mss. 42,500 pp. 46, 48 and 67.
68. G. H. Hodson, *Twelve Years of a Soldier's Life in India; being extracts from the letters of Major W. S. R. Hodson, B.A.* (London, 1859), p. 197.
69. Muir, *Records of the Intelligence Department*, I, pp. 206 and 397ff, II, pp. 2, 9, 10, 11, 16, 25, 30, 117.
70. G. Hutchinson, notes on the disarmament of Awadh, Montgomery papers, Mss Eur D1019/4. OIOC.
71. Bayly, *Empire and Information*, p. 333.
72. For a contrasting view see Arnold, *Police Power and Colonial Rule*, pp. 1–6 and 230–6.
73. James, *Raj*, p. 147.
74. See the brilliant chapter by D. A. Washbrook in 'Orients and Occidents: Colonial Discourse Theory and the Historiography of the British Empire', in Robin W. Winks, *The Oxford History of the British Empire: Historiography* V (Oxford, 1999) pp. 596–610.

Chapter 5. Penetrating Central Asia *(pp. 83–97)*

1. A. J. Barker, *The Vainglorious War, 1854–56* (London, 1970) p. 2.
2. A. J. P. Taylor, *The Struggle for Mastery in Europe, 1848–1918* (Oxford, 1954) pp. 50–1.
3. Peter John Brobst, *The Future of the Great Game* (Ohio, 2005).
4. Taylor, *Struggle*, pp. 63–79; C. J. Bartlett, *Peace, War and the European Powers, 1814–1914* (London, 1996) pp. 52–69; A. Lambert, *The Crimean War: British Grand Strategy, 1853–56* (Manchester, 1990).
5. See Kenneth Bourne, *The Foreign Policy of Victorian England, 1830–1902* (Oxford, 1970); S. Walpole, *The Life of Lord John Russell* (London, 1889) II, pp. 18–30.
6. Peter Morris, 'Russian Expansion into Central Asia', in Peter Morris, ed., *Africa, America and Central Asia: Formal and Informal Empire in the Nineteenth Century* (Exeter, 1984) p. 66.
7. For more details see Fitzroy Maclean, *A Person from England and Other Travellers* (London, 1958) and Kaye, *Lives of Indian Officers*.
8. Report by Consul Keith Abbott, *Journey to the Caspian* (1847) L/P&S/20/A7/2. OIOC.

9. Shakespear later went on to serve W. H. Sleeman. Tuker, *The Yellow Scarf*, p. 141. See also Sir Richmond Shakespear, 'A Personal Narrative of a Journey from Herat to Orenburg, on the Caspian, in 1840', *Blackwood's Magazine*, June 1842.

10. Lieutenant Connolly, *Report of a Journey Overland from Tabreez to the North of India* (Bengal, 1830) F/4/1385. p. 1. OIOC; Morgan, 'Myth and Reality', p. 55.

11. This may have been Naib Abdul Samad Khan. 21 May and 12 November 1883. L/P&S/7/35, 38.

12. Hopkirk, *The Great Game*, p. 279.

13. It was also an inspiration for Joseph Wolff, an eccentric missionary and explorer, who travelled to Bokhara to confirm the Persian's story. Wolff was spared the fate of the British officers because it was evident that he was a cleric, but his published account of his travels and findings was little consolation to the bereaved.

14. J. L. Morrison, *From Alexander Burnes to Frederick Roberts: A Survey of Imperial Frontier Policy*, Royal Academy Lecture, 15 July 1936 (Oxford, 1936) p. 9; see also Edward Thompson, *Life of Charles, Lord Metcalfe* (London, 1937).

15. Allen, *Soldier Sahibs*, pp. 107–16, 119–27, 214.

16. Allen, *Soldier Sahibs*, p. 10.

17. Theodore Pennell cited in Schofield, *Every Rock, Every Hill*, p. 90.

18. Charles Chenevix Trench, *Viceroy's Agent* (London, 1974) p. 39.

19. Charles Chenevix Trench, *The Frontier Scouts* (London, 1985) p. 7.

20. H. M. Lawrence to Lord Stanley, 31 March 1853, in Morrison, *Burnes to Roberts*, p. 12.

21. Nicholas also knew that crushing the Hungarians would end all Polish hopes for liberation; two Polish generals commanded the Hungarian forces and many more served in its revolutionary army. Taylor, *Mastery*, p. 31.

22. Bartlett, *Peace, War*, p. 53.

23. General Duhammel's scheme can be found in *Russian Advances in Asia* (1873) p. 61, WO 106 174. PRO.

24. Chikhachev's and Khruliev's plans are mentioned in R. A. Rittich, *The Afghan Question* (1905) secret, translated by the Intelligence Department, Simla, 1906. L/MIL/7/14/14. OIOC.

25. The plans were passed on by a Berlin correspondent to *The Times* on 26 January 1873.

26. Taylor, *Mastery*, p. 82.

27. Shah Nasir ud-Din had spent two years suppressing a rebellion in Khorassan following his accession in 1848, but a new round of repression began in 1852 when the Babis of Meshed tried to assassinate him. The governor of Herat, Sa'id Mohammed, had allowed Persian troops into the city to help quell disorders which had spilled over the border, but an agreement was concluded with the British envoy that Persian forces would not enter the city unless it was occupied by a foreign power. However, the withdrawal of the British mission under Murray in 1854, increasing Russian pressure, and the rebellion of the Afghan Mohammed Yusuf Sadozai in Herat, had prompted the shah to act.

28. Ian Heron, *The Savage Empire: Forgotten Wars of the Nineteenth Century* (Stroud, 2000) pp. 95–111.

29. The alliance treaty of 26 January 1857 was signed personally by Dost Mohammed at Fort Jamrud. His son had signed a treaty of friendship in March 1855.

30. Hopkirk, *Great Game*, p. 297.

31. The department was formed in 1819. See David Saunders, *Russia in the Age of Reaction and Reform, 1800–1881* (London, 1992) p. 184.

32. See Zara Steiner and Valerie Cromwell, 'The Foreign Office before 1914', in G. Sutherland, ed., *Studies in the Growth of Nineteenth Century Government* (London, 1972); R. A. Jones, *The British Diplomatic Service* (Waterloo, Ontario, 1983).

33. Keith Hamilton and Richard Langhorne, *The Practice of Diplomacy: Its Evolution, Theory and Administration* (London, 1995) p. 123.

34. Hamilton and Langhorne, *The Practice of Diplomacy*, p. 123.

35. B. A. H. Parritt, 'Intelligence Corps to *Intelligence Corps*', *Rose and Laurel* VIII, 29 (1966) p. 50.

36. W. F. Jervis, *Thomas Best Jervis: Christian Soldier, Geographer and Friend of India* (London, 1898) pp. 57, 258, 280.
37. Jervis to J. Peel, 12 June 1855. WO 32/7290. PRO; see also Andrew, *Secret Service*, p. 9.
38. War Office T and S Depot, 'War Office Plans and Reports from the Secretary of War for the seize [sic] of Sevastopol'. WO 28/299. PRO.
39. Jervis, *Jervis*, p. 264.
40. Hopkirk, *Great Game*, p. 295–6.
41. J. R. Godley, Report on the Topographical and Statistical Department, 18 July 1857, p. 8, cited in WO 32/6053. PRO.
42. *Annual Register of Correspondence*, 12 August 1867. WO 139/6. PRO; Parliamentary Papers, XXIII, 2629 (1860) p. 14.
43. Andrew, *Secret Service*, p. 10.
44. Martin Macauley and Peter Waldron, *The Emergence of the Modern Russian State, 1855–81* (London, 1988) p. 176. For the original reference see S. S. Tatischev, *Imperator Aleksandr II; ego zhizn i tsarstvovanie* (St Petersburg, 1903) II, p. 116.
45. Lord Augustus Loftus, *Diplomatic Reminiscences, 1837–1879* (London, 1894) II, p. 47.
46. For details of the debate see David Mackenzie, 'Expansion in Central Asia: St Petersburg vs the Turkestan generals (1863–6)', *Canadian Slavic Studies* 3 (1969) p. 286, n. 1. The Russian debate is summed up by N. S. Kiniapina in *Voprosy Istoii* 7 (1971) p. 174.
47. Saunders, *Reaction and Reform*, p. 295.
48. Trench, 'The Central Asian Question', pp. 191–2.
49. Nikolai Giers to M. de Staal, 1884, cited in A. Meyendorff, ed., *Correspondance Diplomatique de M. de Staal, Ambassadeur de Russie à Londres 1884–1900* (Paris, 1929) I, p. 41.

Chapter 6. The Pundits, Topography and Intelligence *(pp. 98–117)*

1. Morgan, 'Myth and Reality', p. 56.
2. Phillamore, *Historical Records*, II, p. 238.
3. Phillamore, *Historical Records*, V, p. 221.
4. *Journal of the Royal Geographical Society*, 35 (1863) civ.
5. Phillamore, *Historical Records*, V, p. 480.
6. Phillamore, *Historical Records*, V, p. 474.
7. Proceedings of the Government of India, Foreign Department, 1861 P/204/55 pp. 91–101. OIOC.
8. P/204/55 p. 102.
9. *Proceedings of the Royal Geographical Society* 10 (1864–5) p. 184.
10. Waller, *Pundits*, p. 26.
11. *Proceedings of the Asiatic Society of Bengal* 31, II (1862) p. 212.
12. See Henry Yule, *The Late Colonel T. G. Montgomerie* (London, 1878).
13. *Proceedings of the Asiatic Society of Bengal* 32, II (1863) pp. 175–9.
14. Morgan, 'Myth and Reality', p. 56.
15. Waller, *Pundits*, p. 29.
16. Waller, *Pundits*, p. 29.
17. Lt-Col H. A. Sarel, 17th Lancers, led the first China expedition, and Major Edmund Blyth, the Education Officer for Kumaon, led the second. Both had the strong support of the Survey Department, the Indian Army and the Government of India. Letter to the Secretary of State for War, 25 July 1861, Proceedings of the Foreign Department, Part A, 1861, 51; Letter of Lt-Col Ramsay to C. U. Aitchison, 24 August 1861, Proceedings of the Foreign Department, Part A, 1861, 51.
18. Proceedings of the Foreign Department, Part B, Letter from Durand to Smyth, 24 October 1861, 194.
19. *Proceedings of the Royal Geographical Society*, 13 (1868–9) p. 198.
20. Waller, *Pundits*, p. 34; see also Montgomerie Papers, 1866, Royal Geographical Society.
21. *Journal of the Royal Geographical Society* 38 (1868) p. 165.
22. Phillamore, *Historical Records*, V, p. 516.
23. Edmund Smyth in *Proceedings of the Royal Geographical Society* 4 (1882) p. 316.

24. Waller, *Pundits*, p. 40.
25. Indra Singh Rawat, *Indian Explorers of the Nineteenth Century* (New Delhi, 1973) p. 5.
26. 'Report on the Trans-Himalayan Explorations during 1865–7', *General Report of the Grand Trigonometrical Survey of India, 1866–67* (1866). OIOC.
27. Waller, *Pundits*, p. 44.
28. Waller, *Pundits*, p. 47; Charles Allen, *A Mountain in Tibet* (London, 1982) pp. 139–40.
29. T. G. Montgomerie, 'Report of a Route Survey Made by Pundit _____ , from Nepal to Lhasa, and thence through the Upper Valley of the Brahmaputra to its source', *Journal of the Royal Geographical Society* 38 (1868) pp. 129–53.
30. Waller, *Pundits*, pp. 51–2.
31. Letter from the Foreign Department, 23 August 1867, Proceedings of the Foreign Department, March 1868. OIOC.
32. A native agent had passed this way, confirming the existence of the post, in 1853 whilst in search of Lieutenant Wyburd, an officer who had been *en route* to Khiva and was probably murdered there. 'Narratives of the Travels of Khwajah Ahmud Shah Nukshbundee Syud who started from Kashmir on 28th October 1852, and went through Yarkand, Kokan, Bokhara and Cabul in search of Mr Wyburd, communicated by the Government of India', *Journal of the Bengal Asiatic Society* 25 (1856) pp. 344–58.
33. See, for example, Waller who wrote: 'The Survey of India apparently acted as an independent entity', a view based on the conclusion that there was no written directive from the Government of India to explore the Oxus line. Waller, *Pundits*, p. 59.
34. T. G. Montgomerie to Sir Roderick Murchison, President of the RGS, 29 January 1868. RGS Archive. A fourth mission was by Nain Singh, with Mani and his brother Kalian to western Tibet and a subsequent mission was made by Hari Ram further east.
35. Phillamore, *Historical Records*, V, p. 448.
36. Waller, *Pundits*, p. 66.
37. Letter from James Walker to Sir Andrew Waugh, 24 May 1858, *Records of the Survey of India*, Dehra Dun, vol. 710, 203. National Archives of India, New Delhi.
38. Proceedings of the Foreign Department of the Government of India, March 1868. OIOC.
39. Proceedings of the Foreign Department, March 1868. OIOC.
40. Lawrence Papers, Mss Eur F90/53.
41. Proceedings of the Foreign Department, March 1868. OIOC.
42. T. G. Montgomerie, Memorandum, Secret Home Correspondence, 1874, vol. 81, L/P&S/3/92. OIOC.
43. T. G. Montgomerie, 'Report of the Mirza's Exploration from Caubul to Kashgar', *Journal of the Royal Geographical Society* 41 (1871) p. lxvi.
44. Keay, *Men and Mountains*, p. 212.
45. Keay, *Men and Mountains*, pp. 213 and 222.
46. Keay, *Men and Mountains*, p. 224.
47. Keay, *Men and Mountains*, p. 230.
48. *General Report on the Operations of the Great Trigonometrical Survey of India*, (1868) p. 7. OIOC.
49. Montgomerie to Murchison, cited in Waller, *Pundits*, p. 83.
50. Kenneth Mason, 'Kishen Singh and the Indian Explorers', *Geographical Journal* 62 (1923) p. 434.
51. *Proceedings of the Royal Geographical Society* 15 (1871) p. 203.
52. One man had been dismissed because he stole Nain Singh's gold watch during training. The Mirza, their most likely candidate, was still on operational duty.
53. H. C. Thomson, *The Chitral Campaign* (London, 1895) p. 1.
54. *Proceedings of the Royal Geographical Society* 16 (1872) p. 261.
55. *Journal of the Royal Geographical Society* 42 (1872) p. 187.
56. *Journal of the Royal Geographical Society* 42 (1872) p. cxcvi.
57. T. G. Montgomerie to J. Walker, 22 April 1875, cited in Waller, *Pundits*, p. 91.
58. H. Trotter, *Secret and Confidential Report of the Trans-Himalayan Explorations by Employees of the Great Trigonometrical Survey of India, during 1873–74–75* (Calcutta, 1876) p. 4, note 1.

59. Colonel J. Walker, *General Report on the Grand Trigonometrical Survey of India* (1872–3) p. x. OIOC; Captain Henry Trotter, 'The Havildar's Journey from Badakshan to Kolab, Darwaz, and Kubadian', in Trotter, *Secret and Confidential Report of the Trans-Himalayan Explorations*, p. 4. See also note in *Geographical Journal* 48, 3 (1916) p. 229. A gazeteer of information on Bokhara can be found in the military files of the India Office collection. See Captain H. Trotter, *A contribution towards a better understanding of the topography, ethnography, resources and history of the Khanate of Bokhara*. L/Mil/17/12/ pt. 6/2.

60. Lieutenant Wood had tried to get across it in 1837, but this was the first traverse by a British agent.

61. Waller, *Pundits*, p. 93.

62. *General Report on the Operations of the Great Trigonometrical Survey of India* (1874–5) 13, see note, p. 20.

63. *Proceedings of the Royal Geographical Society* 49 (1879) pp. 600–1.

64. Trotter, *Report of the Trans-Himalayan Explorations*, pp. 24–37.

65. Trotter, *Report of the Trans-Himalayan Explorations*, p. 38.

66. *General Report on the Operations of the Great Trigonometrical Survey of India* (1876–7) pp. 21–2.

67. Lieutenant-Colonel H. C. B. Tanner, Deputy Superintendent of the Survey of India, 'The Mullah's Narrative of his journey up the Swat Valley to Kalam and Ushu, and across the Indus Valley via the Kandia Valley in 1878', in Survey of India Records *Report on Trans-Himalayan Explorations to accompany the General Report on the Operations of the Survey of India, 1878–79* (Calcutta, 1880) pp. xix–xxxv. National Archives of India.

68. Lieutenant-General J. T. Walker to Secretary of State for the Government of India, 2 May 1882, L/E/7/17 p. 1. OIOC.

69. Survey of India Records, Dehra Dun, Accounts 1880–1890, p. 594. National Archives of India. For the Boundary Commission see *General Report on the Operations of the Survey of India, 1883–4* (Dehra Dun, 1885) p. 8. National Archives of India.

Chapter 7. The Missions to the Frontiers *(pp. 118–50)*

1. The geographical details of the mission were published in *The Journal of the Royal Geographical Society* 42 (1872) pp. 448–73. See Morgan, 'Myth and Reality', p. 60.

2. The topographical narrative was later published in *The Journal of the Royal Geographical Society* 42 (1872) pp. 440–8. The RGS originally turned down the agent's report as it was, in the words of Sir Henry Rawlinson, 'too political' and 'thus unfitted for publication by our society', letter, Rawlinson, 8 January 1869, Royal Geographical Society Archives.

3. Letters, Political, 1867, vol. 2, 121. L/P&S/5/260. OIOC.

4. Lawrence papers, Mss EurF90/52 and F90/54.

5. This was because the area was claimed by Afghanistan but it was too weak to impose itself there.

6. T. R. Moreman, *The Army in India and the Development of Frontier Warfare, 1849–1947* (London, 1998) p. 8.

7. R. I. Bruce, *The Forward Policy and Its Results* (London, 1900); Andre Singer, *Lords of the Khyber* (London, 1984) pp. 124–32.

8. *General Report of the Operations of the Survey of India, 1883–84* (Dehra Dun, 1885) p. 7; Charles E.D. Black, *Memoir on the Indian Surveys, 1875–1890* (London, 1891) p. 149; *Proceedings of the Royal Geographical Society* 6 (1884) p. 370.

9. *Proceedings of the Royal Geographical Society* 6 (1884) pp. 370 and 750.

10. Keay, *Men and Mountains*, p. 217.

11. Keay, *Men and Mountains*, p. 240.

12. *Selections from the Records of the Government of India* 83 (Calcutta, 1871) p. 5 Index no. 111, ref. V/23/17; T.D. Forsyth, L/P&S/18/C14. OIOC.

13. 'Journey from Peshawar to Kashgar and Yarkand in Eastern Turkestan, or Little Bokhara, through Afghanistan, Balkh, Badakshan, Wakhan, Pamir and Sairkol', *Journal of the Royal Geographical Society* 42 (1872) pp. 448–73; *Selections from the Records of the Government of the Punjab, Confidential* (Lahore, 1873) IOR neg. MF1. OIOC.

14. 'Route of Ibrahim Khan from Kashmir through Yassin to Yarkand in 1870', *Proceedings of the Royal Geographical Society* 15 (1871) pp. 387–92.
15. See Waller, *Pundits*, pp. 151–3.
16. *Journal of the Royal Geographical Society* 47 (1877) pp. 15–17.
17. H. R. Bellew, *Report of a Mission to Yarkund in 1873, under command of Sir T. D. Forsyth, KCSI, CB, Bengal Civil Service, with Historical and Geographical Information regarding the Possessions of the Ameer of Yarkund* (Calcutta, 1875) pp. 214–6 and 249–53.
18. Waller, *Pundits*, p. 155.
19. *Proceedings of the Royal Geographical Society* 18 (1874) p. 433.
20. Captain H. Trotter, 'Narrative of Munshi Abdul Subhan's Journey from Panjeh [Wakhan] to Shignan and Roshan with a short account of his return to India via Kabul', Political and Secret Letters and Enclosures received from India, no. 22 (India, 21 June 1875) p. 394. L/P&S/7/4. OIOC.
21. By then, the Munshi was reportedly in the 'service of the Amir of Afghanistan' although he appears in 1877–8 to have surveyed a particularly hazardous section of Udaipur. Charles E. D. Black, *Memoir on the Indian Surveys 1875–1890* (London, 1891) p. 69.
22. *Report of a Mission to Yarkund*, pp. 22 and 312.
23. See G. J. Alder, *British India's Northern Frontier 1865–95: A Study in Imperial Policy* (London, 1963) pp. 111–12.
24. The series of correspondence between Russia and Great Britain can be found in the Foreign Office records, FO 65/1202. PRO.
25. Firuz Kazemzadeh, *Russia and Britain in Persia, 1865–1914* (New Haven, 1968) p. 7.
26. John Lawrence, minute, 3 October 1867. Correspondence, FO 65/1202.
27. Sir Andrew Buchanan to India Office, secret, no. 28, 26 May 1871. FO 65/1202.
28. Lord Granville to Lord Loftus, 8 January 1873. FO 65/1202.
29. N. N. Knorring, *General Mikhail Dmitrievich Skobelev* (Paris, 1939) p. 26; Kazemzedah, *Persia*, p. 25.
30. Lord Augustus Loftus, no. 304, 28 August 1874. FO 65/1202.
31. Lord Northbrook, minute on Persia, 20 May 1875. Government of India Foreign department, no. 123 L/P&S/7/3/4.
32. Napier, Government of India Foreign Department, no. 123 L/P&S/7/3/4.
33. B. Mallet, *Thomas George, The Earl of Northbrook* (London, 1908) pp. 42 and 48.
34. Lord Northbrook to Edward Cardwell, 26 October 1870, no. 141. PRO 30/48/4/19.
35. C. W. Wilson, *Russian Advances in Asia* (25 March 1873) pp. 49–53.
36. A. C. Cooke, *Russian Advances in Asia* (London, 1869) p. 10.
37. Northbrook to Cardwell, 23 April 1873, no. 60, PRO 30/48/4/21.
38. Mansfield, 24 December 1868, quoted in *Parliamentary Papers*, 1878, C2190, 'Correspondence respecting the relations between the British Government and that of Afghanistan since the accession of Ameer Shere Ali Khan', p. 77.
39. Salisbury to Northbrook, letter 18, 22 May 1874 and letter 27, 19 June 1874. Salisbury Papers C/2/69. Hatfield.
40. Salisbury to Disraeli, 2 January 1875, cited in Lady Gwendolen Cecil, *Life of Robert, Marquis of Salisbury* (London, 1921) II, p. 71.
41. Salisbury to Northbrook, letter 33, 10 July 1874 and letter 86, 11 December 1874. Salisbury Papers C/2/69.
42. Lady MacGregor, ed., *The Life and Opinions of Major General Sir Charles Metcalfe MacGregor* (Edinburgh, 1888) II, p. 3.
43. Wellesley to Loftus, 7 January 1875, no. 4, Wellesley Papers FO 519/278/273.
44. Wellesley to Loftus, 13 April 1875, FO 519/278/412, enc. Report of the Russian Consul at Astrabad to General Kaufman.
45. Cecil, *Salisbury*, II, p. 71.
46. Salisbury to Northbrook, 19 February 1875, cited in Cecil, *Salisbury*, II, p. 72.
47. Salisbury to Northbrook, 22 January 1875 and reply, *Parliamentary Papers* C2190/2 pp. 128 and 130.
48. Robert (Lord) Blake, *Disraeli* (London, 1966) p. 561.

49. Thomson to Lord Derby, 8 December 1875 and Derby to Treasury and India Office, 23 November 1875, Treasury Records, T/1/7615A/15533/1877.
50. Captain Frederick Burnaby, *A Ride to Khiva* (London, 1876, repub. Oxford, 1997).
51. M. A. Terentiaev, *Russia and England in the Struggle for the Markets of Central Asia* (Calcutta, 1876) cited in Burnaby, *Ride to Khiva*, p. xi.
52. Captain E. H. H. Collen, 'Objects of an Intelligence Branch', in *Report on the Intelligence Branch, Quarter Master General's Department, Horse Guards* (1878) p. 115. PRO.
53. Cited in Collen, *Report on the Intelligence Branch*, pp. 126–7.
54. Collen, *Report on the Intelligence Branch*, p. 136.
55. Waller, *Pundits*, p. 248.
56. Viceroy's minute, 23 February and 13 March 1876, *Proceedings of the Foreign Department of the Government of India*, July 1877, secret, nos. 1–20. Colonel Walker was sent a copy of the minute on 28 February.
57. Foreign Department of the Government of India to Secretary of State for India, 5 October 1876, no. 46, secret, L/P&S/7/10 (1876).
58. Walker to A. O. Hume, 27 March 1876, no. 16, secret, in *Proceedings of the Foreign Department of the Government of India*, July 1877, P/Section 3 Part 1, P/1035. OIOC.
59. Minute by F. H., 13 April 1876, in no. 16, secret, in *Proceedings of the Foreign Department of the Government of India*, July 1877. P/1035.
60. Foreign Department of the Government of India to Secretary of State for India, 5 October 1876, no. 46, secret, L/P&S/7/10 (1876).
61. Foreign Department of the Government of India to Secretary of State for India, 5 October 1876, no. 46, secret, L/P&S/7/10 (1876).
62. Waller, *Pundits*, p. 256.
63. Political Department minute, 30 October 1876. L/P&S/7/322.
64. Salisbury, no. 16, secret, 16 February 1877. L/P&S/7/343.
65. *Geographical Magazine*, 4, no. 7 (July 1877) p. 191.
66. A. O. Hume to Walker, 11 July 1878, no. 3, in *Proceedings of the Foreign Department of the Government of India*, October 1878. P/1219.
67. A. O. Hume to Walker, 7 September 1878, no. 7, in *Proceedings of the Foreign Department of the Government of India*, October 1878. P/1219.
68. FO 65/1205.
69. Kazemzedah, *Persia*, p. 37.
70. Someone either purchased or stole the document from the Russian Legation in Teheran, but there is also a chance that the report was an invention for profit, even a deliberate Russian *canard*. The tone of the document is nevertheless in keeping with Miliutin's other writings.
71. R. F. Thomson to Salisbury, 26 April 1876, no. 16, secret, FO65.
72. Lord Lytton to Salisbury, 2 July 1877, no. 21, secret, Government of India Foreign Department (1877).
73. W. T. Thomson, to Lord Derby, 26 July 1877, no. 114, Letters from India /16, 1877; FO 65/1202.
74. Salisbury to Lytton, 18 October 1877, no 68, secret. FO 65/1202. See also R. L Greaves, *Persia and the Defence of India, 1884–1892* (London, 1959) p. 30.
75. Report of the War Minister to the Tsar, 8/20 April 1878, A. Iliasov, ed., *Prisoedinenie Turkmenii k Rossii* (Askhabad, 1960) no. 177, pp. 332–6, cited in Kazemzedah, *Persia*, p. 46.
76. M. A. Terentiaev, *Istoriia zavoevaniia Srednei Azii*, II, pp. 428–30, cited in Kazemzedah, *Persia*, p. 47.
77. The text of the treaty is reproduced in Terentiev, *Istoriia*, II, pp. 451–4.
78. L/P&S/3/25 (1878), cited in L. P. Morris, 'Anglo-Russian Relations in Central Asia, 1873–1887', unpublished PhD thesis (University of London, 1968) pp. 375–9.
79. Captain F. C. H. Clarke, *Memorandum on Recent Russian Military Preparations* 26 July 1878. PRO.
80. A. E. Gathorne-Hardy, ed., *Gathorne Hardy, First Earl of Cranbrook* (London, 1910) II, pp. 88–9.

81. Report of the Meshed Agent & Correspondence at Herat and Merv, 1879. L/P&S/7/23.
82. R. F. Thomson to Lord Salisbury, 6 July 1878, no. 84, secret, Letters from India /20, 1878; see also telegrams from Ronald Thomson to Viceroy, Letters from India /19, 1878.
83. Thomson to Salisbury, 14 August 1878, no. 123, secret, Letters from India, /20, 1878.
84. E. H. H. Collen, *Report on the Intelligence Branch, Quarter Master General's Department, Horse Guards* (1878) p. 100.
85. See Treasury Records, T/1/7615A/15533/1877. PRO.
86. Kazemzadeh, *Persia*, p. 51.
87. *Military Parliamentary Papers 1881* C2811, part III, Lytton's no. 79, 9 September 1878, p. 31.
88. E. Baring, *Memorandum on the Central Asian Question* (London, 8 January 1877) FO 633/16. PRO.
89. R. A. Johnson, '"Russians at the Gates of India?" Planning the Defence of India, 1884–1899', *Journal of Military History* 67, 3 (2003) p. 711.
90. The limits of the available space do not permit a full analysis of the war here. The war has been examined thoroughly by Brian Robson in his *Road to Kabul: The Second Afghan War, 1878–1881* (London, 2004).
91. Cavagnari was the former Deputy Commissioner of Peshawar.
92. Captain Conolly, Political Agent, to Roberts, 4 September 1879, telegram, L/MIL/17/14/44 and Roberts, Field Marshal Lord, *Forty-One Years in India* (London, 1897) p. 383.
93. Lord Lytton to Roberts, 9 September 1879, very confidential, Roberts Papers, 37/212. National Army Museum; see also, Brian Robson, ed., *Roberts in India* (London, 1993) pp. 119–22.
94. Viceroy to Roberts, 15 October 1879, telegram, Roberts Papers, 37/42.
95. Roberts, *Forty-One Years*, p. 429.
96. Roberts, *Forty-One Years*, pp. 429–30.
97. Roberts, *Forty-One Years*, p. 453.
98. Roberts, *Forty-One Years*, pp. 453–4.
99. Government of India to Secretary of State for India, no. 81, 31 March 1880, FO 65/1099; Lord Ripon to Lord Hartington, 9 May 1880, British Library, Add Mss 43565.
100. In the event his funeral was cancelled, and he was buried hastily beside his death bed. David B. Edwardes, *Heroes of the Age: Moral Fault Lines on the Afghan Frontier* (California, 1996) p. 124. His cruelties have been well documented. See F. Martin, *Under the Absolute Amir* (London, 1907) p. 157; Edwardes, *Heroes of the Age*, p. 111; and Schuyler Jones, *Afghanistan* (London, 1992) p. 76. Sir Percy Sykes was more sanguine, and believed that 'His justice was grim and cruel ... but, in dealing with his stubborn, treacherous subjects, his methods were the only methods that would have secured law and order. It was typical rough justice of the only kind that his people understood.' Sykes praised his system of espionage and likened his state-building achievements to those of William the Conqueror. Sir Percy Sykes, *A History of Afghanistan* (London, 1940) II, pp. 198–200.
101. Further details of this fear that rebellion would lead to Russian interference can be found in Government of India to India Office, April 1885, L/P&S/7/44 and L/P&S/7/47.
102. Cited in Sir Percy Sykes, *Sir Mortimer Durand* (London, 1926) p. 198.
103. 'Memorandum on Division of Duties between Home and Indian Intelligence Departments', 5 March 1878, in Collen, *Report*, p. 112.
104. Collen, *Report*, p. 127.
105. Major-General Sir Archibald Alison, 'Memorandum on the Choice of a Military Frontier for India on the Northwest', 9 December 1878. FO 358/5.
106. Intelligence reports from Asian agents, which had been collected by newswriters and sent to the Government of the Punjab during the period of the Second Afghan War, can be found at FO 65/1060–2.
107. Minute by Sanderson (initialled by Salisbury), War Office to Foreign Office, 17 April 1879 and 30 April 1879. FO 65/1063.

108. F. H. W. Milner, 'Herat, with reference to the British Occupation of Kabul and Kandahar', 6 November 1879. FO 65/1191.

Chapter 8. An Intelligence Screen (*pp. 151–64*)

1. Lord Dufferin to Lord Salisbury, 15 July 1879, no. 321, FO 65/1202.
2. This was the view of the Intelligence Division in London and a memorandum was sent to this effect to Teheran, the India Office and St Petersburg. 20 February 1880. FO 65/1098.
3. Kazemzedah, *Persia*, p. 67.
4. Greaves, *Persia and the Defence of India*, p. 50.
5. Alison, Memorandum, 16 April 1880. FO 65/1100.
6. Military Parliamentary Papers, C-2811, Memorandum on our future policy in Afghanistan, 16 August 1880, no. 7, pp. 43–4.
7. R. F. Thomson to Foreign Office, 19 June 1880, no. 145. FO 65/1100.
8. Lord Hartington to Lord Ripon, 11 November 1880, no. 45, secret, Political and Secret Despatches to India, L/P&S/7/6 (1880) pp. 379–86.
9. Memorandum of the Chief of Staff of the 21st Infantry Division of the Caucasus Military District, 21 December/2 January 1880, in A. Iliasov, ed., *Prisoedinenie Turkmenii k Rossii* (Askhabad, 1960) no. 240, pp. 463–4.
10. N. I. Grodekov, *Voina v Turkmenii* IV (St Petersburg, 1884), cited in Kazemzedah, *Persia*, p. 75.
11. See Edmond O'Donovan, *The Merv Oasis: Travels and Adventures East of the Caspian, 1879–80–81* I (London, 1882).
12. See C. E. Stewart, 'Report on the North-Eastern Frontier of Persia and the Tekeh Turkomans', 4 July 1881. L/P&S/18 C32. The purely geographical side of this mission was published as 'The Country of the Tekke Turcomans', in *Proceedings of the Royal Geographical Society* 3 (1881) pp. 513–47.
13. The assassination of Alexander II (March 1881) seemed to make little difference to the policy in Central Asia, suggesting that the more belligerent members of the Army high command and Foreign Ministry were able to direct policy to a remarkable degree. For the Russian calculations in this period see Kazemzedah, *Persia*, pp. 82–4.
14. India Office to Foreign Office, 26 August 1881, copied in FO 65/1202.
15. Government of India to Lord Hartington, 16 January 1882, no. 6, secret, Letters from India . . . /31 (1882); India Office to Foreign Office, 21 February 1882, secret and immediate FO65/1202; Lord Granville to Sir Edward Thornton, British Ambassador at St Petersburg, 22 March 1882, no. 99 FO65/1150.
16. For the latter missions see L/P&S/20/A18. His private journal is in the Hereford County Record Office.
17. John Keay, *The Gilgit Game* (London, 1979) pp. 89–94.
18. Viceroy to Roberts, 15 October and 23 October 1879, telegrams, Roberts Papers, 37/42 and 49. National Army Museum.
19. Keay, *Gilgit Game*, p. 116.
20. Keay, *Gilgit Game*, p. 118.
21. W. W. McNair, 'Confidential Report on the exploration in part of Eastern Afghanistan and in Kafiristan during 1883', enclosure in Secretary of the Government of India to Secretary Political and Secret Department, India Office, no. 1316, Frontier, Confidential. L/P&S/7/44.
22. Cited in Anila Bali, 'The Russo-Afghan Boundary Demarcation, 1884–95: Britain and the Russian threat to the security of India', unpublished PhD thesis (University of Ulster, 1985) p. 28.
23. Earl Granville to Sir Edward Thornton [Ambassador to St Petersburg], 2 February 1882, no. 34. FO65/1150. See the enclosure on General Skobelev's speech at a dinner in St Petersburg, January 1882.
24. Thornton to Granville, 24 October and 1 November 1883. FO65/1175.
25. Thornton to Granville, 14 and 15 February 1884, nos. 3 and 4, FO65/1203.
26. 'Memorandum on Russian Troops at Luftabad and the appearance of the Saiposh

Dervesh in Merv', no. 520. February 1884, Secret, Frontier, nos. 52–3. Foreign Department, Proceedings of the Government of India. National Archives of India. 'Herat Correspondence', January 1884, no. 116, in Secret, Frontier, nos. 113–21, Foreign Department, Proceedings of the Government of India; 'Memorandum concerning events in Merv previous to subjugation' undated, no. 76, May 1884, Secret, External, nos. 52–78; Report by C. E. Stewart, 18 January 1884, no. 144, FO 65/1203.

27. See Lieutenant Nazirov, 'Report on roads between Bokhara and Merv', enclosure in Stewart to O. T. Burne [Secretary of the Political Department of the India Office], 26 December 1883, L/P&S/18/C43.

28. Stewart to Burne, 25 March 1884, no. 380, Foreign Department Proceedings of the Government of India, section 7, nos. 378–80. National Archives of India. See also Newsletters on Merv (routed via Baluchistan) L/P&S/7/42.

29. Argyll to Lord Hartington, 15 March 1881, private, Ripon Papers, Add Mss 43566; Hartington to Ripon, 13 October 1881, private, Ripon Papers, Add Mss 43567; Memorandum by Granville, 11 May 1882, Granville Papers, PRO 30/29/143. Kimberley agreed but felt that Penjdeh, further upriver, that is towards Afghanistan, should be held to prevent an advance on Herat. Kimberley to Gladstone, 4 March 1885. Add Mss 4428. British Library.

30. *Hansard Parliamentary Debates,* 3rd series, House of Lords, 10 March 1884, vol. 285, cols. 1006–10.

31. W. H. H. Waters, *Secret and Confidential* (London, 1926) p. 85.

32. MacGregor, cited in Waters, *Secret and Confidential,* p. 93.

33. For Ripon's objections see Viceroy's minute, 22 September 1884, Ripon Papers, Add Mss 43609, Part B, 99.

34. Letter of the Herat Agent, 27 November 1881, enclosure in R. F. Thomson to Granville, 31 December 1881, no. 93, FO 65/1132; Letter of Herat Agent, 22 May 1882, enclosure in R. F. Thomson to Granville, 17 July 1882, no. 135 FO 65/1152; Report of Lt Col C. E. Stewart on the Perso-Afghan Frontier, FO 65/1171; S. M. Khan, *The Life of Abdur Rahman, Amir of Afghanistan* (London, 1900) II, pp. 259–70.

35. Ripon's Note, 3 February 1883, secret, Ripon Papers, Add Mss 43579.

36. Ripon to Kimberley, 24 June 1884, private, Ripon Papers, Add Mss 43614.

37. 'Note on the Shugnan Frontier' and 'Memorandum on Shignon and Roshan', H. C. Rawlinson, 26 October 1883 and 12 April 1884, FO 65/1175 and FO 65/1205.

38. Thornton to Granville, 26 March 1884, no. 78. FO 65/1204.

39. R. A. Johnson, 'The Penjdeh Incident', *Archives* XXIV, 100 (April 1999) pp. 36–42.

40. Kabul Newsletter, January and February 1883, enclosure in 'Note on some points connected with the north-western frontier of Afghanistan with special reference to Badgheis and Penjdeh', O. T. Burne, 13 March 1885. L/P&S/18/A58.

41. Foreign Department Proceedings of the Government of India, Secret, External, no. 392, cited in D. K. Ghose, *England and Afghanistan: A Phase in their Relations* (Calcutta, 1960) p. 179.

42. Report by Stewart, 19 April 1884, Asia, Secret, 260, L/P&S/18/A53/I.

43. There were 25 European officers, 465 Indian troops, 1,276 camels and 774 horses. For further details on the commission and the Penjdeh Incident see Johnson, 'The Penjdeh Incident'.

44. Foreign Office to Sir Peter Lumsden, 27 March 1885. FO 65/1238.

45. *Records of the Intelligence Party, Afghan Boundary Commission* (Simla, 1888) I, p. 254ff. OIOC.

46. R. F. Thomson to Granville, 12 March 1885. FO 539/25.

47. Condie Stephen to Currie, 1 January 1885. FO 65/1235.

48. See, for example, the effect of this in FO 65/1239.

49. See, for example, FO 65/1235 and FO 65/1207.

50. Major-General Alison had gone to Egypt in 1882 on active service. Cameron had served in the Crimea and the Indian Mutiny during which he was awarded the VC. Later he became the Commandant of Sandhurst and then head of the ID in London in 1883.

51. Johnson, '"Russians at the Gates of India?"', p. 716.
52. A report by Lt-Col Sardar Muhammed Afzal Khan to the Viceroy, 6 March 1885, no. 440, Foreign Department Proceedings Government of India, March 1885, secret Frontier, nos. 440–8; Thornton to Granville, 3 March 1885, no. 4, FO 65/1237.
53. L. A. Gregson and A. C. Cameron, *'The Defence of India' by Sir C. M. MacGregor, QMG India*, (London, 1885).
54. Johnson, 'Russians at the Gates of India?', pp. 711–14.
55. Johnson, 'The Penjdeh Incident', pp. 28–48.
56. Sir Alfred Lyall, *The Life of the First Marquis of Dufferin and Ava* (London, 1905) II, p. 100; Roberts, *Forty-One Years*, p. 507.
57. W. E. Gladstone to Granville, 14 April 1885. PRO 30/29/129; *Hansard Parliamentary Debates*, 3rd series, 297, col.847; Gladstone's explanation to the Cabinet, 20 April 1885 Add Mss 44646, FO 95.
58. J. F. Baddeley, *Russia in the 'Eighties: Sport and Politics* (London, 1921) p. 215.
59. Baba Khan, Native Agent at Meshed, 6, 9 and 18 July 1885, Dufferin Papers, D1071H/M12/13. Public Record Office of Northern Ireland.
60. Newsletter from Samarkand, 6 May 1885, no. 455, Foreign Department Proceedings Government of India, May–June 1885, secret, Frontier, nos. 440–72.
61. Syed Abdullah, Agent in Bokhara, to Amir, 13 April 1885, no. 197, Foreign Department Proceedings Government of India, April 1885, secret, Frontier, nos. 142–98; Haji Muhammed Azim, Agent in Samarkand, to Amir, 15 April 1885, no. 285, Foreign Department Proceedings Government of India, May 1885, secret, Frontier, nos. 252–96.
62. *The Observer*, 12 and 19 April 1885, pp. 12 and 8 respectively; *The Times*, 9 April 1885, p. 5.
63. Field Marshal Lord Napier of Magdala to Dufferin, 1 October 1885, Dufferin Papers, D1071H/M5A/1/13. Information was also relayed by the Turkish authorities, 21 January 1885. FO65/1233.
64. MacGregor, *Sir Charles Metcalfe MacGregor*, II, p. 409.
65. Lockhart, later Lieutenant-General Sir William, was the second director of the Intelligence Branch at Simla from 1881 to May 1885 after Colonel G. E. Sanford (1878–81). He went on to become Commander-in-Chief in India in 1898.
66. Keay, *Gilgit Game*, p. 128.
67. Memorandum, 18 May 1885, no. 1, Foreign Department Proceedings of the Government of India, Secret, Frontier, August 1885, nos. 12–18; Government of India to Lockhart, Instructions, 6 June 1885, no. 50, Foreign Department Proceedings of the Government of India, Secret, Frontier, August 1885, nos. 12–18.
68. Woodthorpe became DQMG in 1889–92, and his assistant was Captain (later Major-General) P. J. Maitland who had served on the Afghan Boundary Commission and eventually he too became DQMG.
69. Colonel W. Lockhart and Colonel R. Woodthorpe, *Report of a Mission to Gilgit, 1885–6*, strictly confidential (London, 1889). L/P&S/20/B57.
70. Keay, *Gilgit Game*, p. 137.
71. Memorandum by Colonel W. Lockhart. L/P&S/18/A79.
72. Lockhart and Woodthorpe, *Report of a Mission to Gilgit*. L/P&S/20/B57.

Chapter 9. On Her Majesty's Secret Service *(pp. 165–80)*

1. Gerald Morgan, *Ney Elias* (London, 1971) p. 171.
2. Morgan, *Elias*, p. 16.
3. In his journal of the Pamirs expedition, he simply noted that he was 'ill' and the neat records of altitude observations give little indication of the extreme cold he endured. (RGS) AR 98–100/33 Journal of the Pamirs Journey 1885–6 and Observations file, number 46, Altitudes in Chinese Turkestan.
4. Ney Elias, *Report of a Mission to Chinese Turkestan and Badakhshan in 1885–6*, strictly confidential, (Calcutta, 1886) L/P&S/20/A27.
5. H. M. Durand to Ney Elias, 26 May 1885, MS letters from and to Ney Elias, 1885–6. Royal Geographical Society archives, AR 98–100/6 and /18. Durand instructed that the

money was to be 'used in rewards for intelligence and to be accounted for by voucher'. Durand to Elias, 943, 26 May 1885.

6. Elias, *Report*, pp. 1–2. Durand believed that Kashgar was the only suitable base in the whole region for a large mission which would cross from the northern Afghan frontier across the Pamirs. Demi-Official Print dated 16 May 1884, forwarded to Elias 23 February 1885. (RGS) AR 98–100/18.

7. Durand to Elias, 26 May 1885 (RGS) AR 98–100/6.

8. See Morgan, *Elias*, p. 208.

9. Elias to Durand, 27 September 1885. (RGS) AR 98–100/19.

10. Durand had suggested that the trade agreements with the Chinese follow the same pattern as that proposed with the Kashgar authorities in the 1870s. Durand to Elias, 23 February 1885 (RGS) AR 98–100/18.

11. Durand to Elias, 26 May 1885. (RGS) AR 98–100/6 and /18.

12. O'Conor to Dufferin, 17 April 1885; Cunningham to Elias, 11 June 1885. AR 98–100/18. Correspondence to and from Ney Elias, 1885–6.

13. The attempt to improve relations via commerce in Kashgar was not new. The explorer Robert Shaw had established a Central Asian Trading Company in 1874, but the company had folded and Andrew Dalgleish, an entrepreneur, continued trading as a private enterprise for fourteen years.

14. Hopkirk, *Great Game*, p. 434.

15. Secretary of State to Viceroy, 5 December 1884, Dufferin Papers, Mss Eur F.130/3.

16. Keay, *Men and Mountains*, p. 261. Daud Mohammed was discovered in the 1890s in Samarkand and arrested by the Russians after enquiries by Hamilton Bower. He then disappeared.

17. Durand to Elias, 28 January 1885 (RGS) AR 98–100/18.

18. Elias, *Report*, L/P&S/20/A27 ch. 1.

19. Elias to Lockhart, 5 December 1885, (RGS) AR 98–100/18 and MS Journal of Journey to the Pamirs. Elias wrote to Durand on 21 January 1886 that letters were not getting through, having written on 16 January that the dak system in Afghanistan was 'unsafe'. It was not inconceivable that Abdur Rahman was trying to obtain information on the British intentions, since he feared annexation or partition.

20. Durand to Elias, 948, 26 May 1885 (RGS) AR 98–100/6; Elias to Durand, 14 April 1886, AR98–100/18.

21. Elias, *Report*, p. 28. Unfortunately, Elias did not include the Alichur Pamir in this assessment, and subsequently it became a source of dispute.

22. See Government of India to Secretary of State for India, secret, no. 212, 16 December 1891, enclosure no. 8, Amir Abdur Rahman to Government of India, 16 October 1891. L/P&S/7/64.

23. Elias, *Report*, pp. 25–6, Elias to Durand, 2 November 1885, (RGS) AR 98–100/19.

24. 'Memorandum on the determination of a military frontier line for India', H. Brackenbury, 7 August 1887, enclosure in War Office to Foreign Office, 16 August 1887, secret, FO 65/1321.

25. Minute on Brackenbury's secret memorandum, 7 August 1887, by Salisbury, 19 August 1887, FO 65/1231; Salisbury to India, Secret, no. 17, 21 July [?] 1887. L/P&S/7/332.

26. Government of India to Secretary of State for India, no. 145, enclosure no. 3, 20 August 1886, L/P&S/7/47/1233.

27. Government of India to Secretary of State for India, 28 May 1886, enclosure no. 5, Viceroy to Amir Abdur Rahman, 18 May 1886, L/P&S/7/47/243; 25 June 1886, enclosure no. 1, 28 May 1886, L/P&S/7/47/463.

28. Elias to Durand, 14 April 1886, (RGS) AR 98–100/18.

29. Elias, *Report*, p. 100.

30. Morgan, *Elias*, pp. 210–12.

31. Gottlieb Wilhelm Leitner was an ethnologist of the Dard peoples and a linguist. Born in Budapest but educated at the Malta Protestant College, he served as an interpreter in the British Army commissariat in the Crimean War in the rank of colonel even though he was only fifteen, before moving to Turkey where he engaged in

educational experiments with language teaching. He returned to Britain and took up a number of posts at King's College, London, where he also studied Islamic law. He was appointed principal of the new college of Lahore in 1864, which he converted to a university college in 1872. His promotion of an Indian renaissance, and his outbursts of criticism of the system of administration in India, earned him few friends. His travels in Kashmir in 1866 were pioneering even if his disguises were wholly unconvincing. He was instructed by the Government of India in 1886 to examine the languages of Hunza and Nagar, prior to intelligence work there, although he was officially 'retired' from the Indian service. However the study took three years to complete and was partly written from the 'Oriental University Institute', a self-styled attempt to set up his own university in Woking. He died of pneumonia in 1899. J. F. L. Stocqveler, *The Life and Labours of Dr Leitner* (London, 1875).

32. F. Beaufort, 'Memorandum on Herat', 17 March 1885; A. Cameron, 'Memorandum on Herat', 28 March 1885. WO 106 PRO.

33. Captain James Wolfe Murray and A. Cameron, 'Estimate of Russian Forces in Trans-Caspia', 2 April 1885. WO 106 PRO.

34. Major J. S. Rothwell, 'England's means of Offence against Russia', 7 July 1884, passed to Cameron 27 January 1885. WO 106 PRO.

35. Wolfe Murray, 'Military Operations in the Event of War with Russia', 17 April 1885. WO 106 PRO.

36. W. H. Smith [Secretary of State for War] to Salisbury, 9 November 1885; Smith to Salisbury, 18 November 1885; Salisbury to Smith, 19 November 1885. WO 110/9.

37. See FO 539/28 and Cameron's 'Memorandum', 13 October 1885. FO 65/1251.

38. Intelligence Division to Permanent Under-Secretary, India Office, 15 February 1886, p. 81. WO 106/12.

39. H. Brackenbury to General Roberts, 22 July 1886. Roberts Papers. 7101 23/11/1.

40. H. Brackenbury to General Roberts, 16 December 1886. Roberts Papers. 7101 23/11/3–4.

41. See, for example, H. Brackenbury, 'General Sketch of the Situation Abroad from a Military Point of View', 3 August 1886. WO 33/46. This assessment was also sent to the British ministers at Teheran and St Petersburg.

42. Captain H. L. Nevill, *Campaigns on the North-West Frontier of India* (London, 1912) pp. 94–104, 122–23.

43. Lord Northbrook to Ripon, 27 May 1881. Northbrook Papers, Mss Eur C. 141/1. OIOC.

44. 'Insufficiency of the existing garrison of India to meet our actual and prospective military requirements, in the event of a conflict with Russia', Frederick Roberts, CAB 6/1 CID 7. PRO.

45. Copy of the Indian Financial Statement for 1885–6, prepared by the India Office, April 1885, Parliamentary Papers, LVIII (1884–5) no. 151. These figures show that the mobilisation of 1885 in India had cost £3,060,000. The cost of the amir's subsidies, railways and frontier defence, and the telegraph link from Bushire to Jask, had come to £3,918,000. An estimate for a further £2 million was prepared by the Mobilisation Committee. 'The Army in India: Increase and Reorganisation of the Army in view of the possibility of war with another European Power'. L/MIL/7/120; 'Indian Army: Increase and Reorganisation of the Native Army owing to Russia's advance in the East'. L/MIL/7/156.

46. Callwell, *Small Wars*, pp. 49–50.

47. W. S. A. Lockhart and R. G. Woodthorpe, *Confidential Report of the Gilgit Mission, 1889*. L/P&S/20/B57.

48. Popplewell, *Intelligence and Imperial Defence*, p. 21.

49. L. P. Morris, 'British Secret Service Activity in Khorassan, 1887–1908' *Historical Journal* 27 (1984) p. 658.

50. Colonel Stewart's Reports L/P&S/3/242, Finn's Reports L/P&S/3/242, 649, 737,789 and L/P&S/8/11. Successively, Captain G. E. Napier (1874), Colonel C. E. Stewart (August 1881–August 1882, March 1883–June 1884), A. Condie Stephens (1882–3), and Alexander

Finn (*c.* 1884), all manned the Meshed post. Finn also served as consul of Resht.

51. Dufferin had wanted two British officers on the northern border of Afghanistan, but Kimberley had objected on grounds of their personal safety, and he feared the complications that might result if they tried to challenge a legitimate Russian claim in a future boundary dispute. Secretary of State to Viceroy, 9 May 1885, Dufferin Papers, Mss Eur F.130/3. Nevertheless, Asian newswriters were established in Kandahar, Kabul and Herat.

52. *General Kuropatkin's Scheme for a Russian Advance upon India*, June 1886, CID 7D CAB6/1.

53. H. M. Durand to Colonel C. S. Smith, No. 514F, 21 March 1885 L/P&S/3/262. R. F. Thomson to Lord Rosebery, No. 44, 29 March 1886, FO 65/1284. See also Home Department, HD 2/1. PRO. It has been suggested that Maclean's orders were given orally, but this is refuted by Durand's instructions. H. M. Durand to Brigadier-General C. S. Maclean, 6 October 1887. L/P&S/8/2/1121.

54. Lord Dufferin to Secretary of State for India, 5 August 1887. L/P&S/3/294.

55. Morris, 'British Secret Service', p. 662.

56. *The Great Game*, Meshed, Home Department, HD 2/1 p. 2.

57. HD 2/1, 4 January 1887. p. 4.

58. HD 2/1, 18 February 1887. p. 6.

59. HD 2/1, 18 February 1887, p. 9. Maclean tried to get a house next to the graveyard, which was seldom visited.

60. C. S. Maclean, Demi-Official letter to H. M. Durand, 'Memorandum on the Russo-Afghan Question', 1 September 1887. L/P&S/8/2.

61. HD 2/1, p. 10.

62. HD 2/1, pp. 20 and 23. It seems that the Foreign Office failed to appreciate Maclean's position or his anxieties. Salisbury was reported as having described Maclean's desire for more information and advice about his role as somewhat akin to 'an Oriental', implying that he lacked the capacity for self-reliance the appointment required. L/P&S/8/2/1120.

63. Government of India to India Office, Memorandum, 8 September 1888. L/P&S/7/55/133.

64. Maclean to Durand, Demi-Official letter, 'Memorandum on the Russo-Afghan Question', 1 September 1887. L/P&S/8/2, p. 2.

65. Maclean to Durand, Demi-Official letter, 'Memorandum on the Russo-Afghan Question', 1 September 1887. L/P&S/8/2, p. 9.

66. Kuropatkin explained that Afghanistan was not the 'target', but he merely desired 'a direct route to India'. Note by Secretary, 25 July 1891, National Archives of India, Foreign Department, Secret, Frontier, August 1891, nos. 140–79 in Bali, 'The Russo-Afghan Boundary Demarcation', p. 280.

67. HD 2/1, p. 30.

68. HD 2/1, p. 34.

69. HD 2/1, pp. 23 and 55. Entry for March 1889.

70. HD 2/1, p. 97–8, 107, 109.

71. HD 2/1, p. 127.

72. Morris, 'British Secret Service', p. 668.

73. HD 2/1, p. 30.

74. FO 65/1347, pp. 1–2, 40–6, 47–8, 54–7.

75. There is evidence that, in this period, intelligence missions grew more extensive. A secret despatch from the Secretary of State for India to the Government of India, dated 11 May 1888, requested information on 'the number of Secret Agents now employed in Turkey' which was referred to the Intelligence Branch on 22 June 1888, Durand to Bradford. L/P&S/8/2.

76. See L/P&S/3/297.

77. Durand to Sardar Mohammed Afzal Khan, 14 July 1891, L/P&S/7/63/1039.

78. Peshawar Confidential Diary, 22 April 1891, in Government of India to India Office, no. 611, 4 May 1891; Peshawar Confidential Diary,14 July 1891,Government of India to

India Office, 27 July 1891. L/P&S/7/63/1041.
79. See for example, 6 July 1891. L/P&S/7/63/1079.
80. His secret letters were enclosed with those of General Amir Ahmadkhan, the Kabul envoy. Mustan Shah dressed himself as a mendicant, and was accompanied by a group of 'religious followers'. Government of India to India Office, 29 August 1888. L/P&S/7/55/175.
81. Lt-Col Picot to H. M. Durand, 1 July 1895. FO 65 1506.
82. Lt-Col Picot to H. M. Durand, 1 July 1895. FO 65 1506.
83. FO 65/1213 p. 45. See also L/P&S/20/A70.

Chapter 10. Closing the Gap *(pp. 181–97)*

1. Halik Kochanski, *Sir Garnet Wolseley: Victorian Hero* (London, 1999) p. 62.
2. Andrew, *Secret Service*, p. 18.
3. Gleichen, *A Guardsman's Memories*, pp. 77–8.
4. Sir George White to John White [father], 7 April 1898. P3/132.
5. H. Brackenbury to John Charles Ardagh, 7 April 1896. PRO 30/40/2; see also H. Brackenbury, *Some Memories of My Spare Time* (Edinburgh, 1909) p. 352.
6. H. Brackenbury, 'General Sketch of the Situation Abroad from a Military Point of View', 3 August 1886. WO 33/46.
7. Brackenbury to Thompson, 15 July and 4 August 1886, 'General Sketch', pp. 84–7. WO 33/46/2.
8. J. Wolfe Murray, Memorandum, 8 September 1886. WO 106/11.
9. Brackenbury to Foreign Office, 4 October 1886, enclosure Wolfe Murray's Memorandum. FO65/1281.
10. H. Brackenbury, 'Report on the Russian Pacific Provinces', 1 May 1886, pp. 3–11. WO 106–11; see also CAB 37/16/7.
11. See Brackenbury Memorandum, Appendix I, 19 August 1889. CAB 37/25/43. PRO.
12. Salisbury to de Staal, 7 July 1892, FO 65/1439, 887.
13. M. S. Bell, 'British Commercial Enterprise in Persia and Communications required to develop it', 30 November 1887, p. 2.
14. Wolff to Salisbury, 14 November 1888. FO 539/40.
15. E. Law [commercial attaché to Teheran] to White, 13 December 1888. FO 539/40.
16. Brackenbury to Foreign Office, 9 February 1889. FO 65/1377.
17. Wolff to Salisbury, 19 February 1889. FO 65/1377. See also Jennifer Siegel, *Endgame: Britain, Russia and the Final Struggle for Central Asia* (London, 2003).
18. Major H. A. Sawyer, 'Summary of Events for the year 1888', 4 January 1889 in FO 65/1377.
19. Major Wolfe Murray [Intelligence Division], 'Memorandum by Intelligence Department on a projected line of Railway from the Caspian through Teheran to the Persian Gulf', 15 March 1889. FO 539/41.
20. Brackenbury to Currie, 28 March 1889. FO 78/1378.
21. Salisbury to Wolff, 9 January 1890. FO 539/44.
22. Morier to Salisbury, 12 November 1890. FO 539/50.
23. Gabriel Bonvalot was accompanied by Messieurs Capus and Pepin. They had crossed Persia in 1886 and reached Meshed but had been turned away by the Afghans and consequently wintered in Samarkand. They arrived in India in May 1887. Major Wolfe Murray, *Russian Advances in Central Asia: 1885–89, 1890*. WO 33 50.
24. E. F. Knight, *Where Three Empires Meet* (London, 1897) p. 353.
25. When Younghusband met Grombtchevsky the following year, the Russian explained this as having been forced to part with his possessions by the Hunza Kanjutis. F. E Younghusband, *Report of a Mission to the Northern Frontier of Kashmir in 1889*. L/P&S/20/150, pp. 58–9. However, a Kanjut mission to Osh in 1891 secured arms and ammunition from Petrovsky, and Russian rifles were used against the British in the Hunza campaign of 1891. L/P&S/7/64, 1c and 4.
26. DMI to Foreign Office, 11 September 1890. FO 65 1394; Foreign Office to George Macartney, 22 August 1891. FO 65 1415. Safdar Ali also claimed to be the descendant of

both Alexander the Great and a mountain spirit. Government of India to India Office, no. 165, 3 December 1889. L/P&S/7/58/731.

27. Government of India to India Office, no. 165, 3 December 1889, L/P&S/7/58/731.
28. North-West Frontier Diaries, 1890, L/P&S/7/59/1057, L/P&S/7/60/427, L/P&S/7/61/943.
29. H. M. Durand, Government of India to India Office, 25 October 1891, L/P&S/7/64/899; Algernon Durand, *The Making of a Frontier* (London, 1899) pp. 238–9.
30. Knight, *Three Empires*, pp. 353–4, and 381; Durand, *Making of a Frontier*, p. 252.
31. Alder, *Northern Frontier*, p. 220.
32. Grombtchevsky's map shown to Francis Younghusband in 1889 showed just such a plan. The Russian Army had expressed this desire as early as 1880, in Kostenko, *The Turkestan Region*, II, (1880) p. 241, cited in Alder, *Northern Frontier*, p. 220. In addition, a Russian Army map entitled the Turkestan Military District, 1887, shows the Russian border reaching as far south as the passes of the Hindu Kush. The map is annotated 'Intelligence Division, War Office, received 18 December 1891'. RGS Map Collection, 'Khyrghzstan' D8.
33. Lansdowne to Roberts, 17 February 1889, Lansdowne Papers, Mss Eur D.558 1/82.
34. Government of India to India Office, Political and Secret Correspondence, 3 December 1889, no. 165, vol. 58, 731.
35. Colonel Mark Sever Bell, VC, was Director of the Intelligence Branch at Simla in 1887. His interest in China as a theatre of operations was matched by his concern for the Persian frontier. He wrote a memorandum entitled 'British Commercial Enterprise in Persia and Communications required to develop it', in November 1887, advocating measures be taken against Russian commercial and communications penetration. FO 65/1327. Younghusband, an officer of the King's Dragoon Guards, enjoyed a distinguished career as a Great Gamer before joining the Indian Political Service. He served as resident of Chitral, Tank and Bannu and was selected by Curzon to lead the invasion force of Tibet in 1904. He went on to become the President of the Royal Geographical Society and founded the World Congress of Faiths in the 1930s.
36. P. French, *Francis Younghusband* (London, 1994) pp. 51–4; A. Verrier, *Francis Younghusband and the Great Game* (London, 1991) pp. 99–100.
37. Notovich was clearly desperate for fame. An untitled article in the press, dated 19 June 1894, showed that Notovich had claimed to have discovered a link between Christianity and Buddhism, which was proved to be false. See also *Daily News*, 2 July 1894, for the same story. Durand to Bradford, Demi-Official, 10 October 1887. L/P&S/8/2/1091.
38. F. E. Younghusband, *Report of a Mission to the Northern Frontier of Kashmir in 1889*, L/P&S/20/150.
39. French, *Younghusband*, p. 70; Keay, *Gilgit Game*, p. 182.
40. There are some discrepancies in Younghusband's accounts of the mission which are examined in more detail in French, *Younghusband*, pp. 73–4. The Darwaz mentioned here should not be confused with the province in the western Pamirs.
41. Younghusband to Parry Nisbet, 26 October 1889. L/P&S/8/3.
42. Grombtchevsky's account of the meeting is in B. L. Grombtchevsky, *Relazione del Capitano, sul viaggo negli anni 1889–1890*, translated by Lionello Fogliano (Rome, 1993) p. 19.
43. Younghusband to Parry Nisbet, 26 October 1889. L/P&S/8/3.
44. Younghusband Papers Mss Eur F. 197/646/23 and Younghusband, *Heart of a Continent*, pp. 273–4; Alder, *Northern Frontier*, p. 211; C. Bower, *Confidential Report of a Journey in Chinese Turkestan, 1889–90*, L/P&S/20.
45. Younghusband, *Report*, p. 103.
46. Knight, *Three Empires*, pp. 350–484; peace terms can be found in Government of India to India Office, no. 43, 16 March 1892, enclosure no. 5, L/P&S/7/65/923.
47. *Russian Advances in Asia 1885–9*, vol. VI, WO 33 50; See also G. N. Curzon, *Russia in Central Asia and the Anglo-Russian Question* (London, 1889) and WO 106 33.

48. David Gilmour, *Curzon* (London, 1994), p. 73 and Hopkirk, *Great Game*, p. 446.
49. See F. Bertie, FO Memorandum, 23 January 1893, FO 65/1460.
50. The Chinese claim was based on an inscribed stone marker, hence Somatash (lit. 'inscribed stone'). Ney Elias, *Report*, pp. 22–3; Sykes, *Durand*, p. 179. Government of India to India Office, secret, no. 39, 11 March 1891, enclosure no. 3, Younghusband to Government of India, 23 November 1890. L/P&S/7/62. The discovery of this stone was no doubt of some personal satisfaction to Younghusband who had thus traversed China from east to west. The Russians later removed the stone to deny Chinese claims to the border.
51. Government of India to India Office, secret, no. 39, 11 March 1891, enclosure no. 3, Younghusband to Government of India, 23 November 1890. L/P&S/7/62.
52. The presence of Younghusband and Macartney prompted a series of special conferences in St Petersburg, attended by Vrevsky, Vannofsky, and Obrucheyev. It was decided to secure the Pamirs from British influence by force. The Russian historian, B. I. Iskandarov, described the conferences in *Vostochnnaya Bukara i Pamir Vo Vrory Polovine XIXV* i, (Dushanbe, 1962) p. 213, cited in A. Sheehy, 'Russia and China in the Pamirs in the 18th and 19th Centuries', *Central Asian Review* 16 (1968) pp. 8–9. See also Howard to Foreign Office, 14 October 1891, 239 FO 65/1415.
53. Taotai to F. E. Younghusband, 18 November 1890, secret, Government of India to Foreign Office, 39, in India Office Memorandum, 1 July 1892. FO 65/1439. The Afghan detachment was only twelve men strong.
54. Abdur Rahman to Simla, 17 October 1891, L/P&S/14/1 and FO 539/51. India Office Memorandum, 1 July 1892, FO 65/1439. Abdur Rahman evidently felt that the river Murghab was the boundary of his own territory. Initially, the Government of India supported Younghusband's decision. Government of India, 15 April 1891, no. 56, secret, Frontier, L/P&S/7/63. The Foreign Office was slower in its approval because it feared hostility from the Chinese over the Hunza issue. Foreign Office to J. Walsham, Peking, 29 July 1891, 21, FO 65/1415. Note by Sanderson, 10 September 1890, War Office to Foreign Office, 11 September 1890. FO 65/1394.
55. Francis Younghusband, *Report of a Mission to the Pamirs*, confidential, (Lahore, 1891) Mss Eur F.197/70.
56. French, *Younghusband*, p. 86; Hopkirk, *Great Game*, p. 464.
57. See Younghusband, *Heart of a Continent*, p. 321.
58. Without permission, this young officer had tried to cross the Mustagh Pass in emulation of Younghusband, but only narrowly avoided death through starvation. Some sources seem to suggest that Davison was acting on his own initiative in going to the Pamirs but the comment in a Foreign Office memorandum appears anomalous. FO Memorandum, 23 January 1893, FO 65/1460.
59. Verrier, *Younghusband*, p. 134.
60. See Proceedings in Central Asia, Further Correspondence, Pamirs Correspondence, 1890–1. FO 539/51.
61. Younghusband, *Heart of a Continent*, pp. 322 and 325.
62. Younghusband, Mss Eur F.197/155 in French, *Younghusband*, p. 93.
63. Younghusband, *Heart of a Continent*, p. 327.
64. Younghusband, Mss Eur F. 197/142. *Note on the Pamir Question and the North-East Frontier of Afghanistan*, S. Bayley, India Office, 19 November 1891, L/P&S/18 A82.
65. Younghusband, *Report*, pp. 6–7.
66. Younghusband, *Heart of a Continent*, pp. 330–1.
67. Younghusband, *Heart of a Continent*, p. 331; French, *Younghusband*, p. 94.
68. Proceedings in Central Asia, Further Correspondence, Pamirs Correspondence, 1890–1. FO 539/51, and FO 65/1415.
69. Prideaux (Government of India) to the assistant to the Gilgit agent, Lieutenant Manners-Smith, cited in Verrier, *Younghusband*, pp. 134–5.
70. F. E. Younghusband, *The Light of Experience* (London, 1927), cited in Alder, *Northern Frontier*, p. 227.
71. India Office to Foreign Office, 21 September and 23 October 1891. FO 65/1416.

72. See *The Times*, 30 September 1891.
73. Knight, *Three Empires*, p. 289.
74. Younghusband to Lansdowne, 20 August 1891, enclosure 5 in despatch of 30 September 1891, secret, L/P&S/7/64.
75. Younghusband, Mss Eur F 197/155 in French, *Younghusband*, p. 96.
76. Salisbury to Sir R. Morier, no. 211, December 1891. CAB 37/33/13.
77. Foreign Office Memorandum, 24 January 1893, FO 65/1460; Proceedings in Central Asia, Further Correspondence, Pamirs Correspondence, 1893–5. FO 539/71.
78. 'I can only tell you once again that we accept that the expulsion of Captain Younghusband and Lieutenant Davison was not legal in itself and that we regret it.' Morier to Salisbury, 20 January 1892, most confidential. FO 65/1434. Morier hoped to secure an apology in return for a secure boundary agreement. Morier to Salisbury, 28 January 1892, private. Hatfield House, Mss 3M/A/74/42.
79. Foreign Office to Walsham, 17 July 1891 and 29 July 1891. FO 65/1415.
80. Salisbury to Sir R. Morier, Telegraph no. 21, confidential, 22 February 1892. CAB 37/33/13. Yanov's official 'reprimand' was short-lived. He was selected to lead the next phase of operations in the Pamirs. Morier to Foreign Office, secret, 20 May 1892. Foreign Office Memorandum, 24 January 1893, FO 65/1460.
81. *Novoe Vremya*, 16/28 January 1891. FO 65/1414.
82. *Kavkaz*, 22 November/4 December 1891, extract, National Archives of India, Government of India Foreign Department, secret, Frontier, January 1892, nos. 410–88.
83. Salisbury to de Staal, 7 July 1892, FO 65/1439.
84. Durand, *Making of a Frontier*, pp. 234ff.
85. Major-General Sir John Ardagh, the DMI, whilst stressing his support for the British agent, pointed out that 'this [crisis] must be settled by the diplomatists', 14 September 1891. Mss Eur F.197/70.
86. Verrier, *Younghusband*, p. 136.
87. This was in response to a stand-off between Chinese and Afghan troops at Somatash on 27 April 1892, which had resulted in a Chinese withdrawal, followed by a 'collision' in which it appears a 'Poowei' (probably a Kyrgyz chief) and some tribesmen were kidnapped. Foreign Office to India Office, 27 June 1892, L/P&S/130/131/381.
88. The Russians claimed that the number was nearer 800 with two guns. Viceroy to Foreign Office, 4 August 1892, and Morier to Foreign Office, 26 September 1892 in Foreign Office Memorandum, 24 January 1893, FO 65/1460.
89. India Office to Foreign Office, 23 August 1892, in Foreign Office Memorandum, 24 January 1893, FO 65/1460.
90. Government of India, 16 December 1891, secret, 202, IO Memorandum, 1 July 1892 FO 65/1439. The Russian boundary was expressed as running from Uzbel to Ak Tash (on the Aksu river), then to Somatash to Tash Kurgan (Murghab valley) and along the Kudara valley to the Alai mountains.
91. Morier to Salisbury, 27 January 1892, cited in Verrier, *Younghusband*, p. 138.
92. Pamirs Correspondence, 1893–5. FO 539/71.
93. Rosebery to Howard, 13 November 1893, FO 65/1470.
94. Government of India to India Office, June 1894. L/P&S/7/74; The intricacies of the Pamirs negotiations between 1893 and 1895 are explained in detail in Alder, *Northern Frontier*, pp. 263–87.
95. T. H. Holdich, *The Indian Borderland* (London, 1901) p. 313.
96. Andrew, *Secret Service*, p. 22.
97. Cited in Antony Wynn, *Persia in the Great Game* (London, 2003) p. 6.
98. Lars Erik Nyman, 'The Great Game: A Comment', *Royal Central Asian Society* 60, new series IV (1973) pp. 299–331.
99. *Kashgar Diary* 1919. FO 371/3698. F155286/40378/10.
100. Andrew, *Secret Service*, p. 22.
101. Maclean to Salisbury, 21 February 1889. FO 539/41.

Chapter 11. Pulling the Bear's Teeth *(pp. 198–216)*

1. Brian Bond, *War and Society in Europe, 1870–1970* (London, 1984), 37. See also John L. H. Keep, *Soldiers of the Tsar: Army and Society in Russia 1462–1874* (Oxford, 1985).
2. Lieutenant-General Brackenbury DMI and Major-General Newmarch, Military Secretary India Office, Memorandum, Secret, 1889 (PRO) CAB 37/25/43, 253.
3. This view was shared by Colonel M. S. Bell, vc, *The Defence of India and Its Imperial Aspect*, private circulation only (London, 1890) L/P&S/20/G2. OIOC.
4. Roberts, *Notes on the Central Asian Question*, L/MIL/17/14/80. OIOC.
5. Lord Salisbury to General Roberts, 6 July 1885. Roberts Papers 80/4. NAM.
6. Brackenbury and Newmarch, 19 August 1889. CAB/37/25/43. PRO.
7. Cited in D. S. MacDiarmid, *The Life of Lieutenant General Sir James Moncrieff Grierson* (London, 1923) p. 88.
8. *Memorandum on the Relations between the Intelligence Departments of the War Office, Admiralty and India*, strictly confidential, 1890, WO 33 50, 4. PRO. Brackenbury to Sir George White, 5 December 1892, Brackenbury Papers, Royal Artillery Institution, Woolwich, London. MD 1085/1 f439.
9. Sir George White to John White, 7 April 1898 P3/132; cited in Ian Harvie, 'A Very Dangerous Man: A Profile of Henry Brackenbury', *Soldiers of the Queen* 96 (1999) p. 16.
10. T. G. Ferguson, *British Military Intelligence, 1870–1914* (London, 1984) p. 78–100.
11. *Notes on the Proposals for the defence of the North West Frontier by the Defence Committee, 1885.* L/MIL/17 OIOC.
12. General Roberts to Charles Marvin, 14 May 1887. Roberts Papers (PRO) 100–1/CXIX.
13. Roberts referred to the expeditions led by General Verevkin and Colonel Lomakin against Khiva. Roberts to Marvin, 14 May 1887. Roberts Papers 100–1/CXIX.
14. Sanderson minute, to Currie and Salisbury, 27 September 1888. FO 65/1353. PRO.
15. Intelligence Division to Foreign Office, 12 May 1887, FO 65/1317; War Office to India Office, 30 April 1889, FO 65/1373. PRO.
16. Intelligence Division to Foreign Office, 5 January 1887. FO 60/538.
17. Wolfe Murray, 'Russia's Power to Concentrate Troops in Central Asia', 4 May 1888. FO 65/1349. PRO. Copies were sent to Salisbury, Teheran, and the embassies at St Petersburg and Constantinople.
18. Wolfe Murray, 'Russia's Power to Concentrate Troops in Central Asia', p. 15.
19. Salisbury to de Staal, 7 July 1892, FO 65 1439. The second small, but significant, commission was on the Kushk in 1893. The Russians had complained that the Afghans had constructed canals on the Afghan side of the border which had diverted much of the water from the irrigation of the lower Kushk. In stark contrast to the Commission of 1885, a compact party assembled to decide on the course of action, consisting of Major Yate who was temporarily detached from Meshed, Lt H. D. Napier, M. Ignatiev and Colonel Atamanov. They found in favour of the Russians, and a hundred Afghan families were moved south, whilst the canals were closed. The intelligence assessment can be found in *Russian Advances in Asia*, WO 33 56. PRO.
20. Salisbury to Cross, 6 November 1890. Cross Papers Add Mss 51264, II.
21. Ardagh to Lansdowne, paper 27 (undated). PRO 30/40/12; Ardagh, 'Draft Note on 'Procedure in India respecting Secret matters' (undated). PRO 30/40/11. PRO.
22. Major-General E. Chapman to Brackenbury, September 1892. WO 106/16.
23. Brackenbury to Lansdowne, 19 October 1892. MS 113 cited in W. C. Beaver, 'The Development of the Intelligence Division, and its role in aspects of policy making, 1854–1901', unpublished DPhil thesis (Oxford University, 1976) p. 186.
24. See, for example, Chapman's letter books, 9 December 1892. WO 106/16. PRO.
25. Wynn, *Persia in the Great Game*, p. 13.
26. Morgan, *Elias*, p. 270.
27. The was carried out by Leontiev in 1891, and Atamanov and Slievnitsky in 1892.
28. Something of the urgency for surveying the area and the harshness of the climate is revealed by the tragic death from thirst of all but one of a seven-man survey party near Seistan in 1900. Sykes, *A History of Afghanistan*, II, p. 209; Morgan, *Elias*, p. 274.
29. Kazemzadeh, *Persia*, pp. 314–5.

30. J. Rabino to Colonel Picot, 14 May 1898, confidential. FO 60/601. PRO.
31. H. M. Durand to Lord Salisbury, 31 March 1899, FO 60/630. PRO.
32. *Novoe Vremya*, 9/21 May 1899 in FO 65/1593. PRO.
33. Kazemzedah, *Persia*, pp. 326–7.
34. India Office, Enclosure A141, 1 September 1899 FO 65/1593. PRO.
35. Kazemzedah, *Persia*, p. 334.
36. 'Dnevnik A. N. Kuropatkina', *Krasnyi Arkhiv*, 2 (1922) p. 31 cited in Kazemzedah, *Persia*, p. 339.
37. Sir John Ardagh, DMI, Memorandum, 5 February 1900, secret, Intelligence Division FO 65/1614.
38. G. N. Curzon to Mrs Cragie, cited in Earl of Ronaldshay, *The Life of Lord Curzon* (London, 1928) II, pp. 100–1.
39. Peter Fleming, *Bayonets to Lhasa* (London, 1961) p. 29.
40. In fact, a Russian mission under Colonel Kozlov and consisting of twenty-one men had entered Tibet in 1899 and returned after several skirmishes with Tibetan troops in 1901. He did not reach the capital.
41. Fleming, *Bayonets*, p. 43.
42. Hopkirk, *Trespassers on the Roof of the World*, p. 160. Fleming, *Bayonets*, p. 45.
43. F. E. Younghusband to Lord Curzon, 18 June 1904, cited in Fleming, *Bayonets*, p. 82.
44. Article III, The Anglo-Japanese Treaty, 23 January 1902 CAB 37/60/17. PRO.
45. Fleming, *Bayonets*, p. 271.
46. Younghusband was later honoured for his part in the mission. Fleming, *Bayonets*, p. 279.
47. Peter King, *The Viceroy's Fall* (London, 1986) pp. 74–5, 151ff.
48. Britain concluded a separate agreement with China, recognising its sovereignty there, but there was widespread disgust when the Chinese invaded Tibet and pursued a policy of brutal repression until the revolution of 1910–11.
49. E. F. Chapman and Cyprian A. G. Bridge, 18 March 1895, *Joint Report of the DMI and DNI*. CAB 37/31/10. PRO.
50. Quoted in K. Schilling, *Beitrage zu einer Geschichte des radikalen Nationalismus in der Wilhelminischen Ara* (Cologne, 1968) p. 60.
51. *Nauticus* (1900) p. 73, cited in Volker R. Berghahn, 'On the Social Function of Wilhelmine Armaments Policy', in Georg Iggers, *The Social History of Politics* (Leamington Spa, 1985) p. 166.
52. Müller to Tirpitz, 8 February 1905, V. R. Berghahn, *Germany and the Approach of War in 1914* (London, 1973) p. 53.
53. Berghahn, *Germany and the Approach of War*, p. 143.
54. Berghahn, *Germany and the Approach of War*, p. 144.
55. Gottfried Hagen, 'German Heralds of Holy War: Orientalists and Applied Oriental Studies', *Comparative Studies of South Asia, Africa and the Middle East*, 24, 2 (2004), p. 145.
56. Andrew, *Secret Service*, p. 29.
57. Gleichen, *A Guardsman's Memories*, pp. 77–8.
58. Lieutenant-General Sir Robert Baden Powell, *My Adventures as a Spy* (London, 1915) pp. 88 and 159.
59. Andrew, *Secret Service*, p. 25.
60. Report of Lord Hardwicke's Committee, 1903, p. 56. TI 10966/617/09. PRO. Cited in Andrew, *Secret Service*, p. 27.
61. Waters, *Secret and Confidential*, p. 248.
62. Andrew, *Secret Service*, p. 29.
63. Ferguson, *British Military Intelligence*.
64. Alan Judd, *The Quest for C: Mansfield Cumming and the Foundation of the Secret Service* (London, 1999) p. 83ff.
65. Andrew, *Secret Service*, p. 80.
66. Andrew Cook, *On His Majesty's Secret Service: Sidney Reilly* (Stroud, 2002) pp. 52–9.

Chapter 12. War and Revolution, 1914–1919 *(pp. 217–34)*

1. Peter Hopkirk, *On Secret Service East of Constantinople* (Oxford, 1994) pp. 55–6; See also intercepted letter from Bethmann Hollweg [Chancellor of Germany] to the Maharaja of Jodhpur, Chelmsford Papers Mss Eur E 264/52. OIOC.
2. The German War, Persia and Afghanistan. L/P&S/10/592,593 and 594. OIOC.
3. Judith M. Brown, *Modern India: The Origins of an Asian Democracy* 2nd edn., (Oxford 1985) p. 200.
4. James, *Raj*, p. 445.
5. See Christopher Sykes, *Wassmuss: 'The German Lawrence'* (London, 1936).
6. C. J. Edmonds, 'The Persian Gulf Prelude to the Zimmermann Telegram', *Journal of the Royal Central Asian Society* I (1960).
7. Weekly Report, 21 December 1915 Home Department, Political Proceedings, B series (December 1915) 709–11. POS 9841. OIOC.
8. It proved difficult to get intelligence from Europe directly. Popplewell, *Intelligence and Imperial Defence*, p. 185.
9. Revolt in Persia: Expenditure of Secret Service Funds. L/P&S/8/71,72,73 and 75.
10. Bushire, Operations in Persia, L/P&S/10/650, file 464, and O'Connor and the Shiraz Prisoners, L/P&S/10/582 file 334 (1916).
11. Hopkirk, *On Secret Service,* p. 222.
12. Brigadier-General F. J. Moberly, History of the Great War, Operations in Persia, 1914–1918, Historical Section CID, 1929 L/Mil/17/15/28.
13. Oskar von Niedermayer, *Unter der Glutsonne Irans* (Hamburg, 1925) cited in Hopkirk, *On Secret Service,* p. 126.
14. Report on the Working of the Military Mission in East Persia, L/Mil/17/15/34 & 35.
15. Wynn, *Persia in the Great Game*, pp. 258–62; The South Persia Rifles, L/P&S/10/690.
16. Wynn, *Persia in the Great Game*, p. 265; Sykes Mission, L/P&S/10/579, see also Despatch by Brig Gen Sykes on Minor Operations in South Persia, Nov 1917–Mar 1918 and May–Jul 1918, L/Mil/17/15/29 & 30.
17. F. J. Moberly, *The Mesopotamia Campaign, 1914–18* (1923–7). L/Mil/17/15/66–72.
18. Roos-Keppel to Hardinge, 13 February 1915, Hardinge Papers, Printed Letters and Telegrams, vol. 89, p. 69. Cambridge University Library.
19. Undated and unsigned letter, Hardinge Papers, Printed Letters and Telegrams, vol. 91, p. 21. Cambridge University Library.
20. Mehendra Pratap, *My Life Story of Fifty-Five Years* (Dehra Dun, 1947) p. 51.
21. James Campbell Ker, *Political Trouble in India, 1907–1917* (1917, reprintd., Calcutta, 1973) p. 307.
22. Sir Michael O'Dwyer, *India as I Knew It* (London, 1925) p. 179.
23. Afghanistan: The Silk Letter Case, L/P&S/10/633; Popplewell, *Intelligence and Imperial Defence*, p. 186.
24. Popplewell, *Intelligence and Imperial Defence*, pp. 42 and 48–9.
25. Popplewell, *Intelligence and Imperial Defence*, p. 63.
26. See Judical and Public Department records, J&P 2222/06 in L/PJ/6/770.
27. See V. N. Datta, *Madan Lal Dhingra and the Revolutionary Movement* (Delhi, 1978).
28. Weekly Report, 23 January 1909, Home Department, Political Proceedings, B Series (January 1909) 106–12 IOR POS 8960. OIOC.
29. Expenses for S. R. Banerjea to watch Indian Students in London, 1909–1913, L/P&S/8/67.
30. Popplewell, *Intelligence and Imperial Defence*, p. 140.
31. Richard Popplewell, 'The Surveillance of Indian Seditionists in North America, 1905–1915', in Christopher Andrew and Jeremy Noakes, eds., *Intelligence and International Relations, 1900–1945* (Exeter, 1987) p. 52.
32. 3000/08 L/P&S/3/438 cited in Popplewell, 'Surveillance', p. 53.
33. Employment of Agents in America, 17 August 1911. Home Department Political Proceedings HD (D).
34. JP 275/12 (1257).
35. Popplewell, 'Surveillance', p. 68.

36. J. A. Wallinger, Memorandum, (undated), cited in Popplewell, 'Surveillance', p. 66.
37. See T. G. Fraser, 'The Intrigues of the German Government and the Ghadr Party against British Rule in India, 1914–1918', unpublished PhD thesis (University of London, 1974).
38. Popplewell, *Intelligence and Imperial Defence*, p. 5.
39. H. W. Blood-Ryan, *Franz von Papen* (London, 1940).
40. Rayment, Newby and Wallinger, Memorandum, 13 November 1917. FO 3713069. PRO.
41. Popplewell, *Intelligence and Imperial Defence*, p. 264.
42. See T. G. Fraser, 'Germany and Indian Revolution, 1914–18', *Journal of Contemporary History* 12, 2 (1977).
43. Eliezer Tauber, *The Arab Movements in World War I* (London, 1993); P. Knightley and C. Simpson, *The Secret Lives of Lawrence of Arabia* (London, 1969); The Arab Bureau and Intelligence in the Middle East, 1919–20, L/P&S/10/576 file 4744.
44. Barbara Tuchman, *The Zimmermann Telegram* (London, 1959) p. 21.
45. Robert Service, *Lenin* (London, 2000) p. 256.
46. Service, *Lenin*, pp. 284–5, 294.
47. Andrew, *Secret Service*, p. 194.
48. Andrew, *Secret Service*, p. 206; British Intelligence Missions to Petrograd, 1., II 'Russia', Templewood Papers, Department of Manuscripts, Cambridge University Library.
49. Andrew, *Secret Service*, p. 216.
50. Brian Moynahan, *Comrades: 1917 – Russia in Revolution* (London, 1992) pp. 340–2.
51. R. H. Ullman, *Intervention and the War: Anglo-Soviet Relations, 1917–21* (London, 1961) I, ch. 8.
52. Ullman, *Anglo-Soviet Relations*, II, p. 23.
53. Wynn, *Persia in the Great Game*, p. 299.
54. Report by General Malleson on Operations in Transcaspia, including the battle of Dushakh (Delhi, 1919) L/Mil/17/14/88; The Turko-German Advance into the Caucasus, Secret, War Office, 1918, L/Mil/17/14/88.
55. Peter Hopkirk, ed., *The Spy who Disappeared: Diary of a Secret Mission to Russian Central Asia in 1918; Reginald Teague Jones alias Ronald Sinclair* (London, 1991) p. 11.
56. Hopkirk, *The Spy who Disappeared*, pp. 62–8.
57. Hopkirk, *The Spy who Disappeared*, pp. 71–6
58. For Bolshevik propaganda see L/P&S/10/836–7 and L/P&S/12/2273–2277, Collection 10.
59. Hopkirk, *Secret Service*, pp. 361–5.
60. See Hopkirk, *The Spy who Disappeared*, pp. 205–7.
61. Teague Jones/Sinclair did not completely give up his intelligence career. He returned to Persia in the 1920s and worked in the American consulate in the Second World War.

Chapter 13. Recessional (*pp. 235–50*)

1. V. I. Lenin, *Imperialism, the highest stage of capitalism* [Paris, 1916] (18th edn., Moscow, 1982) p. 118.
2. R. H. Ullman, *The Anglo-Soviet Accord: Anglo-Soviet Relations, 1917–21* (London, 1973) III, ch. 3.
3. *Report of the Hunter Committee: Disturbances in the Punjab* CMD 681, 1920; Alfred Draper, *Amritsar: The Massacre that Ended the Raj* (London, 1981).
4. See also D. George Boyce, 'From Assaye to *The Assaye*: Reflections on British Government, Force and Moral Authority in India', *Journal of Military History* 63, 3 (1999) p. 660.
5. Curzon, 'Kameneff and Krassin' 2 September 1920 in House of Lords Record Office, Lloyd George MSS F/203/1/3, cited in Andrew, *Secret Service*, p. 269.
6. Andrew, *Secret Service*, p. 269.
7. Sir Cecil Kaye (Subodh Roy, ed.), *Communism in India* (Calcutta, 1971) pp. 1–5. National Archives of India, New Delhi.
8. See L/PandJ (S) IPI Records indicated a close co-operation with MI5.
9. Indian intelligence created reports on the connections between Bolshevik and Pan-

Islamic movements, particularly those involving Baraktullah. His pamphlet on the supposed prediction of Bolsheviks in the Quran was described as a 'very clever piece of work'. See Secret Reports on Central Asia, Persia and Afghanistan, 1919, L/Mil/17/14/91/1, p. 15.

10. Kaye (Roy, ed.), *Communism in India, 1924–27* (Calcutta, 1971) pp. 5–9. National Archives of India, New Delhi.

11. Peter Hopkirk, *Setting the East Ablaze: On Secret Service in Bolshevik Asia* (Oxford, 1984) pp. 118–19.

12. Popplewell, *Intelligence and Imperial Defence*, p. 310.

13. Popplewell, *Intelligence and Imperial Defence*, p. 312.

14. 'Violations of the Russian Trade Agreement 1921', Foreign Office Confidential Print 11861. pp. 108–11.

15. Andrew, *Secret Service*, p. 282.

16. F. M. Bailey, *No Passport to Tibet* (London, 1957) p. 25ff.

17. F. M. Bailey, *Mission to Tashkent* (London, 1946) pp. xiii, and 12.

18. Bailey, *Mission to Tashkent*, p. 22.

19. Zimmermann was later shot as a spy by the British at Merv.

20. Bailey, *Mission to Tashkent*, p. 51.

21. Bailey, *Mission to Tashkent*, p. 92.

22. Hopkirk, *Setting the East Ablaze*, pp. 152–167.

23. Bailey, *Mission to Tashkent*, p. 112.

24. See L/Mil/17/14/16 and HoC Papers /62–71.

25. T. A. Heathcote, *The Afghan Wars, 1839–1919* (London, 1980).

26. The Bolshevik Menace to India, 1919–1921, L/P&S/10/16/886

27. Popplewell, *Intelligence and Imperial Defence*, p. 310.

28. Bailey, *Mission to Tashkent*, p. 180.

29. Bailey, *Mission to Tashkent*, p. 231.

30. Petrie, *Communism, 1924–27*, pp. 172–9.

31. Andrew, *Secret Service*, p. 295.

32. Andrew, *Secret Service*, p. 304.

33. Petrie, *Communism, 1924–27*, pp. 72–4.

34. Andrew, *Secret Service*, pp. 308–9.

35. Sir Eyre Crowe (Permanent Under-Secretary of the Foreign Office) to R. MacDonald, 26 October 1924. FO 371/10478.

36. Sir Horace Williamson, *India and Communism*. Mss Eur E251/33. OIOC.

37. Petrie, *Communism, 1924–27*, pp. 95–6.

38. Petrie, *Communism, 1924–27*, pp. 103–5.

39. See Gordon Brook-Shepherd, *The Storm Petrels* (London, 1977).

40. J. Nehru, *Towards Freedom* (London, 1941 edn.) p. 126.

41. Petrie, *Communism, 1924–27*, pp. 171.

42. Note, 15 December 1925. L/P&S/18 A200. OIOC.

43. Andrew, *Secret Service*, p. 327.

44. Minutes of the Interdepartmental Committee on Eastern Unrest, 23 July 1926. FO 371/11678. PRO.

45. CP 54 (34) CAB 24/247. PRO.

46. M. Hauner, 'One Man Against the Empire: The Faqir of Ipi and the British in Central Asia on the Eve of the Second World War', *Journal of Contemporary History* 16 (1981) pp. 199–201, 211.

47. James, *Raj*, p. 554.

48. Richard Holmes and Anthony Kemp, *The Bitter End: The Fall of Singapore, 1941–2* (London, 1982).

49. Adrian Stewart, *The Underrated Enemy: Britain's War with Japan, December 1941– May 1942* (London, 1987) p. 211.

50. For activities of Japanese agents in central Asia, 1936–41, see L/P&S/12/2368.

51. James, *Raj*, p. 562.

52. James, *Raj*, p. 563.

53. Brown, *Modern India*, p. 320.
54. Sir T. Stewart to Lord Linlithgow, 22 August 1942 cited in Nicholas Mansergh, ed., *The Transfer of Power, 1942–47* (London, 1971) II, pp. 789–91.
55. Brown, *Modern India*, p. 326.

Chapter 14. The Great Game Reassessed *(pp. 251–7)*

1. William Roger Louis, *The Robinson and Gallagher Controversy* (London, 1976) pp. 128–51.
2. Cited in Christopher Andrew, 'There is no such thing as full intelligence', *The Times*, 17 September 2001.
3. Popplewell, *Intelligence and Imperial Defence*, p. 5.
4. Andrew, *Secret Service*, p. 337.

Appendix A

Warning from a Chinese Agent

Dated Yarkand, 22nd September 1885.

From—TSENG S LAISUN,

To—N. ELIAS, Esq.

I have the honor to report to you certain information procured by me during a conversation at a dinner given by the Civil Magistrate of the "Hwuy Chêng" or old city which may serve to show in a measure the feelings which Chinese officials entertain towards Great Britain and Russia in these parts.

A statement was made by one of the secretaries of the Sub-prefect that he had heard of a fight between the Afghans and Russians, and that this was likely to lead towards a war between Great Britain and Russia; upon which some of the company advocated an alliance with England, some took sides with Russia, as being the stronger of the two, and finally, and these were by far the majority, others advocated the part of neutrality at the beginning and then, taking the part of the victorious power, came in for a share of the spoils. This would show that England has a few supporters amongst Chinese officials in this part of the world, but as the power of Russia is more apparent here and she has had a Consul in Kashgar for the last few years, and moreover as seeing is believing it is but natural that Russian influence is paramount in the Hsin Chiang or new dominion. I cannot help thinking that this feeling is due in a great measure to the long delay Her Majesty's Government has made in deciding to establish English Consuls in these the newly reconquered dominions of the Chinese Empire. Not only are Consuls required in Yarkand, Kashgar, and Kuldja, but everywhere Russia may have her agents, and more too if possible.

English influence is predominant all along the coast ports of China, through the agencies of English Consuls and traders, and Russia is nowhere, except perhaps in Upper Manchuria and the vicinity of the Amoor river, but there the face of an Englishman is a novelty, and therefore the same rule applies in this case as in Chinese Turkestan. Russian goods, such as chintz, sugar, and candles, keep pouring into the new dominion every year, but I have observed that the people here are also anxious to buy English manufactured goods, and to effect this Consuls are required, in my opinion, to protect the interests of traders who are British subjects against the intrigues of the Russians.

Appendix B

An Intelligence Officer's Secret Orders

To

BRIGADIER-GENERAL C. S. MACLEAN, C.B.,
Khorassan Frontier.

SIMLA, *the 6th October* 1887.

ϝn Dept. SIR,

I am directed to reply to that part of your telegram No. 12 of the 21st March last in which you asked for information regarding the nature of your future duties on the Khorassar frontier.

2. In the correspondence cited in the margin the Government of India communicated to you instructions to the following effect: You were to watch from the Perso-Herat border the course of events in the Afghan frontier districts, and the movements of the Russians beyond, and to collect such information on these subjects as might seem to be useful to your Government. You were instructed, while cultivating friendly relations both with the Afghans and the Persians, to refrain from acting as an intermediary between the former and the Russians, and to give advice only when requested to do so. You were further enjoined, while in Persia, to act at all times in compliance with any advice or directions you might receive from the British Minister at Teheran.

> Letter No. 514 F., dated the 21st March 1885.
> Telegram of the 6th February 1886.
> „ „ 23rd July „

3. The Governor-General in Council considers that the foregoing instructions require little modification. Your organization of an intelligence agency has had a considerable measure of success; and what you have done in this direction has the approbation of the Government of India. The system needs however further extension and improvement, and with this view the additional establishment asked for in your telegrams marginally noted has been sanctioned. With this establishment, and the enhanced sumptuary allowances at your disposal, His Excellency in Council trusts that you will be in a better position than before to gain full and accurate information as to the state of affairs in and around Khorassan, and to promote friendly relations with the local Governors and officials, and with the border tribes. It will, moreover, be a part of your duty to keep yourself acquainted with the movements and attitude of the Afghan refugees residing in Meshed and its neighbourhood. With regard to your intervention in questions between the Afghans and the Russians, you are aware that His Highness the Amir refused to permit the location of British officers on the border for the purpose of settling such differences, and that His Highness declined to allow his

> No. 3 of the 11th January 1887.
> No. 6 „ 27th „ „
> No. 9 „ 9th March „

[2]

officers to consult you. Nevertheless the Governor of Herat has lately asked for your advice with regard to certain important questions concerning the border. In view of this apparent change of attitude the Government of India, while reluctant to accept a responsibility which might, unless carefully guarded and exercised, lead to complications, would not object to your giving friendly and unofficial advice in emergent cases, on the understanding that the matter should be immediately reported to the Amir for His Highness's orders and to this office for the information of the Governor-General in Council. But as you have been directed by Her Majesty's Government to give no advice you should pending further orders avoid expressing any opinion without reference to higher authority.

4. Finally I am to observe that your proceedings should be regularly reported to the Government of India, who will transmit to you any orders which may from time to time be necessary regarding your movements and duties. You will, however, continue to act in compliance with any advice or instructions you may receive from Her Majesty's Legation at Teheran, and you should refer to the Minister in all cases in which it may seem desirable to consult His Excellency. It is understood that you have hitherto forwarded copies of all important reports to Her Majesty's Government through the Teheran Legation, and I am to request that this procedure may be maintained. But you will understand that there is no necessity for you to adopt it as a matter of course with regard to your ordinary correspondence by telegram or letter with the Government of India.

I have the honor to be,

SIR,

Your most obedient servant,

(Sd.)   H. M. DURAND,
Secretary to the Government of India.

Bibliography

Unpublished Papers

Public Record Office
Cabinet Records

CAB 1, 2, 6, 24, 36, 37	Cabinet Memoranda

Foreign Office Records 1880–97, General Correspondence Series

FO 65/1097–1488	Russia and Proceedings in Central Asia
FO 83/814 & 1328	Communication to newspapers
FO 106/1–11	Central Asia, Afghanistan, India
FO 181	Consular letters
FO 343	Germany
FO 418	Russia, confidential print
FO 539/17–52	Asia and Afghanistan

Home Department Records

HD 2	Secret Service Accounts, Meshed
HD 3	Secret Service Correspondence
HM	Home Miscellaneous Series

Official Papers

FO 343/12 & 13	Other Correspondence of Sir Edward Malet
FO 364	Papers of Sir William White
FO 800	Papers of the Fifth Marquis of Lansdowne

War Office Records

WO 3	Administrative Details of Campaigns
WO 28	HQ Records
WO 30/40	Maj-Gen Charles Ardagh, Director of Military Intelligence 1896–1901, Correspondence
WO 30/57	Lord Kitchener papers
WO 30/64	India, Military Campaigns
WO 31	Regulations of 1878, including Conduct of War Correspondents
WO 33	War Office and Intelligence Department Reports
WO 78	Maps of Operations
WO 105	Maps of the North-West Frontier and Afghanistan
	Field Marshal Lord Roberts, Maps of service in India
WO 106	Directory of Military Intelligence (after 1837)
	Campaigns on the North-West Frontier, Central Asia and Afghanistan
WO 110	W. H. Smith Papers

WO 181	Map Collection
WO 704/2/13	Director of Military Operations and Intelligence
WO 704/2/21	Director of Military Survey
WO 704/2/23	War Office Responsibilities for Mountain Warfare

India Office Library

Political and Secret Department

L/P&S/3	Home Correspondence
L/P&S/7/1–89	Correspondence from India
L/P&S/7/90–253	Correspondence with India, without indexes
L/P&S/7/320–341	Despatches to India
L/P&S/8	Demi-official Correspondence, including Secret Service Records and Accounts
L/P&S/9	Letters relating to areas outside India
L/P&S/14	Correspondence with Asian Rulers (1796–1920)
L/P&S/16	Consul Papers, 1885–1930
L/P&S/18	Memoranda
L/P&S/20 A-H	Reports
L/P&S/20 CA	Confidential Abstracts
L/P&S/20 FO	Foreign Office Prints
L/P&S/44	Letters to the Foreign Department
L/P&S/75	Home Correspondence

Papers, Memoirs and Diaries

Mss Eur C 141	Papers of Lord Northbrook
D 727	Papers of Sir Henry Mortimer Durand
D 958	Papers of the Fifth Marquis of Lansdowne
D1019	Papers of Robert Montgomery
E124	Papers of E. A. Reade
E 218	Papers of the First Earl of Lytton
E 234	Papers of Lord Cross
E251	Papers of Sir Horace Williamson
E 264	Papers of Lord Chelmsford
F 84	Papers of the Ninth Earl of Elgin
F 90	Papers of John Lawrence
F 111–2	Papers of George Curzon
F 130	Printed copies of papers of First Marquis of Dufferin and Ava
F 132	Papers of Sir Alfred Lyall
F 157	Papers of Frederick M. Bailey
F 197	Papers of Sir Francis Younghusband

Military Department

L/Mil/7	Collections of papers relating to NW Frontier and Afghanistan
L/Mil/7/6–19	Intelligence Records on Central Asia, Tibet and Afghanistan
L/Mil/17/13	Military Records, North-West Frontier
L/Mil/17/14	Military Records, Central Asia and Afghanistan

Home Department

B and D Series

National Army Museum, London

7101–23   Papers of Lord Roberts (Home and Overseas Correspondence).

Private Papers, The British Library

Add Mss 44086–44835	The Papers of W. E. Gladstone
Add Mss 44178	Correspondence with Earl Granville
Add Mss 44288–290	Correspondence with the 5th Earl of Rosebery
Add Mss 44563–635	Official Papers
Add Mss 44636–648	Cabinet Minutes
Add Mss 44175–179	The Correspondence of Earl Granville
Add Mss 50013–50064	The Papers of the Earl of Iddesleigh (Sir Stafford Northcote)
Add Mss 43574–623	The Papers of the First Marquis of Ripon
Add Mss 43510–511	Royal Correspondence
Add Mss 43513–515	Correspondence with W. E. Gladstone
Add Mss 43524–527	Correspondence with Kimberley
Add Mss 43572–573	Correspondence with Northbrook
Add Mss 43565–569	Correspondence with Hartington
Add Mss 43585	Official Correspondence (India), Military
Add Mss 43592–593	Correspondence with Lieutenant-Governors of the Punjab
Add Mss 43600–606	Correspondence with the Viceroy's Council
Add Mss 43613	Letters from Sir Robert Sandeman
Add Mss 43874–43967	The Papers of Sir Charles Dilke
Mss Eng/13	The Papers of James Bryce
BP/7/6	The Papers of Courteney Ilbert

Hertfordshire Record Office

The papers of Lord Lytton, D/EK 01–16

The Library of Christ Church College, Oxford

The papers of Robert, Third Marquis of Salisbury
Volume 44: correspondence, 1885–6

Hatfield House, Hertfordshire

The papers of Robert, Third Marquis of Salisbury.
3M/Class Correspondence, 140 volumes
Correspondence with the Queen, 1885, unbound volume
E/51/96 (1885). Philip Currie, Notes on negotiations with Germany
3M/Churchill/1; Correspondence with Randolph Churchill
'1885–6' bound volume, private correspondence with Sir Edward Thornton
M485/1–127, Correspondence with Sir Robert Morier
'Drafts, Copies, Minutes and Memos, 1890–92'

Hove Central Library, Sussex

Papers of Lord Wolseley, 19/51 and 'Correspondence (Sir Ralph Thompson, Under-Secretary of State for War)'

Chatsworth House, Bakewell, Derbyshire

Papers of Spencer Cavendish, the 8th Duke of Devonshire, (Lord Hartington).
Correspondence, 1880–94

The Ministry of Defence Library (Central and Army), London

Archives and library of the Intelligence Division. Most of this archive has now been transferred to the Public Record Office, whilst some library materials are held in the Museum of Defence Intelligence, Chicksands, Shefford

The Public Record Office of Northern Ireland

Papers of Frederick Blackwood, the First Marquis of Dufferin and Ava, D1071H, 1885; volume 2, Correspondence to Secretary of State, November 1884–December 1889

The Bodleian Library, Oxford

Papers of the Earl of Kimberley, Diaries, Ms Eng. e. 28 April 1881–10 Jan 1902, 2793, 2794, and correspondence with Ardagh Mss Eng. 4326–86

Papers of James Bryce, Mss Eng/13

National Archives of India, New Dehli, India

Government of India, Foreign Department, Frontier records, 1885, volumes 244–309; 1891, volumes 140–79; 1892, volumes 410–88

Military Proceedings B, October 1885, numbers 1874–1900, proceedings 1887.

Records of the Survey of India (Dehra Dun).

Kaye, Sir Cecil (M. Saha, ed.), *Communism in India* (Calcutta, 1971)

Petrie, Sir David (M. Saha, ed.), *Communism in India, 1924–27* (Calcutta, 1971).

The Directorate of Archives, North-West Frontier Province, Shahi Bagh, Peshawar, Pakistan

Files of the Government of the Punjab in the Foreign Department, Frontier Branch, '1858–1901'.

The Royal Artillery Institution, London.

Papers of Sir Henry Brackenbury MD/1085

The Royal Geographical Society, London.

Map Collection   The Survey of India, Maps 1850–95

Archive   Letters of Robert Shaw and George Hayward
          Papers of Ney Elias

Proceedings of The Royal Geographical Society

Geographical Journal

Unpublished Theses

Bali, Anila, 'The Russo-Afghan Boundary Demarcation 1884–95: Britain and the Russian Threat to the Security of India', unpublished PhD thesis (University of Ulster, 1985).

Beaver, W. C., 'The Development of the Intelligence Division, and its role in aspects of policy making, 1854–1901', unpublished DPhil thesis (Oxford University, 1976).

Christiansen, R. O., 'Conflict and Change Among the Afridis, and Tribal Policy 1839–1947', unpublished PhD thesis (University of Leicester, 1987).

Fraser, T. G., 'The Intrigues of the German Government and the Ghadr Party against British Rule in India, 1914–18', unpublished PhD thesis (University of London, 1974–5).

Harris, J., 'British Policy on the North-West Frontier 1889–1901', unpublished PhD thesis (University of London, 1960).

Moir, I. M., 'A Study of the History and Organisation of the Political and Secret Departments of the East India Company, The Board of Control and the India Office, 1784–1919', Thesis for University College London, Diploma in Archive Administration (London, 1966).

Morris, L. P., 'Anglo-Russian Relations in Central Asia, 1873–1887', unpublished PhD thesis (University of London, 1968)

Onley, James, 'The Infrastructure of Informal Empire: A Study of Britain's Native Agency in Bahrein, c. 1816–1900' (University of Oxford, 2001)

Preston, Adrian, 'British Military policy and the Defence of India, 1876–80', unpublished PhD thesis (University of London, 1966).

Wyatt, Christopher M., 'Afghanistan and the Defence of India, 1903–1915', unpublished PhD thesis (Leeds University, 1995).

Published Documents

Parliamentary Papers

Hansard Parliamentary Debates. 3rd ser. 1879–1898

House of Commons Enquiry, 17 March 1879. Report on Khost Valley expedition. LVI 100.

House of Commons Correspondence since the accession of Shere [sic] Ali. LVI c.2190. 266

Select Committee on Parliamentary Reporting, 1878. XVII 327

Select Committee on Parliamentary Reporting, 1878–9. XII 203

Select Committee on Parliamentary Reporting, 1880. House of Lords VII 66

Correspondence between the Government of India and the Secretary of State in Council, respecting the proposed changes in the Indian Army System (1884–5), LIX

Report from the Select Committee on the Admiralty and War Office, 1887. VII

Report from the Select Committee on the Army and Navy Estimates, 1887. VIII

Memorandum of the Secretary of State relating to the Army Estimates, 1887–8. Cd 4985, 1887, L

First Report from the Select Committee on the Army Estimates, 17 April 1888, VIII

Second Report from the Select Committee on the Army Estimates, 8 June 1888, VIII

Third Report from the Select Committee on the Army Estimates, 15 June 1888, VIII

Fourth Report from the Select Committee on the Army Estimates, 10 July 1888, VIII

Fifth Report from the Select Committee on the Army Estimates, 17 July 1888, IX

Memorandum of the Secretary of State relating to the Army Estimates, 1888–9. Cd 5303, 1888, XXV

Report of the Committee appointed to enquire into War Office organisation, (Cd 580–1, 1901) XL

Royal Commission on the War in South Africa Cd 1789–92 and CO 879

National Documentation Centre Publications, Government of Pakistan

Tribal Cell Records on:

    Administration and management of Tribal Areas during British Rule, 1888–1947

    British Military Operations in Tribal Areas, 1892–1947

Selection from Punjab Record Office:

    Home Department Proceedings (extracts), 1869–84, 1901–43

    Foreign Department Proceedings (extracts), 1883–92, 1920–1

Special Branch of Police records

Secret Police Abstracts of Intelligence:

    Sind, 1940–7; Punjab, 1931–47; N.W.F.P., 1911–47

Native News Papers Reports:

    Punjab, 1884–1924; Bengal, 1876–1911; N.W.F.P., 1896–1901

Papers:

    Charles Masson, 1800–57

British Library, Newspaper Collection, Colindale Avenue, London

Blackwoods Magazine

Delhi Gazette,

Edinburgh Review

The Fortnightly Review

The National Review

The Nineteenth Century

The Pall Mall Gazette

Punch

The Quarterly Review
The St James Gazette
The Saturday Review
The Spectator
The Daily Telegraph
The Times
The Westminster Review

Books

Contemporary Works (*c.* 1875–1945)

Alison, Sir A., *Memorandum on the North-West Frontier of India*. London, 1878

'An Indian Army Officer', *Russia's March Towards India*. 2 vols. London, 1894

Aston, Sir George, *Secret Service*. London, 1930

Baddeley, J. F., *Russia in the 'Eighties: Sport and Politics*. London, 1921

Baden Powell, Lieutenant-General Sir Robert, *My Adventures as a Spy*. London, 1915

____, Major R., *War in Practice; Lessons of the War in South Africa 1899–1902*. London, 1903

Balfour, Lady Betty, *Personal and Literary Letters of Robert, first Earl of Lytton*. 2 vols. London, 1906

Bartlett, E., *Shall England Keep India?* London, 1886

Baxter, William Edward, *England and Russia in Asia*. London, 1885

Bayley, Sir S., *On the Pamir Question*. London, 1891

Beaufort, F., *Memorandum on Herat*. London, 1885

____, *Russian Advances in Asia*. London, 1887

Bell, Colonel M. S., *Afghanistan as a Theatre of Operations and as a Defence to India*. Calcutta, 1885

Bellew, H. W., *Report of a Mission to Yarkand in 1873, under command of Sir T. D. Forsyth, KCSI, CB, Bengal Civil service, with Historical and Geographical information regarding the Possessions of the Ameer of Yarkund*. Calcutta, 1875

Birom, Major, *A Narrative of the Campaign in India Which Terminated the War With Tipoo Sultan in 1792*. London 1793

Black, Charles E. D., *Memoir on the Indian Surveys, 1875–1890*. London, 1891

Blacker, Captain L. V. S., *On Secret Patrol in High Asia*. London, 1922

Blacker, V., *Memoirs of the British Army in India During the Mahratta War of 1817, 1818 ans 1819*. London, 1821

Blunt, W. S., *India Under Ripon*. London, 1909

Bower, Captain Hamilton, *A Diary of a Journey across Tibet*. London, 1894

Brackenbury, H., *Some Memories of My Spare Time*. Edinburgh, 1909

Browne, Major E. C., *The Coming of the Great Queen; a narrative of the acquisition of Burma*. London, 1888

Burnaby, Frederick, *A Ride to Khiva*. London, 1876, reprinted Oxford, 1997

Bruce, R. I., *The Forward Policy and its Results*. London, 1900

Buchan, John, *Greenmantle*. London, 1916

Burnes, Alexander, *Travels into Bokhara: Being the Account of a Journey from India to Cabool* [sic] *Tartary and Persia*. 3 vols. London, 1834

Callwell, C. E., *Instructions for Intelligence Officers Abroad*. London, 1889

____, *Small Wars*. London, 1896

Cameron, Sir A. C., *Memorandum on Herat*. London, 1885

Cecil, Lady Gwendolen, *Life of Robert, Marquis of Salisbury*. 4 vols. London, 1921–32

Churchill, Winston Spencer, *My Early Life*. London, 1941

_____, *Randolph Churchill*. 2 vols. London, 1906

_____, *The Story of the Malakand Field Force: An Episode of Frontier War*. London, 1898

Cobbold, R. P., *Innermost Asia*. London, 1900

Connolly, Lieutenant Arthur, *Journey to the North of India, Overland from England, Through Russia, Persia and Affghaunistaun* [sic]*,* 2 vols. London, 1834

Curzon, G. N., *The Problems of the Far East*. London, 1894

_____, *Russia in Central Asia and the Anglo-Russian Question*. London, 1889

_____, *Persia and the Persian Question*. 2 vols. London, 1892

_____, *The Pamirs and The Source of the Oxus*. London, 1896

Davies, Cecil Colin, *The Indian Frontier*. Cambridge, 1932

Dey, R. S., *A Brief Account of the Punjab Frontier Force*. Calcutta, 1905

Dickson, Brigadier-General W. E., *East Persia. A Backwater of the Great War*. London, 1924

Dilke, Sir Charles,and Spenser Wilkinson, *Imperial Defence*. London, 1892

Dobson, G., *The Russian Railway Advance into Central Asia*. London, 1890

Dunsterville, Major-General M. H., *The Adventures of Dunsterforce*. London, 1920

Durand, A., *The Making of a Frontier*. London, 1899

Durand, Sir Henry Mortimer, *Life of Field Marshal Sir George White*. London, 1915

Dyer, Brigadier-General R., *The Raiders of the Sarhad*. London, 1921

Earle, Meade, *Turkey, the Great Powers and the Baghdad Railway*. New York, 1923

Edwards, H. Sutherland, *Russian Projects Against India from the Czar Peter to General Skobeleff*. London, 1885

Elsmie, G. R., *Field Marshal Sir Donald Stewart*. London, 1903

_____, *Thirty Five Years in the Punjab*. Edinburgh, 1908

Etherton, Lieutenant-Colonel P. T., *In the Heart of Asia*. Boston, 1926

Evans, George de Lacy, *On the Designs of Russia*. London, 1828

_____, *On the Practicability of an Invasion of India*. London, 1829

Feris, Selim, *The Decline of British Prestige in the East*. London, 1887

Fitzmaurice, Lord Edmond, *The Life of Lord Granville*. London, 1905

Foster, W., *England's Quest of Eastern Trade*. London, 1933

Forbes, A., *The Afghan Wars*. London, 1892

Forrest, G. W., *Life of Field Marshal Sir Neville Chamberlain*. London, 1909

Gathorne-Hardy, A. E., ed., *Gathorne Hardy, First Earl of Cranbrook*. 2 vols. London, 1910

Gazeteer of India. Calcutta, 1907

Gleichen, Lord Edward, *A Guardsman's Memories*. Edinburgh, 1932

Gooch, G. and H. Temperley, *British Documents on the Origins of the War*. vols I to IV, London, 1926–38

Gore, Surgeon General Albert A., *A Medico-Statistical Sketch of the Operations on the North-West Frontier of India*. Dublin, 1899

Graves, Philip, *The Life of Sir Percy Cox*. London, 1941

Gregson, L. A. and F. A. C. Cameron, *'The Defence of India' by Sir C. M. MacGregor, QMG India*. London, 1885

Lord Grey, *Twenty Five Years: 1892–1916*. 2 vols. London, 1925

Grodekov, N. I., *Voina v Turkmenii*. ('The War in Turkestan') 4 vols. St Petersburg, 1884

Gubbins, M., *An account of the Mutinies in the Oudh and the Siege of the Lucknow Residency*. London, 1858

Gurwood, J., ed., *The Despatches of Field Marshal the Duke of Wellington, KG*. 13 vols. London, 1837–9

Hanna, Colonel H. B., *The Second Afghan War*. London, 1910

____, *Can Russia Invade India?* London, 1895

Hardinge, Lord, *My Indian Years*. London, 1948

Hensman, H., *The Afghan War*. London, 1881

Hodson, G. H., *Twelve Years of a Soldier's Life in India; being extracts from the letters of Major W. S. R. Hodson, B.A*. London, 1859

Holdich, T. H., *The Indian Borderland*. London, 1901

Howell, Evelyn, *Mizh: A Monograph on Government Relations with the Mahsud Tribe*. Simla, 1931; reprinted Karachi, 1979

Iavorskii, Dr I. L., *Puteshetvie russkogo posol'stva po Avganistanu i Bukharskomu Khanstvu v 1878–79 gg* ('The Journey of the Russian Embassy through Afghanistan and the Khanate of Bokhara in 1878–79'). 2 vols. St Petersburg, 1882

James, Lionel, *The Indian Frontier War*. London, 1898

Jermingham, H., *Russia's Warnings*. London, 1885

Jervis, W. F., *Thomas Best Jervis: Christian Soldier, Geographer and Friend of India*. London, 1898

Kaye, Sir John, *History of the Sepoy War*. London, 1864–7

____, *Lives of Indian Officers*. London, 2nd edn., 1904

Keppel, A., *Gun Running and the Indian North-West Frontier*. London, 1911

Khan, Sir Syed Ahmed, *An Essay on the Causes of the Indian Revolt*. Calcutta, 1860

Khan, S. M., *The Life of Abdur Rahman, Amir of Afghanistan*. 2 vols. London, 1900

Kipling, R., *Kim*. London, 1901

Knight, E. F., *Where Three Empires Meet*. London, 1897

Knorring, N. N., *General Mikhail Dmitrievich Skobelev*. Paris, 1939

Kosogovsky, V. A., *Persiia v Kontse XIX veka*. ('Persia at the end of the XIX Century'), Moscow: Novyi Vostok, 4, 1924

Krause, A., *Russia in Asia*. London, 1899

Landsdell, H., *Chinese Central Asia*. London, 1893

Langer, W. L., *The Diplomacy of Imperialism 1890–1902*. 2 vols. Cambridge (Mass.), 1935

le Meusurier, A., *From London to Bokhara and a Ride through Persia*. London, 1889

Loftus, Lord Augustus, *Diplomatic Reminiscences, 1837–1879*. 2 vols. London, 1894

Lyall, A., *The Life of the Marquis of Dufferin and Ava*. 2 vols. London, 1905

Lyons, Gervais, *Afghanistan: The Buffer State*. London, 1910

MacDiarmid, D. S., *The Life of Lieutenant General Sir James Moncrieff Grierson*. London, 1923

MacDonnell, Ranald, *And Nothing Long*. London, 1938

MacGregor, Major-General Sir C. M., *The Defence of India: A Strategical Study*. Simla, 1884

Lady MacGregor, ed., *The Life and Opinions of Major General Sir Charles Metcalfe MacGregor*. 2 vols. Edinburgh, 1888

Malleson, G. B., *Herat: The Granary and Garden of Central Asia*. London, 1880

Mallet, B., *Thomas George, The Earl of Northbrook*. London, 1908

Malmesbury, Susan, Countess of, *The Life of Major General Sir John Ardagh*. London, 1909

Mariott, J. A. R., *Anglo-Russian Relations*. London, 1944

Martin, F., *Under the Absolute Amir*. London, 1907

Marvin, Charles, ed. and transl., *Colonel Grodekoff's Ride From Samarkand to Herat*. London, 1880

____, *Merv, The Queen of the World, and the Scourge of the man Stealing Turcomans*. London, 1881

____, *The Russian Advance Towards India*. London, 1882

____, *The Russians at Merv and Herat, and their Power of Invading India*. London, 1883

____, *The Russian Railway to Herat and India*. London, 1883

____, *The Russian Annexation of Merv*. London, 1884

____, *Reconnoitring Central Asia*. London, 1884

_____, *The Region of Eternal Fire. A Journey to the Petroleum Region of the Caspian in 1883.* London, 1884

_____, *The Railway Race to Herat.* London, 1885

_____, *The Russians at the Gates of Herat.* London, 1885

Mason, Capt. A. H., *Report on the Hindustani Fanatics.* Simla, 1895

Masson, Charles, *Narrative of Various Journeys in Balochistan, Afghanistan and the Punjab, etc.* London, 1842

Maurice, Sir Frederick, ed., *Official History of the War in South Africa.* London, 1908

Maurice, J. F. and G. Arthur, *The Life of Wolseley.* London, 1924

Meyendorff, A., ed., *Correspondance Diplomatique de M. de Staal, Ambassadeur de Russie à Londres 1884–1900.* Paris, 1929

Mills, H. W., *The Pathan Revolt.* Lahore, 1897

Morrison, J. L., *From Alexander Burnes to Frederick Roberts: A Survey of Imperial Frontier Policy.* Royal Academy Lecture, 15 July 1936, Oxford, 1936

Muir, W., *Records of the Intelligence Department of the Government of the North-West Provinces of India.* Edinburgh, 1902

Nehru, J., *Towards Freedom.* London, 1941

Nevill, Captain H. L., *Campaigns on the North-West Frontier.* London, 1912

Newton, Lord, *Lord Lansdowne: A Biography.* London, 1929

Neidermayer, Oskar von, *Unter der Glutsonne Irans.* Hamburg, 1925

Nixon, Lieutenant-Colonel, *Notes for Staff Officers on Indian Field Service.* Lahore, 1897

North, R., *The Punjab Frontier Force.* Dera Ismail Khan, 1934

O'Connor, Sir Frederick, *On the Frontier and Beyond.* London, 1931

O'Donovan, Edward, *The Merv Oasis: Travels and Adventures East of the Caspian, 1879–80–81.* 2 vols. London, 1882

O'Dwyer, Sir Michael, *India As I Knew It, 1885–1925.* London, 1925

Oliver, E., *Across the Border.* London, 1890

Pokrovskii, M. N, *Diplomatiia i voiny tsarskoi Rossii v XIX stoletii* ('The Diplomacy and Wars of Tsarist Russia in the Nineteenth Century'). Moscow, 1923

Popowski, J., *The Rival Powers in Central Asia.* London, 1893

Postgate, R. and A. Vallance, *Those Foreigners: Newspapers and Foreign Policy.* London, 1937

Pottinger, Lieutenant Henry, *Travels in Baloochistan and Sinde.* London, 1816

Pratt, E. A., *The Rise of Rail Power in War and Conquest.* London, 1915

Prejevalski, N., *Mongolia, The Tangut Country and the Solitudes of Tibet.* London, 1876

Ralph, J., *An American with Lord Roberts.* New York, 1901

Rice-Holmes, T., *History of the Indian Mutiny.* London, 1904.

Rittich, Petr Aleksandrovich, *Zheleznodorozhnyi put cherez Persuii* ('Railway Across Persia'). St Petersburg, 1900

Roberts, Field Marshal Lord., *Forty-One Years in India.* 2 vols. London, 1897

_____, *Is an Invasion of India Possible?* Madras, 1883

_____, *Message to the Nation.* London, 1912

Robertson, Sir George, *Chitral: the Story of a Minor Siege.* London, 1898

Romanov, P. M., *Zheleznodorozhnyi vopros v Persuii i mery k razvitiiu russko-persidskoi torgovli* ('The Railway Question in Persia and Measures for the Development of Russo–Persian Trade'). St Petersburg, 1891

Ronaldshay, Earl of, *The Life of Lord Curzon.* London, 1928

Russell, R., *India's Danger and England's Duty.* London, 1885

Savage Landor, A. Henry, *In the Forbidden Land.* New York, 1898

Schuyler, Eugene, *Turkistan.* 2 vols. New York, 1877

Seeley, J. R., *The Expansion of England*. London, 1902

Seton Watson, R., *Gladstone, Disraeli and the Eastern Question*. London, 1935

Shadwell, Captain L., *Lockhart's Advance through the Tirah*. London, 1898

Showers, Major-General C. L., *The Cossack at the Gate of India*. London, 1885

Skalkovskii, K., *Vneshniania politika Rossii i polozhenie inostrannykh derzhav* ('Russia's Foreign Policy and the Situation of the Foreign Powers'). St Petersburg, 1901

Skrine F. H. and E. Ross, *Heart of Asia*. London, 1899

Stead W. T., *The War in South Africa; Methods of Barbarism*. London, 1901

Stewart, N., *My Service Days: India, Afghanistan, Suakin '85, and China*. London, 1908

Steinberg, E. L., *Ocherki istorii Turkmenii* ('Essays in the History of Turkestan'). Moscow, 1934

Sykes, Christopher, *Wassmuss: 'The German Lawrence'*. London, 1936

Sykes, Sir Percy M., *Sir Mortimer Durand*. London, 1926

_____, *A History of Persia*. 2 vols. 3rd edn., London, 1930

_____, *A History of Afghanistan*. 2 vols. London, 1940

Temple, Sir Richard, *Report showing the relations of the British Government with the Tribes, Independent and Dependent, on the North-West Frontier of the Punjab*. Calcutta, 1856

Terent'iev, M. A., *Istoriia zavoevaniia Srednei Azii* ('The History of the Conquest of Central Asia'). 3 vols. St Petersburg, 1906

Thompson, Edward, *Life of Charles, Lord Metcalfe*. London, 1937

Thomson, H. C., *The Chitral Campaign*. London, 1895

Thornhill, Mark, *The Personal Adventures and Experiences of a Magistrate during the Rise, Progress and Suppression of the Indian Mutiny*. London, 1884

Thornton, I. H., *Sir Robert Sandeman*. London, 1895

Trotter, H., *Secret and Confidential Report of the Trans-Himalayan Explorations by Employees of the Great Trigonometrical Survey of India, during 1873–74–75*. Calcutta, 1876

Vambery, Arminius, *The Coming Struggle for India*. London, 1885

Walpole, S., *The Life of Lord John Russell*. London, 1889

Warburton, R., *Eighteen Years in the Khyber, 1879–1898*. London, 1900

_____, *The Russian Warning*. Peshawar, 1892

Waters, W. H. H., *Secret and Confidential*. London, 1926

Wellesley, A. R., The Second Duke of Wellington, ed., *Despatches of Lord Wellington 1819–32*. 8 vols. London, 1867–80

Wheeler, S., *The Ameer Abdur Rahman*. London, 1895

Wilson, H. H., ed., *William Moorcroft and George Trebeck, Travels in Himalayan Provinces*. London, 1841

Wolf, L., *The Life of the First Marquess of Ripon*. 2 vols. London, 1921

Wolfe Murray, Sir James, *Military Operations in the Event of a War with Russia*. London, 1885

Wolseley, Sir Garnet, *The Story of a Soldier's Life*. London, 1903

Yate, Captain A. C., *England and Russia Face to Face in Asia*. Edinburgh, 1887

Yate, Major C. E., *Northern Afghanistan*. Edinburgh, 1888

Younghusband, F. E., *The Heart of a Continent*. London, 1896

_____, *The Light of Experience*. London, 1927

Younghusband, G. J., *Indian Frontier Warfare*. London, 1898

Younghusband, G. J. and F. E. *The Relief of Chitral*. London, 1895

Younghusband, G. J., *The Story of the Guides*. London, 1909

Yule, Henry, *The Late Colonel T. G. Montgomerie*. London, 1878

Recent Works

Adamec, Ludwig, *Afghanistan's Foreign Affairs to the Mid-Twentieth Century*. London, 1974

Addy, Premen, *Tibet on the Imperial Chessboard*. Calcutta, 1984

Ahmed, Akbar S., *Millennium and Charisma among Pathans: a Critical Essay in Social Anthropology*. London, 1976

____, *Pukhtun Economy and Society: Traditional Structure and Economic Development in a Tribal Society*. London, 1980

Ahmed, A. S., and D. M. Hart, eds., *Islam in Tribal Societies*. London, 1984

Alder, G. J., *Beyond Bokhara: The Life of William Moorcroft, Asian Explorer and Pioneer Veterinary Surgeon, 1767–1825*. London, 1985

____, *British India's Northern Frontier: A Study in Imperial Policy*. London, 1963

Algar, Hamid, 'Shaykh Zaynullah Rasulev: The Last Great Naqshbandi Shaykh of the Volga-Urals Region', in Jo-Ann Gross, ed., *Muslims in Central Asia*. London, 1992

Allen, Charles, *A Mountain in Tibet*. London, 1982

____, *Duel in the Snows: The True Story of the Younghusband Mission to Lhasa*. London, 2004

____, *Plain Tales from the Raj*. London, 1992

____, *Soldier Sahibs: The Men Who Made the North-West Frontier*. London, 2000

Allen, W. D. and P. Muratoff, *Caucasian Battlefields. A History of the Wars on the Turco-Caucasian Border, 1828–1921*. London, 1953

Allworth, C. E., ed., *Central Asia*. New York, 1967

Anderson, D. M. and D. Killingray, eds., *Policing the Empire, 1830–1940*. Manchester, 1991

Andrew, Christopher M., *Secret Service*. London, 1985

Andrew, Christopher M., and Jeremy Noakes, eds., *Intelligence and International Relations, 1900–1945*. Exeter, 1987

Arnold, D., *Police Power and Colonial Rule, Madras, 1859–1947*. Delhi, 1986

Auty, Robert and Dimitri Obelensky, *An Introduction to Russian History*. Cambridge, 1976

Bailey, F. M., *Mission to Tashkent*. London, 1946

____, *No Passport to Tibet*. London, 1957

Bajwa, Fauja Singh, *The Military System of the Sikhs during the period 1799–1849*. Delhi, 1964

Barker, A. J., *The Vainglorious War, 1854–56*. London, 1970

Barth, Fredrik, *Political Leadership among Swat Pathans*. London, 1959

Barthorp, Michael, *The North-West Frontier*. Blandford, 1982

Bartlett, C. J., *Defence and Diplomacy: Britain and the Great Powers, 1815–1914*. Manchester, 1993

____, *Peace, War and the European Powers, 1814–1914*. London, 1996

Bayly, C. A., *Empire and Information: Intelligence Gathering and Social Communication in India, 1780–1870*. Cambridge, 1996

____, *The Raj: India and the British, 1600–1947*. London, 1990

Beaumont, R., *The Sword of the Raj*. London, 1977

Beckett, Ian, *Victoria's Wars*. London, 1974

Beesly, Patrick, *Room 40: British Naval Intelligence, 1914–18*. London, 1982

Beloff, Max, *Imperial Sunset, 1897–1921*. London, 1969

Bennett, Mary, *The Ilberts in India, 1882–1886*. London, 1995

Berghahn, V. R., *Germany and the Approach of War in 1914*. London, 1973

Berridge, P. S., *Couplings to the Khyber*. Newton Abbott, 1969

Blake, Robert (Lord), *Disraeli*. London, 1966

Blake, R. and H. Cecil, *Salisbury*. London, 1987

Bolt, C., *Victorian Attitudes to Race*. London, 1971

Bond, Brian, ed., *Victorian Military Campaigns*. Hutchinson, 1967

Bourne, K., *The Foreign Policy of Victorian England*. Oxford, 1970

Bourne, K. and D. C. Watt, eds., *British Documents on Foreign Affairs*. I, series B, USA, n.d.

Bovykin, V. I., *Ocherki istoriivneshnei politiki Rossii* ('Essays in the History of Russia's Foreign Policy'). Moscow, 1960

Brook-Shepherd, Gordon, *The Storm Petrels*. London, 1977

Brooks, Chris and Peter Faulkner, *The White Man's Burdens*. Exeter, 1996

Brown, Emily, *Har Dayal: Hindu Revolutionary and Rationalist*. London, 1975

Brown, Judith M., *Modern India: The Origins of an Asian Democracy* 2nd edn. Oxford 1985

Brown, Lucy, *The Victorian Press*. London, 1985

Cain, P. J. and A. G. Hopkins, *British Imperialism*. 2 vols. London, 1993

Cannadine, David, *The Decline and Fall of the British Aristocracy*. London, 1990

Caplan, Lionel, *Warrior Gentlemen: 'Gurkhas' in the Western Imagination*. London, 1995

Carey, J., ed., *The Faber Book of Reportage*. London, 1987

Carr, E. H., *The Bolshevik Revolution, 1917–1923*. vol III. London, 1953

Carreuese, Helen d', 'Systematic Conquest, 1865–1884', in C. E. Allworth, ed., *Central Asia*. New York, 1967

Caroe, Sir Olaf, *The Pathans*. London, 1958

____, *Soviet Empire: The Turks of Central Asia and Stalinism*. London, 1953

Chamberlain, Muriel E., *Pax Britannica?* London, 1988

Coen, T. C., *The Indian Political Service*. London, 1971

Cohen, B. S., 'Representing Authority in Victorian India', in T. O. Ranger and E. Hobsbawm, eds., *The Invention of Tradition*. Cambridge, 1963

Cohen, Stuart, *British Policy in Mesopotamia, 1903–1914*. London, 1976

Collins, Joseph J., *The Soviet Invasion of Afghanistan*. Lexington, 1986

Cook, Andrew, *On His Majesty's Secret Service: Sidney Reilly*. Stroud, 2002

Cowles, V., *The Russian Dagger*. London, 1969

Creveld, Martin van, *Supplying War*. London, 1977

Cunningham, Sir Duncan, *The Country of the Turcomans*. London, 1977

Curran, James, George Boyce and Pauline Wingate, eds., *Newspaper History*. London, 1978

Datta, V. N., *Madan Lal Dhingra and the Revolutionary Movement*. Delhi, 1978

David, Saul, *The Indian Mutiny*. London, 2002

Deacon, R., *The History of the British Secret Service*. London, 1969

de Gaury, Gerald and H. V. F. Winstone, *The Road to Kabul*. London, 1981

DeMoor, J. A. and H. L. Wesserling, eds., *Imperialism and War*. Leiden, 1989

Dennis, Peter and A. Preston, *Soldiers as Statesmen*. London, 1976

Dewey, Clive, *Anglo-Indian Attitudes: The Mind of the Indian Civil Servant*. London, 1993

Dobbs, J., *A History of the Discovery and Exploration of Chinese Turkestan*. The Hague, 1963

Donaldson, Robert H., *Soviet Policy toward India: Ideology and Strategy*. Cambridge (Mass.), 1974

Edwardes, David B., *Heroes of the Age: Moral Fault Lines on the Afghan Frontier*. California, 1996

Edwardes, Michael, *Battles of the Indian Mutiny*. London, 1963

____, *Playing the Great Game*. London, 1975

Eldridge, C. C., *Victorian Imperialism*. London, 1978

Elliott, Major-General G. J., *The Frontier 1839–1947*. London, 1968

Ellis, C. H., *The Transcaspian Episode, 1918–19*. London, 1963

Farwell, B., *Armies of the Raj: From Mutiny to Independence*. London, 1990

Featherstone, Donald, *Victorian Colonial Warfare: India*. London, 1992

Ferro, Marc, *Colonisation*. London, 1997

Fieldhouse, D. K., *Colonialism: An Introduction*. London, 1981

_____, *Economics and Empire*. London, 1973

Fleming, Peter, *Bayonets to Lhasa*. London, 1961

_____, *The Siege of Peking*. London, 1959

Florinsky, Michael T., *Russia: A History and Interpretation*. 2 vols. USA: Macmillan, 1947

Fraser Tytler, W. K., *Afghanistan*. Oxford, 1950

French, David, *The British Way in Warfare*. London, 1990

French, Patrick, *Francis Younghusband*. London, 1994

Fuller, W., *Strategy and Power in Russia, 1600–1914*. New York, 1992

Gail, M., *Persia and the Victorians*. London, 1951

Gallagher, J., *The Decline, Revival and Fall of the British Empire*. Cambridge, 1982

Gammer, Moshe, *Muslim Resistance to the Tsar: Shamil and the Conquest of Chechnia and Daghestan*. London, 1994

Gehrke, Ulrich, *Persien in der Deutschen Orientpolitik wahrend des ersten Weltkrieges*. 2 vols. Stuttgart, 1960

Geiss, Imanuel, *German Foreign Policy, 1871–1914*. London, 1976

Geyer, D., *Russian Imperialism*. Leamington Spa, 1987

Ghose, Dilip Kumar, *England and Afghanistan, A Phase in their Relations*. Calcutta, 1960

Gibbs, N. H., *The Origins of Imperial Defence*. Oxford, 1955

Gilliard, D. R., *The Struggle for Asia 1828–1914: A Study in British and Russian Imperialism*. London, 1977

_____, 'Salisbury and the Indian Defence Problem 1885–1902', in K. Bourne and D. C. Watt, eds., *Studies in International History*. London, 1967

Gilmour, David, *Curzon*. London, 1994

Gleason, John Howes., *The Genesis of Russophobia in Britain*. Cambridge (Mass.), 1950

Glover, M., *A Very Slippery Fellow: The Life of Sir Robert Wilson, 1777–1849*. Oxford, 1977

Gopal, S., *British Policy in India, 1858–1905*. Cambridge, 1965

_____, *Modern India*. London, 1967

_____, *The Viceroyalty of Lord Ripon, 1880–84*. Oxford, 1953

Greaves, R. L., *Persia and The Defence of India, 1884–1892*. London, 1959

Grenville, J. A. S., *Lord Salisbury and Foreign Policy*. London, 1964

Guha, A. C., *First Spark of Revolution: The Early Phase of India's Struggle for Independence, 1900–1920*. Bombay, 1971

Guha, Ranajit, *Elementary Aspects of Peasant Insurgency in Colonial India*. New Dehli, 1983

Hall, Lesley, *A Brief Guide to the Sources for the Study of Afghanistan in the India Office Library*. London, 1981

Hamer, W. S., *The British Army; Civil Military Relations 1885–1905*. Oxford, 1970

Hamilton, Keith and Richard Langhorne, *The Practice of Diplomacy: Its Evolution, Theory and Administration*. London, 1995

Hardiman, D., ed., *Peasant Resistance in India*. Oxford, 1993

Harfield, Major A., *The Indian Army of the Empress*. London, 1990

Harris, J., *Much Sounding of Bugles: The Siege of Chitral, 1895*. London, 1975

Harrison, Mark, *Public Health in British India*. Cambridge, 1994

Hartley, Janet M., ed., *The Study of Russian History from British Archival Sources*. London, 1986

Haswell, J., *British Military Intelligence*. London, 1973

Hawkins, Angus and John Powell, *The Journal of John Wodehouse, First Earl of Kimberley for 1862–1902*. London, 1997

Heathcote, T. A., *The Afghan Wars, 1839–1919*. London, 1980

_____, *The Indian Army*. Newton Abbot, 1974

_____, *The Military in British India, 1600–1947*. Manchester, 1995

Heron, Ian, *The Savage Empire: Forgotten Wars of the Nineteenth Century*. Stroud, 2000

Hibbert, C., *The Great Mutiny*. London, 1978

Higham, R., ed., *A Guide to the Sources of British Military History*. London, 1972

Hinsley, F. H., *Power and the Pursuit of Peace*. Cambridge, 1963

Holland, B., *The Life of Spencer Compton, eigth Duke of Devonshire*. 2 vols, London, 1911

Hopkirk, Peter, *Foreign Devils on the Silk Road*. Oxford, 1980

_____, *The Great Game*. Oxford, 1990

_____, *On Secret Service East of Constantinople*. Oxford, 1994

_____, *The Quest for Kim*. London, 1996

_____, *Setting the East Ablaze: On Secret Service in Bolshevik Asia*. Oxford, 1984

_____, *Trespassers on the Roof of the World: The Race for Lhasa*. Oxford, 1992

——, ed., *The Spy who Disappeared: Diary of a Secret Mission to Russian Central Asia in 1918; Reginald Teague Jones alias Ronald Sinclair*. London, 1991

Howard, C., *Joseph Chamberlain: A Political Memoir, 1880–1892*. London, 1953

Howard, M., 'Empire, Race and War in Pre-1914 Britain', in H. Lloyd Jones, *History and Imagination*. Duckworth, 1981

Inden, Ronald, *Imagining India*. Oxford, 1990

Ingram, Edward, *The Beginnings of the Great Game in Asia, 1828–34*. Oxford, 1979

Iskandarov, B. I., *Vostochnaia Bukhara i Pamir v period prisoedineniia Srednei Azii k Rossii* ('Eastern Bokhara and the Pamirs in the Period of Uniting Central Asia to Russia'). Stalinabad, 1960

Jackson, Patrick, *The Last of the Whigs: Lord Hartington*. London, 1994

James, David, *Lord Roberts*. London, 1954

James, Lawrence, *Raj: the Making and Unmaking of British India*. London, 1997

_____, *The Rise and Fall of the British Empire*. London, 1994

James, Robert Rhodes, *Rosebery*. London, 1963

Jeffrey, K., *The British Army and the Crisis of Empire*. Manchester, 1984

Jenkins, Roy, *Gladstone*. London, 1995

Jelavich, B., *The Ottoman Empire*. Indiana, 1973

Johnson, F. A., *Defence by Committee*. Oxford, 1960

Johnson, R. A., *British Imperialism*. London, 2002

Joll, James, *The Origins of the First World War*. London, 1984

Jones, R. A., *The British Diplomatic Service* (Waterloo, Ontario, 1983

Jordan, G., *British Military History: A Supplement to Robin Higham's Guide to the Sources*. London, 1988

Judd, Alan, *The Quest for C: Mansfield Cumming and the Foundation of the Secret Service*. London, 1999

Judd, D., *Empire*. London, 1996

Kakar, Hasan, *Government and Society in Afghanistan: The Reign of Amir Abd-al-Rahman Khan*. Texas, 1979

_____, *The Pacification of the Hazaras of Afghanistan*. New York, 1973

Kaye, Sir Cecil (Subodh Roy, ed.), *Communism in India*. Calcutta, 1971

Kaye, M. M., *Rudyard Kipling: The Complete Verse*. London, 1990

Kazemzadeh, Firuz, 'Russia and the Middle East', in Ivo J. Lederer, ed., *Russian Foreign Policy: Essays in Historical Perspective*. New Haven, 1962

_____, 'Russian Imperialism and Persian Railways', in *Russian Thought and Politics*. Cambridge (Mass.) Slavic Studies, vol 4, The Hague, 1957

____, *Russia and Britain in Persia, 1864–1914*. New Haven, 1968

____, *The Struggle for Transcaucasia, 1917–21*. London, 1951

Keay, John, *The Gilgit Game*. London, 1979

____, *Where Men and Mountains Meet*. 1st ed. 1975; Oxford, 1993

____, *The Royal Geographical Society History of World Exploration*. London, 1991

Keep, John L. H., *Soldiers of the Tsar: Army and Society in Russia 1462–1874*. Oxford, 1985

Kenez, Peter, *Civil War in South Russia, 1919–20*. New York, 1977

Kennedy, Paul, *The Realities Behind Diplomacy*. London, 1985

____, *The Rise and Fall of British Naval Mastery*. London, 1991

____, *The Rise and Fall of the Great Powers*. London, 1988

____, ed., *The War Plans of the Great Powers*. London, 1979

Kerr, Ian J., *Building the Railways of the Raj*. Cambridge, 1995

Khalfin, N. A., *Russia's Policy in Central Asia, 1857–1868*. Trans. by H. Evans. London, 1964

Kiernan, V. G., *Imperialism and its Contradictions*. London, 1995

King, Peter, *The Viceroy's Fall*. London, 1986

Knightley, Phillip, *The First Casualty*. London, 1982

____, *The Second Oldest Profession*. London, 1986

Kochanski, Halik, *Sir Garnet Wolseley: Victorian Hero*. London, 1999

Kumar, D. and M. Desai, eds., *The Cambridge Economic History of India*. vol II, Cambridge, 1983

Lamar, H., and L. Thompson, *The Frontier in History*. New Haven, 1981

Lamb, Alastair, *British and Chinese Central Asia*. London, 1960

Lambert, A., *The Crimean War: British Grand Strategy, 1853–56*. Manchester, 1990

Langer, W. L., 'A Critique of Imperialism', in H. Ausubel, ed., *The Making of Modern Europe* vol II, New York, 1951

Laushey, David, *Bengal Terrorism and the Marxist Left*. Calcutta, 1975

Leach, Hugh, with Susan Maria Farrington, *Strolling About on the Roof of the World*. London and New York, 2003

Lehman, J., *All Sir Garnet*. Cape, 1964

Le May, S. A., *The History of British Supremacy in South Africa*. London, 1965

Lobonov-Rostovsky, A., *Russia and Asia*. New York, 1951

Longer, V., *Red Coats to Olive Green: A History of the Indian Army 1600–1974*. New Dehli, 1975

Lorrimer, D. A., *Race, Race Relations and Resistance: A Study of Victorian and Edwardian Racism*. Manchester, 1994

Lowe, C. L., *The Reluctant Imperialists*. 2 vols. London, 1967

____, *Salisbury and the Mediterranean*. London, 1965

Lunt, James, *Bokhara Burnes*. London, 1969

Lycett, Andrew, *Rudyard Kipling*. London, 1999

Macauley, Martin, and Peter Waldron, *The Emergence of the Modern Russian State, 1855–81*. London, 1988

MacDonald, Robert H., *Sons of the Empire: The Frontier and the Boy Scout Movement, 1890–1918*. Toronto, 1993

Mackenzie, D., 'The Conquest and Administration of Turkestan, 1860–85', in M. R. Rwykin, ed., *Russian Colonial Expansion to 1917*. London, 1988

Mackenzie, J. M., ed., *Popular Imperialism and the Military*. Manchester, 1995

____, *Propaganda and Empire*. Manchester, 1984

McLean, D., *Britain and Her Buffer State, The Collapse of the Persian Empire 1890–1914*. London, 1979

Maclean, Fitzroy, *A Person from England and Other Travellers*. London, 1958

Macrory, Patrick, *Signal Catastrophe: The Retreat from Kabul, 1842*. London, 1966

Mahmud, M., *Tarikhe ravabete siyasiye Iran ba Englis dar qarne nuzdahome miladi* ('The History of Anglo-Persian Diplomatic Relations in the Nineteenth Century'). 5 vols. Teheran, 1328–29 AH

Malhotra, P. L., *The Administration of Lord Elgin in India*. New Dehli, 1979

Mangan, J. A., *The Games Ethic and Imperialism*. London, 1986

Mansergh, Nicholas, ed., *The Transfer of Power, 1942–47*. London, 1971

Marder, A. J., *The Anatomy of Sea Power: A History of British Naval Power in the Pre-Dreadnought Era, 1880–1905*. New York, 1964

Marshall, P. J., *The Oxford History of the British Empire, II, The Eighteenth Century*. Oxford, 1998

Mason, J. K., *Calendar of the Private Foreign Office Correspondence of Robert, Third Marquess of Salisbury*. 2 vols, Oxford, 1963

Mason, Keith, *Abode of Snow*. London, 1955

Mason, Philip, *A Matter of Honour*. London, 1974

____, *The Guardians*. London, 1954

____, *The Men Who Ruled India*. London, 1985

Matthew, H. C. G., *Gladstone*. Oxford, 1997

____, ed., *The Gladstone Diaries*. Oxford, 1982

Maxwell, Col Leigh, *My God – Maiwand!* London, 1979

Menan, K., *The Russian Bogey and British Aggression*. Calcutta, 1957

Menning, B. W., *Bayonets before Bullets: The Russian Imperial Army, 1861–1914*. London, 1992

Metcalfe, T., 'Ideologies of the Raj', in *The New Cambridge Modern History of India*, vol III, iv, Cambridge, 1994

Meyer, Karl and Shareen Brysac, *Tournament of Shadows: The Great Game and the Race for Empire in Asia*. London, 2001

Mitrokhin, Leonid, *Failure of Three Missions. British Efforts to Overthrow Soviet Government in Central Asia*. Moscow, 1987

Mollo, B., *The Indian Army*. Poole, 1981

Monger, G., *The End of Isolation*. London, 1963

Montgomery, J., *1900: End of an Era*. London, 1968

Moore-Gilbert, B. J., *Kipling and Orientalism*. London, 1986

Moreman, T. R., *The Army in India and the Development of Frontier Warfare, 1849–1947*. London, 1998

____, *The North-West Frontier*. London, 1997

Morgan, G., *Anglo-Russian Rivalry in Central Asia 1810–95*. London, 1981

Morgan, Gerald, *Ney Elias*. London, 1971

Morris, Peter, ed., *Africa, America and Central Asia: Formal and Informal Empire in the Nineteenth Century*. Exeter, 1984

Neill, S., *A History of Christianity in India*. Cambridge, 1985

Nish, Ian, *The Anglo-Japanese Alliance*. London, 1966

Nyman, Lars-Erik, *Great Britain and Chinese, Russian and Japanese Interests in Sinkiang, 1918–34*. Malmo, 1977

Omissi, David, *The Sepoy and The Raj*. London, 1994

Owen, Roger and Bob Sutcliffe, *Studies in the Theory of Imperialism*. London, 1972

Pakenham, Thomas, *The Scramble for Africa*. London, 1991

Parritt, B. A. H., *The Intelligencers*. Ashford, 1972

Pasley, R., *'Send Malcolm!': The Life of Major General Sir John Malcolm, 1769–1833*. London, 1982

P. A. T., 'Zheleznodorozhnyi vopros v Persii i Velikii Indiiskii put' ('The Railway Question in Persia and the Great Indian Road'), in *Velikaia Rossiia*. ii, Moscow, n.d

Paul, S. N., *Public Opinion and British Rule*. New Dehli, 1979

Pemble, John, *The Invasion of Nepal: John Company at Work*. Oxford, 1971

Peters, Rudolph, *Islam and Colonialism*. The Hague, 1979

Phillamore, R. H., *Historical Records of the Survey of India*. 5 vols. Dehra Dun, 1945–68

Pierce, Richard A., *Russian Central Asia, 1867–1917*. California, 1960

Platt, D. C. M., *The Cinderella Service: British Consuls since 1825*. London, 1971

Polmar, Norman and Thomas B. Allen, eds., *The Spy Book: The Encyclopaedia of Espionage*. London, 1996

Popplewell, Richard J., *Intelligence and Imperial Defence: British Intelligence and the Defence of the Indian Empire, 1904–1924*. London, 1995

Porter, A. N., *Atlas of British Imperial Expansion*. London, 1991

Porter, Bernard, *The Lion's Share*. London, 1975

Pottinger, George, *The Afghan Connection*. Edinburgh, 1983

Pradhan, Kumar, *The Goorkha Conquests*. Dehli, 1991

Pratap, M., *My Life Story of Fifty-Five Years*. Dehra Dun, 1947

Pratt, Mary Louise, *Imperial Eyes: Travel Writing and Transculturation*. London, 1992

Preston, Adrian, ed., *The South African Journal of Sir Garnet Wolseley*. Cape Town, 1973

Probst, Peter John, *The Future of the Great Game*. Ohio, 2005

Puri, Harish, *Ghadar Movement: Ideology, Organisation and Strategy*. Amritsar, 1983

Ralston, David B., *Importing the European Army; the Introduction of European Military Techniques and Institutions into the Extra European World*. Chicago, 1990

Ramm, A., *The Political Correspondence of Mr Gladstone and Lord Granville 1876–1886*. 2 vols. Oxford, 1962

Rastogi, Ram Sagar, *Indo-Afghan Relations, 1880–1900*. Lucknow, 1965

Rawat, Indra Singh, *Indian Explorers of the Nineteenth Century*. New Delhi, 1973

Rawlinson, H. G., *The British Achievement in India*. London, 1948

Rhodes James, Robert, *The British Revolution: British Politics 1880–1939*. London, 1976

Richards, D. S., *The Savage Frontier: A History of the Anglo-Afghan Wars*. London, 1990

Robb, P., ed., *The Concept of Race in South Asia*. New Dehli, 1995

Robbins, Richard, *The Tsar's Viceroys*. New York, 1987

Roberts, P. E., *A History of British India*. Oxford, 1921

Robins, Keith, *The Eclipse of a Great Power*. London, 1983

Robinson, Ronald and John Gallagher with Alice Denny, *Africa and the Victorians*. London, 1961

Robson, Brian, ed., *Road to Kabul: The Second Afghan War, 1878–1881*. London, 2004

_____, *Roberts in India*. London, 1993

Roy, M. N., *Memoirs*. Bombay, 1964

Said, Edward, *Orientalism*. New York, 1978

Samra, Chattar Singh, *India and Anglo-Soviet Relations, 1917–1947*. London, 1959

Sanyal, Usha, *Devotional Islam and Politics in British India*. Dehli and Oxford, 1996

Saran, P., *Persian Documents, being written, letters, newsletters and kindred documents pertaining to the several states existing in India in the last quarter of the eighteenth century from the Oriental Collection of the National Archives of India*. London, 1966

Sarkar, S., *Modern India, 1885–1947*. London, 1983

Saunders, David, *Russia in the Age of Reaction and Reform, 1801–1881*. London, 1992

Saxena, K. M. L., *The Military System of India, 1850–1900*. New Dehli, 1974

Schofield, Victoria, *Every Rock, Every Hill: A Plain Tale of the North-West Frontier and Afghanistan.* London, 1984

Schumpeter, J. A., *Imperialism and the Social Classes.* New York, 1951

Seaver, George, *Sir Francis Younghusband.* London, 1954

Seth, Ronald, *The Art of Spying.* London, n.d.

Severin, Tim, *The Oriental Adventures: Explorers of the East.* London, 1976

Shannon, Richard, *The Crisis of Imperialism 1865–1915.* part IV. London, 1974

Siegal, Jennifer, *Endgame: Britain, Russia and the Final Struggle for Central Asia.* London, 2003

Singer, Andre, *Lords of the Khyber.* London, 1984

Singh, H. L., *Problems and Policies of the British in India.* London, 1963

Singha, P. B., *Indian National Liberation Movement and Russia, 1905–17.* Delhi, 1975

Skrine, Sir Clarmont, *World War in Iran.* London, 1962

Smith, Vincent A., *The Oxford History of India.* 4th edn., ed. Percival Spear, Oxford, 1981

Snelling, John, *The Sacred Mountain: The Complete Guide to Tibet's Mount Kailas.* London, 1990

Spain, James W., *The Pathan Borderland.* The Hague, 1963

Sparrow, Elizabeth, *Secret Service: British Agents in France, 1792–1815.* Woodbridge, 1999

Spear, P., 'India 1840–1905', in F. H. Hinsley, ed., *Material Progress and World-wide Problems.* Cambridge, 1962

Spiers, E. M., *The Army and Society.* London, 1980

Spratt, Philip, *Blowing up India.* Calcutta, 1955

Stearn, R. T., 'War Correspondents and Colonial War', in J. M. Mackenzie, ed., *Popular Imperialism and the Military.* Manchester, 1992

Steiner, Zara and Valerie Cromwell, 'The Foreign Office before 1914', in G. Sutherland, ed., *Studies in the Growth of Nineteenth Century Government.* London, 1972

Stewart, Adrian, *The Underrated Enemy: Britain's War with Japan, December 1941–May 1942.* London, 1987

Strebelsky, I., 'The Frontier in Central Asia', in J. A. Bates and R. A. French, eds., *Russian Historical Geography.* vol I. London, 1983

Swinson, A., *Beyond the Frontiers. The Biography of Colonel F. M. Bailey.* London, 1971

____, *The North-West Frontier.* London, 1967

Tapper, Nancy, 'Abdur Rahman's North-West Frontier: The Pushtun Colonisation of Afghan Turkistan', in Richard Tapper, ed., *The Conflict of Tribe and State in Iran and Afghanistan.* London, 1983

Taylor, Robert, *Lord Salisbury.* Edinburgh, 1975

Taylor, A. J. P., *The Struggle for Mastery in Europe.* Oxford, 1954

Tikhomirov, M. N., *Prisoedinenie Merva k Rossii* ('The Annexation of Merv to Russia'). Moscow, 1960

Thornton, A. P., 'Rivalries in the Mediterranean, The Middle East and Egypt', in F. H. Hinsley, ed., *Material Progress and World-wide Problems.* Cambridge, 1962

Tomlinson, B. R., *The Indian National Congress and the Raj.* London, 1976

Trench, C. C., *The Frontier Scouts.* London, 1985

____, *Viceroy's Agent.* London, 1987

Tuchman, Barbara, *The Zimmermann Telegram.* London, 1959

Tuker, Lieutenant-General Sir Francis, *The Yellow Scarf.* London, 1961

Ullman, R. H., *The Anglo-Soviet Accord: Anglo-Soviet Relations, 1917–21.* London, 1973

____, *Intervention and the War: Anglo-Soviet Relations, 1917–21.* 3 vols. London, 1961

Vernon, N. P., 'Soviet Historians on the Russian Menace to India in the Second Half of the Nineteenth Century', *Indian History Congress,* Calcutta, 1976

Verrier, Anthony, *Francis Younghusband and The Great Game.* London, 1991

Walder, David, *The Short Victorious War*. London, 1973

Waldron, Peter, *The End of Imperial Russia*. London, 1997

Waller, Derek, *The Pundits*. Kentucky, 1990

Watson, Angus, *The Strange Ride of Rudyard Kipling*. London, 1977

Watt, D. C., *Personalities and Policies*. London, 1965

Weller, Jac, *Wellington in India*. London, 1972

Whitteridge, Gordon, *Charles Masson of Afghanistan: Explorer, Archaeologist and Intelligence Agent*. London, 2003

Wilkinson Latham, R. J., *From Our Special Correspondent: Victorian War Correspondents and their Campaigns*. London, 1979

Williams, R., *Defending the Empire: Conservatives and Defence Policy, 1899–1915*. New Haven, 1991

Winks, R., ed., *The Historiography of the British Empire and Commonwealth*. New York, 1966

____, *The Oxford History of the British Empire: Historiography*. V. Oxford, 1999

Wright, M., 'Treasury Control, 1854–1914', in G. Sutherland, *Studies in the Growth of Nineteenth Century Government*. London, 1972

Wynn, Antony, *Persia in the Great Game*. London, 2003

Yapp, M., *Strategies of British India*. Oxford, 1980

Zaionchkovskii, P. A., ed., *Dnevnik D. A. Milutina* ('The Diary of D. A. Milutin'). 4 vols. Moscow, 1947–50

Journals

Contemporary

Davis, H. W. C., 'The Great Game in Asia', The Raleigh Lecture on History. *Proceedings of the British Academy* (1926)

Durand, Sir Mortimer, 'Sir Alfred Lyall and the Understanding with Russia', *Journal of the Central Asian Society,* vol i, (1914): pp. 20–45

Johnson, W. H., 'Ney Elias's Journey to Ilchi', *Journal of the Royal Geographical Society* vol 37 (1868)

Macartney, Sir George, 'Bolshevism as I saw it in Tashkent in 1918', *Journal of the Central Asian Society,* vol VII (1920)

Malleson, Major-General Sir Wilfred, 'The British Military Mission to Turkestan, 1918–1920', *Journal of the Central Asian Society,* vol IX, (1922)

Popov, A. L., 'Iz istorii zavoevaniia Srednei Azii' ('From the History of the Conquest of Central Asia'), *Istoricheskie zapiski,* 9 (1940): pp. 198–242

Shakespear, Sir Richmond, 'A Personal Narrative of a Journey from Herat to Orenburg, on the Caspian, in 1840', *Blackwood's Magazine,* June 1842

Tod, Colonel J., 'The Malleson Mission to Transcaspia in 1918', *Journal of the Royal Central Asian Society,* vol 27 (1940)

Trench, Captain F., 'The Central Asian Question', *Journal of the Royal United Services Institute,* February 1873

Ullah, Mir Izzet, 'Travels Beyond the Himalaya', *Journal of the Royal Asian Society,* 4 (1837): pp. 283–340

Recent

Ahmed, A. S., 'An Aspect of the Colonial Encounter in the North-West Frontier Province', *Asian Affairs,* 9 (1978): pp. 319–27

Alder, G. J., 'India and the Crimean War', *Journal of Imperial and Commonwealth History,* 11 (1971)

____, 'The Key to India? Britain and the Herat Problem, 1830–63', *Middle East Studies,* 10 (1974) parts I and II

Beckett, Ian, 'Cavagnari's Coup de Main', *Soldiers of the Queen, The Journal of the Victorian Military Society*, 82 (Sept 1995): pp. 24–8

Bryant, G., 'Pacification in the Early British Raj, 1755–85', *Journal of Imperial and Commonwealth History*, 14 (1985): pp. 3–19

Burroughs, P., 'Imperial Defence and the Victorian Army', *Journal of Imperial and Commonwealth History*, 15 (1986)

Caplan, L., '"Bravest of the Brave": Representations of the "Gurkha" in British Military Writings', *Modern Asian Studies*, 25 (1991): pp. 571–97

Chamberlain, M. E., 'Sir Charles Dilke and the British Intervention in Egypt, 1882: Decision making in a nineteenth century cabinet', *British Journal of International Studies*, 2 (1976): pp. 231–45

Darwin, John, 'Imperialism and the Victorians: The Dynamics of Territorial Expansion', *English Historical Review*, 447 (1997): pp. 614–42.

Dewey, Clive, 'The New Military History of South Asia', *International Institute for Asian Studies*, 9: 21 (1996)

Dilkes, David and Roy Bridge. 'The Great Game', *The British Empire*, vol 4 (1972): pp. 309–36.

Edmonds, C. J., 'The Persian Gulf Prelude to the Zimmermann Telegram', *Journal of the Royal Central Asian Society* I (1960)

Fieldhouse, D. K., 'Imperialism; an historiographical Revision', *Economic History Review*, 1961: pp. 169–201

Fritz, P., 'The Anti-Jacobite intelligence system of the English ministers, 1715–45', *History Journal*, 16 (1973): pp. 265–89

Galbraith, J. S., 'The "Turbulent Frontier" as a factor in British Expansion', *Comparative Studies in Society and History*, 11 (1959–60): pp. 150–68

Gerhard, D., 'The Frontier in Comparative View', *Comparative Studies in Society and History*, 1 (1959): pp. 205–29

Gordon, S., 'Scarf and Sword: Thugs, marauders and state-formation in eighteenth century Malwa', *Indian Economic and Social History Review*, VI, 4 (1969): pp. 403–29

Hagen, Gottfried, 'German Heralds of Holy War: Orientalists and Applied Oriental Studies', *Comparative Studies of South Asia, Africa and the Middle East*, 24, 2 (2004)

Hankinson, Alan, 'Man of Wars: W. H. Russell', *Victorian Studies*, 28 (1984–5): pp. 193–205

Hargreaves, J. D., 'Entente Manquée: Anglo-Russian Relations 1895–6', *Cambridge Historical Journal*, 1953: pp. 65–92

Hauner, M., 'One Man Against the Empire: The Faqir of Ipi and the British in Central Asia on the Eve of the Second World War', *Journal of Contemporary History*, 16 (1981): pp. 183–212

Hayes, Paul, 'Conservative Foreign Policy 1885–1905', *History Review*, 13 (1992): pp. 35–40

Hibbett, Chris, 'China Humiliated', *The British Empire*, vol 5 (1972): pp. 57–84

Huttenback, Robert A., 'The Great Game in the Pamirs and Hindu Kush: The British Conquest of Hunza and Nagar', *Modern Asian Studies*, 9 (1975): pp. 1–29

Inden, R., 'Orientalist Constructions of India', *Modern Asian Studies*, 20 (1986): pp. 401–46

Jefferson, M., 'Lord Salisbury's Conversations with the Tsar at Balmoral, 27–29 September, 1897', *Slavonic and Eastern European Review*, 39 (1960–1): pp. 216–20

Jeffrey, K., 'The Eastern Arc of Empire: A Strategic View, 1850–1950', *Journal of Strategic Studies*, 5 (1982): pp. 531–45

Jelavich, B., 'Great Britain and the Russian Acquisition of Batum, 1878–1886', *Slavonic and Eastern European Review*, 48 (1970): pp. 44–66

Jelavich, C., 'The Diary of D. A. Miliutin, 1878–82', *Journal of Military History*, 26 (1954): pp. 255–9

Johnson, R. A., 'The Penjdeh Incident', *Archives*, XXIV, 100 (1999): pp. 28–48

_____, '"Russians at the Gates of India?" Planning the Defence of India, 1884–1899', *Journal of Military History*, 67, 3 (2003): pp. 697–743

Kennedy, P., 'The Costs and Benefits of British Imperialism, 1846–1914', *Past and Present*, 125 (1989): pp. 186–92

Leopold, J., 'British Applications of the Aryan Theory of Race to India, 1850–70', *English Historical Review*, 84 (1974): pp. 578–603

Lynn, John A., 'The Evolution of Army Style in the Modern West, 800–2000', *International History Review*, 18 (1996): pp. 505–45

MacKenzie, D., 'Expansion in Central Asia: St Petersburg vs the Turkestan generals (1863–6)', *Canadian Slavonic Studies*, 3 (1969: pp. 286–311

_____, 'Kaufmann of Turkestan', *Slavonic Review*, 26 (1968): pp. 265–285

Macpherson, J. W., 'Investment in Indian Railways', *Economic History Review*, 2nd Ser, 8 (1955): pp. 177–86

Moreman, T. R., 'The British and Indian Armies on the North-West Frontier, 1849–1914', *Journal of Imperial and Commonwealth History*, 20 (1992): pp. 35–64

_____, 'The Arms Trade and the North west Frontier Pathan Tribes, 1890–1914', *Journal of Imperial and Commonwealth History*, 22 (1994): pp. 187–216

Morgan, G., 'Myth and Reality in the Great Game', *Asian Affairs*, 60 (1973): pp. 55–65

Morris, L. P., 'British Secret Service Missions in Turkestan, 1918–19', *Journal of Contemporary History*, 12 (1977): pp. 363–79

_____, 'British Secret Service Activity in Khorassan, 1887–1908', *Historical Journal* 27 (1984): pp. 657–75

Morris, P., 'Russia in Central Asia', *Slavonic Review*, 53 (1975): pp. 521–38

Naiads, M., 'G. A. Henty's idea of India', *Victorian Studies*, 8 (1964–65)

Narain, P., 'Interaction of Nationalism and Imperialism in India in the 1880s: A Survey of the Vernacular Press', *Journal of Indian History*, 57 (1979)

Nyman, Lars Erik, 'The Great Game: A Comment', *RCAS*, 60, new series IV (1973): pp. 299–31

Omissi, David, 'Martial Races: Ethnicity and Security in Colonial India, 1858–1939', *War and Society*, 7 (1991): pp. 1–26

Onley, James, 'Britain's Native Agents in Arabia and Persia in the Nineteenth Century', *Comparative Studies of South Asia, Africa and the Middle East*, 24, 1 (2004): pp. 129–37

Page, S., 'The Creation of a Sphere of Influence: Russia and Central Asia', *International Journal* (Toronto), 49 (1994)

Peers, D. M., 'Sepoys, Soldiers and the Lash, 1820–50', *Journal of Imperial and Commonwealth History*, 23 (1995): pp. 211–47

Rogger, Hans, 'The Skobelev Phenomenon', *Oxford Slavonic Papers*, 9 (1976): pp. 46–78

Scudiari, J., 'Better Preparation for War: Indian Army Reorganisations during the Victorian Era', *Soldiers of the Queen, The Journal of the Victorian Military Society*, 82 (1995)

Steinberg, E. L., 'Angliiskikaia versiia o 'russkoi ugroze' Indii v XIX–XX v. V.' ('The English version of the "Russian Threat" to India)', *Istoricheskie zapiski*, 33 (1950): pp. 47–66

Surridge, Keith, 'All you soldiers are what we call pro Boer: The Military Critique of the South African War, 1899–1902', *History Journal*, 82 (1997): pp. 582–600

Thornton, A. P., 'British policy in Persia, 1858–1890', *English Historical Review*, 69 (1954): pp. 55–71

_____, 'The Reopening of the Central Asian Question', *History Journal*, (1956): pp. 123–36

Tucker, A., 'The Issue of Army Reform in the Unionist Government 1903–05', *History Journal*, IXI (1966): pp. 90–100

Williams, Beryl, 'The Strategic Background to the Anglo Russian Entente of August 1907', *History Journal*, IX, 3 (1966): pp. 360–73

Glossary

aksakal – elder (lit. 'white beard')

chaukidar – security guard

cossid – courier

dacoit – bandit

dak – postal service

dastur – custom

feringhee – foreigner

gosain – Hindu pilgrim

hajji – pilgrim to Mecca

hakim – doctor/physician; governor; judge

harkarra – runner or courier

havildar – Indian infantry sergeant

jihad – (lit. struggle) holy war

kafilah – caravan of camels

kotwal – officer with police, security or environmental duties in Mughal period

lakh – ten thousand

mehtar – prince/chief

mullah – teacher of law or religion

munshi – translator or clerk

Pathan – tribesman of the North-West Frontier of India

pundit – learned man (of poetry and music); surveyor

sepoy – Indian private soldier

shikar – sport

sirdar – guide, leader

sowar – Indian cavalry trooper

subedar – (Indian) Viceroy's commissioned officer of junior rank

swaraj – home rule (of India)

thuggee – ritual murder and robbery

ulema – Muslim religious community leadership

vizier – chief minister

zemindar – landowner

Index